The Dutch Republic in the Seventeenth Century

The Dutch are 'the envy of some, the fear of others, and the wonder of all their neighbours'. So wrote the English ambassador to the Dutch Republic, Sir William Temple, in 1673. Maarten Prak offers a lively and innovative history of the Dutch Golden Age, charting its political, social, economic and cultural history through chapters that range from the introduction of the tulip to the experiences of immigrants and Jews in Dutch society, the paintings of Vermeer and Rembrandt, and the ideas of Spinoza. He places the Dutch 'miracle' in a European context, examining the Golden Age both as the product of its own past and as the harbinger of a more modern, industrialised and enlightened society. A fascinating and accessible study, this book will prove invaluable reading to anyone interested in Dutch history.

MAARTEN PRAK is Professor of Social and Economic History at Utrecht University. He is the author and editor of a number of books, including *Early Modern Capitalism* (2000).

DIANE WEBB is a translator specialising in the fields of history and art.

The Dutch Republic in the Seventeenth Century

The Golden Age

Maarten Prak

Translated by
Diane Webb

CAMBRIDGE
UNIVERSITY PRESS

CAMBRIDGE UNIVERSITY PRESS
Cambridge, New York, Melbourne, Madrid, Cape Town, Singapore, São Paulo

CAMBRIDGE UNIVERSITY PRESS
The Edinburgh Building, Cambridge, CB2 2RU, UK

Published in the United States of America by Cambridge University Press,
New York

www.cambridge.org
Information on this title: www.cambridge.org/9780521604604

Originally published in Dutch as *Gouden eeuw. Het raadsel van de Republiek* by
Uitgeverij SUN, Nijmegen, 2002 and © Uitgeverij SUN, Nijmegen, 2002.
First published in English by Cambridge University Press as *The Dutch Republic
in the Seventeenth Century: The Golden Age*.

English translation © Maarten Prak 2005

Printed in the United Kingdom at the University Press, Cambridge

Typeset in Plantin 10/12pt.   *System* Advent 3B2 8.07f [PND]

A catalogue record for this publication is available from the British Library

ISBN-13 978-0-521-84352-2 hardback
ISBN-10 0-521-84352-9 hardback
ISBN-13 978-0-521-60460-4 paperback
ISBN-10 0-521-60460-5 paperback

Contents

List of illustrations		*page* vii
Acknowledgements		ix
Chronology		xi
	Introduction: The enigma of the Republic	1
1	A turbulent beginning	7

Part I: War without end

2	An independent state (1609–1650)	27
3	A world power (1650–1713)	45
4	The armed forces	61
5	Financial might	75

Part II: Golden Age: economy and society

6	A market economy	87
7	A worldwide trading network	111
8	Riches	122
9	Toil and trouble	135

Part III: Unity and discord: politics and governance

10	Community	153
11	The authorities	166
12	A dissonant chorus	186

Part IV: An urban society

13 Religious pluralism   201

14 A new approach to science and philosophy   222

15 The Dutch school of painting   234

16 The urban landscape   250

Conclusion: The end of the Golden Age   263

   Further reading   274
   Index   303

Illustrations

1 Abdication of Charles V. Frans Hogenberg; Printroom,
 Rijksmuseum fm 412   *page* 8
2 The plundering of Naarden by Spanish troops after
 they conquered the city on 30 November 1572.
 Amsterdam Municipal Archives d 7920   18
3 The end of the Truce in 1621. Atlas van Stolk 1529   38
4 The peace negotiations in Münster. Atlas van Stolk 1948   43
5 The murder of the De Witt brothers in The Hague on
 20 August 1672. Romeyn de Hooghe; Atlas van Stolk 2456: 2   54
6 The landing of William III near Torbay in southern England
 on 15 November 1688. J. Luiken; Atlas van Stolk 2744: 2   58
7 Soldiers relax during the siege of 's-Hertogenbosch in the
 summer of 1629. C. J. Visscher; *Atlas van Stolk* 1701: 1   67
8 Maurits of Nassau (1567–1625). C. van de Passe, 1600;
 Atlas van Stolk 1099   72
9 The siege of Breda in 1637. Jan van Hilten, 1637;
 Atlas van Stolk 1803   76
10 The naval battle off Dunkirk (11–14 June 1666).
 Atlas van Stolk 2337   81
11 'Floraes Gecks-kap', a print satirising the tulip mania
 of 1637. Atlas van Stolk 1787   88
12 The oil mill in Wormer on fire, after being struck
 by lightning on 5 May 1699. Atlas van Stolk 2832: 68   102
13 Map of New Netherland. 1655; Royal Library, The Hague   113
14 The island of Ternate in the Moluccas. J. Kip 1676;
 Printroom, Rijksmuseum rp-p-ob-47-595)   118
15 House of the Trip family in Amsterdam. Amsterdam
 Municipal Archives n 34855   124
16 The rear façade of the mansion Goudestein in
 Maarsseveen. I. Leupenius, 1690; The Utrecht Archives   129
17 Lek Dyke near Vianen. Esaias van de Velde; Atlas
 van Stolk S.1620/105   136

18 'Woman washing dishes', an engraving made by a woman,
    namely Geertruyt Rogman (1625–51/57), Rijksmuseum
    rp-p-ob-4228/32–5   144
19 A gathering in Amsterdam's Dam Square during
    the Undertakers' Riot in the winter of 1696. Amsterdam
    Municipal Archives d 8916   154
20 Allegory of the inauguration of Ernst Casimir of Nassau
    (1573–1642). Printroom, Rijksmuseum fm 1423 b   179
21 Frederik Hendrik taking the oath in the States of Holland in
    September 1625. Atlas van Stolk 1933: 1   182
22 Print of the 'Manly Militia of Amsterdam'. Amsterdam
    Municipal Archives d 24220   190
23 The Synod of Dordrecht (1618–19). Atlas van Stolk 1365   207
24 The Portuguese synagogue in Amsterdam. Romeyn
    de Hooghe; Printroom, Rijksmuseum fm 2574 a   218
25 Gabriel Metsu, *Woman Reading a Letter, c.* 1662–5. National
    Gallery of Ireland, Dublin   235
26 Johannes Vermeer, *Woman in Blue Reading a Letter,*
    c. 1660–5. Rijksmuseum, Amsterdam   246
27 The network of *trekvaarten*, or canals specially built for
    passenger barges, in 1665. Taken from Jan de Vries, *Barges*
    and Capitalism, Utrecht, 1981   253
28 The Amsterdam Town Hall in Dam Square. Amsterdam
    Municipal Archives d 6258   261
29 Utrecht's town hall at the time of the negotiations for
    the Peace of Utrecht (1713). I. Smit, 1712; Atlas
    van Stolk 3407   266
30 Details of engravings of Venice and Amsterdam.
    Royal Dutch Maritime Museum, Amsterdam   271

Acknowledgements

It was Maarten van Rossem who first suggested I write this book. He thought that the Netherlands was in urgent need of a series of books, each treating one century of its history. I am a specialist on the eighteenth century, but that had already been given to someone else, so I was allotted the seventeenth. My initial trepidation gradually gave way to a feeling of excitement at having accepted the challenge.

That was more than ten years ago. I had promised to write another book first, and that took longer than expected. Though the series was slow in getting off the ground, the seventeenth century remained a stimulating prospect. In 1994 I first gave a course, together with Lex Heerma van Voss, on the seventeenth-century Dutch Republic at the University of Utrecht – in English, because the course was intended for foreign exchange students. After two years my colleague changed jobs and I was left to give the course on my own. Since that first year, I have given the course – in various guises, and in both English and Dutch – to students of history at the University of Utrecht and the University of Exeter in England, to the students of University College Utrecht and to the foreign exchange students for whom the course was originally intended, always in the hope of arousing the interest of all those American, Croatian, Danish, English, Finnish, French, German, Italian, Romanian, Slovakian, Spanish and indeed Dutch participants in the most fascinating period of Dutch history – a period, moreover, of crucial importance to the history of Europe as a whole. I am grateful to all those students, the good and the bad, the lazy and the diligent, the interested and even the not-so-interested, for their contribution – as unwitting guinea pigs – to this project.

In writing this book, I have incurred debts to numerous historians both in the Netherlands and abroad. Here and there I have relied on my own research, but many of the ideas and much of the information in this book have been shamelessly borrowed from others. In the list of sources to each chapter I have attempted to acknowledge that debt, but there is every reason to express my gratitude here as well. Looking back, it is amazing to see how much has been written in the last twenty years about the subject of this book. The literature is extremely engrossing, and I hope that the overpowering sense of excitement I often felt when writing this book will be felt by my readers as well.

Jur van Goor, Peter Hecht, Christine Kooi, Koen Ottenheym, Judith Pollmann and Jan Luiten van Zanden read individual chapters and allowed me to benefit from their expertise. Boudewijn Bakker, Freek Heijbroek, Ger Luijten and Lina van der Wolde helped me to choose the illustrations. Guido de Bruin, Erika Kuijpers, Maarten van Rossem, Hans Wansink and my wife Annelies Bannink read the entire manuscript. Annelies Bannink pointed out, time and again, the needs of the average reader. Guido de Bruin earmarked places in the text where the description of the historical course of events was insufficiently precise or factually incorrect. Erika Kuijpers made considerable improvements to my writing style. I am extremely grateful to them all for their invaluable help, and naturally take the blame for the remaining shortcomings of this book.

I thank Annelies for her willingness to do more than her fair share of the work necessary to run our household while I was writing the bulk of this book, during the spring and summer of 2001, a period which was darkened by the loss of my sister, Agnes van der Burgt-Prak (*8.8.1956–†24.6.2001), to whose memory this book is dedicated.

NOTE TO THE ENGLISH EDITION

This edition differs in a number of ways from the Dutch edition. First of all, it incorporates the improvements suggested by various readers of the Dutch edition, in particular Oscar Gelderblom. I have also clarified a number of things that may not be self-evident to non-Dutch readers. The list of sources has been updated, as well as expanded to include additional publications in English and pruned of the more inaccessible sources in Dutch. The English edition also benefits from an additional chapter on science and philosophy (chapter 14), and I am indebted to Klaas van Berkel, Lodewijk Palm, Theo Verbeek and especially Piet Steenbakkers for their advice on these subjects.

I should also like to take this opportunity to thank Diane Webb for her wonderful translation and her attention to detail, both of which have helped to make the English version superior in many ways to the original Dutch edition. I am grateful to Michael Watson, my editor at Cambridge University Press, for his help and support, and to the Netherlands Organisation for Scientific Research (NWO) for its financial assistance. I dedicate the English edition to someone who would have been particularly proud, but sadly did not live to see its appearance: my father, Niels Prak (*8.8.1926–†1.6.2002).

Chronology

DOMESTIC POLITICS

1579	Union of Utrecht
1584	William of Orange murdered
1585–1625	Stadholdership of Prince Maurits
1619	Johan van Oldenbarnevelt executed
1625–47	Stadholdership of Frederik Hendrik
1647–50	Stadholdership of William II
1653–72	Johan de Witt serves as Grand Pensionary
1672–1702	Stadholdership of William III

INTERNATIONAL RELATIONS

1609	Truce with Spain
1621	End of Twelve Years' Truce
1648	Peace of Münster
1652–4	First Anglo-Dutch War
1665–7	Second Anglo-Dutch War
1672	'Year of Disaster', Third Anglo-Dutch War
1678	Peace of Nijmegen
1688	Invasion of England (William and Mary)
1689–98	Nine Years' War
1702–13	War of the Spanish Succession

ECONOMY

1585	Antwerp falls to Spanish troops
1602	Establishment of the Dutch East India Company (VOC)
1611	Establishment of the Amsterdam Exchange Bank
1612–43	Polders drained in North-Holland
1621	Establishment of the Dutch West India Company (WIC)

| 1632–65 | Inter-urban network of tow-boat canals built |
| 1688 | Zenith of East India Company shares |

OUTSIDE EUROPE

1595–7	First Dutch voyage to the East Indies
1614	New Netherland established
1618	Batavia becomes the Dutch headquarters in the East Indies
1628	Piet Heyn captures the Spanish silver fleet
1630–54	Dutch in Brazil
1639	Dutch become Japan's exclusive European trading partner
1652	Establishment of the Cape Colony in South Africa
1667	New Netherland becomes a British colony; Dutch acquire Surinam

RELIGION

1572	First Calvinist synod in Holland
1579	Union of Utrecht establishes freedom of conscience
1612	Jewish synagogue opens in Amsterdam
1618–19	Synod of Dordt splits Calvinist Church

SCIENCE AND CULTURE

1575	First Dutch university established at Leiden
1637	Descartes' *Discours de la méthode*
1642	Rembrandt paints *The Night Watch*
1656	Christiaan Huygens builds first pendulum clock
c. 1660	Vermeer paints his *View of Delft*
1670	Spinoza's *Tractatus Theologico-Politicus*

Introduction: The enigma of the Republic

In 1908, Dr Johan Prak, a general practitioner in the provincial town of Ter Apel, acquired P. L. Muller's recently reissued book *Onze Gouden Eeuw* (Our Golden Age). The copy bears his name and the date, written in his unmistakably nineteenth-century hand. The book, the first edition of which had appeared in 1897, bore the subtitle *De Republiek der Vereenigde Nederlanden in haar bloeitijd* (The Republic of the United Netherlands in its heyday). Muller's book was not intended for scholars, and perhaps this contributed in some measure to its success. The 'inexpensive reprint' of 1908 – comprising two sizeable volumes, bound and gilt-edged – was still a superb piece of work, containing 967 pages chockfull of information and hundreds of illustrations in colour and black-and-white. My great-grandfather, the doctor from Ter Apel, might even have read it. His son – my great-uncle Wim Prak, who took a keen interest in history, especially naval history – certainly studied the book, as evidenced by the occasional note in his handwriting, marking passages which particularly attracted his attention or with which he disagreed, in which case he wrote 'incorrect' in the margin.

In his history of the Golden Age, Muller, archivist of Rotterdam and *professor extraordinarius* at Leiden University, repeatedly voiced his surprise: first at the fact that a country 'small in size and limited in population was capable of acquiring a measure of power equal to that of the large, traditionally established monarchies',[1] then at the 'unparalleled prosperity' achieved by that 'uncommonly talented generation',[2] and finally at the 'defectiveness of its national institutions',[3] which was made up for only by the quality of its governors. Later historiographers also expressed their astonishment. In his 1941 book *Nederland's beschaving in de zeventiende eeuw* (*Dutch Civilisation in the 17th Century*), Johan Huizinga, the most famous historian the Netherlands has ever produced,

---

[1] P. L. Muller, *Onze Gouden Eeuw: de Republiek der Vereenigde Nederlanden in haar bloeitijd*, 2 vols. (Leiden: Sijthoff, 1908), vol. I, p. 32.
[2] Ibid., p. 63.   [3] Ibid., p. 69.

asked how it was possible 'that so small and relatively remote a country as the young Republic should nevertheless have been so advanced politically, economically and culturally'.[4] Huizinga found the meteoric speed at which the Republic had shot into the lead extremely surprising, all the more so because it happened at a time when the Republic was actually out of step with other countries. 'Our astonishment would be somewhat tempered', continues Huizinga, 'were we to find that, in the seventeenth century, Dutch culture was merely the most perfect and clearest expression of European culture in general. But such was not the case.' The Netherlands, in his view, 'proved the exception and not the rule'.[5]

Such questions have continued to gnaw at historians, who in recent years have put forward various thought-provoking answers. In their voluminous book on the economy of the Dutch Republic, *The First Modern Economy*,[6] the Dutch professor Ad van der Woude and his American colleague of Dutch descent, Jan de Vries, argued that the Netherlands already had a 'modern' economy a century and a half before the Industrial Revolution. This was apparent, in their opinion, from the presence in the Republic of a number of phenomena: well-developed markets for the three factors of production (land, labour and capital); high agricultural productivity, which not only enabled the development of a complicated social structure based on occupation but also facilitated social mobility; the authorities' respect for property rights and their attempts to promote prosperity; and the level of technological development and social organisation which – aided in part by the consumers' market-oriented behaviour – made economic growth possible. In other countries, such trends were either less marked or non-existent. This prompted the English historian J. L. Price to revive the old notion that the Dutch social structure must therefore have been modern as well. Instead of a society of orders, in which birth determined the individual's position, the Republic displayed the characteristics of a class society, in which economic factors were the main determinants. The Dutch Republic was, in Price's view, a bourgeois society, because social life revolved around the cities and their urban elites, whereas in other countries it was the aristocracy who set the tone.

Culturally, too, the Republic is said to have been in the vanguard. Marijke Spies, an authority on Dutch literature, and the cultural historian

---

[4] J. H. Huizinga, *Dutch Civilisation in the 17th Century and Other Essays* (London: Collins, 1968), p. 10.
[5] Ibid., p. 11.
[6] Jan de Vries and Ad van der Woude, *The First Modern Economy: Success, Failure, and Perseverance of the Dutch Economy, 1500–1815* (Cambridge: Cambridge University Press, 1997).

Willem Frijhoff have conducted extensive research into the characteristics of seventeenth-century Dutch culture, labelling it 'a culture of all-pervasive and unremitting debate in which all segments of society took part'.[7] The Republic distinguished itself from other societies in the compulsive exchange of opinion, in the willingness, often seen as an obligation, to take note of the opinions of others. In this sense the Republic's culture could, in Spies and Frijhoff's view, be called 'modern'.[8] Jonathan Israel, the renowned English authority on Dutch history, demonstrated in an exhaustive study of the Enlightenment – which paved the way for our present-day world view – that its roots should be sought not in France or in England but in the Dutch debates of the seventeenth century.

Seventeenth-century Dutch politics is the only thing that still refuses to fit into this pattern. Since the nineteenth century, the Republic's form of government has been denounced in every possible way. Robert Fruin, the first to hold the chair in Dutch national history at Leiden University, considered the period of the Republic a waste of time from a political point of view. While other countries were improving their political structure by centralising government and systematising legislation, the Netherlands was lapsing into medieval chaos. The Revolt against Spain suspended all initiatives for improvement, and the thread was not picked up again until the Kingdom of the Netherlands was established in 1813. The period of the Republic, in Fruin's eyes, was nothing but a sorry spectacle of discord. As mentioned above, P. L. Muller called the government defective. And Huizinga, in 1941, spoke in no uncertain terms of 'a constitutional monstrosity'.[9] In recent years various people have pointed out that the apparently unstable structure of the Dutch state – with a weak political centre but strong local and provincial institutions – was in fact the Republic's strength, as this created a broad base for political decision-making. No one, however, has yet been willing to characterise the Republic as a forerunner of the modern – meaning democratic and bureaucratic – unified state.

This presents a serious obstacle to the notion that the Republic derived its uniqueness from its 'modernity'. It was, after all, to political discord that the Republic owed its culture of debate, its bourgeois social structure and perhaps even a part of its economic success. Overly emphasising 'modernity' obscures the view of the medieval traditions that were often

[7] Willem Frijhoff and Marijke Spies, *1650: Bevochten eendracht* (The Hague: Sdu Uitgevers, 1999), p. 218.
[8] Ibid., p. 221.
[9] J. H. Huizinga, *Verzamelde werken*, 9 vols. (Haarlem: Tjeenk Willink & Zoon, 1948–53), vol. II (1948), p. 432.

eagerly embraced by those living in the seventeenth century. Moreover, in the mid-nineteenth century, when lambasting the Republic's political institutions became fashionable, the Netherlands was in many respects anything but a modern country. This book will therefore paint a very different picture of the Dutch Republic, one in which the emphasis lies less on its relationship to the future (the Republic as precursor) and more on the unique position of the Republic in the seventeenth century itself.

The following pages will clarify to what extent the Golden Age was the product of its own past. In the sixteenth century, before the Republic had emerged as an independent state, the Northern Netherlands was hopelessly divided. Even at that early stage, however, developments already afoot – especially in the coastal areas – were laying the foundations for unprecedented economic prosperity. The Revolt against Spain gave birth to a new state which had to resolve the discord of the preceding period as well as satisfy the need, by now generally felt, for cooperation. The desire to maintain local and regional 'freedoms' had been a major cause of the Revolt against Spanish authority, and the establishment of the Republic had been a triumph for this so-called particularism. The Republic was a league of cities and provinces, each of which derived its identity from its political independence, but the loosely united provinces had to hold their own against one of the most powerful rulers of the time, the king of Spain. Furthermore, the blossoming of its economy caused the young Republic's international interests to increase, making cooperation, especially military cooperation, inevitable. Throughout the seventeenth century, the Republic hovered between unity and discord in a never-ending struggle to maintain its balance.

The discord that frequently prevailed in the Republic was often seen as a shortcoming. Measured against the standards of the modern state, with its centralised decision-making and bureaucratic apparatus, the Republic was indeed a political freak. In the seventeenth century, however, the modern state as such had huge problems to contend with in countries like France and England. Governmental decisions were counteracted in the provinces; the bureaucratic fabric was still very thin in places. The Republic, lacking both an adequate central government and a well-oiled bureaucracy, could, however, boast reasonably efficient local authorities. The proximity of these local authorities to those they ruled meant that people usually had faith in the government, even if they had no right to elect its officials. Such faith was often lacking in other countries. By the same token, local authorities in the Republic lent a willing ear to the opinions of entrepreneurs and merchants, from whose milieu they often stemmed. Thus from the very beginning there was a healthy climate for investment, which was in turn conducive to expenditure and innovation.

The dominant role played by local and urban communities in the social life of the Dutch Republic contributed greatly to the cultural climate that was so characteristic of the Golden Age. Certainly the Calvinist Reformed Church enjoyed a privileged position, but other religious denominations were also allowed to practise their faith. The Republic was not a tolerant country on principle, but in many cities there seemed to be no alternative to the sufferance of all religious persuasions. Rivalries between cities, as well as the variety of cultures brought to the Republic by the steady stream of immigrants, go a long way towards explaining why this very period witnessed such advancements in science and philosophy. The cities were also the most fertile breeding grounds for the innovations which occurred in painting around 1600 in the Republic. This upsurge in artistic production was the answer to the increased demand for paintings by the quickly swelling ranks of middle-class burghers whose financial circumstances were also improving with lightning speed.

By the mid-seventeenth century, therefore, the Republic seemed to have found the golden formula for success. It had its ups and downs, of course, but for a long time its problems were pushed to the background by the revolutions and civil wars raging in other countries. The Republic's small size created problems, the most worrisome being that the sky-high cost of military defence had to be borne by relatively few people. Another recurrent problem was maintaining the political order of the Republic, which depended on the willingness of the ruling elite to compromise – something they were not always prepared to do. Holland, the province in which economic growth was largely concentrated, was called upon to solve many thorny issues, and this created a great deal of friction between Holland and the other provinces. Over the years the problems became more serious, if only because other countries began to put their own affairs in order, enabling them more successfully to confront what was often seen as the impertinence of the Dutch. Opposition from abroad, military threats and lack of cooperation at home, combined with a general decline in the European economy in the second half of the seventeenth century, led at first to increasing tension in the Republic and finally to stagnation and exhaustion. By 1715 there was no longer any doubt that the Golden Age had come to an end.

The end of the Golden Age meant that the Dutch Republic had again become an 'ordinary' country. In future it would be extraordinary only by virtue of having such a glorious past. For much of the eighteenth and nineteenth centuries, Dutch intellectuals continued to be obsessed with the Golden Age and the question of what should be done to revive it. That long period – in which self-glorification, owing to its undeniable successes, and self-loathing, because of its subsequent decline, fought to gain the upper hand – has certainly shown that the Republic cannot be seen unreservedly as the pioneer of modernity. If that had been the case, the Netherlands would have experienced fewer problems between 1700 and 1900. In those two centuries the Netherlands had to rediscover modernity at least twice: around 1800 in politics, with the introduction of the unified state, and around 1900 in economic and social life, with the rise of industry and the industrial proletariat. In the seventeenth century the Republic had been a unique combination of old and new: unique, not because similar combinations did not occur elsewhere, but because of the period of history in which it manifested itself. In the early-modern period, between the Middle Ages and the world of industry and democracy, a voluntary alliance of urban societies was able to combine economic prosperity with international successes – both diplomatic and military – and cultural florescence. The formula that sparked this spectacular chemical reaction is the subject of this book.

The Dutch Republic in the Seventeenth Century is therefore an overview with a particular slant. It encapsulates for everyone interested in Dutch history the results of historical research carried out in recent years. This survey, written from the perspective outlined above, makes no attempt to be complete – that would be impossible even in twice as many pages – but emphasises instead the way society functioned. Comparison with other countries will show time and again that seventeenth-century Dutch society was indeed in a league of its own.

1   A turbulent beginning

On Friday, 25 October 1555, at around three o'clock in the afternoon, an important gathering was convened at Brussels. Representatives of the seventeen provinces of the Netherlands had been summoned to the palace to assemble in the great hall. Also present were the knights of the order of the Golden Fleece, the members of the three Councils of State of the Netherlands, and various higher nobles. Benches had been made ready to seat them all. Interested members of the public were permitted to watch from behind a railing. When the guests of honour had taken their places, the door to the hall opened and Emperor Charles V hobbled in, leaning on the arm of William, the young prince of Orange. They were followed by Charles's son, Philip II, and the emperor's sister, Mary of Hungary, regent of the Netherlands. Even though Charles was only fifty-five years old, he could barely walk without support. Born in Ghent in 1500, he had been forced at the age of fifteen to assume the reins of government, not only of the Netherlands but also of the Spanish and Austrian possessions of the House of Habsburg. King of Spain since 1516 and Holy Roman Emperor since 1519, Charles V had been compelled to criss-cross Europe dozens of times, waging war repeatedly at the head of his troops. Charles had not succeeded in suppressing the Reformation, which had broken out at the beginning of his reign, nor in restoring the authority of the Catholic Church. Deeply disillusioned and plagued by gout and other ailments, Charles, having decided that he could rule no longer, now intended to abdicate in favour of his son Philip. This news was communicated by a councillor, who explained the emperor's decision to the assembled dignitaries. When the councillor had finished, Charles took the floor, clinging to the prince of Orange. He spoke of his love for his native country and the many sacrifices he had made during his forty-year reign. He asked his subjects to pardon his mistakes and entreated them to be as faithful to Philip as they had been to him. According to eye-witness reports, there was not a dry eye in the hall.

It was in fact a minor miracle that a meeting of this kind could take place at all. When Charles assumed control of the Spanish Netherlands in

Figure 1   On 25 October 1555, Charles V abdicated, handing over the Netherlands
to his son Philip II, here depicted kneeling before him (Frans Hogenberg;
Printroom, Rijksmuseum fm 412).

1515, political turmoil and instability, especially in the North, banished
all thoughts of unity. Formal unification did not come about until 26 June
1548, when the Diet of the Holy Roman Empire, assembled in the
German city of Augsburg, decided at the emperor's behest to bring
together the patchwork of Netherlandish provinces under one separate
Kreits, a self-governing entity of states within the empire. The formation
of the Netherlands was confirmed the following year, when all seventeen
provinces endorsed Charles V's Pragmatic Sanction, which stipulated
that Charles's successors were to treat the Netherlands – now separate
from both France and the Holy Roman Empire – as a single entity and not
divide it up among a number of successors, thus guaranteeing the unity of
the seventeen provinces of the Netherlands. When Charles abdicated,
that union was just seven years old.

The resolutions of 1548 and 1549 and the transfer of sovereignty in
1555 represented the tail end of a process that had started more than a
century and a half earlier, in 1384, when the county of Flanders fell into

the hands of Philip the Bold, duke of Burgundy. Philip's wife was the daughter of his recently deceased predecessor, the duke of Flanders. In 1396 Philip acquired the duchy of Limburg. In 1406 the House of Burgundy also gained possession of the duchy of Brabant upon the extinction of the ducal line. Over the course of the fifteenth century, various other territories in the South were acquired: Namur in 1429, Hainault in 1433, Picardy in 1435 and Luxemburg in 1441, to name only the most important. To the north of the Rivers Maas and Rhine, which cut the Low Countries in two, the Burgundians managed in 1433 to annex the rapidly rising province of Holland, thanks to the crisis of succession that ensued when Countess Jacoba of Bavaria died without a legal heir. Zeeland, closely allied to Holland since the thirteenth century, fell into the Burgundians' lap at the same time. Other territories in the North managed to elude their grasp for the time being.

The Low Countries were a valuable asset. Since the twelfth century, Flanders and later Brabant had been developing into the most important commercial centres in north-west Europe. In Bruges, Italian merchants sold luxury goods such as spices and silk, which they acquired from their agents in the Middle East. At first such trade was conducted overland, and merchants met at the annual fairs held in the Champagne region of France. From around 1300, however, there was also a direct maritime route between Bruges and the most important centres of trade in Italy: Venice and Genoa. These trade routes encouraged the emergence of industrial centres which developed spectacularly in such cities as Bruges and Ghent. In the Flemish countryside as well, spinning and weaving were engaged in with an eye to export. The Flemish textile centres also functioned as processing points for English cloth, imported as semi-finished goods to Flanders, there to be dressed and dyed and finally sold. It was this finishing stage in the manufacturing process that yielded the greatest profits.

The Burgundians were well aware of what the Low Countries had to offer. First and most importantly, the flourishing urban economies were a rich source of revenue. The money thus acquired enabled the Burgundian dukes to pursue their great ambition of ruling a territory stretching unbroken from Burgundy to the North Sea. However, the Low Countries would yield up their riches only if they were treated properly, and this required a great deal of tact. The Burgundians exercised provincial sovereignty; they held no claim whatever to the Low Countries as a whole. Since each province had its own political structure and traditions, the only thing binding them was the duke himself. Each time a new duke was sworn in – which took place in each province separately – he reconfirmed the 'privilege' whereby he granted each province certain rights and immunities. Moreover, these provincial governments were under a great deal of pressure from the prosperous cities, especially those in Flanders and Brabant, which had long been used to getting their own way. Anyone hoping to govern the Low Countries successfully, therefore, had to win the confidence of the urban patriciate and persuade them to open their purse strings. The duke's word was not enough, however, to wheedle money out of the cities and provinces: he had to negotiate, and the great number of provinces made such negotiations tedious. This prompted Philip the Good to summon representatives from all the provinces under his rule to discuss common issues such as money. These assemblies evolved into the States General, which met on a fairly regular basis from 1464 onwards. Other government bodies started to take shape at the same time. Many provinces came to have governors, or stadholders, who exercised authority on behalf of the sovereign. The Burgundians underlined this institutional strengthening of their authority by engaging in a forceful, if symbolic, expansion of power. The magnificence of their court, with all the trappings of princely power, gave a strong boost to the arts in the Low Countries.

Not everyone appreciated the splendour of the Burgundian court and the inevitable political intrigues. The power of the opposition became painfully obvious when Charles the Bold died in 1477. The duke had been in the process of consolidating his conquest of Lorraine, which in 1473 had finally linked the House of Burgundy's hereditary lands to its possessions in the north. The people of Lorraine had risen in revolt, and during the siege of their capital city, Nancy, Charles was fatally wounded. His frozen body lay on the battlefield for a week, while the news spread like wildfire. Charles the Bold was survived only by an unmarried daughter, Mary of Burgundy. The French king, Louis XI, promptly sent troops to occupy Burgundy. At the same time, the weakened regime in the Low Countries was inundated with grievances, nearly all of which called for a halt to the policy of centralisation, urging instead the restoration of provincial and local privileges. Mary was forced to yield to many of these demands by signing the *Grand Privilège* of 1477. In the same year, however, she married Maximilian of Austria, of the illustrious Habsburg dynasty. Maximilian was determined to restore authority and, where possible, to extend it. He began to cast his eye upon the North.

Conquering the North, however, was easier said than done. The territories to the north of the great rivers differed in many respects from those to the south. Friesland, never colonised in Roman times, had always been a law unto itself. A central authority had never established itself there, and feudalism was largely unknown. Friesland was in fact a collection of peasant republics. In small districts the law was laid down by *hoofdelingen*, untitled nobles who lived in fortified houses in the countryside. Frisian society was plagued by feuds between these noble families, bloody conflicts that often dragged on for years. At this time the cities in Friesland were still of secondary importance, certainly from a political perspective. Self-government had come to them late, in the second half of the fourteenth century, before which time they had simply been part of the rural district in which they were located. Even in the relatively large city of Leeuwarden (3,000 inhabitants in 1400), the *hoofdelingen* held sway. Economically speaking, Friesland was by no means backward. Indeed, by European standards it was densely populated, and its agriculture was highly developed. The Frisians carried on trade with Scandinavia, but the province was far removed from the most important centres of trade in the South.

Friesland had neither ruler nor provincial institutions. External threats could move the Frisian lords to cooperate with one another, but otherwise their energies were absorbed in dealing with the problems of their own factions. Indeed, it was this partisanship that was mainly responsible for the demise of the highly praised 'Frisian Freedom'. The Hollanders had long been casting a covetous eye at Friesland, but their conquests had been only temporarily successful. In 1498, however, one of the Frisian factions called in the help of the stadholder-general of the Netherlands, Albrecht of Saxony, who had gained a reputation as a formidable military commander. Albrecht conquered the whole of Friesland, and Maximilian of Habsburg appointed him *gubernator*. Straightaway the first provincial institutions were created, naturally with a view to consolidating and safeguarding the newly acquired territory. Even though the *hoofdelingen* who had requested Albrecht's assistance had deliberately restricted his powers, the new situation was not agreeable to many Frisians, who hoped, with the support of the duke of Gelderland, to regain their old freedoms.

In addition to subjugating Friesland, Albrecht of Saxony had gained power in 1498 over Groningen to the east of Friesland, though at that time he was not able to settle down there. Like Friesland, Groningen was essentially a federation of small peasant republics. The Groningen countryside, like that of Friesland, was dominated by *hoofdelingen* who maintained their authority over a small area by employing groups of armed men. Feuds were not uncommon in Groningen either, but it differed from Friesland in one important respect: by the time the *hoofdelingen* had firmly established themselves, the city of Groningen had become too large to control. The result was a great deal of friction between the city proper – which in 1400 had an estimated 5,000 inhabitants – and the rural districts. In 1506, in an attempt to ward off the Saxon threat, the city offered seigniorial rights to the count of East Friesland. In 1515, Karel of

Egmond, duke of Gelderland, was sworn in as sovereign. This drew Groningen into the battle for a sphere of influence on the northern flank of the aggregation of Netherlandish states. In this battle of the giants, the duke of Gelderland was pitted against the House of Habsburg.

The contenders in this fight appeared to be mismatched, the Habsburgs being expected to win hands down. Gelderland was certainly not a promising contestant in a battle between great powers. The duke's territory consisted of four parts which had never been truly unified: the Nijmegen Quarter, the Veluwe (also known as the Arnhem Quarter), Upper Gelderland (the Roermond Quarter, which more or less coincides with present-day North Limburg), and finally the county of Zutphen, officially completely separate from the duchy of Gelderland. During the 1470s and again in the 1480s, Gelderland had been occupied by Burgundian–Habsburg troops. That encounter had not been a happy one, so it is hardly surprising that there was widespread approval, certainly in the beginning, of the duke's anti-Habsburg policies. Karel of Egmond, moreover, had powerful friends. He was supported by the French king, who viewed him, not without reason, as a thorn in the side of the Habsburgs, who were also his strongest opponents. The English, too, regularly offered support to Gelderland, and Karel also set about finding allies in the adjoining territories, in what is now Germany and in the Netherlands itself.

At first Karel of Egmond was on the defensive. By 1505, for example, the Veluwe (with the exception of Wageningen) and most of the cities in the county of Zutphen had fallen into the hands of the Habsburgs, who also occupied Bommel and the Bommelerwaard, the area between the Rivers Maas and Waal. Later the tide turned, however. Between 1508 and 1513, Karel's troops regularly marauded and plundered the Oversticht (Overijssel), the part of the bishopric of Utrecht beyond the River IJssel. In 1513 he recaptured Arnhem and Stralen. A short time later his help was called upon by Groningen, where he was installed as the sovereign, giving him a firm hold on Overijssel as well. Until 1528, Overijssel was ruled by the Gelderlanders, who had established themselves in Friesland even before 1515. The Frisians, however, who had hoped that Gelderland would restore their independence and offer them protection with no strings attached, were in for a rude awakening. They had to put up with increased taxation, not to mention such inconveniences as the presence of foreign troops.

The Gelderlanders were also called upon to fight in the Nedersticht (the province of Utrecht), again owing to internal conflicts. Between 1481 and 1483 Utrecht had been torn by a civil war between the Hoeks and the Cabeljauws, rival factions of the leading noble and patrician families. In 1511 the city of Utrecht, at war with the lord of IJsselstein, called in the help of the duke of Gelderland, Karel of Egmond. In 1527, Karel was again requested to come to the aid of the city in its conflict with the prince-bishop, who exercised both ecclesiastical and secular authority in the provinces of Utrecht and Overijssel. The prince-bishop, forced by the Gelderlanders to pay a huge indemnity for their recognition of his authority in Overijssel, was in sore financial straits. He saw no alternative but to surrender his authority in both Utrecht and Overijssel to Charles V. In 1528 the emperor occupied the city of Utrecht and changed the constitution, ensuring that the guilds (which had dominated the town council since 1304) were completely excluded from politics. Charles V also had a large citadel built within the city walls, which he called – with a flair for public relations – the Vredenborch, or 'stronghold of peace'.

In Gelderland there was increasing criticism of the duke's escapades. In the cities, the patricians regularly complained of the excessive financial burden placed upon them and the damages they suffered from continued military action. By 1536 feelings were running so high that the duke was in danger of being deposed. Revolts broke out in Nijmegen and Zutphen. The Landdag – the provincial parliament with representatives from all parts of Gelderland – seriously considered the possibility of an alliance with the Lower Rhine mini-states of Cleves, Berg, Jülich, Mark and Ravensberg. When Karel of Egmond died in 1537, the Habsburgs immediately tried to placate the Gelderlanders, but the cities of Gelderland, remembering the fate of Utrecht, preferred to stand aloof. The duke of Cleves, proclaimed sovereign of Gelderland in 1539, was just as ambitious as his predecessor in the field of foreign policy. Joining forces with the king of France, he launched an attack on the Southern Netherlands. In the summer of 1542, Gelderland's famous military leader Maarten van Rossum marched in the direction of Antwerp, an action that proved exceedingly rash. The government in Brussels was alarmed at this threat to the most important trading centre in the Netherlands, and there were also fears that Protestantism, following in the Gelderlanders' wake, would gain a foothold in the Low Countries. Determined to prevent this, the emperor advanced with an army towards Gelderland in the summer of 1543. Jülich and Venlo fell almost immediately. In early September the duke of Cleves was forced to cede the sovereignty over Gelderland to Charles V, whom the Gelderlanders themselves recognised a few days later as their ruler. The dream of an independent state on the northern edge of the Habsburg Empire had come to an end.

It is tempting to dismiss this history of feuds, skirmishes, small-scale wars and changing alliances as the death throes of what is sometimes called 'feudal anarchy' and to portray the Habsburg Empire instead as the

prototype of the modern state, with its rule of law, uniform legal procedures and bureaucratic efficiency. Charles V and his counsellors likely
thought of themselves as modern statesmen, and certainly did everything
in their power to implement their agenda. An important step in this
direction was the splitting up in 1531 of the 'Great Council', the most
important government institution, into three separate Collateral
Councils: a Council of State to handle political questions, a Secret
Council to deal with legal matters and a Council of Finance. However,
the façade of apparent order belied the political reality behind it, even in a
province like Holland, which had long been integrated into the
Burgundian–Habsburg state.

Holland was a late bloomer. In the fourteenth, and even as late as the
fifteenth century, the economic heart of the Northern Netherlands
was located more towards the east. In 1400 the cities of Utrecht and
's-Hertogenbosch, on the northern edge of the duchy of Brabant, were
nearly twice as large as Dordrecht and Haarlem, at that time the largest
cities in the county of Holland. The Northern Netherlandish cities allied
to the Hanseatic League were not in Holland but in the east on the River
IJssel. From the fourteenth century onwards, however, the cities of
Holland were on the upsurge. Small towns, often having no more than
several hundred inhabitants, developed rapidly, thanks to thriving agriculture in the surrounding rural districts and growing markets in the
wealthy centres of Flanders and Brabant, where the numerous beer
brewers of Gouda and Delft found most of their customers. Amsterdam's
grain trade with the Baltic countries, initially arising from the impossibility of growing enough of this vital crop in the wet Dutch soil, also
profited from the demand for grain in the South. Holland developed into
a shipping power, and as early as the fifteenth century could boast one of
the largest merchant fleets in Europe. The estimated carrying capacity of
Holland's ships – 40,000–50,000 tons – meant that they could handle
more cargo than either the Genoans or the Venetians.

The cities played an important part in the provincial politics of
Holland. In the fifteenth century the meetings of the provincial States
were still rather informal, but even in those days the cities had most of the
votes. Gradually a practice emerged by which the six large cities –
Dordrecht, Haarlem, Delft, Gouda, Leiden and Amsterdam – had a
permanent seat, next to the one vote held by the *ridderschap* (the nobility).
The *ridderschap* consisted of nobles of Holland who represented the
rural districts. The church had no representative in the States of
Holland (as it did in the States of Utrecht). Like its neighbouring provinces, Holland was torn by the Hoek-and-Cabeljauw conflicts, which
continued throughout the fifteenth century and led to various civil wars

within Holland. It was not until the end of the century that the stad-holder-general Albrecht of Saxony succeeded in bringing about a cease-fire, though this did nothing to unify the cities, which were regularly at loggerheads. The situation changed owing to the Gelderlanders and Charles V, both of whom were a potential threat to Holland's prosperity – Gelderland because it endangered the transport of goods to Holland via the Zuider Zee, which was the only supply route serving all the cities to the north of Amsterdam. This threat was underscored in 1508, 1517 and 1528 when troops from Gelderland made predatory raids through Holland.

The Habsburgs were in a position to do something about this, but only at a price. In 1521–3, when Holland lent aid to the campaigns in Friesland, and in 1527–8, when it assisted in the capture of Utrecht, Holland's contribution to the central coffers in Brussels rose to fourfold that of a normal year. Around the mid-sixteenth century, Holland was paying ten to fifteen times more to Charles V's war budget than it had thirty years before. This caused the tax burden to increase dramatically and with it the complaints voiced by the citizens, especially the merchants and entrepreneurs who held most of the power in the cities and were witnessing the erosion of their competitive position. In an effort to alle-viate the tax burden, the States of Holland developed a new debt instru-ment, the annuity bond, in which the local elites avidly invested. This gave rise in the cities to an awareness, largely lacking until this time, of common interests and responsibilities. The governors of Holland viewed Charles V not as an ally but as a negotiating partner from whom one must seek to gain as many concessions as possible in exchange for financial support. Such concessions were invariably sought in the sphere of local and provincial self-government. In this respect Holland's political culture joined seamlessly with that of the other areas of the Northern Netherlands, where bargaining with the authorities for local and regional autonomy was also a high priority.

The political tension in the Netherlands, already greatly exacerbated by the ever increasing taxes levied to support the war effort, was further intensified by the religious conflicts that flared up in the wake of Luther's attack on the Catholic Church. Quite apart from the question of Charles V's personal views – he was undoubtedly a true believer – it was an axiom of sixteenth-century politics that no state could survive without a com-mon ideology, or in this case a common religion. Suppressing the Reformation and restoring the authority of the Catholic Church was therefore of the utmost importance. To this end Charles's government in Brussels adopted draconian measures. Placards threatened apostates with death, and hundreds of heretics were burned at the stake.

The battle against the Protestant sects was far from successful, however. In the German territories, Luther had received support from a number of princes, and Charles V was forced to come to terms with them, allowing Protestant services to be held in areas where the ruler was Protestant, according to the terms of the Peace of Augsburg concluded in 1555. Charles was so disappointed by this turn of events that he abdicated. His inheritance was divided up between his brother Ferdinand, who was given the German territories, and his son Philip, who received the Spanish and Netherlandish possessions. Born in Ghent, Charles V had always been viewed as a 'Netherlander'. Philip, by contrast, was born and bred in Spain and also chose to spend most of his life there. This was only natural, considering Spain's position as a world power, but from the perspective of the Netherlands it was a catastrophic choice. Philip tried to maintain his grip on the Netherlands by centralising the government even further and by appointing foreign confidants to important posts, policies which met with increasing resistance from the Dutch elite. At the same time, Protestantism was steadily gaining in popularity among the middle and lower classes. One new Protestant movement in particular – Calvinism – was attracting a great many followers. In the summer of 1566 – a year in which the price of grain rose to unprecedented heights – discontent erupted into violence. These outbreaks of disorder, which started in the textile centres of Flanders, quickly spread to the cities and soon engulfed the whole of the Netherlands. Everywhere churches were stripped of their 'popish idols'. While this Iconoclastic Fury raged, images of saints were smashed and church treasuries robbed. The nobles, long dissatisfied at their political marginalisation, demanded a greater political role for the provinces and the relaxation of religious persecution. William of Orange emerged as the leader of the nobles' revolt. Though a native of Nassau in Germany, he had been prince of Orange in southern France since 1544 and also possessed estates in Holland, Brabant and Luxemburg. William was not only a former confidant of Charles V but also the most important noble in the Netherlands. A sovereign prince himself, though of course a less powerful one than Philip II, he was – at least in theory – Philip's equal.

Philip, in Spain, reacted to these protests by doing exactly what the rebellious Netherlanders had hoped he would not do. After lengthy discussions about what was likely to be more effective – a policy of moderation or a heavy-handed approach – Philip decided to send the duke of Alva to the Netherlands at the head of 10,000 very experienced Spanish troops. Alva had always been the Spanish court's leading hardliner. Immediately upon his arrival in the Netherlands, he began to put things to rights. He created a new court of law with the power to prosecute the rebels in the whole of the Netherlands. This Council of Troubles, which soon became known in popular parlance as the 'Blood Council', eventually sentenced more than a thousand people to death. The rebels' property, including that of the prince of Orange, was confiscated, giving them all a personal reason for joining the Revolt, as the only way to recover their possessions. In order to pay his troops, Alva introduced new taxes: the Tenth, Twentieth and Hundredth Penny. Even though they were never actually collected, these taxes were the source of much resentment. Furthermore, Alva, who set off on a tour of the Netherlands to restore the king's authority, did not eschew the use of force. When billeting the Spanish soldiers – known as *tercios* – no distinction was made between cities or individuals who had participated in the Iconoclastic Fury and those who had remained loyal to the king. The foreign soldiers, guilty time and again of serious misconduct, treated all Netherlanders as heretics.

Alva was successful in restoring a semblance of peace. William of Orange, who had managed to raise several small armies which had, however, proved no match for the *tercios*, was forced to withdraw to the family estate in Germany. By 1570 the rebels, much reduced in number, were living in several refugee communities in Germany and England and on a few privateer ships. In the Netherlands, however, dissatisfaction continued to seethe beneath the surface, as became apparent when the privateers (who had come to be called Sea Beggars), landed at Den Briel (Brill) on 1 April 1572 in a desperate attempt to find a safe harbour. Meeting with little resistance, they succeeded in capturing the town and were amazed to see other towns opening their gates as well. Small armies in the personal employ of William of Orange invaded the Netherlands from the east. By the end of the year, most of Holland and Zeeland was in rebel hands. Only Amsterdam remained loyal, for the time being, to Philip. Friesland, Gelderland, Overijssel, Brabant and one or two Flemish towns sided with the Revolt, though not necessarily because the Protestants were in the majority or because they worshipped the prince. In many places opportunism determined allegiances – abhorrence of the Spaniards' behaviour being at least as great as loyalty to the opposition – though many people preferred, quite simply, to remain neutral.

The prince's incursions into the Netherlands were supported by the French, whose threat from the south had forced Alva to withdraw his troops from Holland in the spring of 1572, leaving the province an easy prey to the rebels. A few months later, however, on 24 August, the entire leadership of the Protestant movement in France was massacred in Paris. This wave of violence against the French Protestants, or Huguenots – known as the St Bartholomew's Day Massacre – put an abrupt end to

Figure 2   The plundering of Naarden by Spanish troops after they conquered the city on 30 November 1572. Such acts of violence, intended to intimidate people elsewhere in the rebellious provinces, were actually counterproductive and only fuelled anti-Spanish sentiment (Amsterdam Municipal Archives d 7920).

French support of the rebels, making it easy for Alva to regain control of the southern and eastern parts of the Netherlands. The rebels were now isolated in Holland and Zeeland, and Orange, demoralised, fled to Holland, intending – as he himself said – 'to maintain my affairs over here as well as may be, having decided to make that province my tomb'.[1] Alva was ruthless in punishing those who resisted his authority. The town of Mechelen (Malines), which had joined the Revolt in August, was plundered by Spanish troops when they recaptured it in October, despite promises that it would be spared. Zutphen suffered the same fate in November, when Alva ordered his son, who was in command there, 'to leave no man alive … and to set fire to the town'.[2] Similarly, on 1 December, Spanish soldiers massacred almost the entire population of Naarden before setting fire to the town.

---

[1] Geoffrey Parker, *The Dutch Revolt* (Harmondsworth: Penguin Books, 1977), p. 141.
[2] Henk van Nierop, *Het verraad van het Noorderkwartier: oorlog, terreur en recht in de Nederlandse Opstand* (Amsterdam: Bert Bakker, 1999), p. 82.

The rebels, for their part, did not hesitate to use high-handed means to pressure the population into participating in the Revolt and contributing to it financially. But while the rebels and the Spanish were both guilty of coercive and even violent behaviour, there was one very important difference between them: it was the Spanish who represented the lawful authority – an authority which exacted not only obedience but also tribute in the form of taxes. And the fact that tax revenues were used to pay Spanish soldiers who behaved so badly on Netherlandish soil was an abomination to the Netherlanders. This, more than anything else, strengthened the people of Holland and Zeeland in their resolve to resist Spanish rule, as evidenced during the siege of Haarlem in December 1572. For seven long months the city held out against the Spanish troops, and when the garrison finally surrendered, they were slain almost to the last man. However, in addition to a grim determination provoked by the Spanish, there were one or two things working in Holland's favour. To begin with, its geographical location was advantageous. Tracts of land could be flooded at will to thwart the enemy. Charles V had provided various cities with new fortifications, which the rebels now put to use in their fight against Habsburg authority. Moreover, under Charles's rule the Hollanders had built up, out of sheer necessity, an advanced system of public finance, which proved useful in July 1572 when the States of Holland resolved – in a special, if illegal, session assembled at Dordrecht – to side officially with the Revolt.

All the same, the rebels' prospects in late 1572 and early 1573 were not at all bright. The Revolt was now confined to Holland and Zeeland and was fuelled more by dislike of Alva and his regime than by positive support for the prince of Orange and his family. Philip II was in grave difficulties, however. Though the king enjoyed military superiority, the war in the Netherlands was a disaster from a financial viewpoint. In 1573, Spanish troops mutinied after not being paid for eighteen months. This happened again in April 1574, when the Spanish wiped out the rebel troops and killed Louis, count of Nassau, at Mookerheide. The victorious soldiers promptly mutinied and marched on Antwerp, which they held to ransom until they were paid 1 million guilders in back wages, part of which was advanced by the city's merchants. On 1 September 1575, Philip II suspended all interest payments on the Castilian public debt. Because many of these loans had been negotiated in Antwerp, this national bankruptcy dealt yet another blow to the city's trading community.

Even in Madrid the idea had begun to take root that Alva himself was not the solution but part of the problem. The king's supporters in the Netherlands were convinced that the Spanish would do best to pull out.

To this end the authorities in the South and the rebels in the North began to negotiate an agreement. These talks had reached an advanced stage when new mutinies broke out among the Spanish troops, who then proceeded to march on Antwerp, where defence works had been hastily built. By Saturday, 3 November, only a small gap remained in the ramparts. Sunday was to be a day of rest, but at daybreak the Spanish left their positions and forced their way into the city. For days Antwerp was plunged into complete chaos while the *tercios* wreaked havoc. At least 2,500–3,000 people, and possibly many more, met their death during this Spanish Fury, which confirmed the widely held opinion that the Spanish were cruel and untrustworthy.

The agreement reached between the royalists and the rebels – the Pacification of Ghent, signed on 8 November 1576 – was not long-lived. Differences of opinion, mainly about religious issues, and mutual mistrust were too great for a lasting peace. The States General governed in the absence of any other legitimate authority, even though it lacked the support of the provinces. Provincial revenues were slow in coming, and now the troops of the States General felt compelled to mutiny as well. The Hollanders and Zeelanders strove openly for a confederation based on the Swiss model. On 23 January 1579 representatives of the States of Holland, Zeeland and Utrecht, the Groningen Ommelands (the rural districts) and the *ridderschappen* (nobles) of Gelderland and Zutphen reached an agreement whereby they promised to lend one another military assistance, to raise an army of their combined forces, and to levy taxes collectively to maintain that army. In the weeks and months that followed, their ranks were swelled by representatives from the city of Ghent, the city and *ridderschap* of Nijmegen, various Frisian cities, Venlo, Amersfoort, Ypres, Antwerp, Bruges, the Brugse Vrije (the 'free region' around the city of Bruges), Lier and finally, on 11 April 1580, Drenthe. Since Stadholder Rennenberg had also signed the agreement, the provinces of Friesland, Overijssel, Groningen and the county of Lingen could also be considered part of the alliance. The counterbalance to this Union of Utrecht was the Union of Arras, formed by the Catholic provinces in the South, whose delegates immediately entered into negotiations with the king's representatives. The Low Countries, which had been joined for only thirty years, were already disintegrating.

The first peace talks between the rebels and the king's representatives took place in Cologne. Philip poisoned the atmosphere straightaway by declaring the prince of Orange an outlaw and placing a price on his head. Philip was clearly not prepared to make serious concessions. The States General, still the only authority in the Dutch-speaking provinces, did not wait for him to relent. They invited the duke of Anjou, a younger brother of the king of France, to be their new sovereign, hoping in this way to secure the much-needed support of France. Anjou accepted the offer and was sworn in on 23 January 1581. Half a year later the States General formally renounced Philip II in an Act of Abjuration, in which they took great pains to justify their revolutionary action. Anjou, however, was not recognised as the new sovereign by Holland and Zeeland, which offered the reins of government to William of Orange instead. His appointment as stadholder – first by Charles V and then by Philip II – had been recon-firmed in 1576 and was now renewed by both provinces. Elsewhere, too, Anjou found that the invitation of the States General did not automati-cally guarantee the provinces' support. In fact he had very little real power. Finally, in January 1583, at his wits' end, he attempted to stage a coup by marching on one of the unwilling cities, the ill-starred Antwerp. After this unsuccessful attack, Anjou left for France. Although he even-tually came to terms with the States General, this reconciliation meant nothing in practice. The duke of Anjou died in June 1584.

The death of Anjou precipitated yet another political crisis in the rebel-lious provinces, a crisis that was aggravated by a dangerous military threat which had meanwhile emerged in the Walloon (French-speaking) prov-inces, where the duke of Parma – son of Margaret of Parma, regent of the Netherlands – had assumed supreme command. In 1582 he succeeded his mother as the highest representative of the Spanish king in the Netherlands. Parma, a gifted strategist, also received the necessary mili-tary support from Madrid. His plan was to cut off the rich cities of Flanders and Brabant from their export markets by conquering the coast and the estuary of the River Scheldt. By 1584 he was well on the way to realising his goal. The crisis in the rebellious provinces deepened when, on 10 July 1584, one month after the death of Anjou, the prince of Orange died in Delft of gunshot wounds inflicted by a Catholic fanatic. He was the only politician whose charisma and popularity could have moved the divided provinces to cooperate. Now the rebels were easy prey to the disciplined operations of Parma, who in 1585 conquered one city after the other. In February Brussels opened its gates, in July it was Mechelen's turn, and on 17 August Parma took Antwerp, the biggest prize of all. This time there was no plundering; instead, those who wanted to leave were allowed to go freely. The message was clear: Parma was reason incarnate and it was perfectly safe to surrender to him. This strategy worked. By the end of 1587 the rebels had been pushed back to a position behind the Rivers Waal and IJssel. Yet again, international developments would come to their aid.

At the time of the Revolt in the Netherlands, similar civil wars were raging elsewhere in Europe. The increased availability of firearms had made it easier for Europeans to kill each other, and the Reformation had given them yet another reason to do so. During the whole of the sixteenth century, Europe was torn by armed conflicts caused by religious differences. The Habsburgs, who had interests everywhere, were inevitably involved in most of these conflicts. Philip, in setting out his policy, had to take into account not only the religious wars in France and the power relations in the German empire, but also his claims in Italy (where a keen interest was taken in the progress of the Dutch Revolt) and the necessity of facing the Turkish threat in the Mediterranean. William of Orange and his allies deliberately spurred the king's other enemies to greater efforts. The rebels had already profited several times from French intervention, as well as from the support of England. Queen Elizabeth had been watching the rise of Parma with increasing alarm. At home she feared the Catholic opposition, which, if it were to receive support from the other side of the Channel, could create serious problems for her government. She therefore decided, the day after the fall of Antwerp, to send troops to aid the Dutch. In exchange for her assistance, her confidant, the earl of Leicester, was installed as governor-general of the Netherlands, and the English were given three Dutch cities – Vlissingen (Flushing), Rammekens and Den Briel (Brill) – as a pledge. Two representatives of the queen were given seats on the Council of State. To break up this Protestant alliance, the Spanish resolved upon a daring countermove: an invasion of England and the establishment there, aided by support from Britain's Catholic population, of a pro-Spanish government. A large fleet was fitted out and Parma was ordered to concentrate his troops along the Flemish coast, in readiness to embark for England. The plan failed dramatically. English and Dutch squadrons prevented the Spanish ships in Flanders from leaving port, and the English attacked the Spanish ships in the Channel. After a subsequent attack (the battle of Gravelines), the Spanish tried to escape but were blown back (by what was later called a 'Protestant wind') and forced to sail around Scotland in an attempt to reach the Atlantic. In the summer of 1588 the famous Spanish Armada met an inglorious end when many of its ships foundered off the coasts of Scotland and Ireland.

In France the death of Anjou, the lawful heir to the throne, had caused a royal crisis. Philip II had remained aloof at first, but the Protestant pretender to the throne, Henri of Navarrre, gained the upper hand. Philip decided it was time to act. In the summer of 1590, Parma was ordered to invade France from his position in the Netherlands. France now had top priority on the Spanish agenda. Parma spread himself too thinly by attacking France and the Netherlands alternately, and the rebels consequently found themselves facing a weakened opponent. Moreover, the constant lack of money meant that the Spanish ranks were beset by mutinies, which occurred no less than forty times between 1590 and 1607. In 1596 the Spanish crown again declared bankruptcy.

The rebellious provinces, which had been losing ground since 1579, could at last attempt to recover some of their former territory. Led by the capable but cautious Maurits, son of William of Orange, the rebels scored important victories, especially along the eastern border. In 1591 Zutphen and Deventer were captured, in 1592 Steenwijk and the strategically important Coevorden, in 1593 Geertruidenberg and in 1594 the city of Groningen. In 1597 Maurits captured Twente and a number of fortified cities in the Achterhoek (the easternmost part of Gelderland) and more to the south, along the Rhine. In 1600 the States resolved, at the urging of Holland but against the wishes of Maurits, to put an end to the operations of privateers based on the Flemish coast. The army's march to Nieuwpoort and Dunkirk nearly ended in catastrophe, however. The Spanish troops, though admittedly in turmoil, rallied round their commander in the face of the enemy. On 30 June the Dutch army was forced into a direct confrontation on the beach at Nieuwpoort. Maurits, keeping a tight rein and strict discipline, succeeded in rescuing his army from its perilous position, though at the cost of many lives.

In 1599 the government in Brussels had voiced a desire for peace talks. The rebellious provinces, in an optimistic mood owing to the victories of recent years, had roundly rejected that offer – but Nieuwpoort turned the tide. Its aftermath was marked by a great deal of mudslinging between rebel army leaders and politicians. The victories continued, to be sure, but 1602 saw the arrival in the South of a new commander, Spinola, whose lack of military training was made up for by his organisational skills and his family connections in Genoa, which gave him direct access to the banking houses there. The fortunes of the war changed again, as Spinola put pressure on the line of defence recently erected along the Rivers IJssel and Waal. A number of cities along the eastern border of the Republic fell in 1606.

Finally the States General were willing to talk. In December there was another large-scale mutiny among the Spanish troops. The whole monarchy was threatening to collapse under the financial burden of the war in the Netherlands. The king ordered an immediate halt to all offensives. In February 1607 an official negotiator received the news from Brussels that the king was willing to accept the independence of the rebellious provinces. On 29 March an eight-month ceasefire was agreed upon. In November the Spanish crown again stopped interest payments on the public debt. The negotiations were now simplified by the fact that the king saw no alternative but to end the conflict. Thus on 9 April 1609 a truce was signed for a period of twelve years. The rebels had been given nearly everything they wanted regarding trade with the East Indies (which was to continue), the blockade of the River Scheldt (which would be maintained), and the practice of the Catholic faith (which was to be forbidden in the North). Spain had not yet formally recognised the Republic as an independent state, but its agreement to the truce made it appear to have done so. Other countries also saw it this way. Immediately after the ratification of the Twelve Years' Truce, the representatives of the rebellious provinces were recognised by France, England and Venice as full ambassadors. The Dutch Republic had become a fact.

A century of conflicts thus led to an unexpected outcome. A combination of diplomacy and military might had enabled Charles V to bring the Northern provinces under his control. In 1548 the Netherlands was formally recognised as a separate entity, but the desire to govern it from Brussels soon met with resistance. Charles's successor, Philip II, refused to compromise with the opposition, trying instead to suppress resistance by violent means. He did not succeed. In the interim, the rebels had set their hearts on restoring the independence they had known in their provinces before the arrival of the Habsburgs. Any victory over the Habsburgs, however, would require a joint effort, and the cooperation this demanded would inevitably compromise provincial autonomy. Though the rebellious provinces had succeeded in freeing themselves of the Habsburg yoke, it was no longer possible to return to the old situation in which Friesland, Groningen, Overijssel, Gelderland and Utrecht had all been independent states. Within the framework of the new Republic, the now united provinces were forced to seek a compromise between their dream of regional autonomy and the hard necessity of cooperation. Their attempts to maintain a delicate balance between the two were to last the whole of the seventeenth century.

Part I

War without end

2   An independent state (1609–1650)

In 1609, at the beginning of the Twelve Years' Truce, the young Republic was still a country with a split personality. The coastal provinces, which were experiencing spectacular economic growth, were overrun with immigrants, fleeing the violence elsewhere or in search of a better life. Ever since the Spanish had vacated Geertruidenberg after the Dutch recaptured it in 1593, the violence of war had been nothing more than a frightening memory and a financial burden to the people of Holland. The inhabitants of Friesland and Zeeland could also reckon themselves safe. In the inland provinces, however, people were still suffering from the ravages of war. Twente was in Spanish hands and would remain so for years to come. Groenlo was still Spanish, whereas the rest of the county of Zutphen had already surrendered to the States General. Elsewhere, too, the borders were in dispute. Limburg lay completely outside the authority of the States General. The Republic occupied the north-western tip of the duchy of Brabant, including Bergen-op-Zoom and the Orangist city of Breda, but 's-Hertogenbosch and the Meierij (one of the four parts of the duchy of Brabant) were completely under the authority of the king of Spain. By contrast, States Flanders (the part of Flanders now known as Zeeuws-Vlaanderen) was controlled by the Republic.

The west had made an amazingly quick recovery from the trauma of war. Leiden's textile industry had been in serious trouble before the Revolt, but by 1586 the civic authorities were already worrying about the housing shortage. Between 1582 and 1609 the population of Leiden had tripled, owing mainly to the immigration of textile workers and manufacturers from Flanders. Rents rose accordingly. To alleviate the housing shortage, an ambitious plan to expand the city was realised two years later, in 1611. In Amsterdam small expansion projects had already been carried out in 1585 and 1593, but in 1609 the authorities began to give serious thought to plans for a substantial enlargement to the city. That year the need for expansion was clearly demonstrated when more than three thousand dwellings were counted outside the city walls, representing a danger in times of war and a loss of revenue in times of peace.

In August 1609 the States of Holland granted the Amsterdam civic authorities permission to move the city wall a considerable distance to the west. Even so, it was another four years before work was begun on this urgently needed extension. The population of Amsterdam, like that of Leiden, had grown sharply, increasing from over 30,000 in 1585 to approximately 70,000 in 1609. Here, too, the influx of immigrants had been the main cause of the population explosion.

These immigrants had been drawn to Holland by the upsurge in the economy, which in turn was boosted by their labours. This process could be clearly traced in Leiden, where the Flemish introduced their 'new draperies': woollen cloth that was lighter and less expensive – and therefore easier to sell – than the traditional, heavy cloth for which Leiden had become famous. In Amsterdam it was the traders from Brabant and especially Antwerp and its environs who were responsible for the flourishing of the staple market. Some of these immigrant merchants were so rich and successful that it was tempting to think that Amsterdam owed its prosperity to them alone. This, however, would not be doing justice to the contribution made by the city's native traders. Especially remarkable was the fact that Hollanders and Brabanters worked together to explore new markets and to expand old ones. Their new markets included the Mediterranean region, which Dutch merchants did not penetrate until 1590, and the East Indies. In 1595 a first fleet of four ships was fitted out for direct trade with East Asia. In 1602 the Dutch East India Company was founded with capital investments coming mainly from Holland and Brabant. A reluctance to antagonise the Spanish caused the founding of the Dutch West India Company – plans for which were taking shape in 1606–07 – to be postponed until 1621. Nevertheless, one sign of progress was the opening in January 1609 of the Amsterdam Exchange Bank, which greatly simplified trade payments. Such developments provided clear proof that Amsterdam had overtaken Antwerp as the leading centre of trade in north-west Europe.

The eastern part of the Republic was much less prosperous. Deventer, conquered by the armies of the States General in 1591, had since been the most important base of operations in the defence of the eastern border. Further south, the front undulated in the area between the River IJssel and the Rhine. The Republic's conquest in 1597 of Rheinberg, Moers, Groenlo, Bredevoort, Goor, Enschede, Oldenzaal and Lingen seemed to secure a buffer zone, but in 1598 the Spanish troops advanced again. In October, Deventer was told to prepare for a siege, a warning that was issued again in January 1599, although the threat abated in the spring. Finally, in 1605, the Spanish launched a new offensive, capturing Wachtendonk, Oldenzaal and Lingen. In August and September,

Deventer served as the headquarters for the commanders of the armies of the States General. In 1606 Spinola and his troops regrouped and attacked, conquering Rheinberg, Groenlo and Lochem. The inhabitants of these stricken areas were often forced to pay heavy taxes, levied by both the Spanish and the Dutch simultaneously, under threat of pillaging and fire-raising. Instead of the sharp rise in population seen in Leiden and Amsterdam, here there was a serious drop in the number of inhabitants. Deventer, which had 8,000–10,000 inhabitants in 1579, had only half that number in 1600. To be sure, some recovery was noticeable by 1609, but it would be another century before the city reached its former size. Between 1550 and 1600, Twente lost at least one-quarter of its population, a loss which would be recovered only in the last decade of the seventeenth century.

These highly visible differences in the provinces' economic conditions, and the extent to which they suffered from armed conflicts, partially eclipsed another difference lurking below the surface: ideologically, the Republic was seriously divided. The Revolt had given a boost to the Calvinists, but only a small part of the population had officially joined their ranks. Probably no more than 10 per cent of the entire population had become members of the Reformed Church, while an unknown number attended Reformed services without actually joining the congregation. These informal churchgoers had not been confirmed and could not take part in celebrations of the Lord's Supper, nor were they subject to the disciplinary authority of the church council, which kept a close watch on the conduct of its flock. In 1609 the Republic had nearly equal numbers of Catholics and Calvinists, as well as members of smaller Protestant groups, such as the Mennonites. Many Lutherans and Jews also settled in the Republic in these years.

Although the Union of Utrecht had promised freedom of religion to people of all faiths, in fact the Dutch Reformed Church was the only one that was allowed to express its views publicly. Other religious communities were forced to meet secretly, in private conventicles and clandestine churches. The adherents of the Reformed faith were divided among themselves, as evidenced by the conflict that arose in 1604 between two professors of theology at Leiden University, Jacobus Arminius and Franciscus Gomarus, who held differing views on the precise meaning of one of the central tenets of Calvinist teaching, the doctrine of predestination. In Calvin's view, God was almighty and had preordained everything, including who would eventually attain salvation and who would not. Calvin, who rejected the Catholic doctrine of good works, maintained that salvation depended on God's grace alone. In Calvin's eyes, human sinfulness was so great that man could never earn salvation on his own merits. Moreover, the very idea that salvation could be *earned* was anathema to those who believed in the omniscience of God, whose providence could thus be crossed by man's free will. But by placing so much emphasis on predestination, Calvin had raised the thorny issue of whether people could actually be blamed for their sinfulness, and if not, how this affected the article of faith which asserts that Christ died for the sins of all humanity. Arminius attempted to deal with this problem by proposing that God did not confer grace in advance but offered it only on certain conditions. The faithful could either embrace that offer and live accordingly or disregard it and accept the consequences. It was an elegant solution, except that it detracted slightly from the omniscience of God by introducing an element of free will and human virtue. This was the very crux of the argument put forward by Gomarus, who accused Arminius of trying to slip an element of Catholicism into Reformed doctrine.

This professorial dispute could have been confined to academic circles were it not that Leiden University had been founded in 1575 expressly to train ministers of the Reformed Church in the United Provinces. A discussion of fundamental issues of faith among the most important professors at that university therefore involved the church as a whole, not only because it was important that clergymen agreed on the message they brought to society, but also because other fundamental issues were at stake, such as the role the Reformed Church played in the Republic. Without doubt the most important question was where the authority of the church resided: in the church itself, as the followers of Gomarus maintained, or in the Republic's political institutions, as the followers of Arminius reluctantly avowed.

The answer to that question would also settle the matter of how and by whom the correct doctrines of the Reformed Church should be instituted. In 1605 Arminius had petitioned the States General to convene a national synod to settle these differences of opinion. The States, deciding to convene a synod in the spring of 1606, wanted to know ahead of time which points would be discussed, but the parties could not agree on an agenda. In May 1608 the professors were invited to debate their standpoints publicly before the highest court of justice, the Supreme Court (Hoge Raad) in The Hague. The councillors of justice claimed not to understand the finer points of the arguments, declared the matters of dispute of little importance, and ordered the parties to bury their differences and stop stirring up trouble. Both men were invited to elucidate their positions in written statements which, it was agreed, were not to be printed for distribution to the public. Arminius, weakened by illness, never finished his paper. Acting in his place, Johannes Uyttenbogaert – court preacher to Prince Maurits and now the Arminians' foremost champion – set forth the Arminian standpoint. Gomarus, in violation of the agreement, attempted to circulate his treatise on church and state. It was confiscated from a Leiden printer by order of the States of Holland but published a short time later in another city. At Oldenbarnevelt's behest, Uyttenbogaert wrote a counter-treatise that appeared in February 1610 and was dedicated to the States of Holland, with that institution's permission. The conflict had now spilled over into the political arena.

In 1609 it was still not clear who was exercising authority in the United Provinces. A revolution had given birth to the Republic, and the pressures of war had continued to conceal countless contradictions and areas of tension. However, the complexity of internal relations – between the various provinces, between the provinces and the States General, between Holland and the stadholder, between clergymen and city governors – inevitably gave rise to vastly divergent interpretations of the situation. Religious strife – which had become the common denominator of all these tensions, now that the binding agent of war had disappeared, at least for the duration of the Truce – finally led to the outburst that had long seemed inevitable. From the very beginning the ideas of Gomarus had been popular among people of simple faith, who, many regents feared, might be unduly influenced by the church and its ministers. The Amsterdam burgomaster Cornelis Pietersz Hooft, father of the famous poet and historian Pieter Cornelisz Hooft, summed up the views of the clergy as an attempt to 'take over the whole government, in defiance of the rights of the provinces',[1] using the civic authorities as their instruments.

In January 1610 the Arminians submitted a petition to the States of Holland, calling for a provincial synod at which they could defend their standpoint, which had been set forth in their 'Remonstrance'. The very fact that they had called on the political authorities was itself a bone of contention, for it proved that the Remonstrants placed the authority of the state above that of the church. The delegates to the States of Holland were in a quandary and put off discussing the matter until July. Instead of calling a synod, the States decided to give representatives of both sides another chance to air their views. At the new debate, which took place on 11 March 1611, the Gomarists presented their rebuttal in the form of a written declaration, or Counter-Remonstrance. Again the politicians judged their differences to be of little consequence and ordered both sides to reach an amicable settlement, however difficult this had become. The dispute had long overstepped the boundaries of the church. The

---

[1] H. A. Enno van Gelder, *De levensbeschouwing van Cornelis Pieterszoon Hooft, burgemeester van Amsterdam 1547–1626* (Utrecht: Hes Publishers, 1982), p. 126.

opinions of Arminians and Gomarists alike, appearing in print, had now become a subject of public debate. The Counter-Remonstrants were adamant in their view that the integrity of the church and the Reformed faith hung in the balance. Counter-Remonstrants refused to attend services led by Remonstrant preachers, and were even prepared to walk to neighbouring towns every Sunday in the absence of a like-minded minister in their own town. For the Counter-Remonstrants this religious strife was no longer a question of faith but a matter of national import. In their eyes the Revolt had been fought to defend the Reformed faith. Anyone who tried to meddle with the new church and its religion was actually in league with the enemy. Among the Counter-Remonstrants were a great many Flemish refugees, who had left hearth and home because of their religious beliefs. Gomarus himself was one of them. Others, who saw in the truce with Spain a form of treason against the state, had their misgivings confirmed by the price rises that occurred immediately after the signing of the Twelve Years' Truce, when traders resumed exporting grain to the Southern Netherlands.

In the States General a Counter-Remonstrant group began to take shape in 1615 which included delegates from the provinces of Zeeland, Friesland and Groningen. Holland was seriously divided. Oldenbarnevelt – advocate of Holland and formally counsel to the States, but in fact the political leader of both the province and the Republic – supported the Remonstrant cause for reasons that had less to do with religion (he tended to favour the orthodox Calvinists) than with political pragmatism: the church, in his opinion, must not be allowed to play an independent role in politics. In 1614 the States, at his urging, had tried to impose tolerance by decree, but this only aroused new resistance from the Counter-Remonstrants, whose darkest suspicions about political interference in religious affairs were thereby confirmed. The cities of Amsterdam, Enkhuizen, Edam and Purmerend supported the Counter-Remonstrants. The States were unable to enforce a uniform course of action, and by 1616 the cities were actually in a position to determine their own religious policies. In such a volatile situation, a local conflict was all that was needed to spark a national crisis.

The town councillors of The Hague were Remonstrants whose leader, Johannes Uyttenbogaert, was also the court preacher. The leading Counter-Remonstrant preacher, Henricus Rosaeus, had been banned from preaching and expelled from the city for various contentious utterances. He had found accommodation in nearby Rijswijk, whither a flock of faithful followers made their way on Sundays to attend church. These treks through mud and mire, which were undertaken every Sunday all over the Republic, gave such churchgoers the nickname 'Mud Beggars'.

Late in 1616, when winter weather made trudging through the mud even more unpleasant, the Hague Counter-Remonstrants, encouraged by kindred spirits from Amsterdam, requested their own place of worship in The Hague. Their request was granted, provided Rosaeus did not preach there. The authorities placed the Gasthuiskerk (Hospital Church) at their disposal, but refused to give in to the dissenters' demand that they be allowed to choose their own church council, since this in fact amounted to a schism. On 13 January 1617 the States asked the stadholder to provide troops to help preserve law and order. Maurits refused. In the meantime, the Counter-Remonstrants had started holding services in private homes. On 22 January they went ahead and elected a church council – apparently nothing could be done to prevent it – before holding the first service in the Gasthuiskerk. This church was much too small, however, and in April several hundred orthodox Calvinists demonstrated at the Binnenhof – the buildings that housed both the States of Holland and the States General – for a larger church building. Again no action was taken. The States of Holland then decided to recruit 4,000 special peace-keeping troops called *waardgelders*, who swore allegiance to the city that employed them and not to the stadholder. The provinces of Zeeland, Friesland, Groningen and now also Gelderland urged the States of Holland to call a national synod. The majority in Holland, who understood that the Counter-Remonstrants now had the support of most of the provinces, retreated to their second line of defence, based on Article 13 of the Union of Utrecht, which upheld provincial autonomy with regard to religious affairs. On 9 July the Hague Counter-Remonstrants grew tired of waiting and seized the Kloosterkerk (Cloister Church), which had stood empty for many years. This building was practically next door to Oldenbarnevelt's house. Two weeks later Maurits attended a service in the Kloosterkerk. The die was cast.

For years Maurits and Oldenbarnevelt had been able to work side by side thanks to a tacit agreement about the division of labour: Oldenbarnevelt was responsible for political decisions; Maurits was in charge of the army. Their collaboration had not always gone smoothly – one of their differences of opinion had concerned the battle of Nieuwpoort in 1600 – but until 1609 it had worked to their mutual benefit. This relative harmony was disrupted by the Twelve Years' Truce, which the stadholder had not supported, for in effect it made him redundant. He began increasingly to see the foreign policy of Oldenbarnevelt – who was strongly pro-French and even willing to support their Catholic king in his suppression of the Protestant minority – as a threat to the independence of the Republic. The province of Holland was tending more and more to strike out on its own path within the Union, and the prevailing attitude there endangered the unity of the state and hence of the army, the most important product of the provinces' concerted efforts. The orthodox congregation saw in Maurits an ally who could stand up to Oldenbarnevelt, and Maurits decided, after long hesitation, to accept this challenge. His indecisiveness had perhaps been due to a disinclination to embrace either the Remonstrant or the Counter-Remonstrant cause. After Maurits had decided to attend the Counter-Remonstrant church, his father's widow, Louise de Coligny, and his half-brother and intended successor, Frederik Hendrik, were encouraged to stay with Uyttenbogaert, so that the interests of the dynasty would be safeguarded, no matter what the outcome of the conflict. Maurits had also hesitated because he knew that a civil war would fatally weaken the Republic. He therefore set to work with the utmost caution.

The orthodox Calvinists, who ruled the majority of provinces, were much better propagandists than the Remonstrants. Even in cities with Remonstrant governments, the orthodox Calvinists (Counter-Remonstrants) were very active in the streets, where they had been intimidating Remonstrants for years. In Holland the situation was becoming dangerous. The despair of Holland's leadership clearly emerges from the resolution passed by the States of Holland on 4 August 1617. This 'Sharp Resolution', as it became known, declared that a national synod was in conflict with provincial sovereignty and that complaints against city governments were inadmissible on principle. It also granted the cities permission to recruit special troops (*waardgelders*) to preserve the peace, and strongly urged everyone to follow the States' instructions only – 'all other orders notwithstanding',[2] meaning, of course, those of Maurits. This inflamed the Counter-Remonstrant opposition. In Utrecht, the other stronghold of Remonstrantism, the States decided the following month to recruit 600 *waardgelders*. Not only did such a force represent overkill in terms of the numbers needed to put down a disturbance, but there was no trace whatever of unrest in that province. In November, Maurits and his personal guard toured the cities of Holland in an attempt to bully them into submission. Though he failed in this endeavour, he did succeed in proving that both sides were willing to play for very high stakes. On 13 December, Oldenbarnevelt told the States that he was prepared to resign, a proposal he had made to Maurits several months earlier. Maurits thought that Oldenbarnevelt's resignation would solve nothing; the Remonstrant majority in the States did not want to let him go either. The bitter cup of defeat had to be drunk to the last drop.

[2] J. den Tex, *Oldenbarnevelt*, 5 vols. (Haarlem: Tjeenk Willink & Zoon, 1960–72), vol. III (1966), p. 494.

In Nijmegen, the annual election of the magistracy was to take place in January. Since its conversion to Protestantism in 1591, the city had adopted a procedure whereby its governors proposed candidates whose appointments were then confirmed by the stadholder. The Nijmegen authorities were hopelessly divided. The Remonstrant majority expected little good to come of the stadholder's appointments and politely informed him that from now on they would prefer to dispense with his help. The minority enjoyed the support of the garrison commander, despite a resolution passed by the States General ordering the military to take a neutral stand. When Maurits arrived in Nijmegen, it cost him little effort to tip the scales of civic government in favour of the Counter-Remonstrants. Oldenbarnevelt and his supporters, however, viewed Nijmegen as the prelude to a *coup d'état*. The Remonstrant cities in Holland announced that they would discontinue their contributions to the national defence budget and use the money instead to pay their own *waardgelders*. The stadholder considered this yet more proof that his opponents were attempting to dismantle the Union. His views were corroborated by the willingness of the Remonstrant cities in Holland to assume financial responsibility for the Utrecht *waardgelders*. On 31 July Maurits disbanded the Utrecht 'army', which he had viewed from the start as an act of rebellion, 'a conspiracy against himself and the constitution'.[3]

Although Holland still refused to cooperate, the other provinces had meanwhile agreed to convene the national synod on 1 November in Dordrecht. Invitations had been sent to foreign observers, so there was no turning back. The last act of the drama had already begun on 29 August – for Catholics, the feast day commemorating the beheading of John the Baptist – when Johan van Oldenbarnevelt, making his way to the States assembly, was summoned to a meeting with the stadholder. Leaning on his cane, which had become his constant companion, the seventy-year-old advocate of Holland climbed the stairs. When he arrived at the stadholder's quarters on the first floor, he was told that he was under arrest. The pensionaries of Rotterdam and Leiden, Hugo Grotius and Rombout Hogerbeets, were arrested a short while later. His detention in the province of Holland without the consent of the States of Holland was in flagrant violation of the law. The States protested fiercely, but to no avail. Oldenbarnevelt was locked up in a room overlooking the Binnenhof. Four examining magistrates, including two outspoken enemies of the advocate, were put in charge of preliminary inquiries.

---

[3] Ibid., vol. III, p. 618.

Oldenbarnevelt was refused the benefit of counsel and denied access to documents pertaining to his defence. He was not even allowed pen and paper. Elsewhere in Holland, one city after another revamped its town council, removing Remonstrants and appointing Counter-Remonstrant followers of the stadholder. Starting on 15 November, Oldenbarnevelt was questioned at length by the examining magistrates. Their interrogations focused on the imbroglio surrounding the disbandment of the Utrecht *waardgelders*, the contacts he was suspected of maintaining with the enemy (a charge of which he was ultimately acquitted), and his attempts to undermine the religious and political order. Solemn and dignified, he protested his innocence on all counts. His rigidity, aggravated by his arrogance and snobbishness, had not endeared him to people in the past, nor did it induce his adversaries to be kind to him now. Indeed, many of them thought that the Remonstrants' power could be broken only by removing their leader. In February and March 1619, Oldenbarnevelt was again questioned, now by the twenty-four judges appointed by the provinces to give their opinion of his behaviour. On 14 April the interrogation was abruptly discontinued. The final indictment contained 215 points. It took the judges three weeks to formulate their decisions, despite the prevailing view that the verdict had been a foregone conclusion. Only the accused still seemed unaware of the seriousness of his situation. On 9 May the death sentence was pronounced, after which it took three days to add the finishing administrative touches to the verdict. On 12 May Oldenbarnevelt was told of the outcome. Eyewitnesses reported that he seemed surprised, but remained in complete control of himself during his final hours. He sent Reverend Walaeus to ask Maurits to rescind the order to seize his property, at which time the stadholder apparently asked whether Oldenbarnevelt had requested a pardon. He had not. The next morning – a beautiful, sunny day – the elderly advocate of Holland, leaning on his cane, climbed the scaffold that had been erected in the Binnenhof. He reportedly mumbled something about this being 'fine recompense for forty years of faithful service'.[4] Shortly thereafter the executioner, who had travelled from Utrecht for the occasion, carried out the death sentence.

In Dordrecht the synod had meanwhile put religious affairs to rights. The Remonstrant cause had been doomed from the start, since all the delegates but two were Counter-Remonstrant sympathisers. They were supported by the provincial synods, which had been held previous to the national synod. The dispute between the Remonstrants and

[4] Ibid., vol. III, p. 744.

Counter-Remonstrants was only one of the points on the agenda. The synod also resolved to produce a new, authoritative Dutch Bible. This edition, commissioned and approved by the States General, became known as the States Bible and was to prove an important influence on the evolution of the Dutch language. The delegates also discussed church organisation and the procedure to be followed in appointing ministers. The most important subject, however, was the rupture in the ranks of the Reformed Church. The Remonstrants were invited to defend their views, and on 7 December the leader of their delegation, Simon Episcopius, a professor at Leiden University, argued passionately for the Remonstrant cause. The subsequent deliberations, which lasted for months, did nothing to change the outcome. In May 1619 the synod officially condemned Remonstrant notions as heresy and the Remonstrants themselves as 'perturbers' of church and state. Preachers sympathetic to the Remonstrant cause were put on a blacklist until they declared themselves amenable to the doc- trines adopted at the synod. Those who refused were delivered up to the States General and subsequently banished from the Republic. Some 200 ministers lost their livings. In June the synod was concluded. Maurits thus succeeded in putting an end to the disputes marring the period of the Twelve Years' Truce before the Truce itself came to an end.

The Twelve Years' Truce was by its very nature a temporary arrange- ment. Lurking in the background was the important question of what was going to happen in 1621: lasting peace or a resumption of war. Maurits's *coup d'état* and the beheading of Oldenbarnevelt had completely dis- mantled the peace party in the Republic. In Spain, the duke of Lerma – chief minister and foremost champion of a continuation of the Truce – was dismissed from office, which made a resumption of hostilities almost certain. Still, no significant military operations were reported in April 1621 when the Truce officially expired. The preparations in the Republic were of an economic nature. The Flemish coast was blockaded, the high import duties – stipulated in a law dating from 1603 – on goods from the Southern Netherlands again came into force, the rivers were closed to traffic and investors were encouraged to put their money into colonial trade, the expansion of which could not fail to harm the Spanish empire. The first shots were not fired until August, during an artillery duel near Sluis, in States Flanders.

Both sides had a double agenda. Few people in the Republic believed in the possibility of conquering ten Southern provinces at this late stage. Many did not even think it desirable. Madrid, to say nothing of Brussels, did not seriously expect to recapture the seven rebellious provinces in the North. Moreover, the war that would become known as the Thirty Years War (1618–48) had broken out in Germany, and the Spanish Habsburgs

Figure 3   The end of the Truce in 1621. This emblematic print shows the
Dutch maiden sitting in an enclosed garden (often used to symbolise the Low
Countries and later the Republic), leaning against a tree hung with the provinces'
coats of arms. The commentary of the burgher and the peasant (behind the
garden) on the end of the Truce appears beneath the print. In the middle,
Victory attempts to free Mars – the symbol of war – of his chains. Behind them,
monks try in vain to keep a pyramid (the Truce) upright. On the right, Mars
throws money and weapons to the gathering crowd (Atlas van Stolk 1529).

were heavily involved. Though it was obvious that negotiations were
inevitable, there was still insufficient basis for agreement, and so the
fighting continued. Both sides were willing to continue the struggle,
though neither had a clear-cut strategy apart from wearing down the
opposition and collecting trump cards to place on the negotiating table,
should peace talks ever materialise. Both parties showed remarkable
restraint during military manoeuvres – there was scarcely any plundering,
and few assaults or rapes – in an effort to prevent feelings from running
unnecessarily high.

In January 1622 the Spanish scored their first victory, capturing Jülich
on the Rhine. In the spring Frederik Hendrik marched into Brabant, his
cavalry advancing as far as the walls of Brussels before he was forced to
retreat. In February 1624 Spinola and his troops attacked Groningen and
shortly thereafter Gelderland. On 28 August he laid siege to Breda, and
the city fell nine months later, marking a great triumph for the Spanish
general, the more so because Breda was an Orangist city. Maurits had
kept Spinola dangling in recent years, fobbing him off with vague talk of

peace initiatives, so that the capture of Breda and the destruction of Orange property was the frustrated Spinola's way of exacting revenge. In Spain the elation at this spectacular success led Velazquez, the court painter, to immortalise the handing over of the keys of the city to the Spanish. Maurits himself had been spared that humiliation, for he had died on 23 April at the age of fifty-seven. In his last years the stadholder had lost his grip on the political process in the Republic. On 2 June, Maurits's half-brother Frederik Hendrik, his junior by sixteen years, was sworn in as stadholder of Holland and Zeeland.

The resumption of hostilities caused taxes to skyrocket, which together with the blockades set up by both sides led to a serious economic recession. The situation worsened after 1625, when the Spanish, beset by financial difficulties, resolved to consolidate their territory and focus their attention on the war at sea. A small but effective Spanish fleet operated from its base at Dunkirk, which at that time was still Flemish territory. This fleet was aided by a large number of private ships supplied with letters of marque, which were actually licences granted by the king, giving the bearer the right to hold up enemy ships and escort them, under arrest, back to port. The Republic also availed itself of this means of reprisal; in Zeeland in particular, privateering was a flourishing business. The Dunkirk privateers were much more effective, however, for the simple reason that so many Dutch freighters and fishing vessels plied those waters. Despite all attempts to protect them, they remained an easy prey. In 1628, 245 Dutch ships were captured or sunk; in 1632, a record number of 305 ships were lost. Those living in the harbour cities were at their wits' end. The Republic could make reprisals only in the colonial territories. In 1627 the Dutch West India Company (WIC) seized fifty-five Spanish and Portuguese ships in African and American waters. The following year the WIC struck even harder, when Piet Heyn captured the entire Spanish silver fleet in the bay of Matanzas in Cuba. The booty was an unbelievable 11.5 million guilders, approximately two-thirds of the Republic's annual war budget. Heyn, who received only 7,000 guilders for his efforts, felt so cheated that he immediately resigned. His name lives on, however, at least in the Netherlands, where he is still a famous folk hero.

The financial blow thus dealt to the Spanish crown unexpectedly provided the stadholder, Frederik Hendrik, with the means to launch an offensive. By April 1629 the States army had increased to an unprecedented 77,000 troops. After several diversionary manoeuvres, the States army laid siege to 's-Hertogenbosch, the most important stronghold in the chain of fortified cities protecting the Spanish Netherlands. In July the Habsburgs launched a counter-offensive, attacking the besiegers from the rear. Civic militiamen from Holland and sailors of the WIC were sent as reinforcements, for Frederik Hendrik refused to give up, even on 13 August when General Montecuculi occupied Amersfoort. On 14 September, 's-Hertogenbosch surrendered. Madrid was stunned by the news. Instead of sending his troops to their winter quarters, Frederik Hendrik decided to stay his course. Various strongholds in Westphalia were captured that winter. In 1631 the war seemed stalemated, but the following year the stadholder launched a large-scale offensive in the Southern provinces. On 22 May 1632 the States General issued a general call to revolt against Habsburg authority in the South, but no response was forthcoming. Frederik Hendrik then tried his luck along the River Maas. In early July he captured Venlo, Roermond and Sittard in the Maas valley and a few days later laid siege to Maastricht. This operation was so successful that the city fell into the hands of the States army on 23 August 1632. The Habsburg armies, tied down in Germany, could do nothing to save this stronghold.

The fall of 's-Hertogenbosch made the Spanish much more willing to negotiate. Frederik Hendrik was also inclined to do so, although the provinces were seriously divided. Gelderland and Overijssel, which had suffered from both the military actions and the river blockades, supported the peace initiatives. The city of Utrecht opposed them, but the majority in the provincial States of Utrecht supported the stadholder. Zeeland – mindful of the interests of the WIC, which would certainly be harmed by peace – was completely opposed to negotiations. Friesland and Groningen were also against the idea. It was thus up to Holland to break the dead-lock, but the province was hopelessly divided. In Amsterdam, where regents sympathetic to the Remonstrant cause had again gained the upper hand, there was support for peace talks, likewise in the trading cities of Rotterdam, Delft and Dordrecht. By contrast, the industrial cities of Haarlem, Leiden, and Gouda, together with Gorcum, Hoorn and Enkhuizen, were fiercely opposed to making any concessions. They demanded that the Republic first tend to internal affairs – both political and religious – before making important decisions about war and peace. The war party also held sway in the public debate. Many clergymen did not shrink from issuing warnings from the pulpit against any accord with the godless Spanish. Most of the pamphlets published in these years were opposed to peace, so it was no wonder that the negotiations made little headway. After the fall of Maastricht, Madrid also lost interest, since the Spanish position was now thought to be so weak that no satisfactory results could be achieved.

The fortunes of the war changed in the following years. On 26 July 1635 the Spanish launched a surprise attack on Schenkenschans, capturing this very important stronghold, strategically situated at the fork of the Rivers Rhine and Waal below Lobith. The Hague was up in arms and an all-out attempt was made to recapture this key position, but victory did not come until 30 April 1636. The following year it was the Republic's turn to celebrate: on 7 October 1637 the army of the States General managed to capture Breda, the last link in the buffer encircling the heart of the Republic, within the Rivers IJssel and Maas. The struggle continued to swing back and forth with no significant changes in the balance of power. The basis for talks therefore had to be sought elsewhere. Spain had been at war with France since 1635 and was still involved in the Thirty Years War in Germany. In May 1640 a rebellion broke out in Catalonia when the people revolted en masse against the unbearable tax burden imposed on them by the Spanish crown to finance its wars. When the Portuguese, who had been subjected to Spanish authority since 1580, were called in to help suppress the revolt in Catalonia, they rebelled as well. These events induced the Spanish king to make far-reaching peace proposals to France and the Republic, on the condition that they keep well away from the Iberian peninsula.

In Holland there were mixed reactions to this propitious turn of events. On the one hand, the war party wanted all peace proposals to be shelved until such time as a general settlement of all European differences could be effected. The peace party, on the other hand, argued in the present circumstances for drastic cutbacks in expenditure, urging a reduction in the size of the army. In December 1642 the States General passed the first resolution aimed at troop reductions. The previous January, Frederik Hendrik had already called upon the provinces to enter into peace talks, but it was more than a year before the first delegates were appointed, the procedure being complicated by the necessity of naming delegates from all the provinces to ensure a broad base of support. The war party was not prepared to give up without a fight, and the long-drawn-out process of appointing delegates provided ample opportunity for obstructionist tactics. In March 1644 the six provinces took the position that an accord did not necessarily have to comply with all the wishes of the States General, but Zeeland insisted that a minimum set of demands be formulated. In April 1645 the delegation was still not complete. On 14 July the States General decided that the delegates would travel in August to the German city of Münster to begin negotiations with the Spanish. Zeeland's continued opposition managed to delay their departure until January 1646.

In May 1646, when the peace talks were well under way, things began to proceed quickly. By July the basic text of an accord calling for a twenty-year truce had been agreed upon. The Republic was to be recognised by Madrid as an independent nation and the Spanish crown was to acquiesce in the blockade of the River Scheldt. During the summer and autumn this accord was discussed in the provinces. Friesland and Groningen, after long hesitation, finally agreed to it, but Zeeland kept up its opposition. The States General nevertheless sanctioned the accord on 27 October 1646. In December, Spain recognised the status quo in the East and West Indies and declared itself willing to turn the truce into a lasting peace. On 8 January 1647 the preliminary signing took place. The delegate from Zeeland, Johan de Knuyt, an adherent of the stadholder, signed in defiance of instructions from the States of Zeeland expressly forbidding him to do so. A large Spanish bribe had persuaded him to change his mind. The only problem remaining was the religious order in the Generality Lands – the areas of Flanders, Brabant and Limburg which the Republic had captured. Madrid had always demanded that Catholic worship be permitted there, but the States General found this unacceptable. It was suddenly realised, however, that the treaty did not have to settle this problem, since it was a matter not for the king but for the pope, who had spiritual sovereignty everywhere. When Frederik Hendrik, who since 1642 had strongly backed a political solution, died on 14 March 1647, the war party immediately threw another spanner in the works. Friesland, Groningen, the Utrecht *ridderschap* and the cities of Utrecht and Amersfoort demanded that amendments be made to the treaty. Zeeland persevered in its opposition. To the indignation of the Spanish delegation, new talks became necessary, which led to a number of changes in the treaty. On 30 January 1648 the results were again signed, though with the abstention of the Utrecht delegate. On 4 April both Utrecht and Zeeland refused to ratify the treaty. Utrecht relented after a few days, but an emissary sent by the States General at the end of April was not able to mollify the States of Zeeland. Nevertheless, the official ratifications were exchanged with the Spanish delegation on 15 May at the Münster town hall. The war was at an end. The Republic had at last been recognised by all the powers of Europe as an independent state.

In the Republic, however, the peace treaty brought unexpected events in its wake. Frederik Hendrik had been succeeded in the spring of 1647 by his eldest son, the twenty-one-year-old William. For William II the stakes were considerably higher than they had been for his father, a second-class sovereign whose capacity for military leadership had enabled him to work his way up to the position of informal head of state of an important power. In 1641 a marriage had been arranged between William and the eldest daughter of the king of England, but unlike the other crowned heads of Europe, who exercised considerable power in their dominions, William had very limited authority in the Republic. The peace also threatened to deprive him of the opportunity to prove himself on the field of battle and

Figure 4 A little-known depiction of the peace negotiations in Münster, showing the Dutch and Spanish delegates exchanging the ratified peace treaty. Printed below is 'Glory to God in the highest and peace on earth', a motto taken from Luke 2:14 (Atlas van Stolk 1948).

thus to earn the same esteem in which his illustrious predecessors had been widely held. It is therefore easy to understand why the young stadholder had turned against the peace treaty and recommended that the provinces do the same. That advice had not been heeded, and now William had to face up to the fact that the cities of Holland were determined to reap the benefits of the peace treaty at the earliest possible opportunity.

The first reduction in troops had already taken place in the summer of 1648, and discussions of the desired, or necessary, size of the States army had since dominated the political agenda. In the States General the provinces could not reach an agreement. On 4 June 1650 the States of Holland decided on their own authority to disband some of the troops who were paid from provincial revenues. That a province could take such action on its own was due to the Republic's system of military funding, in which a province usually made payments directly to the companies it had been assigned to support. For a future military leader like William, this was an unacceptable infringement of his authority. At his instigation the States General sent a delegation to tour the cities of Holland. Amsterdam was expected to offer the most resistance, and William had secretly resolved to use violence to bring the city to its knees. A ridiculous slip-up – the approaching army, 12,000 strong, got lost in the fog but were noticed nonetheless by a passing postal courier, who reported it just in time for the city gates to be closed – caused the attempt to fail on 30 July. The parties – the stadholder and the city of Amsterdam – both at a severe loss as to how to proceed, quickly arrived at a compromise. Internal relations were in profound disarray when fate intervened. At the end of October the stadholder was discovered to have smallpox, and ten days later he died, leaving behind a wife heavily pregnant with her first child.

Since 1609 the Republic had been developing rapidly. Its population had increased greatly, keeping pace with the growth in prosperity. Despite great internal rifts, the Republic of the United Provinces had succeeded in enlarging its territory and in forcing Spain to accept a peace treaty confirming its independence. The disputes that had plagued the period of the Twelve Years' Truce were over; all seemed quiet on the home front. Though the provinces regularly disagreed, they nevertheless managed to outline a common policy. The Peace of Münster appeared to usher in a new era. Admittedly, William II's rash attack on Amsterdam had cast a shadow over the political landscape, but his death now went a long way towards dispelling that shadow.

3   A world power (1650–1713)

The year 1650 marked a political turning point for the Dutch Republic: for the first time in its short history, there was no member of the House of Orange who was a suitable candidate for the office of stadholder. This situation posed fundamental questions about the existing political order. At the invitation of the States of Holland, eighteen delegates from all the provinces gathered to discuss the matter on 18 January 1651 in the Knights' Hall (Ridderzaal) at the Binnenhof in The Hague. This Great Assembly, which lasted until 21 August, debated the most important aspects of the Union's form of government and its power structures. On the subject of religion, the Acts of the Synod of Dordrecht were confirmed, including the basic principle that church organisation was a matter for the provinces. A general amnesty was declared for those who had been involved in the attempted coup of 1650. The thorniest issue, however, was what to do about the stadholderate. Friesland, led by the Frisian stadholder Willem Frederik, expressed the view that each province should be required to have a stadholder and that the army needed an 'eminent head', chosen, in the light of recent history, preferably from the House of Orange. Willem Frederik also offered to serve as acting captain-general until his young cousin, the infant Prince William, came of age. Even before the assembly convened, however, Holland had decided not to appoint a new stadholder and had persuaded the other provinces to endorse its point of view. The assembly duly confirmed, in accordance with Holland's wishes, that the stadholderate was also a matter to be decided by each province separately. The Great Assembly thus paved the way for provincial autonomy, at the same time affirming Holland's predominance, for without a stadholder to coordinate their efforts, the other provinces could not possibly hold their own against the Hollanders.

The question of the stadholderate had important ramifications not only for internal power relations but also for foreign affairs. The attempted coup on Amsterdam had shown once again that domestic politics were closely connected with foreign policy, especially where the army was concerned. Moreover, although nothing had changed with regard to diplomatic ceremony – the representatives of the Dutch Republic still followed those of the monarchies and the Republic of Venice, this place having been assigned them by the French king Henri IV in December 1609 – the status of the Republic had been radically altered by the Peace of Münster. During the second half of the seventeenth century, the Republic of the United Netherlands was in fact much more important than many a monarchy. The Thirty Years War had so eroded the power of the Austrian Habsburgs that the constellation of power in Europe was now determined by France, England and the Dutch Republic. In May 1659, for example, these three states dictated the terms of a peace settlement which eventually ended the Northern War between Sweden, Denmark and Poland. The search for a new balance of power was accompanied by a long series of wars. The Dutch Republic and England were at war three times between 1652 and 1674. The year 1672 marked the beginning of forty years of nearly continuous war between France and the Republic. The wars between France and England were not decided until 1815 at the Battle of Waterloo. The Republic had two fundamental interests at stake: preserving its territorial integrity and securing free trade. Many of Holland's politicians saw England as the greatest danger to Dutch trade and France as the greatest military threat. Johan de Witt, acting Grand Pensionary since 15 June 1652 and Grand Pensionary since 23 July 1653,[1] thought that Holland should always let commercial interests take precedence. It was a simple fact, however, that the French threat could not be ignored. De Witt's two-pronged security policy therefore aimed not only at warding off the French threat but also at preventing France and England from forming an alliance against the Republic. The position of the young prince of Orange played an important role in this delicate balancing act.

De Witt was fortunate at first, because the ruling authorities in both France and England were seriously weakened. The English Civil War, which had broken out in 1642, had inflicted deep wounds. In 1649, Charles I was beheaded after a mock trial. Cromwell's government was rather ambivalent towards the Republic, though in some respects it was viewed as an ally that could help to consolidate the young Commonwealth. To this end, in March 1651 Cromwell put forward a plan to form a union between the two Protestant naval powers, but his proposal met with little enthusiasm in the States General, partly owing to

---

[1] After Oldenbarnevelt's conviction, the name of his office, Advocate of Holland (*landsadvocaat*), was changed to Pensionary of Holland (*raadpensionaris*, commonly rendered in English as Grand Pensionary). The term of office was reduced from life to five years, after which the term could be extended.

the friction caused by conflicting commercial interests. The Republic was conducting a great deal of trade which the English thought they could handle just as well. During the war with Spain, the English had been able to expand their activities in the Mediterranean, but in 1648 the Dutch returned in full force. Cromwell attempted to curb this commercial competition by political means, proclaiming in October 1651 the Navigation Act, which stipulated that all goods transported to England be conveyed on English ships or ships from the goods' country of origin. This measure was enacted purely to thwart the Dutch, the most important middlemen and carriers in Europe. Moreover, Dutch vessels were the principal targets of the arrests on the open sea carried out at this time by the English. The Republic's attempts to protect its merchant fleet led to a great naval battle off the coast of Dover on 29 May 1652. Two months later Britain declared war on the Dutch Republic.

Britain's declaration of war included the reproach that the States General had failed to recognise the threat posed by the tyranny of the House of Orange. Once again, international and domestic issues appeared to be connected. Charles I was William II's father-in-law. To be sure, Frederik Hendrik had remained scrupulously neutral during the first phase of the English Civil War, but the republicans in England nevertheless feared that a restoration of the English monarchy might begin in the Dutch Republic with support from the House of Orange. Their declaration of war did nothing to prevent this. On the contrary, it was precisely the threat of war that sparked off a tremendous call in the Republic for a restoration of the stadholderate. In August 1652, Johan de Witt could not walk the streets of Middelburg without a bodyguard, ample proof of the extent to which the tide of popular opinion had turned against his regime. In the summer of 1653 – after several painful defeats inflicted on the Dutch fleet, which proved to be no match for the larger English battleships – riots broke out in many cities in Holland to demonstrate support for young William III. De Witt was warned that an attempt might be made on his life. On 28 July 1653, Zeeland, which chaired the States General at the time, made a motion to appoint the prince supreme commander of the army and navy as soon as he came of age.

Meanwhile England and the Dutch Republic were both coming to the end of their financial tether. England was the designated victor, inasmuch as either side could be said to be victorious, but in England, too, there was a genuine desire for an end to hostilities. On 31 July, Cromwell's Council of State again proposed a union of the two Republics, promising to revoke the Navigation Act in exchange for Dutch cooperation. The States General roundly rejected this proposal. In November, Cromwell made another offer: he was willing to make peace if the seven provinces would promise in the States General never to appoint any member of the House of Orange-Nassau to the office of stadholder or the position of captain-general. This, too, was found unacceptable by a majority of the provinces. Thus followed months of complicated negotiations in London, in which delegates from both the States General and the States of Holland represented the Dutch Republic. The result that emerged in the spring of 1654 was correspondingly ambiguous. The peace treaty looked innocent enough, but it was accompanied by a secret clause (the Act of Exclusion) in which the States of Holland declared that in future the Oranges would be excluded from the stadholdership in Holland. When the States General hastily ratified the treaty on 21 April, they knew nothing of this appendix, which was revealed only a week later in a closed session of the States of Holland. Even though Holland had more to gain than any other province from a settlement promising the restoration of free trade, a number of towns in Holland initially voted against the treaty. After two long days of discussion, however, the majority saw no choice but to ratify the accord. De Witt was instructed to write a defence of the resolution, and this raised further suspicions that he had actually been the evil genius behind the Act of Exclusion. In fact, this Act turned out to be a serious embarrassment to the republican regime in Holland, because it continued to strike a note of discord for years to come.

With France the Republic had fewer dealings at first. The underage Louis XIV had been confronted in 1648 with a huge internal revolt (the Fronde). France was also at war with Spain until 1659, when Spain, no longer able to sustain the war, agreed to the Treaty of the Pyrenees, which meant that the French now had their hands free. This treaty had important consequences for the Republic, because the Spanish subsequently made severe reductions in the size of their military force in the Southern Netherlands, where it had been keeping up a second front against France. The Spanish Netherlands therefore became vulnerable to a French invasion, which would make France the Republic's next-door neighbour. This scenario was greeted in The Hague with considerable trepidation. The peace treaty eventually concluded with Paris in 1662 was negotiated during a time of great tension in Franco-Dutch relations. French pirates were tormenting Dutch ships in the Mediterranean, and the reprisals taken by a Dutch naval squadron commanded by Michiel de Ruyter caused great consternation in Paris. Furthermore, in June 1659, France increased tariffs on imported goods, which mainly affected the products exported by Holland. The death in 1661 of Cardinal Mazarin, who had acted as adviser to the French king during the years of his minority, meant that the time had come for Louis himself to take command.

In England, the monarchy had been restored the previous year. Charles II had been staying in Breda with relatives from the House of Orange when he received the invitation in May 1660 to return to England. He interrupted his homeward journey to stop in The Hague, where he was given a magnificent reception. Although the States General had thereby hoped to gain his favour, their efforts were in vain. Before the year was out, Parliament passed a new Navigation Act. Moreover, Charles II's new ambassador in The Hague was Sir George Downing, a man known for his antipathy to the Dutch. The restoration of Charles II had also given new hope to his sister, Mary Stuart, the mother of nine-year-old William III. On 20 July, Mary petitioned the States of Holland to make her son a 'child of state' and assume responsibility for his education. The States agreed to this and subsequently revoked the Act of Exclusion.

It was at this time that a new conflict with England began to take shape. The Company of Adventurers, supported by the English king, and the Dutch West India Company were competing for the hefty profits to be made in the American sugar trade. Another source of rivalry was the slave trade, so essential for the supply of labour to the sugar plantations in the Caribbean. In the spring of 1664 an English fleet captured most of the Dutch forts on the west coast of Africa; in May the colony of New Amsterdam also fell and was promptly rechristened New York. De Ruyter, following secret instructions, proceeded with his squadron from the Mediterranean to the African coast, where he occupied a number of English trading posts, which outraged the merchants in London. In January 1665 all Dutch ships at English ports were put under embargo and a number of others were seized and brought in from the open sea. This goaded the Dutch into action. On 13 June, in the first armed encounter, which took place off Lowestoft, the Republic suffered a heavy defeat despite the deployment of more than 100 ships and 20,000 men. In the first half of 1666 the Dutch won one naval battle (the Four Days' Fight) but lost another (the Two Days' Fight). The tide did not turn until September of that year, when a great fire which raged for days destroyed a large part of London. The ensuing economic hardship crippled the English fleet by slowing down the repair of old ships and the building of new ones. In June 1667 a Dutch fleet under the command of De Ruyter was able to sail practically unimpeded up the River Medway to Chatham. After suffering such a huge loss of face, the English announced in mid-August that they were willing to negotiate a peace settlement.

While De Witt and the other leaders of the Republic were doing their utmost to bring the war with England to a satisfactory conclusion, others had been trying to profit from the situation. The bishop of Münster, who was fonder of fighting than of praying, invaded the Republic in September 1665. The weakened army of the States General did not succeed in repulsing him; he was eventually persuaded to retreat only by a shortage of funds and the advancing French army. In Orangist circles everything was being done to promote the prince, some of his adherents even going so far as to collude with the English, with whom they were officially at war. A *faux pas* on the part of one of the conspirators, the French *rittmaster* Henri Buat, inadvertently brought the plot into the open. On 18 August 1666, Buat accidentally gave De Witt a letter intended for himself, which revealed their designs so clearly that he was beheaded for high treason on 11 October. Even though the Republic had officially been on friendly terms with France since 1662, their relationship had always been one of mutual distrust. When it became clear to the French that the balance of power between England and the Republic had not been significantly altered by their second naval war, they resumed their policy of aggression and invaded the Spanish Netherlands, conquering a considerable part of the county of Flanders and the duchy of Brabant, as well as Lille and its environs, which capitulated at the end of August 1667.

De Witt attempted to steer the course of events towards a more favourable outcome. The Peace of Breda, concluded in June 1667, had temporarily averted the English threat. The Oranges had been held in check by a Perpetual Edict passed by the States of Holland on 5 August 1667, which abolished the stadholderate and declared that in Holland the offices of stadholder and captain-general (supreme commander of the armed forces) were incompatible. France posed the stickiest problem. January 1668 saw the sudden emergence of a Triple Alliance consisting of the Dutch Republic, England and Sweden. There was such haste to form this coalition that the States General ratified it without consulting the provinces. The intention of this alliance – to halt the expansion of France – was immediately perceived in Paris. It was, however, an act of desperation. Sweden, far removed from the French borders, could scarcely offer effective resistance. England, after two undecided wars, was an unreliable partner. Moreover, the French king was grievously insulted by such behaviour from a state that was, at least on paper, his ally. Secret negotiations were initiated between Paris and London, and on 1 June 1670 the French and English kings signed the Treaty of Dover. Their aim was to reduce the Dutch Republic to a second-rate power. England planned first to defeat the Dutch on land and sea and then to establish a puppet government under the leadership of the young William III. The English originally intended to carry out this plan during the campaign of 1671, but then decided to postpone it for a year. The Dutch ambassador in

London was kept in the dark all this time. In Paris, Pieter de Groot, son of the famous jurist Hugo de Groot (Hugo Grotius), did in fact suspect foul play, but his warnings were not taken seriously in The Hague.

The army of the States General had suffered greatly from both Holland's dominance in domestic politics and the two wars with England. It was not until the autumn of 1670 that The Hague began to worry seriously about its land defences, though it long persisted in thinking that a couple of regiments of foreign mercenaries could close the biggest gaps. The politicians seemed not to understand that time was needed for units to drill and become attuned to one another. Neither did it help that the supreme commander, Paulus Wirtz, did not carry much weight in The Hague. Eventually it was suggested that William III, who had turned twenty-two in November 1671, be appointed captain-general for one campaigning season only. The prince refused this temporary appointment, but on 24 February 1672 the threat of war induced the States General to appoint him captain and admiral-general for life. On 19 April William assumed his post at Doesburg, where the River IJssel functioned as the main line of defence against a French invasion. That such an invasion was imminent had been known since 6 April, when Louis XIV had declared war on the Dutch Republic, albeit for very vague reasons.

The situation on the River IJssel was little less than catastrophic. On 22 May there were 9,200 infantry, 4,800 cavalry and perhaps 1,000 men in the garrison who could be called upon to fight. Two weeks later their numbers had doubled, but many of these reinforcements were civic militiamen and peasants who had been ordered to the front. This ad hoc army was now confronted with a well-drilled, professional fighting force three or four times its size. By 3 June the French army had laid siege to the Netherlandish forts along the Rhine – Jülich, Orsoy, Wesel, Büderich and Rhineberg – all of which surrendered almost immediately. On 12 June the French crossed the Rhine. A dry summer had made it possible simply to wade across the rivers. In Nijmegen and Arnhem there was rioting, testifying to the unwillingness of the populace to undergo a siege. Panic seized The Hague. On 13 June a delegation was dispatched to the French king, who had taken up residence in Keppel Castle, near Arnhem. When asked what his demands were, Louis answered diplomatically that he would wait and see what the States General proposed. The IJssel line was abandoned as indefensible.

There were two rays of hope. First of all, on 7 June the navy, led by Michiel de Ruyter, had inflicted such losses on a combined Anglo-French fleet in Sole Bay, off the coast of Norfolk, that the threat of an invasion from the sea had been temporarily allayed. Secondly, William III had assumed dynamic leadership of the land defences. That he would do so had not been a foregone conclusion, since the politicians, with De Witt in the lead, had done everything they could to keep him on a tight rein, and William had been sorely offended. He could easily have welcomed – as many people did – the Anglo-French manoeuvres as proof that the republicans had been wrong. Besides, the Anglo-French coalition had seemed well disposed towards William. In December, Pieter de Groot had heard in Paris that there were plans to install a monarchy in the Republic, with William as king. His behaviour during the invasion, however, showed that William preferred to be his own master and did not intend to become a puppet whose strings were pulled by neighbouring countries. His appointment as stadholder was of course only a matter of time. In many cities the citizenry protested against the Perpetual Edict abolishing the stadholderate. Windows were smashed in the houses of regents suspected of anti-Orange sentiments. On the evening of 21 June, four young men attacked De Witt as he was walking home from his office. He suffered only superficial knife wounds, but the resulting infections forced the Grand Pensionary to keep to his bed for weeks. It was a bad omen that three of his four assailants managed to escape, finding a hiding place in the prince's army camp. The fourth, Jacob van der Graeff – none other than the son of a judge at the Court of Holland – was arrested and subsequently beheaded on 29 June. Many Orangists viewed him as a martyr.

After abandoning the IJssel line, the army retreated to the Water Line, an improvised line of defence running along the border between Holland and Utrecht. The retreat was chaotic, the burghers of Utrecht refusing at first to open the gates to their own army. On 27 June, by contrast, the French captured the city without a fight. The Water Line marked the boundary of an extensive area that could be flooded at will by opening the dykes and sluices. On this occasion the inundated area filled up very slowly owing to the dry summer, and in some places it was necessary to use force to put down the resistance offered by peasants unwilling to see their land flooded. Now, however, when only Friesland, North-Groningen, Holland, Zeeland and Brabant were still under the authority of the States General, the French, ironically, were being slowed down by the very speed of their advance. Not only were supply lines becoming too long, but Louis was perhaps letting himself be lulled into lethargy by the negotiations. He had brushed aside the States General's offer to hand over Limburg, States Brabant and Zeeuws-Vlaanderen. He continued to lay claim to all the conquered territories and an indemnity of 24 million guilders. These exorbitant demands only strengthened the resistance in Holland, since it was now clear that they were in danger of losing everything. The English also found the advance of the French extremely worrisome, for it was threatening to disrupt the balance of power on the continent.

The French halted their offensive in July and began to prepare for a long occupation. Louis himself decided to return to Paris. In the conquered areas, the local authorities were forced to take an oath of allegiance to the French king, and taxes were levied to maintain the occupying forces. This was the usual practice in such circumstances and it was accepted without too much grumbling. Although in the occupied areas the Catholics were again free to worship and a number of churches – including Utrecht Cathedral – were returned to them, other forms of religious worship were not suppressed. On the opposite side of the front, the prince had moved into new headquarters in Nieuwerbrug, between Gouda and Woerden, on 18 June. On 3 July the Perpetual Edict was formally revoked, and one week later, on 9 July, William was sworn in as stadholder of Holland. De Witt's policy lay in ruins. Everything he had fought for – for twenty long years – had ultimately failed. The alliance between France and England, which he had hoped to prevent, had overpowered the Republic; the expansion of Orange's power, which he had attempted to curb, had proved unstoppable. On 4 August he tendered his resignation to the States of Holland.

For those in the Orange camp this was not enough. On 23 July in Dordrecht, Willem Tichelaer, a village surgeon from Piershil, presented himself at the house of Cornelis de Witt, who was Johan's brother and an important politician in his own right. Tichelaer, who had come to speak to De Witt about a fine that had been imposed on him, later said that De Witt intimated that he would not only waive the fine but also reward him handsomely if he were to get rid of the prince. It was a highly improbable story, but given the panic of the moment, the Court of Holland thought it should be investigated. Cornelis de Witt was taken to The Hague and held in the Gevangenpoort, the prison opposite the Binnenhof, where he was subjected to interrogation under torture, something unheard-of for a man in his position. The Court of Holland referred the case to the stadholder, who on 20 August ordered De Witt to pay a heavy fine and banished him from the Republic. Tichelaer, by contrast, was allowed to go free. For days an angry crowd had been gathering in front of the Gevangenpoort, and they wanted to see blood. Tichelaer was given every opportunity to whip up emotions. Cornelis, in no fit state after the torture he had been subjected to, had asked his brother to send a carriage. Johan arrived in person at half past nine, apparently in the naïve belief that he could calm the crowd. He could not have been more mistaken. The soldiers and civic militiamen, who had mounted guard around the only entrance to the prison, were becoming just as agitated as

Figure 5   The murder of the De Witt brothers in The Hague on 20 August 1672.
In the foreground they are shown being seized as they leave the prison, while
in the background their bodies are being torn to pieces by the frenzied mob.
The portraits above show Cornelis on the left and Johan de Witt on the right
(Romeyn de Hooghe; Atlas van Stolk 2456: 2).

the crowd. Shops started closing in nearby neighbourhoods as people
began to sense trouble. Wild rumours were making the rounds, one of
which maintained that peasants from the surrounding countryside were
on their way to plunder The Hague. After endless waiting, at four o'clock
the militiamen forced the brothers outside, where a scaffold had been set
up. The crowd could no longer be held at bay. The brothers were barely
outside when Cornelis was stabbed by a sailor, while a notary hit the
former Grand Pensionary on the head with the butt of his rifle, after
which someone else shot him through the head. The civic militiamen then
emptied their weapons into the brothers. The bodies were strung up and
mutilated by the furious crowd, some even eating the body parts, according to eye-witness reports. During the night, family members and their
servants collected the brothers' remains and buried them post-haste. It
was never proved that the prince was behind these violent murders,
though he had certainly done nothing to prevent them. As stadholder
he had ordered the banishment of Cornelis de Witt, thereby suggesting

that the accusations contained a kernel of truth. On the eve of the murders he had been in The Hague, and that visit had fanned the flames of rumour. William refused to distance himself from the atrocity. A couple of years later he even appointed Pieter van der Graeff – who had been involved in the earlier attack on Johan de Witt, but had managed to escape – to the town council of Hoorn, a city with which Van der Graeff had no connection whatsoever.

Although the occupation dragged on, in 1673 the theatre of war moved from land to sea. De Ruyter, faced with a superior fleet of French and English ships, nonetheless managed no less than three times to fend off a new invasion. In August the Republic secured the help of the emperor in Vienna and the king of Spain. The costs of the occupation also weighed heavily on the French budget, and their supply lines proved vulnerable. In September the army of the States General recaptured Naarden. Louis needed his troops elsewhere, and so in the autumn of 1673 he began to evacuate important parts of the occupied territory. The French forces left Utrecht at the end of November, after the city had pledged them a huge sum of money. That pattern repeated itself everywhere, the French always taking several prominent citizens hostage to assure payment of the redemption money. Spring was turning into summer before the evacuation was finished but, even so, scarcely a shot had been fired. The French had attempted to hold only Grave, where a three-month siege was necessary before the States army took charge there as well. The three provinces that had been occupied in their entirety were mercifully readmitted to the Union in April 1674, but only after being severely punished for having surrendered so easily in 1672. In Overijssel, Gelderland and Utrecht, a new *Regeringsreglement* – a general constitution defining the procedures to be employed by the province's governing bodies – was imposed which placed severe restrictions on their autonomy by giving the stadholder an important say in provincial politics. The States of Holland had already decided in January 1674 to make the stadholdership hereditary in the male line. Thus William III, who had been in a precarious position for twenty years, emerged from the war more powerful than some of his predecessors had ever been.

William used this position of power to inject new life into the army. The number of troops had been increased in 1673 to more than 100,000, and over 100 million guilders had been spent on the military, five times the normal budget of the States General. Such expenditure could be financed only by going heavily into debt. The Republic's army was successful: in February 1674 the English withdrew from the war, with the bishop of Münster following suit in April. Pressure was put on the French flank by the armies of the Elector of Brandenburg and the emperor, and Spanish troops joined the fight as well. Negotiations began in 1676 in Nijmegen. The treaty that was signed there in August 1678 put an end to hostilities but not to their underlying cause. In the Republic, peace had been imposed by the regents of Holland, who were weary of the high costs of war and satisfied that the French would reduce import duties on Dutch goods – which had been raised again in 1667 – to their 1664 levels. The stadholder, on the other hand, was not at all convinced that the French military threat had abated. He was to be proven right. In an attempt to ensure himself of the support of the English court at any rate, William was married in 1677 to Mary Stuart, the eldest daughter of the duke of York, the brother of Charles II. (It will be remembered that William's mother, Charles II's sister, was also called Mary Stuart.) Since Charles had no children, Mary was second in line to the throne, after her father. Interestingly enough, William, son of the king's sister and therefore his bride's first cousin, could claim the throne in his own right.

The stadholder, who had to work just as hard to enlist support in the Republic, was aided in this endeavour by Louis XIV, who played into his hands. In 1683–4 the stadholder and the Amsterdam regents were still fierce opponents. In pamphlets William received a drubbing as a despot who did not scruple to tread on the cities' traditional rights and privileges, a deadly political sin in the Republic. His desire to expand and strengthen the army was viewed with distrust by those with commercial interests. The French court made overtures to the Amsterdammers, to the point of carrying on secret talks through their ambassador in The Hague. In August 1684 a treaty of friendship proposed by the French was approved by the States General – despite the prince's stubborn opposition – by four votes to three.

The following year, however, Louis revoked the Edict of Nantes, which since 1598 had offered protection to the Protestants in France. Now it was the French king who was being denounced as a tyrant. Tens of thousands of Huguenots fled the country and many of them – some 35,000 – ended up in the Dutch Republic. The churches set up relief funds; cities offered accommodation and waived citizenship fees. The profits reaped by the Republic from this influx of knowledge and capital signified an equivalent loss to the French economy. Dutch products flooded the French market. In an attempt to turn the tide, in September 1687 the French government reinstated the tariff hikes of 1667. This was in flagrant violation of the Peace of Nijmegen and an affront to the Amsterdam traders, who had always viewed France as an ally and the English as their chief enemy. That they had misjudged the situation became clearer in the months that followed, when the French announced further measures to curb Dutch imports. Not surprisingly, objections to the increase in military expenditure were suddenly withdrawn.

The political developments in England were not very encouraging either. The English king – since 1685 James II, William III's father-in-law – and Parliament were embroiled in a furious debate about their respective powers, especially with regard to religious policy. James was a Catholic, whereas the English establishment fiercely defended the Anglican Church. The king was becoming more and more dependent on support from Paris, a development followed in The Hague with increasing fear, since a repetition of 1672 seemed imminent. These fears were confirmed in February 1688 when James demanded the return of the English and Scottish regiments he had hired out to the Republic. To defuse this threat, the stadholder devised a daring plan based on the claims he and his wife held to the throne, which could justify their intervention in English politics, thereby forcing England to side with the Republic. That summer William began in all secrecy to raise troops and fit out a fleet for the crossing, telling only a handful of confidants about his plan. Still having no base of political support, he had to solicit funds from the Amsterdam capital market. A number of Jewish bankers lent him huge sums of money. William, when he informed the States of Holland in late September, pointed out the enormous damage that French tariffs were inflicting on Dutch trade and painted the darkest possible picture of the strategic consequences of an Anglo-French alliance. Again Louis inadvertently came to William's aid. While various town councils, including that of Amsterdam, were dragging their feet in approving his plan, the French government placed all Dutch ships in French ports under embargo. This was just what the stadholder needed to win over the irresolute cities.

The crossing to England was a huge gamble. Even though several members of the opposition in Parliament had invited William to come to England to put things to rights, it would be easy to see William's interference as an out-and-out invasion. Aware of this, he launched a carefully planned propaganda campaign to be carried out alongside the military manoeuvres. Sixty thousand pamphlets, justifying the presence of foreign troops on British soil (for the first time since 1066), were distributed in England. This 'Declaration' played down the role of the Dutch and drove home the fact that William had come at the invitation of the English themselves. Militarily, too, the risks were excessive. In recent years the English king had raised a standing army of 40,000 men. William could cross over with just half that number, and even that would require a fleet of 500 ships. To ensure the success of the enterprise, he had selected the very best regiments of the States army and hired another 7,000 crack

Figure 6   The landing of William III near Torbay in southern England on 15 November 1688. In April 1689 William and his English wife Mary were crowned king and queen of England. Later that year the couple gave their royal assent to the Bill of Rights, which made them subject to the laws passed by Parliament, though this did not prevent William from forging a strategic alliance aimed at curbing the French threat (J. Luiken; Atlas van Stolk 2744: 2).

troops from the king of Denmark. As soon as the invasionary force embarked, however, the Republic would be wide open to attack. The crossing therefore had to take place as late in the year as possible, after the troops of the other powers had gone into winter quarters, even though a late crossing would be endangered by the bad weather to be expected at that time of year. Indeed, several attempts to set sail had to be abandoned at the last minute, but in mid-November the weather suddenly cleared enough to venture the crossing. On 15 November, William landed in Torbay in Devon, whence he advanced on London, which he entered triumphantly on 18 December, having met with scant resistance from James's troops.

In Paris the crossing was seen as an act of aggression, leading to an immediate declaration of war on the Republic. In his first address to Parliament, William emphasised the necessity of English assistance to prevent the French from taking over the continent. His widely distributed 'Declaration' showed to what extent the needs of the English were secondary to the greater strategic plans William had for England. He stressed the necessity of strong parliamentary control of the king's actions (the heart of what later came to be known as the Glorious Revolution), but also demanded cooperation in the 'execution of his designs'.[2] On 23 February, William and Mary were offered the crown and proclaimed king and queen of England after accepting the Declaration of Rights, which established the rights of Parliament and in fact turned England into a constitutional monarchy. At the coronation, which took place in mid-April, William again stressed the Dutch Republic's need for England's support.

William's plea for assistance was prompted by the fact that support for his leadership in England had been on the wane ever since it had become obvious that his coming was not merely a helpful gesture. Indeed, the imperiousness of William and his entourage alienated many people. James still controlled Ireland and was assisted by the French who sent both money and troops. William would have to deal his opponent a devastating blow to prevent his plans from failing at this stage. Only in July 1690 did he score a decisive victory at the River Boyne, to the north of Dublin.[3] The secret negotiations begun with the French court in 1693 resulted in 1697 in the peace treaties of Rijswijk, in which Louis recognised his opponent as king of England and confirmed the tariff list agreed to in the Peace of Nijmegen regarding import duties on goods from the Dutch Republic. The Republic was also given permission to garrison troops in a number of Southern Netherlandish cities, which were to serve as a military buffer.

This last provision was of great importance, for a new conflict was already looming. The Spanish king Carlos II had no direct successor. The French royal house had good claims to the throne, and if they were honoured, Louis XIV would at a stroke become lord and master of both Spain and the Spanish Netherlands, undoing everything achieved thus far by William and his allies. When Carlos died in November 1700, it

---

[2] Jonathan Israel, 'The Dutch Role in the Glorious Revolution', in J. Israel (ed.), *The Anglo-Dutch Moment: Essays on the Glorious Revolution and its World Impact* (Cambridge: Cambridge University Press, 1991), p. 124.

[3] The commemoration of the Battle of the Boyne, on 1 July, is still an important date on the calendar of the Unionists in Northern Ireland, who wear orange scarves on that day to underscore Ulster's Protestant identity.

appeared that he had bequeathed his entire estate to Philip of Anjou, Louis's grandson. War was inevitable. The conflict, which would become known as the War of the Spanish Succession, was to last twelve years, during which French armies fought a long series of battles against a combined force of English and Dutch troops. The war ended with the Peace of Utrecht in 1713, by the terms of which the Spanish Netherlands were turned over to the Austrian Habsburgs. The threat of a French neighbour had once again been averted, but otherwise the outcome was disappointing. England, which was in the process of overtaking the Republic economically, emerged from this conflict as the great victor.

The stadholder–king did not live to see any of this. While riding in Kensington, William III fell from his horse and died of his injuries on 19 March 1702 without leaving any children. In his will he had named the Frisian stadholder Johan Willem Friso as his successor, but after his stadholdership of thirty years, most of the provinces had had enough. In Overijssel, Gelderland and Utrecht (the provinces that had been forced to accept new *Regeringsreglementen* when the Union brought them back into the fold in 1674–5), as well as in Zeeland (where the stadholder's court had been just as heavy-handed), rioting erupted in protest against the regents who had been appointed through the stadholder's intercession. These disturbances, which were to last for more than ten years, caused a great deal of political turmoil. The Republic's foreign policy was also enfeebled. The coffers of the States General and the States of Holland had been depleted by decades of war. The Republic had preserved its territorial integrity, but the price was so high that it could no longer afford to assume the role of a great power. After more than half a century, the Republic was again a state of middling rank.

4   The armed forces

The naval career of Michiel de Ruyter, one of the most heroic figures in Dutch history, very nearly came to nothing. The son of a seaman, De Ruyter entered the service of the Lampsins brothers while still a child, working as a rope maker at their factory in Vlissingen. His great love was the sea, however, and in 1618 his dream came true, when he began to sail on the merchantmen owned by the Lampsins. One of his first voyages was to the West Indies. De Ruyter quickly worked his way up through the ranks, and in the 1620s he was sailing regularly to Ireland, where he also acted as the Lampsins' agent. In 1633 De Ruyter became first mate on a whaling ship, in the service of the Vlissingen Chamber of the Northern Company. In 1637 he was made captain of a privateer, the first ship under his command. Entering the employ of the Lampsins again in 1640, he sailed for them in the following years to North Africa, Brazil and the Caribbean. These were lucrative times. Because it was customary for seamen to engage in private trade, De Ruyter was able to earn a great deal of money. Business was so good that in 1651 he decided to retire from seafaring. It was only under great pressure that he could be per-suaded the following summer, during the First Anglo-Dutch War, to assume the rank of commodore and set out to sea with twenty men-of-war and four fireships, in an attempt to resist the superior English fleet. He made it clear, however, that he was accepting the commission for one expedition only.

The Dutch Republic owed its international status as an independent state and top-ranking power to the respect commanded by both its army and navy in the many armed conflicts of the seventeenth century. The Republic's military role as a naval power was closely tied to its economic role as the goods carrier of Europe. Until the mid-seventeenth century, the boundaries between the merchant fleet and the navy had been very indistinct – De Ruyter's career reflected this pattern – and it was only in the second half of the century that the merchant and naval fleets emerged as separate entities. The interdependence of the merchant marine and the navy was to some extent financial, the navy being partly funded by a separate system of taxes (*convooien* and *licenten*) levied as import and export duties. These revenues, which were collected by the five admiralty colleges, were used to equip the naval fleet.

Although the admiralties were formally subordinate to the States General, local and regional interests had always determined how the fleet was actually organised. In 1576, at a very difficult time in the Revolt, the provinces of Holland and Zeeland had decided to fit out a combined fleet. Zeeland refused to accept Rotterdam as its base, however, and proceeded to organise its own admiralty in Veere, which had already functioned as a naval base in the fifteenth century. The choice of Rotterdam also met with opposition in Holland. Amsterdam had not been picked for two reasons: it had been one of the last Dutch cities to side with the Revolt (in 1578) and its harbour was not easily accessible. It soon became clear, however, that the city's wishes could not be ignored, and Amsterdam thus acquired its own admiralty. This, in turn, was resented by the cities of Holland's North Quarter (Noorderkwartier), which could not accept the South Quarter (Zuiderkwartier) having two admiralties while they had none. A fourth admiralty therefore had to be established, but because its location could not be agreed upon, it was decided that it would rotate quarterly between Hoorn and Enkhuizen. Finally, Friesland was also given its own admiralty, which was founded in 1596 in Dokkum and moved in 1645 to Harlingen.

Because the admiralties were answerable to the States General, they were administered by delegates from every province. Delegates from the 'home' province always had the upper hand, however, so the opinion of the Zeeland delegates carried more weight in Veere, likewise that of the Frisians in Dokkum and later Harlingen, and the Hollanders in the three admiralties in the province of Holland. The admiralty of Rotterdam consisted of delegates from all the provinces except Groningen, five altogether, as well as seven Hollanders, who represented the *ridderschap* (nobility) and the cities of Dordrecht, Den Briel, Delft, Schiedam, Gorcum and Rotterdam itself. In practice, the delegates from the other provinces did not often make an appearance, so the Hollanders usually held sway in their own admiralties.

The consequences of this administrative system were twofold. First of all, there was a marked tendency for each admiralty to think primarily of its own trading interests, one result of which was widespread evasion – with the admiralties' knowledge – of the customs duties. Although this cut into the admiralties' revenues, it was nevertheless a tempting means of making oneself more competitive. It could only be hoped that the States General would cover the deficit. Secondly, the fleet's disjointed organisation hampered coordination. The stadholder functioned as

admiral-general – in other words, as supreme commander of the fleet –
though two lieutenant-admirals, one appointed by the States of Zeeland
and the other by the States of Holland, were in actual command. Until
1648 three essential tasks were carried out under their supervision:
defending the country, escorting merchantmen and blockading the
Flemish coast. Inadequate resources, however, meant that only a few
dozen ships were available to carry out these duties. In 1609, immediately
after the signing of the Twelve Years' Truce, a considerable number of
warships had been sold, which meant that in times of crisis the admiralties
had to hire suitable merchantmen. Moreover, since crews were not available on a permanent basis, they had to be recruited as needed for each
voyage. In contrast to some other countries, where recruits were press-
ganged into service, the Dutch navy depended entirely on volunteers.
Whenever seamen were in short supply, as during the First Anglo-Dutch
War, their wages were increased – in 1653 by no less than 50 per cent. If
higher pay could not tempt enough men to join the navy, the authorities
simply prohibited fishing vessels and merchantmen from leaving port,
and the resulting unemployment usually generated a sufficient number of
volunteers.

The fragmentation of nearly every facet of the fleet's organisation
made it extremely difficult to adopt a uniform policy. It was no wonder,
then, that the admiralties had been considering a change of tack, especially since the 1620s, when the constant loss of ships, cargo and seamen
to the Dunkirk privateers had created an atmosphere of crisis in the
coastal provinces. Under these circumstances Frederik Hendrik
launched a plan in 1631 to gather a central fleet in Hellevoetsluis whose
main responsibility would be to blockade the Flemish coast. The plan
backfired owing to opposition from the admiralties as well as from
the States of Holland and Zeeland. A second attempt in 1636–7 also
stranded on the sandbanks of particularism.

Nevertheless, the fleet was quite successful in the first half of the
seventeenth century. The Dutch navy could boast outstanding seamen,
whose skills had often been honed in the merchant marine. In other
countries, by contrast, the navy was viewed merely as a floating army,
its senior posts being filled by nobles with little understanding of seafaring. This had also been the case in the Northern Netherlands in the 1560s
and 1570s, when the Sea Beggars (Dutch privateers) had been active, but
in the seventeenth century competence became increasingly important.
Moreover, the Dutch navy was fortunate in having a number of very
capable leaders whose names were known all over Europe: Piet Heyn,
Maerten Harpertsz Tromp, Witte de With and, of course, Michiel de
Ruyter. In 1676, when the ship taking De Ruyter's body home for burial

passed the French coast, Louis XIV ordered a salute, despite the fact that De Ruyter had been fatally wounded in a battle against the French near Messina in Sicily.

Until 1648 the Dutch navy had also been fortunate in another respect: it had never had to face a formidable enemy. Spain had been reluctant to engage in large-scale naval operations since the defeat of its Armada in 1588. The Dunkirk privateers were a nuisance, to be sure, but they were not a threat to the Republic's safety. At this time there was simply no other country with a large fleet at its disposal. The fact that the Republic had by far the largest merchant marine in Europe – larger than those of France and England combined – gave it a decisive advantage.

That advantage disappeared shortly after 1648, the year in which Cromwell put an end to England's Civil War by defeating the Royalists. The English immediately launched an ambitious programme of fleet construction, producing a whole series of specialised warships that were larger than the Dutch ships and could carry more and heavier artillery. In the Dutch Republic, the Peace of Münster had been seized upon as a reason for scrapping part of the fleet, so that it was in a deplorable state when the First Anglo-Dutch War broke out in 1652. The consequences were harsh indeed. The Dutch, suffering one defeat after another, were forced to accept the humiliating terms of the Treaty of Westminster (1654). Johan de Witt, who took a strong personal interest in maritime affairs, instantly ordered a programme of naval reconstruction similar to that of the English. The States General ordered thirty large warships in February 1653 and another series in December, and also resolved that warships could be sold only if the States General agreed unanimously to do so. A permanent naval fleet was eventually launched, consisting in 1654 of sixty-four battleships, armed with forty to sixty guns, and a convoy fleet numbering eighty to ninety ships, which were smaller and less heavily armed.

The heavier weaponry carried by the new warships precipitated a change in military tactics. Traditionally, sea battles had been won or lost by cold steel rather than guns. After manoeuvring into the most favourable winds, ships sailed straight for enemy ships with the intention of ramming, boarding and capturing them. 'Capturing' meant either forcing a ship to surrender or sinking it, though surrender was preferable, because the whole crew shared in the proceeds of the sale of the ship and its cargo, as well as any ransom that could be exacted for the crew. The rise of heavy warships, however, caused the emphasis to shift to cannon. Instead of the so-called mêlée, or skirmish in battle, ships now lined up opposite one another – sometimes forming ribbons six miles long – and exchanged fire. Helmsmanship and coordination came to be of paramount importance, and for this reason the permanent fleet was put under permanent leadership. Officers now began spending their entire careers in the navy, instead of alternating between the navy and the merchant marine, as had been common in the first half of the seventeenth century.

This professionalisation of the war machine, which started in the navy only in the mid-seventeenth century, had begun in the army at least a century earlier. The changes in land warfare, constituting a veritable military revolution, were sparked off primarily by the introduction of firearms to the European theatre of war. The arrival of cannon largely rendered the old, medieval defences obsolete. Upright stone walls could be smashed with a single artillery shot. To combat such force it was necessary to construct much deeper lines of defence: slanting walls, for instance, to which cannon shot could do relatively little damage. Such defence works – bastions, ramparts and moats – were first developed around 1525 in Italy and introduced to the Netherlands soon afterwards. Vredenburg Castle, the stronghold built by Charles V in 1529 after Utrecht had fallen into his hands the previous year, was just such a fortification designed along modern lines. The new methods of warfare, however, actually made castles a thing of the past, quite simply because they were too small to defend. A fortress like Vredenburg Castle had a military future only as part of much more extensive defence works, hence the construction, starting in 1541–2, of five bulwarks surrounding Utrecht. Fortifications on this scale were extremely costly to build and often took years or even decades to complete.

At the beginning of the Revolt, Groenlo (in the province of Gelderland) and Utrecht had modern defence works, as did Antwerp, but medieval walls and ramparts were the rule everywhere else. It was not until the late sixteenth century that work was begun on modernising the defence of a large number of cities in the Northern Netherlands, a good example being Deventer. The River IJssel was an important line of defence for the Republic, certainly up to the time of the Twelve Years' Truce. There were, moreover, no major cities to be found beyond Deventer and Zwolle. Until well into the 1630s, most of the countryside in the province of Overijssel remained disputed territory, where Spanish troops and the Republic's army vied for supremacy. Both demanded the payment of 'contributions', a form of tax often exacted under threat of pillaging and fire-raising. Because the security of Deventer was vital to the national interest, both Maurits and the States General insisted on the improvement of its fortifications. After several years of planning, construction was begun in 1599.

Instead of being built in stone, Italian-style, the fortification walls in the Low Countries were made of turf. There were also other ways in which Dutch fortresses differed from those in southern Europe. In the Netherlands, for instance, ditches were filled with water, almost as a matter of course, rather than being left dry. Instructions for fortress-building were to be found in Simon Stevin's *Stercktenbouwinge*, a reference book written in 1594 for the engineering course introduced around this time at Leiden University. Stevin's colleague David van Orliens drew up the definite plans for the Deventer fortifications, which were to consist of a wreath of eight bulwarks surrounding the town, complete with ravelins, waterworks and new entrance gates. The defence works eventually covered more than 120 acres and took fifty years to complete.

The Deventer defence works were only part of a much more extensive plan. Almost two decades earlier, when the heart of the Republic had been made secure, work had begun in the 1580s on a ring of fortresses and fortified towns designed to protect this core area from further attack. In the sparsely populated north, fortresses were built in Bourtange (1593) and Coevorden (begun around 1579). Further to the south, a cordon was formed by Zwolle (1606–21), Deventer (1599–1646), Zutphen (1592–1605), Doesburg (1607–10), Arnhem (1590–1606, 1619–40), Nijmegen (1598–*c*. 1610), Grave, Heusden, Geertruidenberg, Willemstad (1585) and Steenbergen, as well as Bergen-op-Zoom in Brabant (after 1577–1644), and finally Terneuzen, IJzendijke (1604), Aardenburg (1604), Sluis and Cadzand in States Flanders, which protected the country during the Twelve Years' Truce. In many respects this defensive ring represented the Republic's true boundaries, on the other side of which – certainly until 1648 – a rather ambiguous situation prevailed, characterised by numerous border enclaves and unrestricted travel to and from the adjoining German and Spanish-held territories. This was true in particular of the Generality Lands (States Flanders, States Brabant and Upper Gelderland), which were not seriously considered part of the Republic's territory until well into the eighteenth century, before which time they were viewed more as a military buffer zone. Import duty was even charged on goods sent from Brabant to the North, as though they were coming from abroad.

The Generality Lands had been annexed to the Republic's territory mainly because of their strategic location. This was abundantly clear in the case of Maastricht, which had been captured in 1632 by Frederik Hendrik, but it was no less true of 's-Hertogenbosch, which had fallen to the stadholder in 1629. 's-Hertogenbosch's fortifications had been modernised since the beginning of the Twelve Years' Truce in 1609 – by the Spanish, of course. This city was generally considered the strongest fortress in the Netherlands; the Spanish even declared it impregnable. Its population of around 10,000 was bolstered by a garrison of 3,000

Figure 7   Soldiers relax during the siege of 's-Hertogenbosch in the summer of 1629. The siege was a bold undertaking, for the fortress of Den Bosch, visible here in the background, was thought to be impregnable. Below the print is the inscription 'Wie waecht die wint' ('Nothing ventured, nothing gained') and a verse: 'Den Bos onwinbaer scheen, een burch van 't moedich Spangien / Sijn trots, sijn roem, sijn macht, sijn pochen en sijn roe / Voor 't vereende landt, dit neemt hem wech Orangien' ('Den Bosch seemed unassailable, a valiant Spanish citadel / Its pride, its glory, power, boast and blight / For the united provinces, captured by Orange might') (C. J. Visscher; Atlas van Stolk 1701:1).

soldiers. Nevertheless, on 30 April 1629, Frederik Hendrik succeeded in laying siege to it, more or less by surprise. At first nothing happened, according to an anonymous diarist writing within the city, for the besiegers did nothing but dig. A siege involved not so much fighting as spadework. The besiegers tried to manoeuvre their artillery closer and closer to the walls, hoping eventually to make a breach that would allow them to penetrate the city. It was up to the besieged to prevent this. The besiegers of 's-Hertogenbosch were so busy digging trenches and clearing the field of fire that it was three weeks before the first volley was fired. That same day, 22 May, the city's inhabitants took stock of the remaining provisions. Prices had already soared. By now the city was exposed to daily artillery bombardment. On 31 May alone our informant counted 110 shots, fired from the Republic's 12-pounders, the so-called demi-cartows. By the end of May, no one inside the city had yet been hit, but this state of affairs changed the following month. By 10 June more than a thousand projectiles had been fired at the city; one of these had wounded a man at confession in the Janskerk (the Church of St John). On 15 June the civic authorities commandeered the lead from all gutters, water pipes and even urinals to make much-needed ammunition. The next day the besieged made a sortie and claimed several victims among the besiegers. Such sorties, aimed at demoralising the attackers and checking their approach to the walls, were now being carried out more and more frequently. '[We] boldly attacked the enemy on the outworks of the small sconce',[1] we read in the entry for 21 June. It was not until 4 July, however, that Jan Hendrikszoon, a corn merchant who had been inspecting a granary at the time, became the first civilian victim. Meanwhile the shooting and digging outside the walls continued unabated. The city had to contend with bombs in addition to cannonballs, and the consequences were serious indeed. On 7 August our anonymous diarist noted: 'We were so terribly fired upon with bombs that we scarcely noticed the shooting of the heavy cannon; so many died every day that I'd best keep silent as to their number'.[2]

The mood among the besieged, at first combative, became more depressed every day. A rumour that the emperor's army had arrived in nearby Gelderland and was ready to rescue the city proved untrue. On 7 August a captain, who had been ordered to escort some prisoners of war to the besiegers, seized this opportunity to defect. Having participated in all the tactical discussions, he could now supply the enemy with vital information. The bombardment was stepped up: on 16 August more than 300 projectiles were fired at 's-Hertogenbosch. Outside the gates the defenders were forced to yield strategic positions. On 31 August they 'began to lose courage'.[3] Some refused to dig, while others were no longer willing to keep watch. The immediate cause of their discontent was the threat posed to the Vught Dyke and consequently to their property. They demanded that the commander surrender rather than force them to endure continued destruction, since sooner or later they would be forced to surrender anyway. Feverish negotiations were being conducted within the city, while outside the walls the besiegers, encountering little resistance, managed to seize one of the gates, the Vughterpoort. On 11 September a large mine exploded beneath the fortress of 's-Hertogenbosch.

---

[1] *Negen schoten met grof canon. Bossche oorlogsdadboeken 1629–1794, 1944*, compiled and with an introduction by Coen Free ('s-Hertogenbosch: Adr. Heinen, 1993), p. 15.
[2] Ibid., p. 22.   [3] Ibid., p. 25.

The city surrendered three days later on two conditions: that the Republic promise to respect the city's privileges and that the garrison be allowed to depart with drums beating and colours flying.

A siege was not an unusual occurrence in the seventeenth-century Dutch Republic. Between 1590 and 1609, the cities experiencing sieges included Breda, Zutphen, Deventer, Nijmegen, Hulst, Coevorden, Steenwijk, Grave, Geertruidenberg, Groningen and Groenlo. After the end of the Twelve Years' Truce in 1621, the following cities also suffered sieges: Bergen-op-Zoom, 's-Hertogenbosch, Groenlo, Maastricht and Breda (twice). This burden was shared unequally, for the provinces of Holland, Friesland and Utrecht, as well as the islands of Zeeland, were completely spared the violence of war. Along the borders, moreover, the armed forces were an ever present part of life, not only in times of war but also during periods of relative peace. The cities listed above were besieged because their importance to the defence of the Republic meant that they had been provided with a garrison. The strength of the garrisons varied from a few hundred men in small fortresses like Lillo, below Antwerp, or Steenwijk in the province of Overijssel, to more than 2,000 in such strategic bases as Doesburg and Nijmegen. Comparing these numbers to the number of civilians in these cities – some 3,000 in Doesburg and around 10,000 in Nijmegen – and considering, moreover, that the soldiers did not live in barracks but were billeted in private homes, one can easily imagine how much the presence of a garrison affected the lives of people in border towns. Understandably, there was some degree of ambivalence towards the soldiery. On the one hand, they were felt to be a burden: often young and unattached, these men filled their days in times of peace with routine drills and waiting. Boredom made them prone to mischief. On the other hand, they were an important source of revenue for the local middle classes, who profited from the continuous flow of money from Holland – the most important financial backer of the armed forces – to the border provinces.

Most of these fortresses and their garrisons had been established in the two decades preceding the Twelve Years' Truce, since which time they had formed the backbone of the Republic's armed forces. The army grew considerably during the seventeenth century, its ranks swelling from around 35,000 men at the beginning of the century to three times that number a hundred years later. This growth was not constant, however. In 1608 there were nearly 50,000 men in service, in 1613 just half that number. Under the command of Frederik Hendrik, the number of men in the army grew to 60,000, half of whom had been dismissed by 1650. The greatest increase occurred in 1688, when the struggle against Louis XIV was raging at full force, and the Republic, together with its ally

England, was confronted with a huge French military force on the continent. However, despite these fluctuations in the size and strength of its armed forces, the Dutch Republic remained one of the most important military powers in Europe during the whole of the seventeenth century.

The soldiers who fought for the Netherlands were not all Dutch by any means. The army of the Dutch Republic was a professional army, and the nationality of the soldiers was therefore of little importance. Regiments were recruited in Germany, Switzerland and Scotland, as well as in the French-speaking provinces of present-day Belgium and in France. These foreign regiments brought along their own chain of command and weaponry. In 1635 around half of all the soldiers in the Republic's army were members of foreign regiments. Foreigners served in the Dutch regiments as well, but on an individual basis. Such soldiers are often referred to as mercenaries, but this is misleading. To be sure, these men had made the art of war their profession, but they were not adventurers. Their terms of employment were anything but temporary, and they often served for many years in succession, marrying and settling down in the garrison towns in which they were stationed. In the seventeenth century the army was far and away the most important employer in all European countries. The Dutch East India Company, the most important private employer in the Republic, had some 8,000 people in its service in 1625, less than a quarter of the number serving in the army.

The garrison system – an intrinsic part of which was the potentially disruptive influence of disgruntled soldiers – was one of the reasons Maurits found it so important to pay his troops on a regular basis. In the sixteenth century, arrears of soldiers' wages had created great problems. The Spanish, for example, had been forced to yield crucial positions in the Netherlands when whole companies rose in mutiny because they had not been paid, often for years on end. During the period preceding the Twelve Years' Truce, the States General's annual statement of revenue and expenditure included a list of various companies that were 'not being paid'.[4] Soldiers were expected to live partly from the spoils of war; in other words, they often had to plunder and forage, and to subsist on the pickings. Small wonder, then, that they were hated by the peasantry. Soldiers who became separated from the main force during a campaign were in real danger of being beaten to death by the local populace. Such a thing could not happen in a garrison town. Moreover, army leaders were keenly aware of the need for a strong base of support among the tax-paying public, who had to make great sacrifices to pay for

---

[4] J. W. Wijn, *Het krijgswezen ten tijde van prins Maurits* (Utrecht: no publisher, 1934), p. 117.

their security and thus demanded value for their money. When the burghers of 's-Hertogenbosch began to lose heart in August 1629, grumbling was heard in the streets: 'We are ordered, on pain of high fines, to put our houses at their disposal, and there are no munitions. We have paid fortification money and other taxes for so many years, and what has it brought us? We have a rich governor, a rich chief magistrate, and others who have bled us dry.'[5]

Paying soldiers on a regular basis was also a way of winning their continued allegiance and thereby ensuring an eventual return on the money invested in their training. It took two to three years to turn a raw recruit into a fully fledged soldier. This long period of training was due both to the difficulty of handling seventeenth-century firearms and to the nature of war itself. In addition to cannon, small firearms had become widespread on the battlefields of sixteenth-century Europe. The infantry, formerly armed with cross bows and pikes, were now supplied with muskets, arquebuses and other guns, all of which had complicated loading procedures. Jacob de Gheyn's illustrated handbook, which appeared in print in 1608, distinguishes more than thirty steps necessary to proper loading. It took several minutes to reload a weapon, even after proficiency had been achieved through long hours of practice. Furthermore, troops had to be able to reload under fire while remaining in formation. The infantry had traditionally operated in square blocks of archers and pikemen, the latter serving mainly as protection against cavalry attack. During a battle, the infantry moved in tightly packed blocks over the battlefield, making it vitally important to stay in formation and to continue to return fire.

To enable volleys to be fired without interruption, Maurits and his cousin Willem Lodewijk, a general in the Republic's army, developed the so-called countermarch: the first line, after firing, moved back through the ranks to make room for the next line. Those in the line that had just fired then began to reload their weapons. This repeated itself with every line, until the line that had fired first was back where it started. This method, however, demanded incredible discipline from the men, who were required to carry out these difficult manoeuvres under fire. The moment a formation fell apart, infantrymen became easy prey to the cavalry. Soldiers under fire therefore had to suppress their natural instinct to flee. Sometimes they were assisted in this by their commanders. At Nieuwpoort (1600), one of the few pitched battles in the seventeenth century that the Republic's army fought to the finish, Maurits made sure

[5] *Negen schoten*, p. 26.

Figure 8   Maurits of Nassau (1567–1625), with the Battle of Nieuwpoort (1600) in the background. Maurits was of great importance to the Republic, not only as a strategist and army commander but also as an instigator of military reforms, whose example was followed in all of Europe (C. van de Passe, 1600; Atlas van Stolk 1099).

that his own men had no avenues of escape, so they were forced to stay and fight. The most important weapon, though, was endless practice. Drilling ensured that the necessary manoeuvres became so routine that they could be carried out automatically.

Exercises and drills were part of a general systematisation of the business of war carried out under Maurits's leadership. This efficiency drive was largely prompted by the constant need to cut costs. The army leadership was forced, for example, to reduce the depth of the infantry lines, which made drills all the more important. It was perhaps for the same reason that Maurits put an end to the chaotic state of the artillery, where lack of standardisation caused huge problems in the supply of munitions. To overcome these difficulties, from 1590 onwards cannon were cast in four diameters only, a national artillery foundry supplying cannon to these specifications having been established in 1589 in The Hague. An artillery handbook was compiled in 1599. At the same time, Maurits – in consultation with the mathematician Simon Stevin – tried to improve the accuracy of artillery by means of advancements based on mathematical calculations and experiments in the field. Jacob de Gheyn's *Wapenhandelinge* (Soldier's Handbook) of 1608 was also part of this more modern approach to warfare. In 1617, Count Johann of Nassau, Maurits's cousin, even founded a military academy at Siegen, in Nassau's hereditary lands, where officers from all over Europe could participate in a six-month course on Dutch military reforms.

Many of these reforms had been inspired by Roman military practice. The standard orders, for instance, another novelty 'invented' by the Republic's army, had been borrowed with only slight modifications from Aelianus, a Greek military writer living in Rome in the second century. The Dutch also continued to build on developments that had started earlier: the standardisation of artillery, for example, had been instigated by Charles V. Maurits and his staff distinguished themselves particularly in their systematic – even scientific – approach to all aspects of the military profession. It was due mainly to their efforts that the army of the Dutch Republic was able to grow into one of the most successful fighting machines of the seventeenth century.

The innovations of the late sixteenth and early seventeenth centuries proved to be of lasting value. A century later relatively little had changed in the organisation of Dutch defences on land, though after 1672 the construction of the Water Line, which made it possible to flood large tracts of land at will, gave Holland an extra belt of protection behind the line of fortresses stretching from Groningen via Twente, Gelderland and Brabant to the coast of Zeeuws-Vlaanderen. Another improvement came in 1672, when the government assumed responsibility for paying troops directly and determining their number, something which had previously been left to officers and middlemen, so-called *solliciteurs-militair*. On the battlefield itself, even fewer lines of infantry were necessary by the end of the century, when the invention of the firelock ensured quicker loading and therefore greater dependability in firearms. Finally, the introduction of the bayonet made pikemen redundant. In 1709 the Republic's army was one of the last to dispense with this weapon.

The garrison system had made the army an inextricable part of society in the Dutch Republic. Even so, in the coastal provinces the elites remained ambivalent towards the land forces, since they were understandably partial to the navy. The whole reorganisation and professionalisation of the fleet had taken shape in the 1650s and 1660s under the leadership of Johan de Witt, who had a strong personal interest in naval affairs. He went on board himself on various occasions, and in July 1665 and again in 1666 he even served – in his capacity as delegate of the States General – as acting supreme commander. De Ruyter was able to operate as effectively as he did because De Witt supported him every inch of the way. De Witt, in turn, always made sure that he had Amsterdam's support in naval matters. After 1672, William III left many practical affairs to Job de Wildt, secretary of the Amsterdam admiralty, whose experience and expertise were widely known. In the navy, the rank of officer was more often held, at least in the second half of the seventeenth century, by regents or members of their circle, causing politics and naval affairs to be closely connected.

Inhabitants of the inland provinces, on the other hand, had little affinity with the navy and were naturally more in step with the army. The officers corps consisted largely of foreigners, mostly of noble descent, who occupied an important place at court. Contemporary observers thought it significant that in Frederik Hendrik's funeral procession in 1647 the numerous foreign officers took precedence over members of the States General and the States of Holland, in whose service the stadholder had performed his glorious deeds. In 1789 it was not Holland, the most populous province, but Gelderland that supplied the largest number of non-commissioned officers in both the infantry and the cavalry, and this had probably been no different in the seventeenth century. The disparity should not be exaggerated – plenty of examples could doubtless be found of nobles serving in the navy, for example, and of middle-class army officers born in the coastal provinces – yet it cannot be denied that to some extent the army and the navy represented two very different social worlds.

Of greater importance, however, was the fact that the land forces and the fleet reflected the geographic fragmentation of the Republic. In Holland and the other coastal provinces, politicians attached the greatest value to the navy, which protected the coast and defended trading interests far from the borders of the Republic. In the east of the country, people were understandably more worried about the threat posed by the armies of their immediate neighbours, and it was here, on the eastern border, that most of the Republic's army had been stationed, making soldiers a ubiquitous part of everyday life. In the seventeenth century, when hardly a year went by without a war somewhere in Europe, a country such as the Dutch Republic could not afford to neglect its defences on either land or sea. Consequently, whether they liked it or not, the provinces were forced to contribute collectively to the maintenance of their military machine.

5   Financial might

In 1673 a book was published in England which explained the success of the Dutch Republic to foreigners. The author, Sir William Temple – who spent several years serving as the English ambassador to The Hague – had set himself the task of explaining the peculiarities of the Republic to his fellow countrymen. In addition to setting forth the proverbial Dutch character – frugal, reserved, hard-working, community-minded – Sir William thought it important to elucidate the international position of the Republic, which at that very moment was at war with England for the third time in twenty-five years. He discussed the Republic's position in a chapter with the revealing title 'Of their Forces and Revenues', for in the eyes of this English diplomat money and military might were closely connected.

That connection may seem logical now, but in the seventeenth century it was not at all self-evident. As Temple explained to his readers, it had previously been customary for sovereigns to raise armies by granting parts of their domain in fief, in exchange for which their vassals owed them allegiance. When called upon to serve their lord in times of war, those vassals brought along their own weapons and sometimes a few brothers-in-arms who were in turn their own tenants. Almost no one waged war professionally. Campaigns were mercifully short, so that everyone would be home in time for the harvest. This situation began to change in the sixteenth century, and in Temple's view this change had been brought about by trading countries such as Venice, and later also the Dutch Republic, which had insufficient land and too few inhabitants to take on the armies of the larger, territorial states. One thing these countries did have, though, was money, which meant they could hire soldiers to fight for them. Money had thus become a decisive factor in military success.

On the face of it, the financial structure of the Republic was anything but solid. The national system of taxation laid down in the Union of Utrecht (1579) would not be instituted until more than two centuries later, in 1805. In the meantime, money had to be collected by all manner of means. The Union, meaning the States General, had only meagre

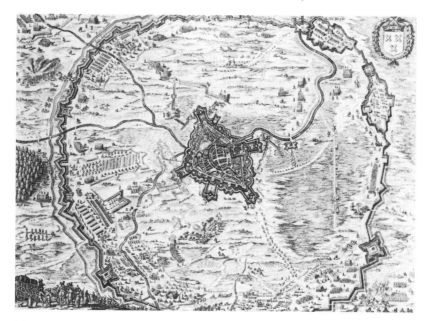

Figure 9   The siege of Breda in 1637. The extensive, semi-permanent siege works surrounding the city are clearly visible. The outermost circle was intended to protect the besiegers against attacks from the rear. Inside the circle the besiegers are busy shoring up positions on newly won ground, from which they bombard the city. The building of siege works, the number of soldiers required to sustain the effort, and their long duration made sieges very costly undertakings (Jan van Hilten, 1637; Atlas van Stolk 1803).

revenues of its own. Most taxes were levied by the provinces, which considered themselves sovereign and were therefore averse to interference in what they thought of as 'internal affairs'. Every year the provinces – each of which had to approve its contribution to the costs of joint defence – were asked to sanction a budget, which was called, significantly, the 'State of War': significantly, because this label emphasised the fact that the States General concerned itself almost exclusively with waging war on land and sea. At first there was an annual quarrel about the amount each province was expected to contribute, but in 1583 Oldenbarneveldt suggested reverting to a formula that had already been tried and tested in the time of Charles V, when the various provinces had contributed money according to fixed quotas set in relation to one another. Holland's contribution, for example, was one-half that of Brabant, Zeeland one-fourth that of Holland, Utrecht one-tenth and Friesland one-fifth that of Holland, while Groningen's contribution was half that of Friesland, in other words the same as Utrecht's. Because the duchy of Brabant was ultimately excluded from the equation, the Holland/Brabant ratio became irrelevant, but the quota system was maintained, with fixed percentages stipulating each province's share in the total budget. The advantage of this system was clear: if the total budget needed to be increased, it was easy to work out how much more each province would have to contribute. Only Overijssel (which had long remained aloof from the Revolt for fear of the financial consequences) and Gelderland – the last two provinces to be admitted to the Burgundian-Habsburg state – still had to be integrated into the system.

One problem posed by the fixed-quota system was deciding what to do when economic changes within the provinces made it necessary to realign the quotas. Some adjustments were indeed made at the beginning of the seventeenth century. Zeeland, for instance, had been put at a serious disadvantage by the war, which had caused the major trade routes to shift from the basin of the River Scheldt to Holland. Not unreasonably, Zeeland called for an adjustment in the province's contribution to the Generality's budget. After years of negotiation, they finally succeeded in obtaining a reduction in their contribution, from 15 per cent to 11 per cent and finally to 9 per cent of the total budget. The adjustment made in 1616 was the last for nearly two centuries. Only in 1792 were the quotas again revised, until which time Zeeland was obliged to pay 9 per cent, Gelderland, Utrecht and Groningen each 5 per cent, Friesland 11 per cent and Overijssel slightly more than 3 per cent. Starting in 1658, the region of Drenthe, which had been recognised as a full province but had no seat in the States General (where it was represented by the Groningen delegates), paid 1 per cent on top of the 100 per cent contributed by the others. Together these provinces contributed just over 40 per cent of the budget of the United Provinces; the rest – 58.3 per cent, to be precise – came from the province of Holland.

Thus the Republic was in large part financially dependent on Holland, the province which fortunately also had the healthiest finances, owing mostly to excise revenues. In Holland nearly every product was taxed in one way or another. Temple had heard it said that by the time a fish ended up on one's plate in Amsterdam, no fewer than thirty separate taxes had been levied on it. In all honesty it must be said that Temple had included in his calculations the taxes imposed on everything from the boats used to catch the fish to the ingredients of the sauce served with it. Still, it cannot be denied that the Hollanders were highly resourceful when it came to tax collection. Even the wind was a revenue-producing commodity, since a tax was imposed on millers for the right to use it. All these taxes, of course, were passed straight on to the consumer, who bore the brunt of the tax burden. In seventeenth-century Alkmaar, bread was 20–35 per cent more expensive than in Kampen because of Holland's higher excise duties, especially those levied on flour-grinding, which together with the tax on beer yielded the greater part of Holland's excise revenues.

During the whole of the seventeenth century, the public coffers of Holland were filled mainly by excise revenues, which were good for approximately two-thirds of all government revenues. An important advantage of this method of levying taxes was its convenience for the authorities. By making the suppliers responsible for collecting the tax, in the same way that tobacco and petrol are taxed today, the authorities had to examine the accounts of only a relatively small group. Since the market economy in Holland was well developed, there was a lot of money in circulation, and it was relatively easy for the authorities to tap that flow in order to raise taxes. The drawback to this system was that it placed a proportionately greater burden on the poor. By taxing consumers – and levying those taxes mainly on their primary necessities – taxation came down hard on the 'man in the street'. The well-to-do, on the other hand, were less severely affected by such taxes. The land tax they paid, for example, was more than offset – certainly in the first half of the seventeenth century when tax rates were fixed – by steadily rising agricultural production and land rents. Theoretically, there were other ways of letting the wealthy pay their share, but the States were reluctant to implement them. The possibility of levying an income tax was rejected time and again, because merchants were unwilling to open their account books and reveal their trading contacts for the purposes of an audit. This argument was enough to dissuade the States of Holland – ever aware of how vital trade was to the province's prosperity – from levying an income tax. In the end, however, there was no escaping direct taxation, which took the form of a property tax. Especially after 1672, during the wars with France, a capital levy – the confiscation by the state of a portion of privately owned wealth or property – was frequently imposed, and property owners were required to deliver goods or money several times a year. The Two-Hundredth Penny, a tax of 0.5 per cent on real estate, securities and other capital property, was levied no less than twenty-eight times in the 1670s, amounting to the seizure of 14 per cent of the total value of such goods. Significantly, business capital was exempt from these levies.

The capital levies imposed in the 1670s were necessary to cover the sharply rising costs of war. The Republic's spending had risen in the first half of the century from less than 10 million guilders before the Twelve Years' Truce to more than twice that amount in the 1630s. After the Peace of Münster, however, a considerable peace dividend could be booked. Expenditure dropped to around 5 million guilders a year, the lowest level since 1600. Though the Second Anglo-Dutch War caused a sharp increase in expenditure, which remained at this higher level, the Year of Disaster (1672) and its aftermath led to unprecedented spending. The heightened vigilance that was now deemed necessary demanded constant investment in the military machine, but the system of taxation could not keep up with such increases. At the beginning of the seventeenth century, the tax burden was such that the average labourer had to work 17–18 days a year to satisfy the tax man. That level was seldom exceeded throughout the seventeenth century, which suggests that the authorities were convinced that a ceiling had been reached. Moreover, the government would not risk placing too great a tax burden on the rich, for fear that they would simply move elsewhere. That such fears were not unfounded emerges from the flight of capital from Amsterdam to London and elsewhere that occurred in 1672 and again a few years later, when William III nearly became duke of Gelderland. Since this would have given him unprecedented power, the merchants were fiercely opposed to it. Their loud protests bore a clear message to the regents: capital is a mobile asset and must be persuaded to stay put.

The States of Holland were thus caught between an increasing need for money and the impossibility of taxing the wealthy more heavily. To escape from this impasse, the States increasingly resorted to another financial instrument: the loan. Loans had the advantage of speed, for in times of war a great deal of extra money was needed in a very short time. Taxation could not supply it quickly, but the capital market could. The States of Holland had begun to borrow money in the sixteenth century, and this policy soon proved successful. This success was based on one very important factor: faith. Why did investors entrust their money to the States of Holland? In the first place, because of the proximity of this governmental body to the public it served. In most countries in sixteenth- and seventeenth-century Europe, it was the sovereign who incurred the largest debts. Ordinary citizens, however, could exert no influence on a king, a fact which sovereigns regularly confirmed by failing to meet their financial commitments. Philip II of Spain, for example, suspended interest payments on his debts in 1557, 1560, 1575 and 1596, and his successors did the same in 1607, 1627, 1647, 1652, 1660 and 1662. As late as 1739, the Leiden millionaire Pieter de la Court van der Voort warned his heirs against investing in such loans: 'He who trusts in the sealed promises of sovereigns often finds himself grossly deceived.'[1] The

[1] M. Prak, *Gezeten burgers. De elite in een Hollandse stad: Leiden 1700–1780* (Amsterdam/Dieren: De Bataafsche Leeuw, 1985), p. 137.

States of Holland, on the other hand, were a representative body. Though its members were not elected directly, one could run into them in the street in any city in Holland. And, even more importantly, these men invested considerable sums themselves in government bonds and could fall victim to corrupt practices or misappropriation just as easily as any other investor.

The faith placed by investors in their government allowed Holland's debt to increase rapidly. In 1600 the province's debt was less than 5 million guilders, but in the next twenty years it increased fourfold. The resumption of hostilities after the Twelve Years' Truce demanded new investments, and by 1648 the debt had increased to 125 million guilders. After this there was little change, until the Year of Disaster (1672) ushered in forty years of more or less continuous war against France, at the end of which Holland's debt had risen to approximately 300 million guilders – a pittance, perhaps, compared with today's public debt, though it must be remembered that 60 per cent of all tax revenues collected in the province of Holland went as interest payments to bondholders. It is therefore all the more surprising that so much money could be raised at a time when the interest on Holland's bonds was continually dropping. At the beginning of the century, the States could attract capital only by promising an interest rate of 8 per cent. By 1655 they were paying a mere 4 per cent, an extremely low rate in comparison with other countries. It is no wonder, then, that foreign governments were full of admiration for the financial policies of Holland's regents. Their success is especially remarkable if one considers the deep-rooted discord between the so-called 'united provinces'.

The façade of financial strength concealed a very complicated inner structure endangered by various shortcomings, one of which was the way the States of Holland obtained its money. Rather surprisingly, there was neither a national nor a provincial tax authority. Throughout the seventeenth century, the job of collecting taxes was farmed out to private individuals, self-employed tax-farmers who bid at auction for the right to collect a certain tax for a period of six months. The advantage of this system was that it guaranteed the authorities a certain amount of money, paid in advance by the tax-farmers, who could take the blame in times of exorbitant taxation and who suffered the financial consequences of failure to collect enough. The disadvantage, however, was that the profits to be gained by more efficient collection ended up not in the public coffers but in the tax-farmers' pockets.

Another shortcoming of this system was the way in which the various cities in Holland contributed to provincial revenues. These contributions were set in relation to one another in much the same way that the

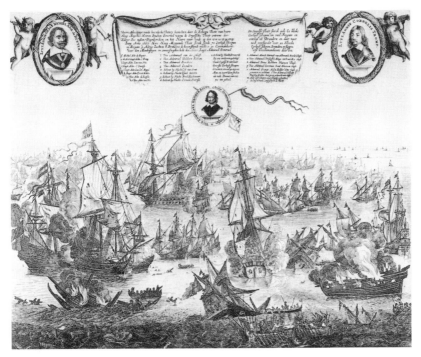

Figure 10   The naval battle off Dunkirk (11–14 June 1666) was one of the many armed clashes between the English and Dutch fleets. During the Second Anglo-Dutch War, the Dutch navy was much better equipped to confront the English, since they now had specially built warships. Michiel de Ruyter is portrayed at the upper left and Maarten Tromp at the upper right; in the middle, below the inscription, is Sir George Ayscue, the captured English admiral. Special taxes in the form of import and export duties were levied to finance the navy. These taxes went to the five Admiralty Colleges, which were responsible for outfitting and maintaining the fleet (Atlas van Stolk 2337).

provinces contributed fixed quotas to the Generality's revenues. This turned the cities into rivals: those which managed to keep their contribution low – and, by extension, the taxes they imposed on their citizens – could maintain a more favourable tax environment. This was abundantly clear in the granting of *convooien* and *licenten*, which were import and export duties levied to provide money for the maintenance of the fleet. Although the five admiralties responsible for collecting these taxes were national institutions, the local authorities had a large finger in the pie. Concerned as they were about the local business climate, they turned a blind eye to large-scale tax evasion, which meant that customs duties always yielded far less than they might have done.

A third problem was the disproportionately large amount contributed by the province of Holland to national revenues. In the area of government bonds, this imbalance was even more extreme, for neither the bonds issued by the other provinces nor those of the Union inspired as much confidence as those of Holland, which continually urged the other provinces to step up their efforts. This was easier said than done, since in the other provinces market traffic was not so dynamic and excises brought in less money. The inland provinces relied more on the land tax to fill their coffers, but because they also had a less dynamic agricultural sector than Holland, their revenues remained disappointing. Of more importance, however, was the fact that, despite Holland's very large contribution, it was still the other provinces that were overtaxed. This was made plain in 1716 when the Republic was on the verge of bankruptcy and research was done into the actual figures: while the province of Holland contributed nearly 60 per cent of the Generality's budget, 66 per cent of all the revenues collected in the United Provinces were collected in Holland.

In the first half of the seventeenth century the inland provinces also suffered disproportionately from the war, owing to devastation, pillaging and fire-raising, the levying of rather arbitrary taxes, and the building of defence works. In the 1590s, for example, both Maurits and the States General exerted a great deal of pressure on Deventer – a garrison town on the eastern frontier – to modernise its fortifications. Work began in 1599 and was finally completed fifty years later, in 1646, just before the Peace of Münster rendered such fortifications largely unnecessary. The costs of the project amounted to 250,000 guilders. On the basis of Article 4 of the Union of Utrecht, the city could claim compensation for half that amount. Less than 40 per cent was in fact subsidised, nearly two-thirds of the costs being borne by the people of Deventer. In Holland, by way of contrast, there was far less need for costly defence works.

Finally, a fourth problem was the fact that the money which the provinces were forced to contribute to the common coffers often never made it to The Hague. Most of the Generality's revenues – more than 90 per cent – were destined for the army and other forms of military expenditure. The fleet was financed with the money flowing in from customs duties. On paper and on the battlefield the Republic had just one army, but in the financial sense it had seven. In the Generality's budget, specific companies of infantry and cavalry were assigned to certain provinces, which were responsible for their upkeep. In 1653 Holland, for instance, maintained 28 companies of cavalry and 231 of infantry. Gelderland paid for 2 companies of mounted troops and

21 companies of foot soldiers, Utrecht paid for 6 companies of cavalry and 20 of infantry, and so on. Moreover, these companies were not always quartered in the provinces paying for them. Utrecht, for example, had only 2 companies of infantry on its soil; Gelderland, by contrast, had 26. Thus there was a considerable difference between repartition, meaning the apportionment of financial responsibility, and the actual quartering of the troops. Sixty per cent of the troops were quartered in the Generality Lands, which had not even taken part in the repartition.

One obvious problem was the supervision of financial responsibility. As mentioned above, many payments went directly from the provincial coffers to the relevant army units, but the provinces were not always able to fulfil their obligations and sometimes fell into arrears. This could be dangerous, because unpaid soldiers were less reliable and more inclined to mutiny. All kinds of informal arrangements were made to iron out these irregularities in the financial structure. A drastic example was the appeal made in 1688–9 to private persons to support the invasion of England. This daring venture required funds to be raised in great haste and with a maximum of secrecy. The official channels did not guarantee the desired discretion, so an appeal was made to a wealthy individual, Francisco Lopes Suasso. This Portuguese Jew, who had been born in France and trained there as a doctor, had emigrated to the Republic in 1653 and subsequently married a woman by the name of De Pinto. It was probably Lopes's father-in-law who let him try his luck in trade and banking. Lopes quickly grew into a leading figure in the Amsterdam banking world, extending loans that enabled both the Spanish crown and William III to pursue their ambitions. When money was urgently needed in 1688, Lopes proved willing and able to furnish it. He advanced a total of 1.5 million guilders to support William III's bid for the English crown.

The same pattern is discernible in the position of the Doubleth family as receivers-general of the Union. The Doubleths had come from Mechelen (Malines) in the Southern Netherlands. In 1586, Philips Doubleth became the receiver-general of public revenues, having previously fulfilled another function in Holland's financial apparatus. At this time the fate of the Revolt was by no means sealed, and the receiver-general had to possess considerable improvisational skill. At first there were not even clear instructions as to what he was expected to do. The receiver was generally charged with collecting the contributions promised by the provinces and making payments ordered by the Council of State. Moreover, he had to keep the books, which was an extremely difficult job, considering that many payments did not issue from his coffers but directly from the provinces. To complicate matters further, the Republic had no central bank which could build up reserves and advance funds as needed. Inevitably, this task now fell to the receiver-general. Doubleth, acting as an informal banker of the state, had to borrow and pay back money, often when it was in extremely short supply. The whole system demanded a thorough knowledge of business, extensive contacts in the circles of high finance, and a willingness to take great risks. Not surprisingly, the office came to be dominated by one family. After Doubleth's death in 1612, his eldest son, Johan, became receiver-general. In 1629 he was succeeded by his brother Philips, who held the office until 1653, after which a distant relative, another Philips Doubleth, became receiver-general. Only in 1667 was someone from outside the Doubleth family circle appointed to this extremely important post. In the meantime, all kinds of lawsuits had been instituted against the heirs. The States General called their bookkeeping into question and demanded the return of millions of guilders which the Doubleths – whose fortune had increased substantially during their time in office – had supposedly spirited away. In 1628, for example, the books of 1618 had not yet been balanced, an unusual situation even by seventeenth-century standards. Such irregularities, however, were the inevitable result of The Hague's lack of supervision of provincial affairs.

The holes in the financial system had to be stopped up by every possible means. Other countries – with centralised governments – seemed better equipped to deal with such problems, but appearances can be deceiving. It was precisely the small scale and piecemeal nature of the political and financial institutions in the Republic – and in Holland in particular – which inspired investors with confidence, making them willing to lend their money to the state. Moreover, the economy ran smoothly, and that was a boon, of course. The result was a large supply – particularly in Amsterdam – of capital in search of a safe haven. Holland's government bonds offered the security investors were looking for. That they were satisfied with the lowest interest rates in all of Europe is yet another indication that the government, despite its seemingly inefficient organisation, was in fact perceived as a well-functioning machine.

Part II

Golden Age: economy and society

6   A market economy

People came from far and wide to an auction held in Alkmaar on 5 February 1637. The regents of the Civic Orphanage were selling the estate of the innkeeper Wouter Winkel. It was not the furnishings of his inn, however, which made the auction worthwhile. Several years before his death, Winkel had started trading in tulip bulbs, and in a very short time he had become one of the richest men in Alkmaar. He possessed specimens of such rare varieties as Admirael van Enkhuizen and Paragon Schilder, and no fewer than seven bulbs of the highly coveted Gouda variety, all of which were on sale. The Admirael van Enkhuizen bulb alone fetched an incredible 5,200 guilders, and the proceeds of the sale amounted to 90,000 guilders. To put this in perspective, in those days a professor at Leiden University received an annual salary of 1,500 guilders, and a stately house on the Rapenburg canal in Leiden cost less than 20,000 guilders. The tulip auction in Alkmaar was therefore a resounding success, which was all the more remarkable when one considers that half a century earlier the flower had been almost completely unknown in Holland.

In the Middle Ages the tulip, which originated in West China, became a status symbol in Turkey. The son of the Turkish sultan – battling the Serbs on the Field of Blackbirds at Kosovo in 1389 – wore beneath his armour a cotton shirt embroidered with tulips. It was not until the mid-sixteenth century, however, that the first tulips appeared in the Christian part of Europe. In 1562 a merchant in Antwerp received some tulips in a shipment of cloth from Constantinople. Most of them were subsequently chopped up and cooked on the assumption that they were onions, though several of them survived to blossom spectacularly in the kitchen garden the following spring. At the time, the tulip was known only to a handful of enthusiasts, one of whom was Charles de l'Escluse, or Carolus Clusius, who became a professor at Leiden University in 1592. It was he, more than anyone else, who was responsible for the popularity of the tulip in the Northern Netherlands.

At first the tulip remained within the province of flower lovers, but its rarity quickly turned it into an object of desire, and it was not long before

Figure 11 'Floraes Gecks-kap', a print satirising the tulip mania of 1637. The fool's cap serves as a saleroom where people stock up on bulbs in the hope of getting rich. Below the flag we see Flora riding upon a donkey (Atlas van Stolk 1787).

the first tulip was stolen from the botanical gardens at Leiden. By 1621 the tulip had risen so much in standing that the successful Amsterdam physician Claes Pieterszoon started going by the name of Nicolaes Tulp (Tulip), and as such became a member of the Amsterdam town council the following year. In 1632, while publicly dissecting the body of an executed criminal, he was immortalised by Rembrandt in *The Anatomy Lesson Of Doctor Tulp*.

The tulip trade grew steadily. The sandy soil near Holland's dunes proved eminently suited to the cultivation of tulips. Small growers began to produce them, while innkeepers such as Wouter Winkel started trading in bulbs as a sideline. One of the tulip's drawbacks is that the flower blossoms only for several weeks a year, so in order to sell their wares, bulb traders compiled catalogues to illustrate the many varieties on offer. The tulip is by nature uniform in colour, but there were also varieties with flamed patterns. It was not until the twentieth century that scientific research showed these colourful patterns to be the result of viral infections in the bulbs. In the seventeenth century it was not possible to distinguish these freaks of nature from the regular varieties, apart from observing that the 'broken' varieties were rarer. The most coveted variety was Semper Augustus – a red flame on a white background – of which there were only a few dozen specimens in the Netherlands. Other 'broken' varieties – including the Root en Gheel van Leyden, the Paragon van Delft and the previously mentioned Admirael van Enkhuizen – were sold in the markets. Their names alone reveal that these tulips were cultivated near Holland's cities.

The tulip's rise in value kept pace with its growth in popularity. In 1636 prices soared. The high point was reached in 1637 at the sale in Alkmaar, where buyers paid unheard-of sums in the expectation that prices would rise even more. Such wild, speculative trading could not remain profitable for ever. Shortly after the Alkmaar auction, the bubble burst. Prices plummeted and scores of speculators – who had been dealing in futures and now had to pay for bulbs that had dropped dramatically in value – suddenly found themselves in desperate financial straits. The States of Holland set up an investigation and issued debt-payment guidelines, but it was years before the last accounts were settled. For Holland, the outcome was not all negative. The speculation in bulbs had drawn attention to the tulip both at home and abroad, and the Dutch tulip mania had actually been the best possible way of advertising the flower. Holland had been put firmly on the map as the land of tulips and would continue to profit from that reputation for centuries to come.

The tulip craze of 1636–7 was the logical outcome of the flourishing Dutch economy, which had experienced huge growth in the previous fifty years, growth which had left the province of Holland with an abundance of ready money. The well-to-do could afford to pay large sums for luxuries such as flowers. At the same time, there were countless people – not all typical capitalists by any means – willing to invest in this promising product. Relatively little capital was necessary to set oneself up as a cultivator and trader of tulip bulbs. It was rumoured that one of the two black tulips in the Republic had been grown by a cobbler in The Hague. Although apocryphal, this story says a great deal about the prevailing investment climate. That the product in question had come from abroad was also typical of the Dutch economy at this time. What makes the case of the tulip especially interesting, however, is that Holland's farmers quickly got the hang of tulip cultivation and started producing bulbs themselves. In other words, not only was the Republic's economy highly commercialised and internationally oriented, but it also had a broad social base.

The Northern Netherlands is situated in the delta formed by three important European rivers: the Scheldt, the Meuse and the Rhine. Its geographical location inevitably left its mark on the economy of the pre-industrial Netherlands, partly because of the opportunities afforded by these waterways – easy accessibility, for example, at a time when it was cheaper to transport goods on water than over land – and partly because of the limitations it imposed. The difficulty of overcoming these limitations contributed greatly to the success of the Dutch economy in the seventeenth century. In 1600 a large part of the western Netherlands was literally new land. Such place names as Nieuwvliet (New Brook) in Zeeuws-Vlaanderen, Nieuwveen (New Peat Bog) in Zuid-Holland, and Nieuwwolde (New Fenlands) in Groningen bear witness to the land reclamation which had taken place in these areas by damming up the mud flats on the coast, as well as by draining and empoldering the marshes behind the dunes. These developments, which had started in the Middle Ages, picked up again in the seventeenth century. But as impressive as medieval land reclamation had been from a technological point of view, it soon reached its limits economically. Particularly in the parts of Holland where water-logged peat bogs were prevalent, drainage was a problem, because it caused the peat – and therefore the level of the land – to subside and the groundwater to well up with redoubled force. In the course of the fourteenth century it became clear that it would not be possible to drain the land sufficiently to make grain cultivation profitable.

This forced the Hollanders to choose between moving to drier regions or finding an alternative. The solution – importing their basic foodstuffs instead of growing them – gave them the time and the wherewithal to engage in a host of other activities, such as increased peat production, shipping and fishing, and textile manufacturing. The grain trade, which now became the lifeblood of the Dutch economy, had not been a viable alternative before the fourteenth century, when the high cost of transport had limited long-distance trade mainly to luxury products, which combined small volume with large profits. Many areas of the Republic were self-supporting, meaning that most of their food came from the surrounding countryside. Only in times of scarcity was it necessary to search further afield for provisions, something the Hollanders were now forced by circumstances to do on a regular basis. At first Holland acquired its grain from adjoining regions in the Low Countries: Zeeland, and probably Utrecht and Gelderland as well, shipped their surpluses to Holland. England and especially northern France were equally important suppliers. Finally, there was the Baltic, which in the mid-fifteenth century was a relatively minor source of grain – though the Hollanders were involved in Scandinavian wars aimed at keeping the Danish Sound open to their shipping traffic – since at least three and perhaps even four times as much grain was imported from France. In the last quarter of the century, however, it was becoming increasingly difficult for French grain to reach the harbours of Holland, owing to the consequences of war and shortages in France itself. Since at this time grain production was being stepped up in eastern Europe, trade naturally shifted to that area. It emerges from the oldest register (1497) of the toll collected at the Danish Sound that already at that time more than half the ships passing through the Sound came from Holland.

Holland's ecological problems had repercussions on other provinces in the Republic. Agriculture in Zeeland had been highly commercialised since the Middle Ages. Wheat, the most important crop, had yields of between 40 and 70 bushels per hectare, whereas in the area around Maastricht not more than 20–35 bushels were harvested from the same amount of land. In a famous farming region such as Norfolk in England, it was not until the eighteenth century that farmers achieved yields comparable to those common in medieval Zeeland. Zeeland's agricultural prosperity was due in part to the fertility of its clay soil, which did not subside like the peat bogs of Holland. Despite this advantage, farming in Zeeland was far from easy. Maintenance of the seawalls was costly, the groundwater was often brackish, and frequent shortages of drinking water made it difficult to breed cattle. The profitability of farming in this region was boosted, however, by the proximity of urban markets. This pattern was repeated all over Europe: where demand was strong, traditional means of production were abandoned and agriculture was commercialised.

The farmers of Zeeland found their markets partly in Zeeland itself. By the beginning of the seventeenth century, more than half the population of Zeeland lived in towns or cities. These were often modest in size – in 1622, Tholen, for instance, had around 1,600 inhabitants and only Middelburg had more than 10,000 – but altogether town-dwellers accounted for a sizeable percentage of the population. Every farmstead in Zeeland therefore had to feed not only itself but also one urban household. It seems likely that in the Middle Ages the farmers of Zeeland had fed, in addition to Zeeland's town-dwellers, quite a few families in Flanders, Brabant and Holland. By the seventeenth century, however, it was primarily the Hollanders who made their bread from wheat grown in Zeeland.

In the second half of the seventeenth century grain prices dropped all over Europe, and the farmers in Zeeland inevitably suffered. Again, it was the Hollanders who came to their aid, though this time it was not the consumers but the merchants. As early as the fifteenth century, farmers in Zeeland had started to grow madder, the roots of which were dried to produce a red pigment used in dyeing leather and textiles. Madder was thus a perfect example of a commercial crop destined for industrial use. Madder growing, however, was not only labour-intensive but also extremely capital-intensive. It took several years before the plants could be harvested, and the processing, which involved drying the roots in a madder-stove, required investments in material as well as specialist labour. A madder-stove cost more than 20,000 guilders, a sum plainly beyond the means of small farmers. The stoves were therefore built and run by consortia, usually consisting of sixteen participants. The preparation and quality of madder were subject to provincial regulations designed to prevent the dissemination of the plant and knowledge of its preparation – to no avail, of course. Madder was processed under the supervision of specialists, all of whom came from Tholen. The madder was taken from the madder-stoves and shipped to Rotterdam, where most of it – more than 90 per cent, according to figures from 1690 – was exported to other countries. The capital-intensive aspect of madder processing meant that the traders were also deeply involved in the production phase. Merchants bought the crops while they were still in the fields and had the entire harvest processed at their expense. The intensification of madder cultivation in Zeeland, after grain prices dropped in 1660, was no doubt made possible by injections of investment capital. Thus agriculture in Zeeland was determined completely by commerce.

Farming on the sandy soils in the east of the country was an entirely different story. Here commercialisation was far less advanced, though not entirely absent. In 1650 fewer than 20,000 people were living in the rural areas of Drenthe, a province that had no cities of any importance. The largest concentrations of people were to be found in Meppel, which had 1,200 inhabitants, and the fortified town of Coevorden, with a population of 800. There were no large markets in the area, the nearest being the city of Groningen to the north and the cities of Kampen and Zwolle on the River IJssel. Consequently, Drenthe's agriculture was mainly self-supporting, meaning that the farmers consumed a large part of their own produce. Their main crop was rye, as evidenced by a statement made by the provincial government of Drenthe in 1622: 'The wealth and prosperity of this Landtschap [as Drenthe was commonly called] ... consists in agriculture or the growing of rye.'[1] This alone distinguished it from the western part of the country, where one customarily ate wheat bread. In the sandy areas in the east and south, however, one had to be content with dark rye bread.

Much of the land in Drenthe was not cultivated and cattle grazed there undisturbed, in stark contrast to the western Netherlands, where the land was worked intensively. Cattle were in fact Drenthe's most important

[1] J. Bieleman, *Boeren op het Drentse zand: een nieuwe visie op de 'oude' landbouw*, AAG-Bijdragen (Wageningen: Afdeling Agrarische Geschiedenis, Landbouwuniversiteit Wageningen, 1987), pp. 520–1.

export product, especially in the seventeenth century, when cattle were bred in Drenthe and sold to farmers in Holland to be fattened up and slaughtered. Some cattle were sent to fattening-up farms in the Groningen countryside before being exported to Germany. The wool of small, shaggy Drenthe sheep was woven into blankets in Kampen and Leiden, and Drenthe horses supplied industries and especially households in the west with horsepower. Elsewhere on sandy soil farmers undertook the cultivation of marketable crops, the most remarkable of which turned out to be the tobacco grown in the Veluwe region of Gelderland.

In the first half of the seventeenth century, the farmers in the Veluwe region, urged on by Amsterdam traders, began to grow tobacco, which was then blended with superior tobacco from the English colonies and consumed as snuff, pipe tobacco and chewing tobacco. Tobacco cultivation grew spectacularly in the second half of the century. Prompted by dropping grain prices, farmers – often no more than smallholders – switched over to tobacco, a very labour-intensive and completely commercial crop. Not only was its sale dependent on the market, but its cultivation also called for intensive market traffic. When properly fertilised, tobacco could be grown continually. Experience had shown that the best manure consisted of sheep dung mixed with pigeon droppings. Dutch merchants did a brisk trade in this commodity. For the most part the Veluwe region imported Frisian pigeon droppings, while sheep dung was shipped in from Holland, Zeeland, Friesland and Groningen. When tobacco cultivation in the Veluwe region peaked shortly after 1700, around half of the farmland in the vicinity of Wageningen was planted with tobacco. Although Veluwe tobacco was gradually supplanted in the marketplace by the American product, the crop was still being grown in the Veluwe region as late as the mid-twentieth century.

In Holland, nature itself forced agriculture to commercialise, a process that was accelerated by the proximity of expanding urban markets. Holland's farmers supplied urban consumers in the Republic as well as markets abroad. They also grew industrial crops, such as rape, the oil of which was used to produce lamp oil and soap, while the pulp was given to cattle as fodder. In Holland's North Quarter (Noorderkwartier) – the area above the River IJ – grazing grounds were established in response to the demand for dairy products in the cities of Holland. Oxen, many of which had been driven from Denmark in herds of 40–100 head, could eat their fill of Holland's grass before being sold for slaughter. Of the approximately 50,000 oxen exported from Denmark every year, 60–80 per cent went to Holland. Cattle farmers living close to cities naturally specialised in milk production.

Butter and especially cheese were also produced, partly for export. The process of preparing hard cheese had been perfected in Holland as early as the twelfth or thirteenth century. Hard cheese, which has a long shelf life, was eminently suited to long-distance transport. Most of the cheese shipped from Hoorn was destined for France and, to a lesser extent, southern Europe. In addition to milk, most cattle farms produced hemp – sold to rope-yards – which was cultivated in small, very intensively worked 'hemp gardens'.

The increased demand from neighbouring cities and foreign markets led in the first half of the seventeenth century to a sharp rise in the price of agricultural products. Dutch merchants began to realise that they could invest their capital profitably in agriculture, and this in turn led to the large-scale creation of polders, especially in the North Quarter. Even if there had been a demand for more arable land in Noord-Holland, the technology needed to drain such large lakes was lacking before this time. Improvements in windmill technology helped to overcome this obstacle, leading to the empoldering in a relatively short time of the Beemster (1612), Wieringerwaard (1617), Purmer (1622), Wijde Wormer (1626), Heerhugowaard (1631) and Schermer (1635). Such large-scale empoldering increased the surface area of Noord-Holland by one-third, but the drop in agricultural prices around mid-century put an abrupt end to these drainage schemes.

The search for supplemental foodstuffs, as well as regional surpluses of labour – both arising from the difficulties of farming in Holland – had led early on to the development of sizeable fisheries. In many villages in Holland people alternated farming with fishing. A 1494 survey revealed that most of the villages in the North Quarter had people who engaged in herring fishing 'for a wage'.[2] The herring catch was destined for both domestic consumption and export. Herring gutteries had existed since the first half of the fourteenth century, but now fishermen began to gut and preserve fish on the open sea, leading to better quality and longer storage life. Herring-busses, with a crew of 18–30 men, stayed at sea for weeks on end, during which the catch was brought to port by fish-carriers. In this way the fishing fleet could maximise its catch by staying close to the schools of herring. In the sixteenth century, herring-busses operated mainly from the estuary of the River Meuse, where the crews from Noord-Holland gathered. This location was connected with important outlets in the Southern Netherlands. The increasing demand for herring

---

[2] A. M. van der Woude, *Het Noorderkwartier: een regionaal-historisch onderzoek in de demografische en economische geschiedenis van westelijk Nederland van de late middeleeuwen tot het begin van de negentiende eeuw* (Utrecht: Hes Uitgevers, 1983), p. 403.

in Holland prompted fishermen to sail out from a number of harbours. By the mid-seventeenth century, Holland had approximately 500 herring-busses, which supplied most of the herring in the European market. Their success and high standards were due in part to the effective organisation of the herring industry, which was supervised by the Board of Commissioners for Sea Fishing (College van Commisarissen van de Groote Visserij), which was responsible for quality control.

For a long time herring was the most important product exported to the Baltic, where proceeds from its sale were used to buy grain. The increase in the herring catch also had significant side effects in the Netherlands itself. Fishermen were of course important clients of shipbuilders and rope makers. To preserve their catch they also required large quantities of salt. Salt was obtained in Holland's coastal areas through the evaporation of seawater, but this did not supply enough to meet the growing demand. In the course of the sixteenth century, therefore, more and more salt was imported from Portugal, Spain and France. Dutch traders also imported wine from southern Europe which they then sold to the Baltic countries. The contours were thus emerging of a trading network that would exploit Holland's central location to the full.

In the sixteenth century, however, Antwerp was still the largest centre of commerce in the Low Countries. Brabant and Flanders had an age-old tradition of international trade, which had enabled first Bruges, then Ghent and finally Antwerp to grow into commercial centres of European and even global importance. Since the discovery of a direct sea route to the East Indies and the European conquest of Central and South America, the focal point of international trade had shifted more and more from the Mediterranean to the Atlantic. Until that time the cities of Italy had been the arrival point of spices coming from the Middle East, which were then shipped by land or sea to the other markets of Europe. Shortly after 1500, Antwerp became the official entrepôt for Portuguese spices, which meant that all spices shipped by Portugal from the East Indies were first unloaded at Antwerp and then transported to other parts of Europe. By the mid-sixteenth century, Antwerp was handling around 80 per cent of all the trade conducted by the Habsburg Netherlands.

From a commercial standpoint, Holland was at this time little more than a satellite of Antwerp. The province did have its strong points, how-ever, one of which was a fine-meshed commercial infrastructure which owed its early development to the trade in bulk goods with the Baltic. Numerous Dutch merchants, who had a direct interest in trade but lacked large amounts of capital, had developed the so-called *partenrederij* (part-ownership of shipping firms) as a means of sharing the risk and attracting capital. Ships, as well as such things as windmills, were financed collectively by dividing their ownership into eight, sixteen, thirty-two and sometimes as many as sixty-four or ninety-six shares.

Another of Holland's strengths was its large merchant fleet, which was necessary for the grain trade. As early as the fifteenth century, Holland's fleet – with a cargo capacity of 40,000–50,000 tons – was twice as large as that of powerful Venice. In 1530 the Hollanders had approximately 400 large sea-going vessels, more than France and England combined. Owing to the relatively high cost of transporting bulk goods such as grain, Dutch shipbuilders were continually developing more efficient models, a process that culminated in the flute, a type of ship first launched around 1595 in Hoorn. The flute combined a large carrying capacity with the need for only a small crew. In the mid-seventeenth century, a 200-ton flute could sail with a crew of nine or ten, whereas a comparable English ship needed a crew of thirty. This superior technology, coupled with great consumer demand, allowed the Hollanders to set themselves up as the freighters of Europe.

The Antwerp entrepôt was also threatened in the sixteenth century by developments taking place elsewhere in the Spanish empire. South American silver – necessary to buy spices in the East Indies – arrived in Seville, which was gradually ousting Antwerp as the centre of the Portuguese spice trade. Antwerp suffered further setbacks when the Spanish crown, having borrowed huge amounts of money in the city, declared bankruptcy in 1557 and 1575, which undermined faith in the Antwerp capital market.

The Dutch Revolt exacerbated these problems. Antwerp's wealth made it a desirable asset, and the Habsburgs were determined to use every means possible to conquer the city, which finally fell in 1585. The rebels in Zeeland, who controlled the access route to Antwerp's harbour, subsequently blockaded the River Scheldt, forcing ships destined for Antwerp to anchor in the roadstead at Vlissingen and tranship their goods. Both the Habsburgs and the rebels levied high excises on goods transported via the Scheldt. To avoid paying these taxes, the merchants of Antwerp moved their shipping activities to the coast, where the Republic's warships did everything in their power to obstruct traffic, with the result that the Flemish coast was blockaded for most of the Eighty Years War. The fall of Antwerp prompted an exodus of traders, who moved to a variety of commercial centres in north-western Europe, including Rouen, Hamburg, Cologne, Frankfurt, London, Middelburg and Amsterdam. Within a few years, however, the majority of Antwerp's merchants had congregated in Amsterdam, creating a wondrous synergy that not only enabled Amsterdam to succeed Antwerp as the centre of international trade but also lifted that trade on to a higher plane.

Antwerp's trade had traditionally been based on annual fairs at which luxury goods were sold by merchants who flocked to the city from far and wide. Dutch traders, by contrast, were specialised in the transport and processing of bulk goods and had long been forced to look for grain and salt in foreign markets. The Antwerp merchants now in Amsterdam therefore had ample capital and wide-ranging trading networks at their disposal. The Hollanders controlled one region – the Baltic – and had the carrying capacity, as well as the knowledge of shipbuilding and sea-faring, to sail great distances. This combination of know-how and con-tacts, together with unprecedented concentrations of goods and services, allowed merchants from the Low Countries – Hollanders and Brabanters alike – to open up new markets and to integrate the flow of goods, making the Republic the greatest economic power in the world and enabling it to maintain this position for several decades. A memorandum signed by Amsterdam merchants in 1629 stated, with a note of satisfaction, 'that by virtue of our good management and shrewdness throughout the Truce we have driven the ships of all other countries out of the water, attracted nearly all the business from other countries, and served the whole of Europe with our ships'.[3]

The trade with the Baltic (particularly Poland) – of such importance that it was called the 'mother trade' – long remained an essential part of the Republic's trading network. A 1636 estimate of European goods arriving in Amsterdam, the total value of which amounted to 30 million guilders, reckons the share of the Baltic trade to be 12.5 million guilders, or more than 40 per cent. In comparison, the goods shipped from Norway, North Russia and North Germany together were worth 5 mil-lion guilders, or 15 per cent. Throughout the sixteenth century, however, trade with the Baltic had been one-sided, since the Baltic had little demand for Dutch products. Two-thirds of the ships passing through the Danish Sound were commanded by Dutch captains, but it was mainly the ships sailing westward that were carrying cargoes. As late as the 1580s, 70 per cent of the Dutch ships sailing eastward were filled with ballast, usually in the form of bricks and roof tiles of little commercial value which served mainly to stabilise the ship. Only in the seventeenth century were the Hollanders able to offer a much wider range of goods. Shortly before 1600, Dutch merchants managed to obtain access to new markets in and outside Europe, and this brought about a change in the Baltic trade, which gradually shifted from one-sided trading in bulk goods to trading in both bulk and luxury goods.

---

[3] Joost Jonker and Keetie Sluyterman, *Thuis op de wereldmarkt. Nederlandse handelshuizen door de eeuwen heen* (The Hague: Sdu Uitgevers, 2000), p. 35.

In 1589 a group of merchants from the Southern Netherlands sent their first ship, *Den Swerten Ruyter* (The Black Horseman), from Holland with a cargo of grain to Italy, where poor harvests had caused serious food shortages. The following year the Spanish crown, at war with France, suddenly lifted – for political reasons – the trade embargo on ships sailing for the rebellious provinces in the Netherlands, thus opening up the Mediterranean to Dutch traders. In the 1590s, between 200 and 300 ships sailed annually from the Republic to the Mediterranean, carrying grain at first and gradually textiles as well. They made the return voyage loaded with spices, silk and other luxury goods, which had either been produced in the region or shipped there from Asia via the Middle East. Such goods were in great demand in the Baltic, where grain exports had brought wealth to many a landowner. Moreover, the Dutch had recently begun to engage in the rapidly expanding trade with Russia – meaning the merchants of Muscovy (the principality of Moscow), who were now also eager to acquire southern European products. Finally, to the consternation of the Venetians, the first Dutch merchantman, heavily laden with silver, appeared off the coast of Syria in 1595 with the intention of stocking up on spices and silk in Aleppo.

The lifting of the Spanish trade embargo also put the Dutch in a position to do business directly with non-European territories. In the 1590s, Dutch merchantmen began to appear off the African coast, where they bought precious metals and sugar from the Portuguese. In 1593–4 the Dutch began to trade directly with the Caribbean. In 1596 they built a fort in the estuary of the River Essequibo (in present-day Guyana). It was destroyed several months later by the Spanish, but trade continued nonetheless. In 1599 a fleet arrived at Punta de Araya, the vast salt flats along the Venezuelan coast. No fewer than 768 Dutch merchantmen would put in there in the next five years. The States General granted the New Netherland Company (Nieuw Nederland Compagnie), founded in 1614, a monopoly of North American trade, a privilege it enjoyed for a number of years. Even though the Twelve Years' Truce led to the postponement of plans to found a West India Company (WIC), it was finally established when the Truce ended in 1621. After initial setbacks in Brazil, the Caribbean and Africa, where bases were lost in Bahia, Puerto Rico and St George d'Elmina, the WIC succeeded in 1630 in establishing a bridgehead on the Brazilian coast, where it remained an important producer of sugar and tobacco for fifteen years. On the African coast at this time, the Dutch established (or captured from the Portuguese) a number of forts, many of which would continue until well into the nineteenth century to serve as a base of operations for the Dutch slave trade. The conquest of Aruba, Curaçao and Bonaire in 1634 had already assured the

WIC of a distribution point for slave labour in the Caribbean. Though Brazil was lost in 1654 and the English captured New Netherland in 1664, these losses were made up for from the 1670s onwards by the enormous increase in the production of sugar, a most profitable crop, in such places as Surinam, where the number of plantations doubled between 1672 and 1700. In these years Dutch traders also supplied English, French and Spanish plantations with slaves. Between 1685 and 1689 an Amsterdam consortium even enjoyed for a brief time the Spanish *asiento*, the sole right to act as a supplier of slaves.

The most extensive of all these trading networks, however, was the Dutch trading imperium in Asia, the foundations of which had also been laid in the 1590s. Before this time, the Portuguese had been the main supplier of spices to the Low Countries. Their deliveries could not always be relied upon, but fortunately the Levant offered an alternative supply. A number of enterprising traders, however, dreamt of playing a greater role in the trade between Asia and north-western Europe. Their idea was to avoid confrontations with Spanish and Portuguese competitors by dis-covering a route to the East along the northern coast of Russia. In June 1594 the first expedition set sail from the roadstead at Texel. This attempt, and another the following year, failed when the ships were stranded in the ice. The third voyage, under the command of Willem Barentszoon, yielded only the spectacular tale of the long, harsh winter months spent on Nova Zembla. There was now little hope of finding a northern route. At almost the same time, in 1595, a group of Dutch merchants fitted out four ships – under the command of Cornelis de Houtman of Gouda – for a voyage to the East Indies via the southern route around Africa. The voyage lasted more than two years. One ship perished and only 87 of the 240 crew members returned. The proceeds from the sale of the cargo – 290,000 guilders – did not even cover the costs, but the expedition had proved that direct trade with East Asia along the southern sea route was indeed possible.

In 1598 the Spanish imposed another embargo, which cut the Republic off almost completely from its supply of spices. This prompted the founding of new companies in Amsterdam, Middelburg, Veere and Rotterdam, all aiming to open up trade with the East Indies. Between 1598 and 1602, the Dutch sent sixty-one ships to the East, while the Portuguese sent only forty-six. Thus, from the very beginning, the Dutch became serious competitors in Asian waters, though their continued success was far from certain. The profits from spices, which had risen spectacularly, could plummet just as spectacularly as a result of sudden oversupply, while the suppliers in the East Indies could easily raise their prices in response to competing demand. The long sea route to the

East Indies was also full of peril. These risks, both material and economic, could, however, be minimised by mutual agreements among merchants. Moreover, Oldenbarnevelt saw the trade with the Indies as an opportunity to strike a blow at the Spanish. In 1602 he brought about a merger of the various companies in Holland and Zeeland, forming a new joint-stock company, the Dutch East India Company (Verenigde Oost-Indische Compagnie, or VOC), which in the coming two centuries would leave its mark on all of Asia. Because the VOC had been formed by combining a number of local initiatives, the company always retained a hybrid structure consisting of six chambers – which were in fact subsidiaries that were largely independent of one another – in Middelburg, Rotterdam, Delft, Amsterdam, Hoorn and Enkhuizen. The Board of Governors – known as the Gentlemen XVII (Heeren XVII), consisting of representatives of all six chambers – were clearly dominated by the Amsterdam Chamber, which not only supplied eight of the board's members but also put up more than half the share capital. At the VOC's founding the States General granted it the monopoly of trade with the territories to the east of the Cape of Good Hope.

There was, almost inevitably, a negative balance of trade with Asia, because the Asians were not interested in European products. The goods bought in Asia therefore had to be paid for in cash in the form of precious metal. The Europeans' main sources of silver were the Spanish mines in South America, and for this reason alone the trade with Spain was of great importance. To reduce their dependence on Spanish silver, the VOC bought goods in Asia for which there was a demand in the Indonesian archipelago. The VOC quickly claimed a share of the trade with India's Coromandel coast, where cotton cloth was produced that was popular in the East Indies. Japan was the principal source of silver in Asia itself, hence the importance of good trade relations with that country. This was notoriously difficult, because the Japanese authorities pursued a policy of isolation. There was, however, a great demand in Japan for Chinese silk. By means of systematic intimidation, the VOC managed to acquire a position as a principal trader of this product from 1624 onwards. After the English, Spanish and Portuguese had been driven out of the country, the Dutch were granted the sole right to trade with Japan. In the years between 1630 and 1660, Japan was the VOC's most important source of silver.

The geographic expansion of Dutch trade was also noticeable in the Republic itself. Existing industries, such as textiles and shipbuilding, saw the demand for their products increase many times over both at home and abroad. New industries sprang up owing to the availability of raw materials previously unknown in the Northern Netherlands. These included processing industries, which processed goods directly connected with trade in the Dutch staple market. A typical example of this is sugar refining. By 1597 there were three sugar refineries in Amsterdam, processing cane sugar from Central and South America, which would remain the Netherlands' source of sugar for the whole of the seventeenth century. This industry grew quickly. In 1650 there were forty sugar refineries in Amsterdam; by 1661 their number had grown to sixty. Holland had now become Europe's largest centre of sugar production, and in other countries as well it was mainly Dutch know-how that helped to get the industry off the ground. In the second half of the seventeenth century, Amsterdam's sugar refineries provided work for approximately 1,000 people. Refineries were also established in other cities, such as Rotterdam (1593), Middelburg (1627) and Dordrecht (1686).

The tobacco industry, although increasingly dependent on home-grown leaves, was in fact a true processing industry. From around 1600 onwards it owed its development to the raw tobacco imported from America; before this time only processed tobacco had been imported. Consumers bought their tobacco in rolls called 'carrots', which were produced in tobacco-spinning works by rolling the tobacco leaves together. The partial mechanisation introduced in the seventeenth century – rolling tables, tobacco wheels, spindles and presses – enabled tobacco-spinning works to grow into medium-sized businesses employing dozens of workers. In 1669, Jacob van Emden had forty workers in his warehouse-cum-spinnery on the Vlooienbrug in Amsterdam, and Abraham Levy had just as many workers in his tobacco cellars in the timber yards behind Anthoni Breestraat. Jacob Franco Drago employed 50–60 people. As these names suggest, Portuguese Jews were very active in this sector. At the beginning of the eighteenth century, the tobacco industry, which was largely concentrated in Amsterdam, reportedly employed some 4,000 workers, while tobacco-related industries offered employment to another 3,000. Similar developments were seen in the diamond industry, in silk-spinning and silk-weaving, in cotton-printing and in other industries dependent on imported materials.

The expansion of the trading network also gave a big boost to old established industries. Between 1625 and 1700 the increasing demand for cargo space required the yearly production of 400–500 sea-going vessels. These ships, mostly flutes, took four months to build from a standard design. Until 1600, shipbuilding had mainly been an urban industry, but after 1600 the area around the River Zaan became the largest supplier of newly built ships. This sector offered work to some 10,000 people. In other ways, too, the Zaan district developed into an industrial region of unparalleled importance. In 1582 the first industrial

Figure 12   The oil mill in Wormer on fire, after being struck by lightning on 5 May 1699. Dozens of mills were built for industrial purposes in the area around the River Zaan. Before the invention of the steam engine, wind was an important source of energy in both shipping and industry. This print featured in a book that included high praise for the fire pump, an invention of the Amsterdammer Jan van der Heyden (Atlas van Stolk 2832: 68).

windmills were built in Alkmaar, in Holland's North Quarter. In 1630, there were 191 such windmills in the area, 30 of which were in cities and 128 on or near the River Zaan, where the proximity of water and the availability of free wind energy offered ideal conditions for establishing an industry. It was here that windmills sawed timber for shipbuilding, pressed oil out of seeds, husked grains and pounded rags into pulp to make paper. By the early eighteenth century the number of industrial windmills in the cities had increased only slightly, but on the River Zaan there were far more than before. Most of these windmills were used in shipbuilding, since Cornelis Corneliszoon of Uitgeest had succeeded in 1592 in using a crankshaft to change the circular motion of a mill into the back-and-forth movement of a saw. Of the 584 industrial windmills counted in 1731, 256 were used for sawing timber. The windmills were highly efficient at cutting up Norwegian timber into ship parts which were taken directly to the shipyards. This availability of parts was primarily responsible for the concentration of shipbuilding yards on the River Zaan. The shipyards in nearby Amsterdam generally confined themselves to carrying out repairs.

In addition to the free and unlimited supply of wind energy, Dutch industry also profited in the seventeenth century from the abundance of peat. The Republic, otherwise poorly endowed with raw materials, had an ample supply of peat. The peat bogs in the north-east of the Republic were easily accessible by boat, which made it possible to transport peat quickly and inexpensively to the markets in the west of the country. In Holland itself, peat digging was undertaken on a large scale, enabling the Republic to consume what in those days was a considerable amount of energy-producing fuel. To obtain the same amount of energy from wood, one-quarter of the country would have had to be forested.

The increased employment opportunities in agriculture, trade and industry stimulated the growth in population. Lacking exact figures, we must make do with estimates, but it seems likely that the Republic had more than 1 million inhabitants by the beginning of the seventeenth century. Slightly more than half of these people lived in the province of Holland, whose population increased in the next twenty years to 672,000, according to tax records from 1622 which give us a better idea of the actual figures. The province of Utrecht had 76,500 inhabitants, and Zeeland approximately the same number. Friesland cannot have had a population of more than 125,000 at that time, and Overijssel at most 71,000, the number recorded in 1675. Drenthe's population numbered 22,000 in 1630. We have no reliable figures for Gelderland and Groningen. The Generality Lands in Brabant and Limburg, which were conquered between 1629 and 1632, certainly added another 150,000 and perhaps as many as 200,000 to these figures. By the end of the seventeenth century, the Republic's population had increased to nearly 2 million. A great deal of this growth had taken place in Holland, where the population had increased between 1622 and 1680 by approximately 30 per cent. In the last quarter of the century, however, the inland provinces began to show strong growth, much of which was due to immigration. The city of Utrecht grew relatively little in the seventeenth century – its inhabitants increased in number from approximately 25,000 to 30,000 – but its population actually declined if one discounts the number of immigrants. In other words, there were more deaths than births in seventeenth-century Utrecht. This was mainly due to epidemic diseases such as the plague and dysentery. In 1624, 8.5 per cent of the population of Utrecht died. Other cities suffered far greater losses: Delft and Leiden, for example, lost 16–17 per cent of their population during the same epidemic. Between 1634 and 1637 the plague again claimed 4,000 lives in Utrecht, while in Leiden one-third of the population was swept away. That the cities of Utrecht, Leiden and Delft managed to grow at all during this period was therefore due entirely to immigration.

The growth of export industries, the population boom and the rise in immigration had in turn a positive effect on the service industries. This is evident from the increase in the number of guilds and shopkeepers' organisations. Guilds were particularly important in those sectors serving a local market. In Amsterdam alone, twenty-five new guilds were founded in the course of the seventeenth century, giving Amsterdam around twice as many guilds in 1700 as in 1600. Similar developments occurred elsewhere. In 1600 there were approximately 650 guilds in the Republic, whereas by 1700 their number had risen to more than 1,100.

Formally, each guild had a monopoly of the production and sale of certain products. For example, only members of the furriers' guild, founded in 1613, were allowed to dress fur in Amsterdam, while members of the bakers' guild had the exclusive right to sell bread. Men's clothing had to be ordered from members of the tailors' guild, clothes for women and children from seamstresses belonging to the dressmakers' guild. In practice, though, it often proved difficult for a guild to secure the monopoly it had been granted. Amsterdam was the only city with a dressmakers' guild. Elsewhere these women had been excluded from the guild system and were continually at loggerheads with their male counterparts. Although the Haarlem tailors had started in the sixteenth century to expel women from the guild – a process that was taking place everywhere in Europe at the time – they did not succeed in driving women out of dressmaking completely, largely because female customers were reluctant to have themselves measured by men. The civic authorities in Haarlem continually vacillated between tolerating the dressmakers' activities – another argument in their favour being that they provided many women with a respectable means of earning a living – and protecting the tailors' share of the market. It was not until the beginning of the eighteenth century that a clear line was drawn between the specific work tailors and dressmakers were authorised to do.

The result of such territorial tiffs meant that the monopoly a guild possessed on paper was impossible to secure in practice. Many guilds were supported by the town council in their attempt to gain complete control of the market, an endeavour which was often well worth the effort. In Amsterdam the local Guild of St Luke (whose members included painters of all descriptions, ranging from house-painters to artists) managed to secure more than half of the market for paintings. This was no easy task, since mid-seventeenth-century Amsterdam had more than 150,000 inhabitants. In Delft and Haarlem the local artists' share of the market was considerably higher: 66 and 79 per cent, respectively. Such figures suggest that the guilds were not completely powerless in the game of supply and demand, even if they did not succeed in monopolising the market.

At the end of the eighteenth century it became fashionable to think that guilds were detrimental to the economy. Adam Smith, the father of economic theory, disparaged the guilds, claiming that they obstructed free trade and impeded economic development. Many economists and historians later adopted his line of reasoning, and for a long time the guilds' reputation suffered accordingly. Even so, the history of the Republic suggests that the guilds did not exert such a negative influence after all. The growth and modernisation of the economy that took place in the seventeenth century coincided with the foundation of a great many guilds, providing a clear indication that the two developments were not necessarily at odds. The presence of guilds might well have been a blessing in some sectors. In many cities in the province of Holland, for example, artists' guilds were founded in the early seventeenth century: in Gouda and Rotterdam in 1609, in Delft in 1611, in Leiden in 1615. Only in Amsterdam (1579) and Haarlem, where the Guild of St Luke dated from the Middle Ages, were the artists' guilds considerably older. The founding of these guilds not only corresponded with an unprecedented demand for paintings but also ushered in the development – in Delft and Leiden, for instance – of local schools of painting. In all likelihood, the renowned Dutch school of painting – in all its diversity – owes its very existence to the relatively protected economic environment which allowed it to flourish.

The local authorities were happy to cooperate in the creation of a favourable business environment. In a manuscript circulated among the regents of Leiden in the 1660s, Pieter de la Court, a wealthy textile manufacturer, pointed out that their power and standing rose in equal proportion to their city's increase in population. The civic authorities, adhering to this principle, tried to entice entrepreneurs to set up businesses in the city by offering them attractive conditions. The city of Deventer, which suffered greatly from nearby hostilities, waived citizenship fees for immigrants intending to set up in business. In particular the Deventer magistrates tried to lure textile manufacturers to their city. Consequently, no fewer than 83 of the 187 persons granted free citizenship in Deventer between 1591 and 1609 were active in this branch. These privileged citizens could also request exemption from civic guard duty. In 1639 the Deventer town council paid 400 guilders for a building they intended to turn into a dye works. The magistrates also offered subsidies to German entrepreneurs in the hope that they would come to Deventer to manufacture fustian, a coarse cloth made of cotton and flax that had become very popular around 1600. In Leiden the civic authorities had done the same after the catastrophic siege of 1572. They succeeded in persuading a group of Flemish textile manufacturers, who had fled to Colchester in 1577, to leave England and move to Leiden, promising them free citizenship and the absence of guilds. Various schemes to enlarge the city were approved, on the grounds that the shortage of housing would otherwise force entrepreneurs to settle elsewhere. Other cities subsequently attempted to lure these manufacturers away from Leiden, whose town council vigorously objected to the offers made by Gouda (1586), Den Briel (1587), Delft (1595) – the States of Holland even had to mediate in this dispute – Alkmaar (1593), Haarlem (1596), Middelburg (1597), Franeker (1601) and finally Amsterdam (1616). In the 1680s various cities offered favourable conditions to French Huguenots who had fled to Holland, even going so far as to advertise in French newspapers in an attempt to attract the cream of the refugees. Town councils tried to guarantee conditions favourable to trade. The Amsterdam Exchange Bank was founded in 1609 to enable merchants to give money into safekeeping, to transfer funds and to exchange foreign currencies. Not surprisingly, this bank was housed in the town hall. At the behest of the civic authorities similar banks were also established in Middelburg (1616), Delft (1621) and Rotterdam (1635). Most cities also had a Municipal Pawn Bank, supervised by the authorities, where credit was extended upon the deposit of collateral, not only to the poor but also to tradesmen and small businesses.

Town councils were understandably sympathetic to the needs of local trade and industry, for in many cities – certainly in the first half of the seventeenth century – the town councillors came from those circles themselves. The cities' delegates to both the provincial States and the States General persuaded these government bodies to take trading interests seriously. We have seen how closely Oldenbarnevelt was involved in the founding of the Dutch East India Company (VOC) in 1602. The capital contributed by the Zeeland Chamber of the VOC came mainly from Southern Netherlanders, who had settled in Zeeland after the fall of Antwerp in 1585, and from town councillors from Middelburg, Vlissingen, Veere, Goes and Zierikzee, as well as from various officials in the provincial government. In 1614, when the Guinea Company (Guinese Compagnie) was founded, the same combination of merchants and regents came forward to finance the enterprise. At the end of the seventeenth century it was the regent families who were the principal investors in the Zeeland Chamber of the Dutch West India Company. It is therefore no wonder that as a rule the national authorities also let their policies be determined by the interests of these groups. In 1613 the Danish king was threatened with military intervention if he continued to obstruct the passage of Dutch ships through the Sound. In 1656–9 his successor was forced by a large Dutch fleet to make important concessions concerning trading vessels passing through the Sound. The wars against England and France in the second half of the century were waged in part to safeguard interests considered vital to Dutch trade.

The intervention of the local authorities often helped to perpetuate a previously existing pattern of specialisation which the accelerated economic growth of the seventeenth century had made even more pronounced. In Holland, cities without a harbour developed into centres of industry. Leiden had traditionally been a centre of textile production, specialising in the manufacture of woollen cloth, but this specialisation became even more marked in the seventeenth century, owing to the massive influx of Flemish and later Walloon immigrants. Leiden – along with the French city of Lyons, known mainly for its silk industry – became one of the most important industrial centres in Europe in the seventeenth century. Similarly, Haarlem's reputation for linen-bleaching spread far beyond the borders of the Republic. In the mid-seventeenth century, its bleaching fields offered employment to some 1,000 people, mostly women. Haarlem also boasted a large number of linen-weavers; no fewer than 3,350 looms were counted in 1643. Gouda, formerly a regional centre of service industries, developed in the course of the century into an important centre of pipe-making. The pipe-makers' guild, founded in 1660, had 223 members in 1686. At the beginning of the eighteenth century, Gouda – a city with a population of just under 20,000 – had more than 4,000 people working in the pipe industry.

The port towns had their own specialisations. Those in Holland's North Quarter, in particular Hoorn and Enkhuizen, had profited greatly from the Baltic trade. Rotterdam had traditionally traded with France and England, and these relations were again confirmed in 1635, when the town council lobbied extensively – and offered a considerable bribe to the English sovereign – to ensure the establishment in Rotterdam of the Dutch branch of Merchant Adventurers, which had been granted the exclusive right to export woollen cloth from England. French wine, too, usually entered the Republic at Rotterdam. Dordrecht, by contrast, was a centre of river trade, which arrived in the city via the Rivers Meuse and Waal. The Dordrecht authorities, who placed great value on this trade, regularly carried out inspections at Schenkenschans, on the Republic's border with Germany, where the River Waal and the Lower Rhine fork.

This fork was claimed by various interested parties in both Gelderland and Holland. The Dordrecht authorities were worried that too much water was being tapped from the River Waal. To prevent this, Dordrecht, in collaboration with Nijmegen, destroyed on several occasions hydraulic works near the fork in the river.

Local specialisation was especially conspicuous in Holland. In the other provinces the cities were characterised by service industries which had sprung up in response to demand from the surrounding countryside. The limited success of Deventer's attempt to attract fustian manufacturers is therefore hardly surprising. Yet there did exist a certain division of labour among the provinces. Zeeland, for instance, was involved mainly in trade with countries on the Atlantic seaboard, whereas the Hollanders were more interested in trade with northern Europe and Asia. Friesland, of course, traded heavily with the countries of northern Europe. Draught animals and beasts of burden were bred in Drenthe; Gelderland and Zeeland both produced a number of industrial crops. These specialisations brought some measure of unity to the Dutch economy. In the seventeenth century, for example, the fluctuation of grain prices in the markets of Arnhem and Amsterdam showed exactly the same trends. At the same time, however, conflicting interests created by local and regional specialisation could be resolved only by means of political compromise.

Foreign observers, for whom these differences were not always discernible, thought the growth and flourishing of the Republic's economy nothing less than a miracle. William Temple wrote in 1673 'that no Countrey can be found either in this Present Age, or upon Record of any Story, where so vast a Trade has been managed, as in the narrow compass of the Four Provinces of this Commonwealth'.[4] This situation was all the more surprising when one considers that the Dutch had scarcely any raw materials of their own and even had to import much of their food. Historians, equally amazed, have attempted to explain this miracle. One thing is certain: the developments in the Republic were part of a much larger process of economic change that was taking place in this period in the whole of Europe. These changes have sometimes been characterised as 'modernisation', or as 'the rise of capitalism', and both points of view can be defended to some extent. The expansion of the market economy, which had been taking place in Europe since the late Middle Ages, had both an internal and an external dynamism. The cities were growing, and with them the demand for agricultural products.

---

[4] Sir William Temple, *Observations upon the United Provinces of the Netherlands*, edited by Sir George Clark (Oxford: Clarendon Press, 1972), p. 108.

Particularly in the rural hinterlands of urbanised areas, farmers began to specialise in commercial crops and to develop increasingly efficient means of cultivation. Such specialisation and expansion meant that many small farmers lost their independence and were forced to hire themselves out as wage labourers to their more successful neighbours. Migration increased. At the same time an integrated network of cities sprang up in Europe which offered further possibilities for specialisation. In the Republic these developments attained new heights. Agricultural production in the west of the Netherlands was and still is among the most efficient in the world. Hired labour became very common in the Republic. The labour markets in the cities of Holland absorbed large numbers of migrants – from the surrounding countryside, from the inland provinces and from neighbouring countries. Throughout the seventeenth century, Dutch industry was propelled by technological innovations.

Around 1500 a number of European countries began to explore the possibility of establishing trading contacts with overseas countries. In the sixteenth century, the flow of goods, people, and money started to connect Africa, Asia and America by means of trading systems dominated by the Europeans. Holland contributed to this process by exploiting the possibilities offered by economic integration, which it was able to do thanks to the carrying capacity of Dutch ships and the seafaring expertise of Dutch captains, developed as a result of Holland's need from as early as the fifteenth century to import grain on a large scale from the Baltic. The Low Countries had already become a centre of international trade in the Middle Ages. During the sixteenth century, the merchants of Brabant and Holland had come into more intense contact, and the ties between them became even stronger after 1585, when the fall of Antwerp caused a flight of capital and expertise, much of which ended up in Holland, turning Amsterdam into a hotbed of free-market and popular capitalism.

Did these developments give Holland a modern economy? The answer depends entirely on the definition of the word 'modern'. The Republic had reached an unusually high level of urbanisation, with non-agrarian occupations strongly represented in the rural districts as well. There were highly developed and well-integrated markets for goods, as well as for capital and labour. Growth was not confined to one city or even to one province, but encompassed the entire country. The rise in productivity in all sectors of the economy made the division of labour possible, bringing about the development of a dynamic labour market. The high standard of living in the Republic created a great demand for goods and services. Authorities respected property rights and actively promoted economic development. In all these respects the seventeenth-century Dutch Republic can be said to have been modern. In several important respects, however, its economy remained an old-fashioned one. Economists generally consider modern economic growth to have two defining features: it leads to a long-term and substantial increase in per capita income, and it is self-propelling, the self-propulsion being due to the fact that modern economies function within a larger economic system. The economy of the Dutch Republic had a strong internal dynamism, since many sectors were interlocked, yet it was surrounded by more or less traditional economies, which in the long run made it difficult to sustain growth.

Modern economic growth began in many Western countries in the first half of the nineteenth century and has continued until the present day, showing average annual growth rates of several per cent. Between 1580 and 1650, Holland's economy grew by 1.5 per cent annually, though the rate of growth for the Republic as a whole was undoubtedly less. This was impressive in comparison with other countries, but relatively little compared with economic growth since the Industrial Revolution. Moreover, Holland's economy stopped growing in the second half of the seventeenth century, when a period of stagnation set in that lasted approximately 150 years. Seen in this light, the Republic's – and particularly Holland's – economy was not so very modern after all. In the end, it remains a question of semantics, though this does not alter the fact that the seventeenth-century Dutch Republic played an important part in developments leading to a high level of prosperity in Western European countries, a prosperity which enabled them to dominate the world economy. The silent witnesses to the Republic's remarkable role in these developments are still scattered across the globe.

7   A worldwide trading network

On 23 February 1631, Evert Willemszoon, who had begun his journey in the Dutch city of Woerden, arrived in hell. For this seventeenth-century Dutchman, hell was a very real place. It was located on the west coast of tropical Africa, in Guinea, parts of which were tellingly called the Gold Coast and the Slave Coast. For Evert Willemszoon, hell also had a name: Fort Nassau in Mouree. Most of the people who went there had but one objective, to get rich quickly. In Mouree there were two ways of doing this: trading in precious metals and trading in people.

Evert Willemszoon arrived on the eve of a new phase in Dutch colonial history. Until this time the Dutch had been only marginally involved in the slave trade. The Dutch West India Company (WIC), founded in 1621, had so far failed to establish a viable colony in South America. Thanks to an unexpected stroke of luck, however – the WIC's commander, Piet Heyn, had captured the Spanish silver fleet in 1628 – the Company could now afford to launch a large-scale attack on the Brazilian mainland. In the autumn of 1629, a fleet of sixty-seven ships sailed for the region of Pernambuco, the easternmost part of Brazil. The most important town, Recife, soon fell into Dutch hands. Many of the inhabitants fled, setting fire to the town's sugar warehouses before they left, which was all the more unfortunate because sugar had been the WIC's reason for going there. Recife was fortified in the following months, but the skirmishes with Portuguese guerrillas in the interior continued. In 1636 the States General appointed a governor, Johan Maurits, count of Nassau-Siegen, a cousin of the stadholder, who relaxed trading restrictions for merchants outside the WIC in the hope of stimulating economic growth in the territory.

Brazil, then, was a sugar-growing region. After the flight of the Portuguese planters, a large number of Amsterdam Jews of Portuguese descent settled in the territory. The indigenous population could not supply them with enough hands to work their plantations, making it necessary to import labourers, some of whom came from Europe. Until the mid-seventeenth century, Brazilian plantations regularly used contract labourers from the Low Countries. After 1650 almost exclusive use was made of African slaves, but even before this time the slave trade had been gaining momentum. Between 1637 and 1642, the WIC acquired six new bases on the African coast with the intention of providing slaves to work the Brazilian plantations. In the decade after 1635, Hollanders and Zeelanders transported to Central and South America some 25,000 African slaves, their numbers swelling by the end of the century to approximately 3,000 per year. The Dutch continued to play a prominent role in the slave trade until well into the nineteenth century. Strangely enough, this trade was not very lucrative. The slave trade with Brazil was plainly a loss-making venture; economically speaking, it was only interesting because it saved the plantations from complete bankruptcy. To these economic disadvantages were added the risks to life and limb, for the Europeans directly involved in the slave trade – whether on board ship or based in Africa – died just as frequently as the slaves themselves. The mingling of two bacteriological systems in the cramped quarters on the transport ships had a devastating effect on Africans and Europeans alike.

In mainland Africa conditions were little better. A journal dating from 1617 reveals that of the 125 soldiers sent out that year, twenty succumbed within three weeks of their arrival to 'Guinea fevers', meaning malaria or dysentery. Moreover, of the sixty men sent out on the previous ship only twenty were still alive. Impatient to board the storm-beaten ship that would take them back to the Netherlands, they told the surprised newcomers, 'When you have served your time here as we have, you will no longer fear the dangers of the return voyage, for you could not be worse off than you are at the fort.'[1] One year after his arrival, Evert Willemszoon was therefore extremely pleased to be alive and well enough to undertake the return voyage. In June 1632 he was back in Amsterdam, where he applied for admission to the ministry of the Reformed Church. Following his ordination one month later, he was nominated by the WIC to the position of spiritual leader of the colony of New Netherland in the New World.

New Netherland was, by the sound of it, a veritable Land of Cockaigne. 'New Netherland is one of the most wonderful lands under the sun ... There is plenty of everything. One can catch birds by the neck, wild and domesticated game birds in abundance. Grapes grow wild there.'[2] To Evert Willemszoon, New Netherland must have seemed like paradise compared with Africa. Discovered in 1609 by Henry Hudson, an Englishman in the service of the Dutch East India Company who was

[1] Willem Frijhoff, *Wegen van Evert Willemsz. Een Hollands weeskind op zoek naar zichzelf, 1607–1647* (Nijmegen: SUN, 1995), p. 509.
[2] Ibid., p. 563.

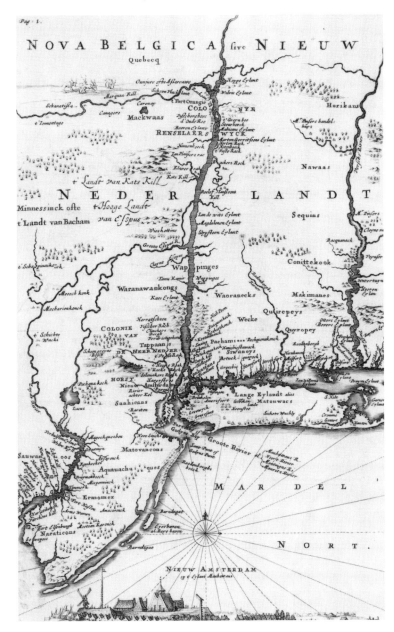

Figure 13   Map of New Netherland used to illustrate Adriaen van der Donck's
Beschryvinge van Nieuw Nederlant (Description of New Netherland) of 1655.
The map indicates the locations of various tribes of Indians. Depicted below is
New Amsterdam (present-day New York City) 'on the island of Manhattan'
(1655; Royal Library, The Hague).

searching for a western route to the Indies, the territory of the present-day state of New York had been systematically colonised since 1614 by Amsterdam merchants. Their most important commercial product was fur, which they bought from the Indians. The Dutch first settled in the area of present-day Albany, where Fort Nassau was built in 1624, and in 1626 they acquired the island of Manhattan from the local Indians in exchange for goods worth 60 guilders. Evert Willemszoon – who had started calling himself Everardus Bogardus, a more fitting name for a preacher – ended up in New Amsterdam, as the settlement on the island of Manhattan had been named. In 1638, Bogardus married a Norwegian widow, who had probably come to the New World via Amsterdam. Through her, Bogardus became the owner of a farm (*bouwerij*, hence the Bowery in New York), situated between the Hudson River and present-day Broadway. He rented out a plantation with a tobacco house, which meant that even this clergyman was inevitably involved to some extent in the colonial economy and its agricultural production.

The Dutch colonists were on an intimate footing with the Indians, which was unavoidable considering the size of the settlement. In a territory the size of the state of New York (the population of which is now more than 19 million), there lived in 1640 fewer than 2,500 Europeans, their numbers having risen by 1664 to no more than 7,000. New Amsterdam alone had 2,500 inhabitants, representing by far the largest concentration of immigrants. One thousand more lived in Beverwijck (Albany), and the remaining 3,500 Europeans were scattered over some twenty small farming communities. The Indians were free to come and go, but this unrestricted traffic had ruinous consequences for themselves and their families, for the diseases they contracted from the Europeans, such as smallpox, proved to be fatal. Of the 90,000 Native Americans estimated to have been living in the area around 1600, probably no more than 14,000 were left half a century later. The white settlers undeniably played an active role in this wholesale slaughter. In 1643–4, the 'New Netherlanders' waged a bloody war against the Indians, in which the Dutch did not hesitate to stage nocturnal raids on their adversaries, killing them all – including the women and children – by cutting their throats in their sleep. To protect themselves against the Indians' reprisals, a wall was built that later gave Wall Street its name. The colonists' brutality can perhaps be explained by the fact that, despite their close contact, they never regarded the Indians as fellow human beings. In written accounts of the conditions in New Netherland, the colonists usually described the Indians as 'wild men', and sometimes also as *naturellen*, 'the naked ones'. They had no religion that was recognisable as such to the Dutch settlers, and their marriage customs and views on the ownership of property were so foreign that the colonists could see no similarity to their own society, which of course they took to be the norm.

The war against the Indians was also the result of differences of opinion among the colonists themselves. A large number of them, including the Reverend Bogardus, saw New Netherland as a colony which should be able to expand, if necessary at the expense of the Indians. Others viewed the settlement primarily as a trading post, whose interests were best served by peaceful relations with the indigenous population. The dilemma in New Netherland reflected the predicament of the WIC as a whole. At the time the Company was set up, some of its founder members had envisioned a combination of trade and private production, to be engaged in by the colonists themselves, whereas others wanted to limit activities to trade only. It was much more difficult in America than it was in Asia to acquire desirable products through barter. Such products would have to be produced in America through the Europeans' own efforts. Colonisation promised considerable profits, but the necessary investment also entailed great risks. It was in the first half of the 1640s that the WIC's colonisation policy suffered several setbacks. In Maranhâo (northern Brazil), the Portuguese settlers revolted against Dutch authority in October 1642, spurred on by the revolt in their native country against Spanish rule. By 1645 the WIC could no longer finance the colonial army. Hostilities continued until finally, in 1654, Brazil had to be given up. Not surprisingly, the WIC – suffering from its abandonment of Brazil and confronted with problems in New Netherland – now found itself immersed in difficulties.

The Company was compelled to concentrate more on trade. The Leeward Islands in the Antilles had been conquered in 1634 and had since served as the WIC's trading base in the Caribbean. Curaçao, in particular, came to be the distribution point for the Dutch slave trade. The Dutch not only supplied African slaves to Dutch planters but also met the great demand for slave labour on the Spanish plantations. The Dutch planters, mostly of Portuguese–Jewish descent, concentrated their activities in the deltas of the Essequibo, Berbice and Pomeroon rivers on the 'Wild Coast' of Guyana, where in the 1650s they rapidly established sugar plantations dependent on slave labour imported from Africa. By 1663 there were 4,000 people living in this area. Between 1683 and 1713 the number of plantations in Surinam increased fourfold, from 50 to 200. Around the turn of the century, approximately 2 million guilders' worth of goods were shipped every year from the Caribbean to the Dutch Republic.

The WIC shareholders, however, did not benefit much from all this activity. The attempts to hold on to Pernambuco had cost a great deal and yielded nothing. In 1664 the English appeared off Manhattan with a large fleet. Pieter Stuyvesant, the governor-general, saw that it would be useless to resist and immediately surrendered New Netherland to them. Although in 1673 the Dutch regained possession of their settlement on the Hudson – which the British had dubbed New York – this victory was only temporary. A year later it changed hands again, when the second Treaty of Westminster awarded it to Britain in return for British recognition of the Netherlands' claims to Surinam, which had been conquered by the Zeelanders in 1667. At the time it was an advantageous exchange, though the WIC did not benefit greatly by it. Surinam was exploited by a conglomerate of entrepreneurs from Amsterdam and Zeeland. It is therefore hardly surprising that in 1674, when the WIC's charter expired, the decision was made to dissolve the Company. By then share prices had dropped to a mere 10.5 per cent of their nominal value. A new WIC, set up almost at once, had from the start much more modest objectives.

Compared with the unfortunate fall in WIC shares, the Dutch East India Company (VOC) was doing remarkably well. Since 1639, VOC shares had usually been traded on the Amsterdam Stock Exchange at four times their nominal value. On the eve of the Year of Disaster (1672), it was perfectly normal to trade shares at five times their nominal value. The events of 1672 dealt a crushing blow to investor confidence, but share prices recovered quickly, reaching their seventeenth-century high in August 1688. That the VOC so outpaced the WIC was due to three factors. First of all, the Dutch had come to America relatively late. The Spanish, Portuguese and English were already established there by the time the WIC was founded in 1621. The Company was therefore forced to expend a great deal of time and money in carving out a place for itself. Moreover, a relatively small country like the Dutch Republic could not send out as many colonists as its larger rivals. When the Company postponed its founding because of the Twelve Years' Truce, private investors in the Netherlands jumped the gun and established their own companies in the Americas. After all, the voyage to the West was much shorter and less dangerous than the voyage to the East – an inducement to groups of merchants to trade in the West on their own terms. The WIC was never in a position to secure the monopoly it had been promised in its charter. In both New Netherland and Surinam, the Company was forced to find a modus vivendi with competitors from its own country, which ate into the WIC's profit margins.

The most important factor limiting the success of the WIC was undoubtedly the fundamental difference in the economic structures the Europeans encountered in America and Asia. The American Indians, whose economy was comparatively underdeveloped, produced relatively little that interested the Europeans, and of the few goods that did interest them (mainly precious metals and sugar), they produced far too little to meet European demand. From the very beginning, the Europeans were forced to take production in America into their own hands. Asia, by way of contrast, had a highly developed economy that produced a great number of products, both agricultural (pepper, cloves, nutmeg, mace, cinnamon) and industrial (silk, cotton, porcelain), which were much in demand in Europe. The Asians were also in a position to react to an increase in demand. The difference between Eastern and Western trade was obvious from the fact that in Asia there was little demand for European goods, making it necessary for Europeans to pay for their purchases in cash, whereas in America (and in Africa as well) it was precisely the European goods – and not only the proverbial mirrors and beads – that were very much in demand. While the Europeans generally showed Asians a certain degree of respect, they considered the indigenous populations of America and Africa to be inferior and treated them accordingly. Moreover, it was much more lucrative to trade with the economically developed areas of Asia than with the more primitive economies of Africa and America.

In Asia the VOC preferred to enter into agreements with the local sovereigns, thereby continuing a long-standing tradition. When Europe was experiencing its Dark Ages, Asia could already boast an extensive trading network, which supplied spices to Europe via intermediaries in the Middle East. After the Portuguese discovered a direct sea route to East Asia, first they and then the Spanish, the English and finally the Dutch could join the existing commercial structures. For example, in Bantam (or Banten), a sultanate in western Java, the VOC bought pepper from the sultan. In the seventeenth century the sultan also sold pepper to the English East India Company. Most of Bantam's pepper came from fields – also belonging to the Bantam sultanate – in south-eastern Sumatra, where peasants grew rice for their own consumption and pepper for export. In the sixteenth century, a large number of relatively small merchants had dominated trade in this area. The VOC, which could exercise far greater power, occasionally resorted to force in an attempt to secure a larger share of the Bantam pepper export. Their efforts did not really succeed until 1682, when the sultan became involved in a civil war that he could not win without the aid of the VOC. In exchange for its support, the Company was granted an exclusive contract that gave it the right to determine unilaterally the price of Bantam pepper.

Pepper cultivation was so widespread in the archipelago that no single company could hope to gain a monopoly. In fact, the VOC monopoly in the East meant only that Dutch merchants were constrained to trade under the flag of the VOC. The Company, moreover, turned a blind eye

Figure 14   The island of Ternate in the Moluccas, where cloves are cultivated. The Dutch East India Company tried to secure a monopoly of this product by such methods as the periodic destruction of new plantings (J. Kip 1676; Printroom, Rijksmuseum rp-p-ob-47–595).

to employees' engaging in private trade. In the case of some products, however, a monopoly was indeed within reach. The Moluccas were the only producers of cloves, nutmeg and mace. Cloves came mainly from the Central Moluccas, i.e. Ambon and the surrounding islands. A few years after concluding supply contracts with local sovereigns, the VOC managed in 1605 to capture the Portuguese fort on Ambon. At first the Dutch were welcomed as rivals of the Portuguese, but as soon as they tried to secure the exclusive right to export cloves, they met with fierce resistance. The trade in contraband cloves flourished as a result. The VOC repeatedly used force to coerce the Ambonese into honouring contracts concluded under duress. Finally, a bloody war broke out in 1641 which lasted until 1646, during which the VOC eliminated the recalcitrant ruling elites on North Ambon. On Ternate, in the North Moluccas, the Company purchased from the sovereign the right to carry out the periodic destruction of clove-tree plantings. In the Central Moluccas, plantings were monitored just as closely, to ensure that production remained low enough to keep prices high in Europe. The peasants who grew the cloves, however, were paid a fixed price set by the VOC.

The VOC acted much more ruthlessly on the Banda Islands in the South Moluccas, where the peasants had long specialised in the cultivation of nutmeg. Foodstuffs were imported from Java and elsewhere, so the local economy was thoroughly commercialised, largely because the Banda Islands were the only place in the world producing nutmeg. This situation was perfectly suited to the VOC, which as early as 1602 had entered into an agreement promising to protect the Banda Islands against the Portuguese and the English in exchange for the sole right to export nutmeg. Here, too, the contract gave rise to a flourishing trade in contraband. Jan Pieterszoon Coen, the governor-general, decided in 1621 to put an end to this situation. The VOC used its superior strength to occupy the islands. Those of their population of 5,000 who did not manage to flee were either massacred or taken as slaves to the recently founded city of Batavia. The Islands were divided into sixty-eight plantations and leased to employees of the VOC. Only a few hundred of the original inhabitants were allowed to stay, to teach the new managers the tricks of the trade, while the plantations were worked with the help of slave labour.

Elsewhere the VOC confined itself to trade. In Japan the merchants in the Company's service were completely isolated on the artificial island of Deshima in the bay of Nagasaki. The Japanese authorities provided them with food and female companionship, but the Dutch were allowed to leave their gilded cage only once a year, to journey to the imperial court. The situation in Japan was an extreme version of the conditions prevailing in most of the settlements governed by the VOC. Only the colony at the Cape of Good Hope, officially established in 1652, served another purpose. Here the Company had no prospect of trading with the surrounding countryside. Instead, it founded a farming community that was expected to grow enough food to provision passing ships. In terms of outlook, the Cape colonists were more like the colonisers of the WIC territories than like the Europeans in the East Indies.

Because the VOC was primarily a trading company, it could make do with relatively few employees. In 1687–8, exactly 11,551 Europeans were stationed in Asia in the service of the VOC. In most places the Dutch community, augmented by considerable numbers of Germans and Scandinavians, amounted at most to several hundred people. Even Ceylon and Batavia, the largest settlements, had only just over 2,500 European inhabitants, far fewer than New Netherland twenty years earlier. Moreover, two-thirds of the VOC's personnel in Asia were soldiers employed to protect the valuable trading goods. In 1687 fewer than 1,000 people were necessary to administer the Company and supervise trade. Such small numbers meant that the VOC was forced to rely on the help of the indigenous population. These contacts were naturally encouraged and intensified by the fact that the European communities overseas were predominantly male. Cornelia van Nijenroode, who in 1652 married the Amsterdammer Pieter Cnoll, junior merchant and later first senior merchant of the VOC in Asia, was the daughter of Cornelis van Nijenroode, the head of the above-mentioned trading post on Deshima, and his Japanese concubine. Cornelia, born and raised in Japan, was taken after the death of her father to Batavia, where she continued to correspond with her mother in Japanese. Her mixed parentage did not prevent her from playing a prominent role in Batavian society in the second half of the seventeenth century. After the death of her husband, she was married in 1676 to another Dutchman, Johan Bitter, who had come to the Indies after being appointed to a seat in the Batavian Court of Justice. Many Dutchmen married and had children with Indonesian women, and often took their families back to Europe when their stay in the East came to an end. Trade required contact, not seclusion. Merchants, if they were to be successful, had to build up and maintain trade relations. They were less interested in territorial conquest, not because they were opposed to it on principle, but because it was too costly. Even in America, where there was no alternative, the attempts to found colonies were only partially successful.

The spectacular success of colonial trade has attracted attention on all sides. The VOC was the first joint-stock company and as such the forerunner of Shell, Unilever, Philips and a host of other multinationals that are promoting economic globalisation in our own day. But was colonial trade actually all that important to the economy of the Dutch Republic? It depends on how one looks at it. The VOC – which in 1689 had approximately 22,000 employees – was in its time the largest company in the Dutch Republic and perhaps the largest in the world. To put things in perspective, however, one should realise that in those days four to five times as many people were serving in the Dutch army. As in the army, a considerable number of the VOC's European personnel – certainly in the seventeenth century – came from other countries. Another similarity between the army and the colonial trading companies was that these jobs cost many people their lives. Two-thirds of those who sailed to the East in the service of the VOC never returned to Europe. Surprisingly, one's chances of survival were probably much greater in the army. In the first half of the century, the VOC made enormous profits, though it was also forced to invest huge sums of money. The first investors also benefited from considerable increases in share prices. In the second half of the century, however, the return on VOC shares was not substantially higher than the return on government bonds. By then, spectacular increases in share prices were a thing of the past. The value of WIC shares actually dropped, and when the first Company was dissolved in 1674, it had millions of guilders of debt. Around 1700 the value of imports from Asia averaged 4–5 million guilders annually, while imports from America were worth approximately one-third that amount. The volume of colonial trade must therefore be estimated at around 10 per cent of the Republic's total foreign trade, a not inconsiderable portion. It is important to remember, however, that most of the Republic's trade was conducted within Europe. Moreover, only one-third of the Republic's population earned a living in the service sector. Far more people worked in industry and agriculture. Nevertheless, colonial trade was of great importance in the Golden Age, for without its colonial products the Republic could never have played a key role in European trade. And trade, after all, was by far the most dynamic sector in the Dutch economy in the seventeenth century.

Of equal importance, perhaps, were the political and cultural consequences of the activities of the VOC and the WIC, whose trading posts and settlements enabled the Netherlands to grow into a world power, a status it maintained until the mid-twentieth century. The Netherlands' trading imperium had the inadvertent side effect of disseminating Dutch culture around the globe, allowing it to mingle with the cultures of other continents. Multatuli's *Max Havelaar* (1860), arguably the most significant work of Dutch fiction ever written, is set in the East Indies, as are many twentieth-century Dutch novels.

Evert Willemszoon Bogardus was not destined to witness the full flowering of the Dutch Golden Age. He drowned in September 1647, when the ship carrying him back to Holland from New Netherland foundered off the coast of England. His fate underlines the price the Dutch paid for the adventure of overseas expansion.

8   Riches

Elias Trip, who died at the beginning of January 1636, was a very successful man. The son of a barge captain from the town of Zaltbommel, he rose to become one of the wealthiest and most powerful merchants in Amsterdam. His trading contacts extended to the remote corners of Europe and far beyond. The scale of his transactions was often astounding, and his fortune no less so. The total value of his estate is estimated to have been around 1 million guilders, a tremendous amount in those days, when a labourer earned only 200–250 guilders a year. Such wealth had not been amassed overnight, however. Elias's precise date of birth is unknown, but he was probably born in 1570. In 1592 or 1593 he married Maria de Geer, the sister of the Liège merchant Louis de Geer. It was around this time that Trip moved to Dordrecht, where he began trading in iron – he acquired his stock in trade from the rural areas around Liège – a line of business that had just begun to flourish. Trip's contacts with De Geer stood him in good stead, for by 1602 he had become the largest iron merchant in Dordrecht. In that year Elias Trip signed a contract with the States General in which he agreed to supply 90,000 guilders' worth of bullets, which he obtained in Liège, as well as farther afield in Germany and France. Trip's trading network grew rapidly. He began to trade in saltpetre, a scarce but essential ingredient of gunpowder, making the gunpowder trade the next logical step in the expansion of his business activities. Trip was well on the way to becoming an all-round munitions dealer. In 1612 he first imported 200 cannon from England, at that time the leading producer of artillery. In 1614 he was appointed – on behalf of Dordrecht – to the board of governors of the Amsterdam Chamber of the Dutch East India Company (VOC). The following year Trip moved to Amsterdam, but continued to run a salt-extraction works in Zwijndrecht, near Dordrecht. In 1628 he and several business partners attempted (unsuccessfully) to secure a monopoly of the Muscovite grain trade. He also traded in West Africa, and had been involved since 1623 in the lading of ships for the Dutch West India Company (WIC). These were only sidelines, but they paint a colourful picture of the man's entrepreneurial vitality.

The trade in iron and armaments remained the heart of Elias Trip's business empire, which was given a boost in the 1620s when his brother-in-law Louis de Geer succeeded in gaining a monopoly of Swedish copper production. The Swedish economy was lacking in revenue, but the young king Gustavus Adolphus did not let this stop him from launching an ambitious military programme which would eventually enable him to play a leading role in the Thirty Years War. To pursue these military objectives, Sweden was compelled to step up its production of weapons, but it also needed money to pay its troops. Starting in 1616, the States General granted loans to Gustavus Adolphus, with the profits from copper-mining serving as collateral. Around 1620, De Geer – who in 1618 had moved from Liège to Amsterdam – contrived to become part of this relationship by co-financing with Trip the Dutch loans to the Swedish crown, in return for which the king granted concessions to Trip and De Geer for the export of Swedish copper. A company was formally set up, the shares of which were held by De Geer, Elias Trip and his second cousin Pieter Trip. In 1626 the company's working capital amounted to an extraordinary 400,000 guilders. From 1629 the company made annual cash payments of approximately 750,000 guilders to the Swedish crown. Investment on this scale could be considered wise only under conditions in which the company controlled both the supply and the sale of the copper. Trip and De Geer had been able to fulfil these conditions by having De Geer in Sweden, overseeing the copper-mining and arms production, and the Trips in Amsterdam, supervising sales. De Geer, in Sweden, relied in part on the technical expertise of skilled metal workers from Liège, who were recruited by Trip. The armaments were not only sold in the Netherlands but also exported to such countries as France and the Republic of Venice. Merchants of Elias Trip's stature were even in the position to deliver, upon request, a small naval squadron.

The company formed by the Trips and De Geer was dissolved in 1631, by which time Elias had made his fortune. This did not put an end to the collaboration between the two families, however. In 1646, Hendrick Trip, a son of Elias's brother Jacob, married Johanna de Geer, a niece of Louis. Her father, Mathias de Geer, supervised various iron foundries which were part of the family holdings in Sweden. In Amsterdam, Hendrick Trip, together with his brothers Jacob and Louis, founded a new trading company which was to prove very successful indeed. The company still ran the salt-extraction works in Zwijndrecht and traded in tobacco, grain, fish, whale oil and wine, as well as providing banking services – in 1666 alone the company made and received payments amounting to more than 7 million guilders through the Amsterdam Exchange Bank – but it remained chiefly a company trading in iron and armaments. Between 1648 and 1662, the company also held a monopoly of trade in Swedish tar. These were lucrative years. The return on Louis Trip's share – according to his accounts, which have survived – was more than 13 per cent annually, and his lifetime earnings from trade amounted to more than 2 million guilders.

Society did not fail to recognise Trip's achievements. A daughter of Louis Trip was married to a son of Gillis Valckenier, the man who lobbied in Amsterdam for the appointment of William III as stadholder. In 1672, Trip became a magistrate, an appointment he owed to the good offices of Valckenier, and in 1674 he was appointed burgomaster of Amsterdam, a very influential post. Louis served as burgomaster again in 1677 and 1679, in the meantime having decided to live in an appropriately grand style. Louis, together with one of his brothers, had a house built on the Kloveniersburgwal. It was designed by Justus Vingboons, the younger brother of the leading architect Philips Vingboons, who was much sought after as a designer of houses for Amsterdam's elite. The young Vingboons had just been awarded a very prestigious commission in Sweden, which perhaps explains why he was approached for the job. In any case, he

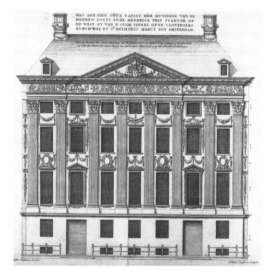

Figure 15   Between 1656 and 1664 the brothers Louis and Hendrick Trip built a magnificent house on the Kloveniersburgwal in Amsterdam. It was designed according to the precepts of classicist architecture by Justus Vingboons, the brother of the famous Amsterdam architect Philips Vingboons. The house, which once housed the collection of the Rijksmuseum, is now the home of the Royal Dutch Academy of Sciences (Amsterdam Municipal Archives n 34855).

designed a magnificent double house in classicist style, a style that had been applied with such success in the design of Amsterdam's new Town Hall. The roof of the Trippenhuis sports chimneys in the shape of cannon barrels. On 24 May 1661 the first stone was laid and two years later the 250,000-guilder house was finished. The Trip brothers had just lost their tar monopoly and it seems that from now on they did business on a more modest scale. A balance sheet drawn up on 1 January 1682, two and a half years before Louis Trip's death, shows his assets to have been 850,000 guilders, with 200,000 guilders invested in real property, 255,000 in bonds and 115,000 in shares in the Dutch East India Company. By this time he had only 101,000 guilders tied up in trade, in addition to owning a cargo of pepper worth 50,000 guilders. Finally, his debtors owed him 33,000 guilders. This shift from active trade to passive investments was a trend that was becoming increasingly noticeable among the wealthy in the Republic.

Vigorous economic growth brought about an enormous increase in prosperity, though not at all levels of society, for there were a great many people who never shared in the Republic's new-found wealth. The rich, however, only grew richer. Around 1600, the wealthiest 1 per cent of Leiden's population owned one-fifth of all capital holdings; in 1623 their share was one-third and around 1700 one-half. In Amsterdam, a fortune of more than half a million guilders was highly unusual until the mid-seventeenth century, after which time such wealth was hardly exceptional. In Gouda, although the number of people with sizeable fortunes decreased between 1625 and 1675, the number of those with extremely large capital holdings increased, their share of the total capital doubling in fifty years. This increase in wealth and the lack of a corresponding improvement in the conditions of the working class resulted in a widening of the social gap.

These extremely wealthy individuals maintained close ties with the ruling class. As we have seen, Louis Trip was appointed to the Amsterdam magistracy in 1672, thanks to connections which had led to the marriage of his son to a daughter of Gillis Valckenier. Earlier, in 1652, a son of Elias Trip had married Elisabeth Bicker, who also belonged to a regent family and was, moreover, the sister of the future wife of the Grand Pensionary Johan de Witt. Such ties bound money and political power tightly together. Thirty-one of the forty-one members of the Amsterdam city government appointed between 1600 and 1625 were involved in one way or another in trade. Often their trading interests were very sizeable indeed. A good example is Andries Bicker – the son of one of the founders of the VOC and himself active in the trade with Russia – who in 1622 was appointed to the town council. He and his three brothers had trading contacts that spanned the globe: Jacob concentrated on the grain trade with the Baltic; Cornelis, the youngest, had invested all his money in America and the Dutch West India Company (WIC), while Jan was in charge of the brothers' trading interests in southern Europe. Vondel fittingly praised their efforts in verse:

> As far and wide as Bicker's flag o'ershadowed the vast ocean
> And plied those waters with his mighty vessels richly laden
> To tow the golden harvest of the world to Holland's bosom ... [1]

Cornelis Pieterszoon Hooft – the father of the famous man of letters, P. C. Hooft, and himself a grain merchant and burgomaster of Amsterdam – had a brief but powerful political programme: 'Most of our power and prosperity is due to the *Imperium maris* and to foreign trade.'[2]

The close ties between trade and politics slackened over the years. In the last quarter of the seventeenth century, only one-fourth of Amsterdam's regents were active in trade. The regents' decreasing involvement in economic life was noticeable everywhere, though it must be said that nowhere were commercial and political ties so close or enduring as in Amsterdam. In Leiden, for example, the number of textile manufacturers with seats on the town council dropped, and despite a momentary rise at the end of the century in the number of merchants, the proliferation of jurists and professional administrators was the most pronounced trend in Leiden's city government. Similar developments took place elsewhere.

This professionalisation of the governing bodies was directly connected with another remarkable development, namely the closing of local government to newcomers. In Zwolle, the percentage of 'new' families with positions in the city government dropped from two-thirds at the end of the sixteenth century to one-fourth a hundred years later, with the percentage of established families – who had been represented for generations – rising in inverse proportion. The same thing occurred in the town of Zierikzee in Zeeland. To ensure the continuation of this process, in 1652 a group of closely related regents entered into a so-called 'contract of correspondence', in which they promised to appoint one another to the most powerful and best-paid posts. Such contracts, which would become increasingly popular in the coming decades, always had the same objective: to clarify the claims of the established families to the various civic offices. On the one hand, these contractual agreements reflected the ever greater interest these families doubtless had – now that they were less involved in business – in gaining access to influential and lucrative posts. On the

---

[1] Johan E. Elias, *Geschiedenis van het Amsterdamsche Regentenpatriciaat* (The Hague: Martinus Nijhoff, 1923), p. 116.

[2] P. C. Hooft, *Memoriëen en Adviezen van Pieter Corneliszoon Hooft*, 2 vols. (Utrecht: Kemink, 1871–1925), vol. I, p. 236.

other hand, these agreements were prompted by fears that such jockeying for political positions would lead to conflicts that could be resolved only by outside intervention – from the stadholder, for instance – and this, in the regents' view, was to be avoided at all costs.

The rise of a specialised class of regents is beautifully reflected in the ups and downs of the Teding van Berkhout family. In the sixteenth century, when they were making their fortune in shipping and trade, they were called simply Berkhout, after their native village near Hoorn. In 1553 Pieter Janszoon Berkhout was known as a 'cheese merchant at Hoorn'. Pieter had first become a magistrate in Hoorn in 1523, and shortly thereafter a member of the town council. His son Jan married Cornelia Jan Tedingsdochter, thus acquiring the second part of the family name. Cornelia came from a well-born family in Holland. After settling in Monnickendam, Jan was appointed to the town council there. When his wife died, he moved back to Hoorn, so that his son could assume his seat on the Monnickendam town council, since father and son were not allowed to hold office simultaneously. Upon his death, Jan Berkhout left the very respectable sum of 30,000 guilders. His son Jan Teeng, or Teding, did in fact become a member of the Monnickendam town council and continued his father's trading activities. In 1571, in the midst of the Revolt against Spain, his first son, Adriaan, was born.

Adriaan Teding van Berkhout was destined for something other than trade. He was sent to school in Leiden, where in 1588 he enrolled at the university, which had been founded in 1575. After completing his studies, he travelled around Europe, and on 10 April 1595 he obtained his doctorate in law from the University of Orléans, a place much favoured by the sons of Dutch regents. The following year he became pensionary of Monnickendam, a position that marked the beginning of his career in public office. In his capacity as pensionary, he accompanied the Monnickendam delegates to assemblies of the States of Holland at The Hague, and it was probably these contacts that gained him a position in the National Auditing Office (Generaliteitsrekenkamer) in 1605. Of equal or greater importance was his marriage in 1604 to Margaretha Duyst van Beresteyn, the daughter of an extremely wealthy and powerful regent of Delft. Adriaan, a faithful follower of Oldenbarnevelt, made a successful career for himself, eventually being appointed to the Council of State in 1613. He died in 1620, but his political career had foundered shortly before that, owing to the ascendancy of the Counter-Remonstrants. By then, however, the Teding van Berkhouts' position had been firmly established. They would continue until the end of the Republic in 1795 (and after) to hold high offices in the cities of Holland (especially Delft and Leiden) and in the government institutions in

The Hague. Adriaan had also greatly increased his fortune: his estate is estimated to have been worth at least 450,000 guilders.

The success stories of such families as the Trips and the Teding van Berkhouts were based not only on the achievements of individuals but on the concerted efforts of the family as a whole. Marriages were much more than the happy union of two people: they were meant to forge alliances between two families, each of whom hoped to gain an advantage through its link with the other. Merchants preferred to have relatives as partners in their trading firms; regents always took family ties into consideration when conferring offices. Newcomers to public office, such as Louis Trip in 1672, had nearly always married into a regent family before their appointments. It was therefore of the utmost importance to main-tain family ties and uphold the family's reputation, and it was for this very reason that the entire Coymans family protested vehemently against the intended marriage of Aletta Coymans and Carel Voet, a man of such low birth as to be described as the descendant of 'a scabrous race'. His father was said to have been 'an impostor and cheating dice player', and 'the reputation of his mother and sister [were] very bad', wrote Johan Huydecoper, who was married to one of Aletta's elder sisters. His fierce opposition to the marriage was hardly surprising, because it would mean, as he said, 'a scandalous alliance for all of us'.[3] The Coymans family ran one of the most distinguished trading houses in Amsterdam; the Huydecopers were a prominent regent family. The honour of both was at stake. But Aletta Coymans had the support of her mother, Sophia Trip, the eldest daughter of Elias Trip. It was a small world. The marriage eventually took place, but only after the relatives had taken steps to safeguard the family fortune.

Huydecoper – who after the death of his father was allowed to call himself Huydecoper van Maarsseveen, after the family manor – became a member of the Amsterdam town council in 1662. He had applied for the position in the same letter in which he invited one of the burgomasters to his father's funeral. His appointment was unchallenged: 'Maerseveen stood firmly in the place of his father'.[4] He first became burgomaster in 1673. These appointments elicited numerous congratulations from friends and relatives who hoped to profit from Huydecoper's influential position. In January 1676, for instance, he received a request from his sister Constantia, whose young brother-in-law Coenraad van Westerhoff was falling into bad ways. He had broken off his studies and was drifting

[3] Luuc Kooijmans, *Vriendschap en de kunst van het overleven in de zeventiende en achttiende eeuw* (Amsterdam: Bert Bakker, 1997), p. 127.
[4] Ibid., p. 132.

Figure 16   The rear façade of the mansion Goudestein in Maarsseveen, which was turned by the Huydecopers, lords of Maarsseveen, into an idyllic retreat for well-to-do Amsterdammers (I. Leupenius, 1690; The Utrecht Archives).

aimlessly through life. Constantia wondered if Johan could perhaps find Coenraad some sort of useful employment. Johan wrote back, saying that although he was willing to receive Coenraad, it appeared that the young wastrel had so abandoned himself to dissolute ways that he would be incapable of holding down a job. Constantia then sent another brother-in-law, one whose financial situation had suffered greatly during the French occupation of 1672. If he were given a job, he would be able to support poor Coenraad as well as himself. Bestowing such favours upon members of one's family was an everyday occurrence. Huydecoper kept complete records of all the services he rendered as well as all the favours granted him. Only in this way could he control the network – a network based on family ties – that was one of his greatest social assets.

The obsession of merchants and regents with maintaining their families' positions also existed, though to a lesser extent, among the class often referred to as the 'broad bourgeoisie'. This class included members of the various professions, as well as military officers. The connections among people of this milieu emerges from a study of the social background of clergymen's wives. Through their marriages, clergymen found themselves in the society of other clergymen, teachers at Latin schools, physicians, civic administrators, merchants, booksellers and military officers. Clergymen and physicians alike enjoyed the status conferred by a university degree. The *doctores medicinae*, the university-trained physicians, were often social climbers whose fathers or grandfathers had been artisans or tradesmen. In the practice of their profession, they refrained from performing actual surgery, which was considered an inferior occupation. The scalpel was wielded by the practitioners of internal medicine, the surgeons, who knew no Latin and therefore could not read classical medical treatises. Surgeons followed a course of training and practised a profession whose members belonged to a guild. University-trained physicians felt compelled to establish a similar organisation, which led in many cities to the founding of a Collegium Medicum intended to preserve the distinction between qualified doctors and trained surgeons. Similarly, in 1643 the jurists in Zwolle founded a fraternity of 'jurists and *costumiers*' which included the *jurisperiti promoti* (jurists with a doctorate in law) and the *non promoti*: in other words, the barristers and the solicitors. Unfortunately, little is known about the barristers, except that their salaries were comparable to those of doctors of medicine.

Though clergymen earned only half as much as physicians, their salaries were not at all bad. In the rural districts, however, there was sometimes cause for complaint, as witnessed by the Drenthe clergyman Johannes Picardt, who in 1650 exclaimed melodramatically: 'Why, O Lord Jesus Christ, is this venerable office so scandalously despised and we, your beloved servants, so belittled that many of the lowest servants who handle the stinking filth of this world are held in higher esteem than the holy servants of God?'[5]

Even a village clergyman, however, could count on a minimum annual income of 450 guilders plus a considerable number of gifts from his congregation. In the countryside, a parsonage often included a piece of land, which the minister could cultivate to his heart's content. From the complaints of parishioners it emerges that some clergymen who took advantage of this opportunity did not hesitate to bring in the hay on Sundays. In the cities, clergymen's salaries started at 600 guilders, but even in a small town like Den Briel the clergyman was earning as much as 900 guilders by 1684. In Amsterdam, where efforts were made to attract the best ministers, clergymen's salaries were sometimes as high as 2,000

---

[5] G. Groenhuis, *De predikanten: de sociale positie van de gereformeerde predikanten in de Republiek der Verenigde Nederlanden voor ±1700* (Groningen: Wolters-Noordhoff, 1977), p. 125.

guilders or more. To put Picardt's lament in perspective, it is important to know that his wife was a noblewoman, his daughter married a country squire, and his cousin Hendrik Picardt married a woman of the noble Rengers family, becoming lord of Fraylemaborg in Slochteren.

Such marriages between burghers and nobles were unusual, but they draw our attention to the fact that clergymen did enjoy a certain amount of prestige. They also point to the presence of 'old money' amidst the unprecedented prosperity of the Republic's middle classes. Admittedly, the fortunes of the nobility paled in comparison with the meteoric rise of trading dynasties like the Trips', but the aristocracy nevertheless continued to play a role of some importance, especially in areas at some distance from the coastal cities of Holland. Not just the landscape but the whole of society changed to the east of Utrecht, where the urban population was proportionately smaller and agriculture much more important. It was in such provinces as Gelderland and Overijssel, as well as in eastern Utrecht and the two provinces to the north, that the nobility played a more prominent role.

In the Veluwe region of Gelderland, 15 per cent of the land was owned by the nobility, and the percentage was considerably higher near the cities. In Overijssel in 1600, nearly one-third of the land was in the hands of the nobility. The fortunes of these nobles were for the most part smaller than those of the wealthiest merchants of Amsterdam. Abel Coenders Lewe van Ulrum – who, together with his wife, was estimated in 1664 to be worth at least 400,000 guilders – would have cut a fine figure even in Amsterdam. Many noble families also possessed manorial rights, meaning feudal privileges which gave them the right to appoint functionaries in the villages in their domain. In the mid-seventeenth century in Holland, approximately 60 per cent of these rights – which were a source of income and prestige – had been conferred on aristocratic families.

The land in their possession was almost always leased to tenants, but wherever possible, the aristocracy reaped the benefits of property owner-ship in other ways as well. For example, the Ewsums, a powerful family of *hoofdelingen* (untitled nobles) living in the Groningen countryside, had begun as early as the sixteenth century to exploit the Nienoord peat bogs in the border area between Groningen, Drenthe and Friesland. Even though the expansion of their peat business had been financially unsound, causing them to fall deeply into debt, they nevertheless man-aged to pay off most of this debt in the seventeenth century. George Willem van In-en Kniphuizen, husband of Anna van Ewsum, prided himself on having paid back a debt of more than 150,000 guilders with the profits from the Nienoord peat excavation. He also had Nienoord House, which had been destroyed during the French invasion in 1672, restored to its former glory. The Isendoorn à Blois family, who lived in the charming moated castle 'De Cannenburch' (built by Maarten van Rossum, see p. 13) near Vaassen in the Veluwe region of Gelderland, tried to gain a share of the region's rapidly growing paper industry. This entailed digging mill streams and building paper mills, which were then leased or sold to paper manufacturers.

In addition to enjoying an income from their land, the nobility came to depend more and more on another source of income: holding public office. The nobles of Holland were always included in the provincial delegation to the States General and the Council of State. One noble of Holland had a seat on the admiralty boards of Rotterdam and Amsterdam. Nobles also filled the following positions: two councillors of justice at the Court of Holland, one of the curators of Leiden University, two members of the board of governors of the VOC and the chairman of the delegated representatives (Gecommitteerde Raden) of Holland's South Quarter. In the seventeenth century, the most important offices in the Veluwe quarter in the province of Gelderland, such as the bailiff of the Veluwe and the judge of Arnhem and the Veluwezoom, were reserved for members of the landed nobility. Other offices, such as those of dyke-grave and local judge, which they did not hold by virtue of their nobility, were almost automatically awarded to nobles anyway. Their influence in the village councils tended to increase in the course of the seventeenth century. In Gelderland, moreover, it was not unusual for a nobleman to hold a seat on the town council. In Arnhem, for instance, the Bentincks and the Van Arnhems, both noble families, regularly held seats on the council. In Holland this practice became uncommon after the Revolt. Catholics – such as the Isendoorn à Blois family – found it very difficult to be appointed to public office, but Protestant members of the nobility steadily expanded their sphere of influence.

The nobility, in any case, were on the decrease in every province. In Holland, their number was halved in the seventeenth century, dropping from nearly a hundred to just a few dozen. In Friesland, the number of noble families dropped from fifty-eight to thirty-four between 1600 and 1700; only five of Groningen's forty-five families of landed nobility were left in 1800. The Utrecht nobility had only six members in 1667. This process of extinction was the result of a natural development, not in itself unusual. In the past, the ranks of the nobility had been continually filled by the elevation of new families. In the Republic this failed to take place, owing to a conscious strategy on the part of the aristocratic families themselves. In principle the provincial States, acting as sovereigns, could raise commoners to the peerage. During the whole period of the

Republic, however, they refrained from doing so, especially since the nobility were reluctant to admit newcomers with whom they would be forced to share the plums of political privilege. In 1666, the *ridderschap* of Holland – the political delegation of the nobles of that province – adopted more stringent requirements for admission to their ranks by stipulating that new members could be admitted only by unanimous decision. At the same time it was laid down that the eldest son of an incumbent family would automatically become a member upon the death of his father.

Most of the aristocracy in the Dutch Republic consisted of untitled nobles, the princes of Orange being the most notable exception. In Holland, the Wassenaers and the Brederodes were counted among the higher nobility, but the main branch of the Wassenaers had died out in the sixteenth century, and it was a younger branch, the Wassenaers van Duvenvoirde, who were prominent in the seventeenth century. Moreover, in June 1679 the Brederodes' coat of arms had to be broken over the grave of the family's last male descendant, when twenty-nine-year-old Wolfert van Brederode died unmarried and childless.

The nobility, however, enjoyed a measure of prestige that far surpassed their comparative paucity in numbers. This was due to their economic and political influence, to the prominent role they played in the army and at court, and especially to the social climate prevailing in Europe at the time. In most countries, aristocrats were the undeniable trendsetters. Commoners who had become wealthy did everything in their power to acquire a country estate and a title. The latter was out of the question in the Dutch Republic, but it was possible to flaunt other aristocratic status symbols: possession of a manor included the right to call oneself a 'lord' of that manor, a country house in the right location could exude aristocratic allure, and a marriage to the descendant of an ancient noble family provided access to aristocratic circles. Not everyone could resist these temptations. In 1566, Johan van Oldenbarnevelt enrolled at the University of Louvain as a *nobilis*, a pretence that was immediately called into doubt by whoever it was who jotted in the margin *sub specie nobilis*: posing as a nobleman. Later on he called himself 'lord of Tempel', after one of his manors, and it was often said that he preferred the company of nobles to that of the regents to whose milieu he belonged. One of his daughters married a Brederode, another the noble Cornelis van der Myle. Taking such an interest in things aristocratic, however, was the exception rather than the rule. Of the many men who in the course of the seventeenth century held seats on the *Veertigraad* – the town council of Leiden – only two or three possessed a manor. In 1682, Adriaan van Bredehoff became the first member of the Hoorn town council to own a manor when he acquired Pijlsweert near Utrecht. In 1686 he also bought the manor of Oosthuizen for 20,000 guilders. Such investments were unprofitable and thus served mainly to boost the family's prestige. The fact that most regent families found manor houses too expensive says something about the bourgeois nature of Holland's most prominent citizens. One's chances of marrying a member of the landed gentry were in fact very slight, since nobles tended to marry within their own circle. That the Oldenbarnevelt girls were welcomed into that circle was due entirely to the power wielded by their father. Whether one liked it or not, the nobility and the patriciate remained divided in the seventeenth century. In the northern and eastern provinces, the nobility played a prominent, often even a leading, role. In the urbanised west, however, wealthy merchants and influential regents could think of themselves as the nobles' equals, and there is every reason to believe that they did so.

As early as the Middle Ages, the cities and urban elite of the Low Countries had acquired a highly influential position. Especially in the coastal provinces – Flanders, Brabant, Holland and Zeeland – the cities played a very prominent role, owing mainly to the success of trade and industry. After the Revolt, the prosperity brought about by the booming economy further strengthened the position of merchants and entrepreneurs, as well as that of the regent families recruited from their midst. Although this lent Dutch society a middle-class character, there was still room for the nobility. In comparison with the European norm, however, their role was limited. The European norm was more closely reflected by the situation prevailing in the northern and eastern provinces. Social relations in the Republic thus mirrored to a great extent the country's economic divide.

9   Toil and trouble

Great fortunes were amassed in the Golden Age, but only the lucky few actually struck it rich. Hermanus Verbeeck of Amsterdam, who lived from 1621 to 1681, was one of the many for whom life was a struggle. The son of a furrier, Verbeeck was twenty-three years old when his father died and he took over the business. He could never manage to run it successfully, however, complaining that stiff competition made it impossible for him to earn a decent living. Verbeeck was not cut out to be an artisan. His father had sent him to the Latin School, where he had taken an interest in literature. Although he wrote the occasional poem and play, the most interesting of his writings to have survived is his autobiography, written in 7,000 lines of rhyming verse. It is mainly a story of trials and tribulations, as he himself said:

> The story of my life sadly contains nothing but woe,
> For the mantle of disaster doth fit me from top to toe.[1]

Verbeeck's life was marked by setbacks and ordeals. After four years as a furrier, he sold the business and became a shopkeeper in the employ of his wife's parents. He then worked as a bookkeeper in a trading company owned by his brother-in-law, after which he became a wine broker and finally a clerk at the weigh-house in Dam Square. He did not do particularly well in any of these occupations: the shop was soon left in the care of his wife, his incompetence as a bookkeeper led to his dismissal, and when at last he managed to acquire a much-coveted wine brokership (by paying his predecessor's pension), he was confronted with the death of the brother-in-law who had promised to help him to secure orders. To make matters worse, Verbeeck was sickly all his life. He could hardly make ends meet, and for the last twenty years of his life he was nearly always dependent on the sickness benefits he received from the wine brokers' guild.

---

[1] Hermanus Verbeeck, *Memoriaal ofte mijn levenraijsinghe*, edited by Jeroen Blaak (Hilversum: Verloren, 1999), p. 197.

Figure 17   On 10 January 1624 floating ice exerted so much pressure that the Lek Dyke near Vianen broke, allowing water to flood as far as Amsterdam. An all-out effort was made to repair the dyke (Esaias van de Velde; Atlas van Stolk S.1620/105).

Hermanus Verbeeck was by no means a poor man. His father, who had achieved a certain measure of prosperity, had left 6,400 guilders, a small fortune in those days. Verbeeck owned a house, though for most of his life it was let to others. He probably earned around 400 guilders a year, one and a half times as much as a skilled worker. The Verbeeck household knew no luxury, but at least no one went hungry. The guild was to thank for this, since the small supplemental allowance it gave him – 3 guilders a week – was enough to spare his family the humiliation of asking for charity. The Verbeecks were decent folk, a true middle-class family in every respect. Mrs Verbeeck, née Molenaer, was – as we have seen – the daughter of a shopkeeper. Verbeeck's mother held up her husband as a good example to her son:

> Your father raised his offspring with due honour and respect,
> With food and drink and clothing they grew up not in neglect.[2]

For people like Verbeeck, life in the Republic definitely changed in the seventeenth century. The population grew and with it the demand for a

[2] Ibid., p. 51.

variety of products, the supply of which kept pace with demand. Verbeeck remembered that when his father settled in Amsterdam around 1600 there had been no more than a dozen furriers in the city. By the time he took over the business, however, there were probably a hundred. The enormous influx of foreign furriers naturally influenced his earnings. We have no precise figures for Amsterdam, but research carried out in the tax registers of Gouda has shown that the number of people with assets of between 1,000 and 10,000 guilders – the group to which Verbeeck belonged – remained about the same from 1625 until the end of the seventeenth century. Their average wealth, which increased slightly at first, dropped by around 10 per cent after the middle of the century. These people were not much better off at the end of the century than they had been at the beginning. Their situation contrasts sharply with the picture presented by the wealthy, that is to say, people with property valued at 30,000 guilders or more. This group grew in size throughout most of the seventeenth century, and their average assets rose by approximately 40 per cent. These were the people who succeeded in profiting from economic growth.

The guilds helped to boost the low incomes of people like Hermanus Verbeeck, who received sickness benefits for years on end. The number of guilds increased by leaps and bounds in the seventeenth century, and Hermanus Verbeeck was just one of many who benefited from his guild's insurance scheme. Nowhere was the payment of benefits better organised than in Amsterdam. In the eighteenth century no fewer than thirty Amsterdam guilds were paying supplemental allowances on a weekly basis to sick or needy members. Occasionally only the widow received such benefits, but usually the man was entitled to them as well. The wine brokers were especially generous in giving their disadvantaged members 3 guilders a week, but they were not the only guild to do so. The surgeons' and the gold- and silversmiths' guild also gave their sick or unemployed members 3 guilders a week, whereas the guilds of the tailors, booksellers and confectioners could afford to dispense only half that amount. This lower amount was customary in towns where the guilds did not have the well-filled coffers of some of Amsterdam's guilds. These guild funds, called *gildenbossen*, generally contained funds contributed by the members themselves. They were insufficient to protect one against complete loss of income, but they helped, as in the case of Hermanus Verbeeck, to make up the difference between a labourer's income and that of a middle-class family, thus preventing people from sliding down the social scale. This was also the aim of various other institutions, such as *gasthuizen* (originally hospices for pilgrims, these had evolved by the seventeenth century into homes for the sick or elderly) and *hofjes* (small, privately endowed houses for the elderly, built around a *hof*, or courtyard), which admitted people upon payment of sums of up to several hundred guilders. This was beyond the means of labourers' families.

The care given by the orphanages followed a similar pattern. Members of guilds could rest assured that, if they were to die prematurely, their children would be well looked after, for they would be admitted to the Civic Orphanage (Burgerweeshuis). This institution opened its doors only to the children of citizens – not mere residents, but people with full rights of citizenship – which all guild members were by definition, since citizenship was a prerequisite to guild membership. The Civic Orphanage likewise tried to protect children from social decline by giving them a good education. In the Amsterdam Civic Orphanage most of the boys learned a trade and were expected to become independent masters in one of the guilds. Many boys ended up in the building trade, but other popular choices were cooper, shoemaker, sailmaker and ship's carpenter. The girls, who were not allowed to work outside the institution, were taught to perform various household duties. The poorer children, who were housed in the Almoners' Orphanage (Aalmoezeniersweeshuis), were seldom taught a trade. Instead, they were sent out at a young age to work as servants or day labourers. Many of them ended up in the service of the Dutch East India Company, a large employer, but one of last resort.

The difference between the two milieux was also noticeable in the care given to orphans. The children in the Civic Orphanage were given good, nutritious food. Their ample and varied diet regularly included meat, fish, dairy products and eggs. Such food was also served at the Almoners' Orphanage, but less frequently and in much smaller portions. In terms of calorie intake, the food consumed by these less fortunate orphans contained half as many calories as the fare enjoyed by the children in the Civic Orphanage. Not surprisingly, the mortality rate among the poor orphans was more than five times that of the orphaned children of citizens.

This seems inevitable when one considers the living conditions of the destitute. Hendrickje Slackebaarts of Zwolle lived in a rent-free house on the grounds of a former monastery. In a row of sixteen houses – eight up and eight down – there was only one family not receiving alms. In 1686, Hendrickje was living there with her three children and her eighty-six-year-old mother, Maaike Slackebaarts, who had been a widow since her husband, the skipper Jan Slackebaarts, had died in 1652. She and her seven children had immediately been thrown upon charity and had continued to receive it for the next forty years. Hendrickje had returned to her mother's house – which was, after all, rent-free – when she herself became a widow. They would not have been able to pay the rent in any case, for the household income was extremely low. Between 1684 and

1690, Hendrickje sewed regularly for the Chamber of Poor Relief (Armenkamer), probably making clothes for poor people like herself and thereby earning half a guilder a week. As soon as her children reached their teens, they were sent out to work; together they contributed a guilder a week to the family income. Each year the family received 20 guilders from the municipal fund for poor relief and another 10 guilders from the Reformed diaconate (the Board of Deacons responsible for the distribution of parochial alms). Each of the children was also entitled to one new shirt a year. In monetary terms the family income amounted to approximately 100 guilders a year, barely one-fourth of the income of Hermanus Verbeeck.

As permanent recipients of charity, the Slackebaarts were at the lower end of Zwolle's social scale. They and the 250 families who shared their fate made up 6 per cent of Zwolle's population. Another 4 per cent received alms on a temporary basis, but altogether the alms recipients probably accounted for less than 10 per cent of the city's population. Elsewhere their number may have been as high as 15 per cent, but this was still relatively low by contemporary European standards. One rung higher on Zwolle's social ladder were the labourers who could generally get by on their own earnings. The size of this group can be determined only indirectly. The middle class made up 20–30 per cent of the urban population, the upper middle class and the elite another 8–10 per cent and the poor 10–15 per cent. Then there was a very sizeable group of household servants, who are estimated to have made up another 10 per cent. If we add up these figures, we find that the working class accounted for the remaining 35–50 per cent of the population.

Very little is known about the working class, though on the face of it labourers did not fare too badly. In the last years of the sixteenth century and the first decades of the seventeenth century, wages rose dramatically, increasing threefold between 1580 and 1620. Although prices also rose sharply, the increase in real wages was nevertheless 20–40 per cent, depending on the worker's job, training and place of residence – in Holland, for example, wages were considerably higher than in Overijssel. After around 1640 the growth curve levelled off, and a period of wage stagnation set in which was to last for approximately 200 years.

Despite this substantial rise in wages, it is still questionable whether Dutch workers were better off than their counterparts abroad. The information available is inconclusive. A comparison between real wages in Holland and in southern England suggests a significant difference, to the advantage of the Dutch. Nonetheless, a comparison of the purchasing power – expressed in pounds of bread – of unskilled building workers in Amsterdam, London and Paris reveals that the differences were in fact very slight. It is certain, however, that workers in Holland profited from the thriving economy in two other ways. First of all, the Republic was a country with a stable food supply. Elsewhere, town-dwellers were dependent on agricultural products from the surrounding countryside, a source which could easily dry up when shortages occurred. Poor harvests, for instance, made it necessary to take emergency measures, but such measures often took effect only after grain prices had skyrocketed, and this meant – at a time when workers spent around 40 per cent of their income on bread – that many people went hungry. However, the Republic's long-standing practice of importing grain from the Baltic largely shielded it from food shortages, soaring prices and threats of famine.

Secondly, workers could also profit from the Republic's seemingly inexhaustible demand for labour. In the seventeenth century, the potential of the European labour force was seriously underexploited, which not only kept wages low but also meant that people were regularly unemployed. Permanent contracts were the exception; most workers were hired on a daily or at most a weekly basis. Fortunately, the Republic's strong economic growth meant that there was always a demand for labour. The Dutch East India Company (VOC), an enterprise that did not even exist at the beginning of the seventeenth century, had by 1625 a total of 4,500 Europeans working in Asia, 2,500 employees en route to Asia, and 700 making the return voyage. In the Republic itself the VOC employed another 2,000–3,000 people. By the end of the 1680s the VOC's European employees in Asia numbered 11,500, and by 1690 the number of voyages between the Republic and the East Indies had increased by 70 per cent. We have already seen how Amsterdam's tobacco-spinning works, an activity first recorded in 1627, employed at least 4,000 people at the end of the seventeenth century, with another 3,000 working in tobacco-cutting and stem-crushing operations, which were carried out in large workshops, each employing as many as 200 workers. Between 1603 and 1661 the number of sugar refineries in Amsterdam rose twentyfold, increasing in number from three to sixty and continuing to grow after that. The first pottery in Delft was recorded in 1581. A century later – by which time blue and white Delftware had become famous both at home and abroad – the industry employed 1,500 people, providing 5 per cent of Delft's population with a livelihood. In 1581 Leiden had 12,000 inhabitants, but in 1667 there were 36,000 people working in the local textile industry alone. Finally, in the course of the seventeenth century, those serving in the army grew in number from approximately 35,000 to more than 100,000. All these people needed food and clothing and a place to live, which likewise gave a boost to all manner of service industries.

The domestic market could not meet the demand for so much labour. Perhaps the most convincing proof of the comparatively attractive situation in the Republic is the great influx of wage labourers from abroad. We can only guess at their number, but the most reliable figures place the number of foreigners who settled in the Republic in the seventeenth and eighteenth centuries at half a million, meaning that 6–8 per cent of the population were of foreign descent. This percentage was considerably higher in the west of the country, where the great majority of foreigners settled. In Amsterdam, one-third of those marrying in the seventeenth century were immigrants, who probably constituted an even greater percentage of the population as a whole. Only 44 per cent of the men marrying in Leiden in the 1640s had been born in the Republic, while most of the others came from the Southern Netherlands or Germany. And although two-thirds of Utrecht's brides were Dutch, only half of the city's bridegrooms had been born in the Republic.

These people had certainly not come to the Netherlands for economic reasons only. The Jewish immigrants hoped to find a less hostile climate in the Republic. The approximately 100,000 Southern Netherlanders, largely from Flanders and Brabant, who moved north between 1580 and 1620 were fleeing the Inquisition. In 1685, when Louis XIV revoked the Edict of Nantes – which until then had guaranteed French Protestants a certain measure of religious freedom – 130,000 Huguenots fled the country. At least 30,000 of them came to the Republic, lured by the promise of help from the Dutch. In the first half of the seventeenth century, many German migrants fled the violence of the Thirty Years War raging in their own country. Their choice of a place to settle often depended on the prospects it offered. Indeed, for many refugees this was the most important criterion. Hermanus Verbeeck's father, for instance – who had arrived in Amsterdam shortly after 1600 with the great stream of immigrants coming from the South – was Catholic and therefore had nothing to fear from the Inquisition. Many immigrants, in fact, came from areas such as Scandinavia where there was a high degree of religious tolerance.

Migrational patterns also suggest the importance of economic motives. Those patterns were not at all arbitrary, as one would expect when people abandon house and home in panic. One stream of migration, for example, was clearly directed at Leiden, where the textile industry had gone through a period of depression in the sixteenth century. During the 1570s the civic authorities had taken great pains to entice Southern Netherlandish textile workers to Leiden. Their efforts had been crowned with success: the resurgence of the industry was due entirely to these immigrants and their technical know-how. A particularly successful innovation was the production in Leiden of the 'new draperies', various qualities of light-weight woollen cloth developed in and around Hondschoote in Flanders. In the decades just before and after 1600, thousands of textile workers and entrepreneurs emigrated to Leiden from Hondschoote and its environs. However, the manufacture of one of these new fabrics – serge, a woollen fabric favoured by the poorer classes because of its durability – was threatened by increasing competition. Consequently, the focus shifted back to *laken*, the traditional, heavier, high-quality woollen cloth for which Leiden had become famous. *Laken*, which was more expensive and therefore more profitable to produce, re-emerged in a new, light-weight version. This cloth was not the speciality of the Flemish but of the textile workers of Liège. In the first half of the seventeenth century, therefore, increasing numbers of textile workers emigrated from Liège to the North, where it was easy for them to find employment producing *laken*. The Flemish, by contrast, remained active as producers of serge.

In Amsterdam, which continued to attract the greatest number of foreigners, there was also a clear connection between an immigrant's place of origin and his chosen occupation. Most of the immigrants from the Southern Netherlands and France ended up working in the luxury industries, such as silk-twining and hat-making. The coastal provinces of Germany – and, for that matter, those of the Republic itself – mostly supplied builders and dock labourers. Not surprisingly, most of the immigrants from Scandinavia were involved in seafaring. The inland provinces of both the Holy Roman Empire and the Republic, especially Overijssel and Gelderland, supplied for the most part artisans and tradesmen. In Amsterdam, for example, the baking trade was dominated by Germans until well into the nineteenth century. During the seventeenth century, half of all the bakers who married in Amsterdam had come from Germany. Such patterns were presumably linked to economic structures in the immigrants' country of origin. The connection between coastal areas and seafaring is obvious. In the inland provinces, many people combined agriculture with a craft or trade, which may explain why such professions were often practised by immigrants from these areas. Nevertheless, one should not overrate such connections. The Scandinavian seamen and household servants in Amsterdam are known to have come largely from farming families: because farms were usually intended for the eldest son, the other children were often forced to leave home and seek their fortunes elsewhere. Natives of Twente who moved to Amsterdam often ended up in the shoemaking trade, yet Twente was not a centre of shoe production. Such examples suggest that networks also played an important role in patterns of migration: as soon as one group had firmly established itself in a trade, they helped others from the same area to follow suit.

Migration did not confine itself to traffic between countries. Within the Republic people also moved from east to west. Of the 144 children who left the Zwolle Holdehuis (the orphanage for the poor) between 1673 and 1695, 115 left the city. Of the 67 children whose final destination is known, nearly all went to cities in Holland, the girls to work as maid-servants, the boys to seek employment in one trade or another. In the seventeenth century, 1,254 men and 1,105 women from Twente – a region with just over 20,000 inhabitants – married in Amsterdam alone. In the city of Utrecht, less than 20 per cent of those marrying in the Reformed congregation came from the province of Utrecht. Foreigners accounted for some 35–45 per cent, but a considerable number of Utrecht's brides and grooms came from other parts of the Republic, most notably from the adjoining provinces of Holland and Gelderland, a group which accounted for 20–30 per cent, while the other provinces supplied 10–15 per cent.

All of these people, Netherlanders and foreigners alike, had to manage as best they could, and although the circumstances in which they found themselves, certainly in the cities, were not particularly bad, many of them hovered continually around the subsistence level. Any slight setback might plunge them into poverty. An accident, a protracted illness, a congenital defect or anything that made it impossible to earn a living condemned many to the humiliation of asking for charity. The loss of the male breadwinner was a blow many families never recovered from: Hendrickje Slackebaarts was just one of countless widows reduced to dependence on charity. Some men had occupations that involved a high risk of impoverishment for their families. Soldiers' wives, for example, were frequently among those receiving alms in garrison towns, and there were also proportionately higher numbers of textile workers receiving poor relief. In Zwolle, 25 per cent of the men and more than 70 per cent of the women receiving charity in the second half of the seventeenth century were textile workers, mostly spinners or weavers. This was more than twice the average for the population as a whole. In Delft, which could not be considered a textile centre, 25 per cent of the men and 60 per cent of the women receiving charity worked in the textile industry. An equally large number of Delft men dependent on alms were active in the army. The textile industry and the armed forces were, to be sure, typically proletarian professions with a very low standing. In the port towns, sea-men were held in similar low repute, since their occupation was charac-terised by scant schooling and meagre earnings, and their ranks were filled by unmarried men who could not afford to have a family.

Around 1680, a total of 50,000 men were active in the Dutch shipping industry. The VOC was responsible for many deaths, owing to the unhealthy living conditions both on board ship and in the East Indies. There are strong indications that of the more than 300,000 people who left for the Indies in the seventeenth century in the service of the VOC, only 100,000 returned to the Netherlands safe and sound. The high mortality rate among seamen resulted in a large surplus of women in the port cities of Holland, a surplus estimated to have been 39 per cent among the Amsterdam working classes. In other words, for every 100 male workers there were 139 women in the city. Those women, especially

Figure 18 In the seventeenth century, too, a woman's place was in the home. Even though Dutch women had a reputation for being more independent than their counterparts in other European countries, and many lower-class women were forced to work outside the home out of financial necessity, the household remained the woman's domain, as illustrated here by the chore of washing up. This engraving was made by a woman, Geertruyt Rogman (1625–51/7). There were in fact a fair number of women artists in the seventeenth-century Dutch Republic, but few of them made art their livelihood (Rijksmuseum rp-p-ob-4228/32–5).

the foreigners among them, had poor chances of marriage and were paid much less for their labour than men, so it is no wonder that many of them were dependent on charity.

While artisans and tradesmen could arm themselves to some extent against the risk of illness and death by means of the insurance schemes organised by their various guilds, day labourers were powerless to withstand the buffetings of fate. When there was no work to be found or they themselves were injured or otherwise unable to engage in heavy labour, they attempted to earn a living in the 'makeshift economy', doing such things as running errands, setting out the stoves in churches, or guarding the town gates on Sundays. For those who were either very daring or at the end of their tether, there was always crime and prostitution. Sometimes even that was not enough, however, and then help had to be sought from others, not infrequently from relatives or neighbours living in equally impoverished circumstances – witness the Slackebaarts family – who could offer only limited assistance. The truly desperate, of course, were forced to accept charity.

Joost Arienszoon, for example, finally ended up at Delft's Chamber of Charity (Kamer van Charitate) in 1609. Joost, a native of Courtrai in Flanders, had gone north with the great stream of migrants making their way to the Republic. He had originally registered as a bricklayer, but that was perhaps more his ambition than his trade, because later on we encounter him as a hod-carrier – carrying mortar and bricks to the artisans who did the actual building – an occupation requiring no training whatsoever. In 1605 he married a girl from Delft, Neeltge Michielsdochter, and they soon had a number of children. This stretched their budget so much that in 1609 Neeltge applied for poor relief. It is remarkable how often women requested charity, probably because those reviewing the applications were more readily persuaded by domestic need. Neeltge, moreover, was a native of Delft. She was given 3 stuivers a week (there were 20 stuivers to the guilder), but in 1614 this assistance was cut off, because the overseers of poor relief were convinced that she could get by on her own. Besides, it was rumoured that Neeltge earned money filling barrels with peat. From 1616 the family received a few loaves of bread every week, at least during the winter months, but at the end of the 1620s the alms came with more regularity, because Neeltge had a 'weak chest' and later also suffered from an 'aching arm'. It was not until 1645, by which time all their children had left home, that Neeltge and Joost were again able to care for themselves.

The Chamber of Charity was an institution which coordinated the efforts of the civic authorities and the Board of Deacons of the Reformed Church. The Reformed poor received alms from the church deacons; others were dependent on public relief. The poor relief on offer in Delft seemed much the same as the poor relief to be had elsewhere, but the way in which it was administered differed from city to city. The city of 's-Hertogenbosch, for example, offered public relief for which people of all faiths were eligible. The Table of the Holy Spirit (Tafel van de Heilige Geest) – named after the table from which alms had formerly been distributed and now popularly known as the Give-house (Geefhuis) – had originally been a parochial institution, but the civic authorities had already begun to exert a powerful influence on it in medieval times. In addition to relief offered by this civic fund, administered by the city magistrates, each of 's-Hertogenbosch's nine neighbourhoods distributed funds of their own to small groups of neighbourhood residents. From 1629 the poor who were members of the Reformed Church could also request aid from the parish welfare fund administered by the Board of Deacons. Because these benefits were handed out independently of one another, the poor of the Reformed congregation could hope for three separate allowances. Each was so little, however, that all three together could not always guarantee a full stomach. In Amsterdam there was a separate fund for people who had lived in the city for a specified period of time. The Amsterdam *huiszittenmeesters* had traditionally been responsible for administering poor relief, but they gave alms only to fully fledged citizens or to those who had lived in the city for at least five years. Others had to apply to the Board of Almoners, created in 1613.

In the villages of Holland – which seemed more urban than rural, owing to their limited agricultural activities – the system of poor relief resembled that of the cities. Alms distribution in the village of Graft in North Holland was like that of the cities in both organisation and level of benefits. In rural Drenthe, however, things were done differently. All poor relief was in the hands of the Reformed Church, because the province had so few people of other religious persuasions. These Reformed diaconates attempted to put the poor back on their feet by setting them up as smallholders, giving them some land and perhaps some tools and seed for sowing. The abundance of wasteland in Drenthe made this easy to do, but in the highly commercialised west this solution was much more expensive. In Rotterdam the Catholic almsgivers occasionally set someone up as a tradesman or the keeper of a boarding-house. This meant a sizeable investment, however, and success was far from certain. Indeed, such schemes often seemed more like make-work projects. In 1687, for example, the Zwolle authorities provided the funds to set up a workhouse in the eight upstairs flats in Broerentrans (where the Slackebaarts lived), in which the recipients of alms were required to spin thread to be used in sailmaking. The plan had been devised by a group of merchants from Wormer in North-Holland, who assumed the costs of running the operation. Children were put to work in the workhouse, and their mothers were given a spinning wheel to take home. Once out of their mothers' sight, however, the children were of little use as employees. The parents contrived to obtain loans from the foreman, saying that otherwise they would not be able to work. One foreman, Lodewijk Walraven, complained that even the officials doling out public charity protected the poor and made it impossible for him to keep discipline. Within two years the Zwolle workhouse had closed its doors.

There was nothing for it but to keep the poor alive at the lowest possible cost. To this end the institutions distributing alms handed out an assortment of goods and services. Medical care, for example, was provided to the poor free of charge by municipal doctors. In many places poor families could send their children to school for several years without paying fees. Very poor families, such as the Slackebaarts of Zwolle, were not required to pay rent. The 'Geefhuis' in 's-Hertogenbosch owned a bakery and various farms in rural Brabant, which supplied the grain used to bake the bread distributed daily to the poor. In addition, the poor received a couple of stuivers and the occasional item of clothing or pair of shoes. In the winter they were often given heating fuel in the form of peat. Such alms packages were very common. Nearly all the recipients of poor relief lived on their own and were therefore called *huiszittende armen*, the 'at-home poor'. This solution was less expensive than confinement in workhouses. Nowhere, however, was it possible to *claim* benefits. Charity was not a right, but a privilege graciously bestowed by the administrators of the various charitable funds.

The Republic's system of poor relief caused the Dutch to be admired abroad as paragons of philanthropy. 'Charity seems to be very national among them',[3] wrote William Temple in 1673 in his description of the Dutch national character, and in a certain sense this was true. Whereas England levied special taxes to finance poor relief, in the Republic it was customary to make collections. In Sneek two-thirds of the alms given to the poor were collected every month by the overseers of poor relief, who went door to door with an open collection plate so that a certain amount of social control was possible. This method obviously worked, because for two centuries the proceeds remained at nearly the same level.

The great objection to this system was the limited control it exerted over the activities of the poor. There was already a great awareness in the seventeenth century that poor relief was susceptible to fraud. The fact that charity was financed locally made it all the more important to ensure

---

[3] Sir William Temple, *Observations upon the United Provinces of the Netherlands*, edited by Sir George Clark (Oxford: Clarendon Press, 1972), p. 88.

that the money actually benefited the right people, that is to say, the local poor. All cities restricted the distribution of alms to long-term residents. In Leeuwarden the requirement was initially one year of residence, but in 1630 this was changed to two years and in 1660 the States of Friesland set the requirement for the whole province at five years. The residency problem became more pressing in the last quarter of the century, when the economy took a turn for the worse. The question of who was responsible for which poor then became crucial. Only Friesland managed to coordinate the local systems of poor relief at the provincial level. In 1682 the States of Holland attempted to do the same, stipulating that each locality could be held responsible for a maximum of one year for the support of a native of that place, after which the expenses were to be borne by that person's new place of residence. In 1687 similar laws were enacted in Utrecht and in 1705 in Zeeland. Most cities managed to circumvent such measures, however, and took other steps to safeguard the independence of their own systems of poor relief. Henceforth people were allowed to settle in a new place only after the authorities in their birthplace had stated in writing that they would assume the costs of any future poor relief the new resident might need. Only Amsterdam, the city with by far the greatest demand for casual labour, refrained from insisting upon such assurances.

The civic authorities were intent on monitoring not only the freedom of movement of alms recipients but also their behaviour. Those receiving charity were visited regularly. These visits, the records of which make it possible for us to take a closer look at the household of mother and daughter Slackebaarts, were of course originally intended to give the overseers of Zwolle's poor the opportunity to see whether their money was being well spent. As logical as this seems from the present-day perspective, in the seventeenth century it was a novel idea. In the Middle Ages, charity had been motivated at least as much by the alms-givers' desire for personal salvation as by their concern for the welfare of the poor. It was not until the sixteenth century that a distinction was made between the deserving and the undeserving poor. It became the task of the authorities to ensure that only the former received alms. To this end, the charitable institutions joined forces and were placed under the supervision of the city magistrates. At the same time, the overseers of the poor were instructed to punish those who tried to take unfair advantage of the system.

The increasingly larger scale of almsgiving and alms distribution – the inevitable result of economic growth – turned supervision of the poor into one of the authorities' biggest obsessions, a fact we must bear in mind when considering the founding of the Amsterdam house of correction in 1589.

Amsterdam's example was soon followed by other cities, including Leeuwarden (1598), Groningen (1609), Haarlem (1609), Gouda (1610), Alkmaar (1613), Utrecht (*c.* 1616), Delft (*c.* 1620) and Middelburg (1642). The inmates of the Amsterdam house of correction were put to work rasping Brazilian hardwood from which a red dye was made, hence the institution's name: Rasphuis. For a small fee one could stand in the visitors' gallery and observe the men at work. Some of them were criminals, but many had been arrested merely for begging. The Rasphuis was not designed to house and care for the poor; instead, it was a penal institution that served as a warning to those living on the margins of society. Outside Amsterdam it proved so costly to maintain houses of correction that most closed their doors within twenty years of their establishment.

The Rasphuis was also greatly admired by foreigners, and it was imitated in many places where there were considerable numbers of Dutchmen, especially in northern Germany and along the Baltic coast. The Rasphuis serves as a reminder that the Golden Age was far from golden for everyone. The inhabitants of the Republic, especially those living in the coastal areas, were probably better off than their counterparts in other countries, but it was precisely this advantage that caused the great influx of immigrants that eventually put a damper on the improvement of the living conditions of ordinary people. Despite the great achievements of the Dutch Republic, the seventeenth century was a time of increasing social inequality, inevitably foretelling ills to come.

Part III

Unity and discord: politics and governance

10   Community

From 30 January to 6 February 1696, Amsterdam was the scene of wild rioting. Men, women and children gathered to protest against a proposed change in the burial laws. Not only had the States of Holland introduced a tax on marriages and burials the previous year, but Amsterdammers would soon be required to use only government-approved undertakers. This measure threatened to put many people out of work, while at the same time benefiting the minions of the city governors. It also raised fears of a large increase in the cost of burial.

The new regulations were to come into effect on 1 February. On 31 January, however, the burgomasters were harassed and jeered at in the streets. Municipal soldiers had been posted in various places, but this only made the situation more volatile. There were a great many idle sailors in town who could not leave port at this season, and they too joined the gathering at the Almshouse, where women and children had begun to drum loudly on barrels and buckets. The crowd became so boisterous that the soldiers threatened to shoot. Forming a procession, the protesters marched off to Dam Square, where they posted a placard on the wall of the Town Hall which read 'house to let'. The authorities were about to issue a severe warning, but when they saw the crowd gathering they instantly announced a six-week postponement of the new burial law: to no avail, however, for the crowd had already started to throw paving stones at the soldiers, who fired back with blanks. One of the officers, who had been hit by a stone, was carried away with a gaping head wound. Everywhere soldiers were retreating before the angry demonstrators, who proceeded to lay siege to the house of Burgomaster Boreel on the Herengracht – one of Amsterdam's most fashionable canals – where they broke the windows and wrecked the interior. They also threatened to plunder the house of Sheriff Witsen. Meanwhile the first blood had been spilled: Captain Sparo had stabbed a protester to death on Burgomaster Boreel's doorstep. Clearly, the situation was getting out of hand.

It was more than the soldiers could handle, so the civic militia were called in. The militiamen, unlike the soldiers, were not employed by the city. They were ordinary citizens who kept the night watch once a month

Figure 19   A gathering in Amsterdam's Dam Square during the Undertakers'
Riot in the winter of 1696. Riots were a regular occurrence, but they were
seldom on such a large scale or as violent as this one (Amsterdam Municipal
Archives d 8916).

and were otherwise on call in emergencies. Obviously this was just such
an emergency, but the problem was that many militiamen sided with the
protesters. When they were urged to step up their efforts and put a stop to
the rioting, one militiaman retorted: 'What the devil! Why should we put
a stop to it? These people are doing us a favour. This crowd and the new
law are none of our business.'[1]

---

[1] *Oproeren in Holland gezien door tijdgenoten: ooggetuigeverslagen van oproeren in de provincie
Holland ten tijde van de Republiek (1690–1750)*, compiled and edited by Rudolf Dekker
(Assen: Van Gorcum, 1979), p. 65.

The militiamen's attitude changed only when the mob began to plunder the houses of people who had nothing to do with the matter. The broker Joris Craffurd, an eye-witness to the violence, reported that the crowd broke into the house of a well-to-do Jewish merchant, David de Pinto, in Sint Antoniesbreestraat. At this point several burghers realised that it was not the burial law that was at stake but De Pinto's possessions. 'If things go on like this, it will be our turn next',[2] they are reported to have said, upon which fifteen militiamen entered De Pinto's house, while others formed a cordon outside. They swept the place from top to bottom, 'slashing away … and pushing [the rioters] down the stairs, and those who resisted were killed without mercy'.[3] Anyone trying to escape was captured by the guards posted below, who were not inclined to show pity. Hours later the neighbours were still finding would-be plunderers under their beds, scared to death and begging to be spared. Order was quickly restored. A few weeks later the relieved authorities had a medal struck to commemorate the successful quelling of the riot. The medal, which was to be given to all the civic militiamen, bore the following inscription:

> Through Amsterdam's wise counsel, regents' courage, burghers' valour
> The plunderous rabble are appeased, no longer filled with rancour.

Town and village communities played a more important role in the Republic than they do in modern society. This was not, as is sometimes thought, because people tended to stay in one place. Seventeenth-century trends in migration do not differ significantly from those of our day, certainly not in the cities of Holland. In those days, however, villages and cities attached greater importance to their local identity and did their utmost to maintain it. Regulations were enacted and institutions founded to enable each community to preserve its distinctive character. Proponents of local identity asserted that all the inhabitants of a given locality were equal, but most people knew better. The commemorative medal struck by the city of Amsterdam after the Undertakers' Riot names three social classes: the regents, the burghers and the rabble. The same groups also figure prominently in the account given by Craffurd, whose vision of society emerges from his terms of reference. He not only calls the rioters 'rabble',[4] but also portrays them as the 'very lowest sort of people',[5] 'seafaring folk'[6] and habitués of 'public houses and brothels',[7] and goes on to describe one of them as a cooper's mate who had been raised in the Almoners' Orphanage. But who exactly were the militiamen – referred

---

[2] Ibid., p. 75.   [3] Ibid.   [4] Ibid., p. 45.   [5] Ibid., p. 47.   [6] Ibid., p. 64.
[7] Ibid., p. 98.

to by Craffurd and the authorities as 'burghers' – who played such an important role in these events?

In 1696, at the time of the Undertakers' Riot, the Amsterdam civic militia consisted of sixty companies. Each company had its own officers, and both they and their men were recruited from the same neighbourhood, or district. These militia districts had been carefully apportioned to encompass both rich citizens (for the officers' ranks) and the less well-to-do (for the rank and file). A little more than a century earlier, before the 1578 Alteration – the transfer of power to the Protestants – Amsterdam had had only three *schutterijen*, or militia guilds: small, relatively elite societies of men who practised marksmanship so that they could lend military aid to the sovereign or come to the city's defence, though the militias also served as important social networks.

In the 1570s, when the Revolt seemed to be stagnating, William of Orange and his followers attempted in desperation to turn the militias into inexpensive army units: inexpensive, because militiamen earned their living practising an honourable profession in civilian society and were not paid wages like regular soldiers. To bring this about, the civic militias were stripped of their exclusiveness, and compulsory military service was introduced for all men between the ages of eighteen and sixty, at least for those in a position to buy their own equipment. This effectively excluded the working class, which was undoubtedly the intention. (The outcome of the 1696 riot might have been very different if the 'rabble' had possessed firearms.) The burghers were divided into new companies and charged with defending the city and maintaining public order. This reorganisation of the militias began in Amsterdam in 1578. The civic militias in the other cities of Holland were also reformed at this time, with new guidelines for militia organisation taking effect in Alkmaar and Leiden in 1578 and in the other cities of Holland in 1580. In the words of a Rotterdam chronicler, '[The Prince of] Orange has turned all the militias in town into bands of burghers.'[8]

The militias' tasks were considered supplementary, for a professional army was actually responsible for defending the country, and municipal soldiers functioned as the police force. It was just as well, because despite the militias' apparent financial advantage, their use in the Republic's defence had a distinct disadvantage: the militiamen were no match for professional soldiers. To be sure, the militiamen of Haarlem and Leiden had made a heroic stand when their cities were besieged by the Spanish, but on the battlefield they were practically useless owing to their lack of

[8] Paul Knevel, *Burgers in het geweer. De schutterijen in Holland, 1550–1700*, Hollandse Studiën, vol. XXXII (Hilversum: Verloren, 1994), p. 97.

training. Indeed, as a French contemporary said of the Paris militiamen, 'they are just like dogs, who only bark and bite on the threshold of their own homes'.[9] In 1672, however, there was no choice but to use the civic militia to stop up the gaps at the front during the invasions in that Year of Disaster. Some 6,000 militiamen were sent as auxiliaries to prevent the advance of the French army, but they did not prove to be very effective. The diplomat Hieronymus van Beverningh even went so far as to call them 'completely useless'. As upholders of public order they also had their shortcomings, of which the Amsterdam authorities had become keenly aware in those fearful days of February 1696.

Yet the city could not do without the militias as a policing force. Municipal soldiers patrolled the city by day; militiamen performed this duty at night. In fact, it was this aspect of their duties that prompted Rembrandt in 1642 to depart from the traditional setting of the militia piece – a portrayal of the officers of a company of civic militiamen – and to paint this most famous of group portraits as a nocturnal scene, portraying the officers of the company of Frans Banning Cocq on their nightly rounds. A militiaman was generally called upon to keep the night watch about once a month, which entailed patrolling the streets (along with the others on duty that night), pausing once in a while to play a game of cards or drink a beer. Militiamen could also be called into action during the day, whenever the municipal soldiers faced overwhelming difficulties, such as riots. Sometimes, as in 1696, they sympathised with the rioters; at other times the militiamen themselves instigated the disturbances.

The strength of the civic militias, therefore, did not reside primarily in the sphere of military defence or the maintenance of public order. The militias were, first and foremost, an expression of civic solidarity. When a dignitary – the stadholder, for instance – visited the town, the militiamen filed past as representatives of the civic community. In many cities the militiamen also marched through the streets during the annual fair. Every year at Whitsuntide, Leiden's militiamen gathered at the shooting grounds, where they were inspected at seven o'clock in the morning. The various companies then drew lots to determine the order in which they would parade through town. Amsterdam had too many militia companies to allow them all to march on the same day, so they took turns, a different company parading every Sunday in the summer, despite protests from the members of the Reformed church council, who disapproved of this desecration of the Lord's Day. Their objections are more

---

[9] Robert Descimon, 'Solidarité communautaire et sociabilité armée. Les compagnies de la milice bourgeoise à Paris (XVI-XVIIe siècles)', in F. Thélamon (ed.), *Sociabilité, pouvoirs et société* (Rouen: no publisher found, 1987), p. 601.

readily understood if one considers that such parades were generally followed by great merrymaking. In 1664 no fewer than twenty-two tapsters were hired to supply beer to Leiden's militiamen, who were determined to maintain their reputation as insatiable gluttons and guzzlers. All this ingesting and imbibing was intended to promote comradeship among the militiamen. Many civic militias held an annual banquet at which the officers passed around a beautifully decorated silver drinking horn. One such drinking vessel from Leiden bore the following inscription:

> Discord and mutiny are fiends most clever
> My officers will manfully defeat them
> And let union crown Batavia for ever.[10]

It was precisely because these banquets so aptly expressed the community spirit of the militias that they were often depicted in militia pieces: group portraits made for display in the *doelen*, the building where target practice and assemblies were held, and often the scene of boisterous drinking. These *doelens* generally had a large hall with correspondingly large walls. In the sixteenth century civic militias had started to have their portraits painted as a group, and this tradition was continued in the seventeenth century. After the reorganisation of the militias, however, the size of the companies made it impossible to portray all the men in one painting. Henceforth such portraits included only the officers, who often had to pay princely sums to have themselves portrayed in dress uniform. Occasionally, though, the return on the investment was eternal fame, for who today would know the name of Frans Banning Cocq if he were not the luminous focal point of Rembrandt's *Night Watch*? Such group portraits were expressly intended for public display, thus emphasising the militiamen's dedication to the community. Naturally the officers portrayed were well aware that such exposure would enhance their reputations. Banning Cocq, a second-generation immigrant, had a copy of the *Night Watch* drawn for his private album, where it figured alongside a drawing of his country estate and a copy of a militia piece featuring his father-in-law.

Thus the militiamen liked to think of themselves as the backbone of urban society, or – as Hadrianus Junius, the rector of the Latin school in Haarlem, had called them in 1588 – as '*robora et nervos reipublicae*', the strength and nerves of the Republic, 'republic' meaning 'civic community' in this context. In terms of political strength, the armed militiamen could be formidable opponents, despite their lack of soldierly discipline in battle. The nerves of the city, however, were more likely the 'burghers', a term with a great many meanings. Burghers could mean *poorters*, those

---

[10] Knevel, *Burgers in het geweer*, p. 301.

people who possessed full rights of citizenship. In a more general sense it also referred to established folk, people firmly rooted in society. Militiamen were popularly known as burghers, and the guilds organised the burgher trades (*burgerneringen*). Burghers of all descriptions, therefore, were the property owners who comprised the middle classes.

In Amsterdam those with full rights of citizenship had either inherited this status or purchased it. Occasionally the burgomasters granted an individual honorary citizenship. In 1655, the burgomasters of Amsterdam expressed the high esteem in which they held Michiel de Ruyter by making him an honorary citizen. Clergymen had citizenship rights conferred on them free of charge, but others were forced to pay increasingly large sums for these rights in the course of the seventeenth century. In 1600 the price of citizenship in Amsterdam was 8 guilders, but the rate was raised repeatedly until it reached the 1650 level of 50 guilders. That money was earmarked for various institutions: 13 guilders for the Civic Orphanage, 22 for poor relief, 10 for the civic militias, and, finally, 5 for the city itself. Newly naturalized citizens were therefore compelled to support the various civic institutions, thus becoming pillars of society from the moment they acquired citizenship.

No one was obliged to acquire citizenship, however, and its considerable cost would have caused many people to question its value. Life as an ordinary resident, as opposed to a fully fledged citizen, was not necessarily disadvantageous, but it did prevent one from enjoying certain privileges. Citizens had the right to be judged by their fellow citizens, the magistrates, and only the children of citizens could be admitted to the Civic Orphanage. Citizens were also exempt from certain tolls. More importantly, only citizens could enrol in the guilds. Anyone intending to set himself up in a craft or trade governed by a guild had no choice but to acquire citizenship. The same was true of people who hoped to pursue a political career in the municipal government: the better positions were open only to citizens.

Burghers, therefore, were the very embodiment of civic society, though it was not always clear to whom the word referred. A publication appearing in Amsterdam in September 1672, *Wachtpraetje ... gedruckt voor de Liefhebbers des Burger-Rechts* (Watch talk ... printed for the lovers of citizenship rights), quotes a man who maintains that he read the following in the Citizenship Law of 1578: 'The Councillors shall be elected from among the citizens.'[11] This was correct inasmuch as regents had to be citizens, but the speaker took these words to mean that the burghers had the right to elect their governors. This had happened only once, in 1578,

---

[11] *Wachtpraetje 1. September 1672; Gedruckt voor de Liefhebbers des Burger-Rechts* (Knuttel 10564), p. 5.

when the civic militias had drawn up a list of candidates for the new town council after driving out the Catholic council. Now, in 1672, it was suggested that the burghers, meaning the militiamen, should do this again: 'The burghers must pay municipal and national taxes, take an oath declaring themselves ready, day and night, to prevent all disasters, take turns on guard duty and even march against the enemy outside the city. Why, then, should citizens not enjoy their lawful rights and privileges?'[12] This implies that citizenship rights, militia duty and tax liability were somehow connected, but although all Amsterdammers were liable to taxation, not all militiamen were citizens. Further on in the *Wachtpraetje* another subset was added to the equation: 'in addition to the Bible, he [the militiaman, or burgher] should have a charter in the house',[13] meaning a list of the municipal privileges to which all citizens were entitled. Citizens and militiamen were therefore expected to be Christians who read the Bible regularly.

This mingling of the various milieux – citizens, militiamen, guild brothers, Christians – was to be found in all the cities of the Republic, in some places much more overtly than in Amsterdam. Everywhere the guilds were open only to those who had 'obtained' the rights of citizenship. In Deventer, from 1658 onwards, anyone hoping to acquire citizenship was required to present himself at the town hall, display a firearm and declare himself its owner. In the seventeenth century, Jews applying for citizenship in Arnhem were invariably turned away. In Utrecht and further to the east, increasingly stringent restrictions were introduced in the course of the seventeenth century, even in Christian circles. In some cities Catholics were barred from citizenship with increasing frequency, with the result that they could no longer establish themselves as independent shopkeepers or craftsmen. Those discovered to have declared falsely that they were members of the Reformed Church were deprived of both citizenship rights and guild membership and ordered to shut down business.

The guilds hosted the same kind of convivial gatherings as the militia companies, and the founding of many new guilds in the seventeenth century meant that such conviviality was on the increase. On a fixed day every year, usually the feast day of the guild's patron saint, the guild's assets were counted and announced, and a new board of governors was chosen. In nearly every guild the chairman was called a *deken* (dean), while the other members of the board had a variety of titles. In Arnhem they were called *gardianen* (guardians), in Utrecht *oudermans* (elders), in Amsterdam *overlieden* (senior officers) and in Haarlem *vinders* (wardens).

[12] Ibid., p. 6.   [13] Ibid., p. 7.

In most cities their appointment had to be approved by the town council, which also issued and amended guild regulations, though this generally occurred at the express request of the guild in question. In the summer of 1642, for instance, the Haarlem Guild of St Luke, whose members included the painters, requested that lotteries and sales of estates by public auction be more strictly regulated. According to the guild, they served to cover up the import of 'illegal' art, meaning works produced by artists who were not members of the city's Guild of St Luke. A petition was drawn up at the behest of nine painters and presented to the authorities by the guild's board of governors, who met regularly with the burgomasters and supplied them with the information needed to settle the matter. Even though a decision was not taken until August 1644, the Guild of St Luke eventually got what it wanted, having exerted the necessary influence by means of petitions and informal consultation at the town hall.

Like the civic militias, the Haarlem Guild of St Luke held an annual banquet. In 1643, however, their day of wining and dining had to be called off, because after contributing towards the cost of a new chandelier in the Church of St Bavo, the guild found itself short of funds. In Nijmegen, the baker's guild consumed 71 guilders worth of food and drink on 11 June 1693 – the *keurdag*, the day on which a new board was chosen – and music was even provided for the occasion. In 1686 the baker's guild in Arnhem entered into a long-term arrangement with the innkeeper Jan Mossel, who agreed to host all future 'meetings and refreshments' of their guild in his establishment. Solidarity was promoted not only by regular meetings but also by the funeral rites performed under the guilds' auspices. Most guilds organised funerals for their members, the coffin being carried by guildsmen and covered with the decorations of the guild, usually a black cloth with silver shields. All guild members were expected to be present at the funeral of a fellow guildsman. In the Great Church in Dordrecht, moreover, the drapers, merchants, furriers, dyers, shoemakers, fishmongers, smiths, carpenters, cabinetmakers and surgeons could be buried in their guild's communal vault, and space would even be made available in those vaults for their wives and children. Various Utrecht guilds also had such vaults. The Dordrecht and Utrecht guilds in particular functioned as a kind of substitute family, in which context the terms 'guild brother' and 'guild sister' took on a special significance. It is known, however, that not all members made use of these communal vaults. It was probably the poorer members who preferred a guild vault in the church to a dishonourable grave among the poor in the cemetery outside.

The guild model served as the example for the formal neighbourhood organisations existing in such cities as Leiden, Haarlem, Delft, Rotterdam, Utrecht and even The Hague, which had no municipal rights and so was not, strictly speaking, a city. In the mid-seventeenth century, Haarlem had a hundred such organisations, ninety within its walls and the others beyond the town gates. These neighbourhood organisations had their own rules and regulations: they exacted contributions from their members, kept a treasury and held annual meetings, at which they chose a board of governors, consisting in Haarlem of the dean (chairman) and wardens, the same titles as those used for guild officers. The members of these organisations dined together once a year, helped one another in times of need, and carried their fellow neighbours to the grave. Sometimes they tried their luck collectively, as in 1609, when the city of Haarlem held a lottery to collect money for an Old Men's Home. There were 300,000 tickets for sale, and many neighbourhoods took collections to buy lottery tickets on behalf of all the 'neighbours'. The draw – in which one could win costly silverware and splendid paintings, as well as large sums of money – was accompanied, just as draws are today, with much fanfare. The rules of seventeenth-century lotteries required everyone buying a lot to submit a rhyme, and these rhymes reveal the same thirst for riches that prompts people to take part in the national lottery today. The 'neighbours' in Bakenesserstraat, who combined their resources to buy sixty-seven lottery tickets, wrote the following rhyme:

> Good neighbours of Bak'nes, by this agreement do abide,
> Verily I tell you, we have saved and now subscribe
> The money of the neighbourhood, sheer madness it is not,
> May it please the good Lord now to let us hold a winning lot.[14]

At the draw, all the rhymes were read aloud and this continued around the clock, lasting in the case of this particular lottery for a full fifty-two days.

Seventeenth-century neighbourhoods often had very poetic names. Among the names of the eight militia districts in Utrecht were Pitch Sticks (Pekstokken), Blood Pit (Bloedkuil) and Turkey (Turkije). The neighbourhood opposite the town hall, in the curve in the canal called the Oudegracht, was named Under the Flight of Snipes (Onder de Snippevlucht). In Haarlem the names of the neighbourhoods usually corresponded to street names, but in Leiden they were called such things as The Realm of Pallas (Het Rijck van Pallas), County of Jersusalem and Jericho (Graeflicheyt van Jerusalem en Jericho) and Compostelle (after Santiago de Compostela). Sometimes these names were corruptions of other names – Barbariën, for example, derived from the former Convent

---

[14] Gabrielle Dorren, *Het soet vergaren: Haarlems buurtleven in de zeventiende eeuw* (Haarlem: Arcadia, 1998), p. 25.

of St Barbara – while others seemed to be fanciful inventions. The residents of the Snippevlucht neighbourhood in Utrecht could hardly avoid close association with one another. Of the approximately sixty families, fourteen fulfilled an administrative function. The neighbourhood's rules and regulations stipulated the rights and duties of its residents. In the winter, for example, they had to brave the cold and take turns collecting for the poor. The neighbourhood also mediated in the event of conflicts. When a resident died, the whole neighbourhood attended the funeral and fellow neighbours carried the coffin. Once a year the money in the cash box was counted and promptly spent on food and drink. One interesting bit of information that has come down to us is that smoking was banned during their meetings in 1630. The residents of Snippevlucht saved all year for a neighbourhood banquet that lasted three days. Twenty-four married couples attended the banquet of 1639, and together they polished off 180 guilders worth of ham, veal, lamb, poultry, rabbit, sausages, pasties, salmon, shrimp, tarts, bread, cracknel, cinnamon bread, cream cheese, Edam cheese, sheep's cheese, butter, apples, hazelnuts, radishes and lettuce. A meal shared by the 150 residents of Haarlem's Koningstraat neighbourhood cost no less than 600 guilders. Fifty rabbits were among the food consumed. Unity and solidarity were extremely important: at these banquets, for example, the wealthier neighbours paid the share of their poorer brethren. By all accounts they were lively events, marked by much singing and the recitation of verses specially composed for the occasion.

One drawback of such a close-knit neighbourhood was the suffocating effect of so much social control. Neighbourhood supervisors were called in to determine the tax liability of all residents, who in turn kept a sharp eye on one another. In 1695 the husband of Anna Nagtegaals of Rotterdam was brought before the magistrates and accused by the neighbours of beating his wife and cheating on her with other women. The adulterous husband was banished from the city, despite urgent pleas from his wife to let him come home. The court eventually consented to his return, but he was not permitted to show himself anywhere near his house, evidently to spare the feelings of the neighbours, which were probably prompted less by sympathy with the unhappy Anna than by concern for their own honour and the reputation of the neighbourhood as a whole. In the seventeenth century, honour – both individual and collective – was immensely important. A preoccupation with proper conduct from the cradle to the grave was shared by people from all walks of life.

The various corporate bodies – the citizenry, the civic militias, the guilds and the neighbourhoods – had a number of characteristics in common. They were invariably local institutions which justified their existence in terms of such localism. For example, guild members claimed that they provided the bulk of local tax revenues, militiamen that they defended the city, and citizens that they were the backbone of society.

Secondly, these corporate bodies were self-governing, at least in principle. The guilds and neighbourhoods were self-governing in practice as well: they held assemblies at which decisions were taken and leaders chosen, and they had the financial means to carry out their plans. The members themselves, however, were not always in charge. Though cities were self-governing, the citizens exerted little influence on the choice of governors or their policy-making. The officers of the civic militia were often appointed by the town council, even though the militiamen claimed the right to choose their leaders themselves. These departures from the rule of 'democratic' decision-making were a frequent source of conflict throughout the seventeenth century.

Thirdly, the members of these bodies stemmed largely from the middle classes. Guilds were organisations of small, independent tradesmen and craftsmen, for whom citizenship was a prerequisite to guild membership. Militiamen were required to own their own firearms and equipment; in some places prospective citizens could acquire full citizenship only after contributing a weapon to the city's arsenal.

Fourthly, the membership of these bodies was overwhelmingly male. There were no 'militiawomen'. Most guilds had accepted only men since the fifteenth or sixteenth century. Even when women were not explicitly excluded, they made up only a small fraction of the membership. Women could possess full rights of citizenship, but they nearly always obtained them by descent, seldom by purchase. Citizenship evidently had little to offer them. Within the neighbourhood organisations, women and men worked on more or less equal terms, but there, as well, administrative posts were filled almost exclusively by men.

Last of all, corporate bodies were an overwhelmingly urban phenomenon. Villages seldom had such institutions, though this had nothing to do with size. Graft, a village in Holland's North Quarter, had approximately 1,500 inhabitants in the second half of the seventeenth century. This was two and a half times as many as Delden, a small town in the province of Overijssel, but despite its smaller size, Delden had three guilds and Graft had none. The inhabitants of Graft, only a minority of whom worked the land, were prone to bourgeois airs and called themselves 'burghers of Graft'. Official bodies would have none of it, however, and refused to use the term. Official Graft documents refer to *buren*, or 'neighbours', the customary term for those living in the countryside. Though guilds were not completely unknown in rural areas, they were in fact rare, partly because the administration of a small organisation was often disproportionately expensive. A number of bakers were needed to keep a baker's guild running; two or three were not enough to make it worthwhile. The rarity of country guilds also had to do with the fundamentally different status of villages, which were often ruled by the lord of a nearby manor. In Brabant there were rural militias, but they had a primarily social character, providing not only entertainment, such as archery competitions, but also help for the needy and burials for their members. The yearly banquet was the most important thing on their agenda. The rules and regulations laid down in 1645 by the 'brotherhood or militia of John the Baptist' in Leenderstrijp, south of Eindhoven, stipulated that 'a communal banquet or gala, prompted by love and friendship, shall be held every year'.[15] Such rural militias were unknown outside the province of Brabant, which, together with Flanders, was the cradle of the European civic militia.

In the eastern Netherlands, and more particularly in Drenthe, Twente and the county of Zutphen (also known as the Achterhoek), one could take pride in an institution unknown in the cities: the mark society. Its members were farm owners who administered collectively the communal lands of the village, on which the members of the corporate body – the mark – were allowed to graze cattle, gather wood and cut peat. Like the guilds, these mark societies were organisations of property owners, and here and there they are even referred to as 'guilds'. Some marks also provided burials for the members of their community.

Together these corporate bodies formed a tightly knit fabric of social organisations. Since it was common to be a member of more than one of these organisations, many people were well integrated into the economic, social, religious and political life of local society, as well as taking part in its defence. The corporate bodies of the Dutch Republic were important, but not at all unique, since they were also to be found elsewhere in Europe. Their special significance in the Republic derived from the specific power relations prevailing in the Low Countries, which lent local communities – and more particularly those in urban settings – an importance unknown in other countries.

---

[15] Max Farjon, *Het gilde St.-Jan Baptista en Leenderstrijp: 350 jaar historie en gebruiken* (Leenderstrijp: no publisher, 1995), p. 6a7.

11 The authorities

On 15 August 1652, Coenraad van Beuningen left for Sweden, charged by the States General with the important task of persuading Sweden to side with the Dutch Republic in its conflict with England, later known as the First Anglo-Dutch War. Van Beuningen was thirty years old and by no means a professional diplomat. The grandson of an Amsterdam burgomaster, he had been appointed secretary to the Amsterdam town council in 1643 and to the highly influential post of pensionary (chief municipal magistrate and legal adviser) in 1650. This made Van Beuningen the most important adviser to the Amsterdam authorities and, by virtue of his office, a member of Amsterdam's delegation to the States of Holland. Van Beuningen thus combined a position in local government with a role in foreign policy. As a public servant in the employ of the city of Amsterdam, he was naturally a prominent figure in local politics, and his ambassadorial travels in the service of the Republic lent him both national and international prestige.

Although Van Beuningen's two-year stay in Sweden was not in fact successful, he was asked to travel to Scandinavia again, in January 1656, to safeguard the Republic's interests in the war between Sweden and Poland. In this case the Republic's interests largely coincided with those of Amsterdam, the centre of the grain trade with the Baltic. Because Van Beuningen had, in the interim, been unable to devote enough time to his duties as pensionary, he decided to resign his office. In January 1660 he was elected to the *vroedschap*, Amsterdam's thirty-six-member town council. Less than three months later, however, he was travelling again, this time to France, where he was sent to urge the relaxation of trade restrictions detrimental to the Dutch, a mission that was essentially a failure. The most notable result of his efforts was a lifelong distrust of the French king's intentions, a distrust that proved to be well founded when the French invaded the Republic in the spring of 1672, while Van Beuningen was in Paris on yet another diplomatic mission. When he returned to Holland on 28 July, the French occupation was well under way. On 17 September, Van Beuningen was chosen as one of

Amsterdam's four burgomasters, which allowed him to devote all his energy to saving the Republic. He became a delegate to the States General, where he emerged – together with Caspar Fagel, at that time *griffier* (clerk) of the States of Holland, and William III – as a leading figure in the field of foreign policy. Not only was he directly involved in the peace negotiations with France, but he also consulted Michiel de Ruyter about strengthening the fleet and later managed to persuade the Spanish to carry out a diversionary action against the French.

Van Beuningen thus had ample opportunity to hone his diplomatic skills. He nonetheless continued, for the whole of his active life, to be part of Amsterdam's municipal government. This was not unusual in the Dutch Republic: while Van Beuningen was sojourning in Sweden in 1652, Nanning Kaiser, pensionary of Hoorn, was sent to the Danish court; Johan Meerman, a member of Leiden's town council, travelled as a special envoy to England in 1667–8; Jacob de Witt – burgomaster of Dordrecht and the father of Johan de Witt, the future Grand Pensionary – served as a special envoy to Sweden in 1644–5. These men, and others like them, combined international diplomacy with local public office. Such posts were considered to be positions of crucial importance to anyone aspiring to power in the Republic.

The Republic's political system can seem very confusing to modern-day observers, as indeed it was for many people in the seventeenth century. It certainly appeared to have no clear plan. Authority resided in places where one would least expect it. Institutions and offices that we take for granted – such as a head of state or cabinet ministers – were unknown in the Republic. This confusion is largely due to the fact that the Republic's political system was based on a compromise between two contradictory principles. In fact, these contradictions emerge clearly from Article 1 of the Union of Utrecht of 1579, which states that the 'provinces will form an alliance, confederation, and union among themselves ... in order to remain joined together for all time, in every form and manner, as if they constituted only a single province'.[1] In other words, there would be unity in government. However, the article goes on to say how such unity is to be understood: 'Nevertheless each province and the individual cities, members and inhabitants thereof shall each retain undiminished its special and particular privileges, franchises, exemptions, rights, statutes, laudable and long practised customs, usages and all its rights, and each shall not only do the others no damage, harm or vexation but shall help to maintain, strengthen, confirm and indeed protect the others in these by all

---

[1] Herbert H. Rowen (ed.), *The Low Countries in Early Modern Times* (London: Macmillan, 1972), p. 70.

proper and possible means.' In other words, unity of government would not be instituted at the expense of local and regional privileges and customs. Furthermore, the signatories to the Union – representatives of provinces and cities alike – promised to help one another in the event of infringement upon those privileges and customs. Because there were a great many of these in the Low Countries, this stipulation in the Union of Utrecht had far-reaching consequences.

The Low Countries had experienced unity of government only briefly. Charles V's attempts to consolidate the Low Countries by establishing a central government had been more successful in the South than in the North. Friesland, Groningen, Drenthe, Utrecht, Overijssel and Gelderland had only recently become Habsburg possessions. Until that time they had resisted, often by force of arms, all attempts to incorporate them into the Habsburg Empire. No sooner had they been annexed than the Revolt broke out, giving them ample opportunity to display their local and regional loyalties, as the Union of Utrecht makes clear. The same text also reveals that what was closest to the heart of the rebellious elites were their 'own particular privileges' and 'customs' and that their rather reluctant cooperation had been born of necessity, for only by a concerted effort could they hope to withstand the powerful armies of Spain. Later on, in the seventeenth century, necessity again forced the United Provinces to work together, but their primary loyalty was still to local and regional government.

The power of the local governments was, in their own eyes at least, practically unlimited. The opening of the charter of the city of Zwolle left no room for doubt on this score: 'The city of Zwolle is a free city which is dependent on no one'.[2] Like Kampen and Deventer, the other two Hanseatic cities in the province of Overijssel, Zwolle claimed to be an Imperial City, i.e. a city which paid tribute directly to the Holy Roman Emperor. In the constitutional sense, Imperial Cities were the equals of sovereign rulers. During the Revolt, the cities in Overijssel had considered annexing the entire province to the Holy Roman Empire. For the whole of the seventeenth century Kampen, Deventer and Zwolle continued to repudiate the sovereignty of the provincial States, and naturally they considered the States General's claims to sovereignty nothing less than ludicrous. So it was only logical, in the eyes of Zwolle's governors, that they should be consulted on affairs of state. Thus the city of Zwolle solemnly ratified the Peace of Münster in February 1648, the Treaty of

---

[2] J. C. Streng, '*Stemme in staat*': de bestuurlijke elite in de stadsrepubliek Zwolle, 1579–1795 (Hilversum: Verloren, 1997), p. 88.

Westminster in February 1654 and the Peace of Breda in July 1667, and gave its stamp of approval to other treaties as well.

The municipal government of Zwolle consisted of two departments: the magistracy and the *meente* or *gemeente* (representatives of the citizenry), elsewhere also known as the *gezworen gemeente* (sworn representatives). The Zwolle *meente* was chosen from the city's four districts, or 'streets': Voorstraat, Waterstraat, Diezerstraat and Sassenstraat. Each street had twelve representatives in the *meente*, which therefore had a total of forty-eight members, who were chosen for life. Every year on 13 December, the feast day of St Lucy, the members themselves voted to fill the vacancies in their ranks. Each year on the day of St Paul's conversion (25 January), called 'Pauli' for short, the *meente* chose the eight magistrates who formed the executive branch of the municipal government. On that day the town gates were locked at half past eight in the morning, thus eliminating – at least symbolically – any outside influence. The keys were then brought to the town hall, where the retiring magistrates – already assembled in the council chamber – were now joined by the *meente*. The twelve men from each district drew lots to choose three electors (*keurnoten*) per street, who swore an oath before the magistrates, promising to elect only competent men. The twelve electors of the *meente* were then entrusted with the keys to the city, whereupon they withdrew to the tower to elect the new magistracy.

The magistracy was both an administrative and a judicial body. Not only was it responsible for the daily running of the city, but it also functioned as the municipal court. Every four weeks, the two magistrates serving as burgomasters stepped down and two others took their place. The burgomasters functioned as 'presidents for the duration', in other words as chairmen of the magistracy. This continual change of staff – annual elections of the magistracy, a monthly change of burgomasters – was aimed at minimising the excesses of public office. If a burgomaster overstepped his bounds, he could be brought to account relatively quickly, and unacceptable regents could easily be passed over when new magistrates were elected.

The *meente* thus played a vital, supervisory role, and was – as expressly stated again in 1690 – 'representative of the entire body of burghers'.[3] What was meant by 'burghers' is not entirely clear, though it must refer at the very least to those who possessed formal rights of citizenship, since this was a requirement for election to the Zwolle *meente*. In addition to choosing the magistrates, the *meente* could exert its influence by approving

---

[3] Ibid., p. 114.

or vetoing all manner of resolutions. The Zwolle *meente* was more than a mere electoral college: it met regularly in its own building next door to the town hall. Many resolutions could be passed only with the approval of the *meente*. The magistracy was required to consult the *meente* on questions of war and peace, and no new taxes could be imposed without the permission of its members. The *meente* also audited the accounts every year to ensure that the magistracy was handling the burghers' money properly.

The existence of a *meente* or other representative body was typical of governmental organisation in Overijssel and Gelderland. The cities of Brabant had no *meente*; instead, the guilds elected their own representatives to the municipal government. In 's-Hertogenbosch this practice was stopped when the city was captured by Dutch troops in 1629. Perhaps there were fears that Catholics, acting as the guilds' representatives, would continue to take part in the municipal government. The government of Bergen-op-Zoom consisted not only of magistrates and ex-magistrates but also of councillors elected by the seven 'nations', each of which represented a number of guilds. In Utrecht the guilds had dominated the entire municipal government, but Charles V had put an end to this when he assumed sovereignty over the province of Utrecht in 1528. Something similar had happened in Groningen in 1536, though informally the guilds long retained a strong hold on the municipal government. In 1657 they even threatened to seize power, but the Frisian stadholder Willem Frederik took action to thwart their intended coup. In 1662 Willem Frederik again deployed troops in the city, this time to put down a guild uprising. Afterwards, guild members were no longer permitted to hold seats on the Groningen council, and the council was given the right to appoint the guilds' boards of governors.

In the coastal provinces the middle classes had little to say about who was elected to public office. In Middelburg there was an electoral college consisting of twelve of the 'most notable' burghers, who, together with the twelve councillors (ex-magistrates), drew up a list of twelve names from which the stadholder then appointed two burgomasters and half the magistrates' court. In 1586 the States General granted the city of Leeuwarden the right to have a twelve-member magistracy chosen by nine electors, who were appointed by drawing lots from a pool of eighteen burghers. In 1657, however, the voices of the burghers of Leeuwarden were stifled by the introduction of a very complicated electoral system.

In most cities in the province of Holland the middle classes had no say whatever in their municipal government. The *vroedschappen* were permanent town councils whose members were chosen for life and varied in number from fourteen (Medemblik) to forty (Delft and Leiden). The town councillors filled the vacancies in their ranks by means of cooptation, or election by the votes of the existing members. The magistrates and burgomasters, who were replaced yearly, were usually members of the town council. Only Amsterdam departed from this practice, for there the burgomasters could be chosen by the ex-burgomasters, thus circumventing the town council. In Amsterdam the ex-burgomasters formed a kind of back-up council which greatly influenced local policy. The citizenry exerted a noticeable influence only in Dordrecht and a few cities in West-Friesland. In the seventeenth century the Dordrecht guilds appointed Eight Good Men (*Goede Lieden van Achten*) who took part in the annual elections of the burgomasters. In Hoorn, Enkhuizen and Medemblik the burghers participated in the election of the magistrats, though they had no say in the composition of the town council, from whose ranks they were required to choose the magistrates.

The cities in the coastal provinces enjoyed less formal independence than the cities in Overijssel. Though municipal claims to sovereignty were out of the question in the coastal provinces, foreign observers did not find their superior airs much different from the imperious attitude of the high-and-mighty cities of Overijssel. In his *Observations upon the United Provinces* of 1673, the well-informed English ambassador Sir William Temple blithely refers to the 'Soveraign Authority of the City of Amsterdam',[4] adding that even though formal sovereignty resided in the provincial States, 'to discover the nature of their Government from the first springs and motions, it must be taken yet into smaller pieces, by which it will appear that each of these provinces is likewise composed of many little states or Cities, which have several marks of soveraign power within themselves'.[5] The truth of Temple's words is borne out by the apportionment of votes in the provincial States, where the cities were treated as equals, regardless of their size, as though they were sovereign. This meant that, in the province of Holland, Amsterdam with its 200,000 inhabitants had just as much (or as little) influence, formally speaking, as Schoonhoven with its population of 3,000. In deliberations, of course, Amsterdam's opinion carried more weight. A seeming contradiction to their formal equality, however, was the fact that motions could be passed in the States of Holland by a majority vote, whereas if the cities really had been sovereign, unanimity would have been called for. In Overijssel, on the other hand, a unanimous vote was required for certain decisions,

---

[4] Sir William Temple, *Observations upon the United Provinces of the Netherlands*, edited by Sir George Clark (Oxford: Clarendon Press, 1972), p. 53.
[5] Ibid., p. 52.

which indeed suggests a greater degree of independence than the cities of Holland enjoyed.

The independence of the cities created serious problems in the provincial States, problems that were exacerbated by the need for the cities to work together with the *ridderschappen*, the colleges of nobles. This was easy in Holland, where the nobility had only one vote, as did each of the eighteen cities that were allowed to send delegations to the States of Holland. The *ridderschap* had the prerogative of voicing the first reaction to proposals and casting the first vote. Owing to the prestige of individual noblemen, the *ridderschap* exerted an influence out of all proportion to its numbers. There was no doubt, however, that the cities represented the dominant force in the States of Holland. This was not necessarily the case in Zeeland, where the *ridderschap* was represented by the First Noble (*Eerste Edele*), a position firmly held since 1559 by the House of Orange, who also held sway in the cities of Veere and Vlissingen, each with a vote in the States assembly, which meant that the Orangists controlled three of the seven votes in the States of Zeeland. Even so, the cities were in the majority.

In Utrecht, Overijssel, Gelderland and Groningen, a delicate balance was maintained between the nobility and the cities. In Groningen's provincial assembly, the States Assembly of City and Countryside (Statenvergadering van Stad en Lande), only two votes were cast: one by the city of Groningen – also on behalf of Oldambt and Westerwolde, which were under its jurisdiction – and the other by the landowners in the districts of Hunsingo, Fivelingo and Westerkwartier. Groningen had no *ridderschap*, and the landed gentry (*jonkers*), untitled nobles (*hoofdelingen*) and landowners who held a free and unencumbered title to their land (*eigenerfden*) were allowed to attend assemblies of the provincial States on behalf of the Ommelands (Groningen's rural districts), provided they owned a minimum amount of land. Sometimes more than 200 of them showed up, though more often than not only a few made the effort. Since the city of Groningen usually sent its entire delegation, consisting of four burgomasters and twelve councillors, it nearly always had the upper hand.

Gelderland did not have a proper States assembly. The old duchy of Gelderland was divided into four quarters, three of which were in the Republic: Nijmegen, Arnhem and the county of Zutphen. Most of the fourth quarter, Roermond, remained in Habsburg hands. Each quarter had its own States assembly, in which the cities and the *ridderschap* were entitled to one vote each.

In the States of Utrecht the *ridderschap* had one vote and the cities of Utrecht, Amersfoort, Rhenen, Wijk bij Duurstede and Montfoort had one vote among them. The five Utrecht collegiate churches, representing the clergy, also had one vote. After the Reformation, the property of the collegiate churches was expropriated, but the churches continued to elect a representative, which sparked off a fierce struggle between the nobles and the city of Utrecht, both of whom demanded the right to this tie-breaking vote in the States assembly. In 1618 it was decided that the *ridderschap* and the city of Utrecht would exercise joint control over the churches' vote.

Only in Friesland did the rural districts hold sway. The States of Friesland voted on resolutions at separate assemblies held in each of the four quarters, the eleven cities combining to form one quarter. The delegates to the assemblies of the other three quarters were elected by the more than 10,000 farmsteaders and householders in the countryside who were eligible to vote. Thus the component parts of the provincial States were the same everywhere, consisting always of representatives of town and country, though governmental organisation differed from province to province.

This diversity was scarcely compensated for by a central government. The Republic had no national legislation and no national judicial system. Lawbreakers could be sentenced to banishment from a province or even a city, thus depositing the problem on the neighbours' doorstep. Taxation was the responsibility of the provinces, whereas most other administrative matters were strictly a local affair. The States General, Council of State and other government institutions had no choice but to confine themselves largely to foreign policy. Domestic policy was the prerogative of the provinces.

Despite the fact that the Generality scarcely formed a threat to provincial autonomy, the question of sovereignty was hotly disputed, largely because domestic and foreign policy were inextricably entwined. In the international sphere, there were certain interests to defend, but their priority was contested. Such issues had caused a deep rift between the cities of Holland during the peace negotiations with Spain. The strong arm of foreign policy – the army and the naval fleet – was costing a great deal of money. Who should finance them, and what power accrued to those who assumed this responsibility? In 1650 the States of Holland, acting on its own authority, disbanded troops which it considered unnecessary after the Peace of Münster. This decision prompted William II, supported by the other provinces, to attempt to occupy Amsterdam. The question of where authority in the Republic ultimately resided was therefore of vital importance, but the answer depended on one's perspective. In 1652, Johan de Witt, shortly before being appointed to the post of Grand Pensionary, voiced the opinion that 'these provinces do not together constitute *a republic*, but each province *alone* is a *sovereign republic*, and as such these United Provinces should not bear the name of *republic* (in the singular) but rather the name of *federated* or *united republics*, in the plural'.[6] Those 'republics' were of course the independent provinces. In official documents the provinces referred to one another as *bondgenoten* – 'allies' or 'confederates' – as though they were independent states, bound to one another only by virtue of the wording of a treaty. Although De Witt thought this an important matter of principle, one must bear in mind that in 1587 one of his predecessors, Oldenbarnevelt, had unhesitatingly defended the sovereignty of the States General above that of the provinces. De Witt's opinion must therefore be considered within the context of the traumas of 1618 and 1650, when two stadholders, claiming unlimited federal powers, had brushed aside Holland's independence in the interest of the general good.

As a matter of fact, everything did revolve around the province of Holland, though this was not immediately apparent on paper. In the States General each province had one vote only, even though the city of Leiden had just as many inhabitants as the whole province of Overijssel and Amsterdam more than the provinces of Utrecht and Groningen combined. Moreover, important matters could be settled only by a unanimous vote, making it impossible for one province to impose its will on another. To emphasise their equality, the chairmanship rotated among all the provinces, so there was a different 'president' every week. In the Council of State, which was responsible for preparing policy for the States General and implementing the decisions taken, the apportionment of seats did somewhat more justice to the balance of power between the provinces – and to their contribution to the Generality's coffers – by giving Holland three seats and Gelderland, Zeeland and Friesland two each, while the remaining provinces had only one each. In 1674, Gelderland lost one of its two seats to Groningen. However, considering that Holland contributed nearly 60 per cent of the Generality's revenues, even this apportionment went a long way towards preserving the formal equality of the provinces.

In practice Holland was at a great advantage, not least because the government institutions were located in The Hague. Their establishment there had encountered resistance, however. In the Middle Ages, The Hague had developed into the most important administrative centre in the county of Holland. Although its enormous growth had been due to the presence of governing bodies, it had never been granted municipal rights. In fact, The Hague was, as the Florentine writer Lodovico

[6] Guido de Bruin, *Geheimhouding en verraad: de geheimhouding van staatszaken ten tijde van de Republiek (1600–1750)* (The Hague: Sdu Uitgevers, 1991), p. 129.

Guicciardini wrote in 1567, 'the loveliest, richest, and largest unwalled village in all of Europe'.[7] Unfortunately, little was left of its beauty several decades later. Because The Hague was a village and not a city, it could not be defended. In 1528, nearly half a century before Guicciardini saw it, The Hague had almost been plundered by Maarten van Rossum (see p. 15), but its inhabitants had prevented this disaster by paying a huge ransom. During the Revolt, The Hague proved easy prey to both the rebel armies and the Spanish, and consequently suffered much devastation. In the 1570s, when it was time to decide where the government of the rebellious provinces should be established, The Hague was no longer the first choice by any means. The city of Delft – where William of Orange frequently stayed and the States of Holland now assembled – seemed a likely candidate. In a meeting of the States which took place on 29 May 1575, the Delft delegates proposed razing The Hague to the ground in an attempt to improve their city's chances. The other cities were not inclined to give Delft the advantage it was manoeuvring for, and so 'to prevent all jealousy among the cities',[8] they resolved to keep The Hague as the seat of government. In 1577 the Court of Holland and the Auditing Office of Holland returned to The Hague, followed the next year by the States of Holland and in 1585 by the States General and the Council of State.

Thus the governing bodies of the Generality were housed directly opposite the assembly hall of the States of Holland, whose delegates could drop in on meetings of the States General any time they liked. The delegates from the other provinces had to travel much further to attend these meetings, and because most of the provinces did not maintain guesthouses in The Hague, their delegates were forced to lodge with private individuals or in public boarding-houses, where they were exposed to pressure from Holland's many special interest groups. Moreover, the delegates from outside Holland were often called away to attend elections or other important events in their home provinces, which were, after all, their seat of power. It is hardly surprising, therefore, that delegates to the States General often thought of such a post as a form of banishment, despite its lucrative nature. In 1624, for example, when the Amsterdam regents wanted to rid themselves of their pensionary Adriaen Pauw, they found him a position in one of the government offices in The Hague.

---

[7] Paul Knevel, *Het Haagse bureau: zeventiende-eeuwse ambtenaren tussen staatsbelang en eigenbelang* (Amsterdam: Prometheus/Bert Bakker, 2001), p. 29.
[8] Ibid., p. 30.

Holland could throw its weight around in many ways, but its financial might supplied the most persuasive arguments. Some provinces – especially those along the Republic's borders – received much more from the Generality's coffers than they gave in return, and so could not afford to offend Holland. This dependence was a great source of frustration. In 1652, Friesland was furious that the country had plunged into war with the English 'at the desire of the province of Holland, without waiting for our consent or that of any other province'.[9] In 1666, Zeeland was incensed at the appointment of 'delegates at sea' – representatives of the States General who kept an eye on the activities of the fleet – which had taken place when 'the province of Holland deemed it timely to insist upon it',[10] whereas Holland took a long time to deliberate upon the proposals of the other provinces. The Hollanders, moreover, did not hesitate to send representatives of the States General on surprise visits to other provinces whenever they were suspected of shirking their obligations to the Generality.

The bureaucracy at The Hague could scarcely compensate for the dissension among the provinces. Until 1585, The Hague had been a centre of regional government only, but the Revolt against Spain had unexpectedly turned it into a centre of national government as well. It had no experience of government at this level, however, for the administrative centre of the Low Countries had hitherto been Brussels. It was only natural, therefore, that the Republic's first high-ranking officials were recruited in Brabant: Cornelis Aerssens, who became *griffier* of the States General in 1584; Christiaan Huygens, secretary to the Council of State, who was appointed in the same year; and Joris de Bie, the treasurer-general, a post more or less equivalent to Minister of Finance. It was not until around 1620 that Northern Netherlanders finally gained the upper hand.

The bureaucracy at The Hague was sadly lacking in both experience and revenue. The regents who wielded power in the Republic thought, probably rightly so, that enlarging the bureaucracy at The Hague would curtail their own influence. Civil servants, who were therefore kept to a minimum, were usually forced to pay their staff out of their own pockets. To defray these expenses, they often earned money in other ways. A popular sideline was copying documents, a widespread practice undertaken at the behest of foreign envoys, who found this an easy way to gain knowledge of even the most secret resolutions of the States General. Many officials asked for 'unofficial' payment for all kinds of services.

⁹ Ibid., p. 149.   ¹⁰ Ibid., p. 123.

No one went so far in this respect as Cornelis Musch, who as *griffier* of the States General from 1628 to 1650 held one of the most important positions in the Republic. Musch was thoroughly corrupt. He once invited the wife of an office-seeker to his house and asked her what was missing in his reception room. She gave it some thought, said he needed a tablecloth and some cushions for the chairs, and was promptly invited to remedy the situation. Although she presented Musch with five silk tablecloths and various cushions – worth more than the annual salary of the position her husband was seeking – Musch gave the job to someone else, presumably a person of greater generosity. Musch's reputation was of course well known in his lifetime, but his protectors included the stadholders Frederik Hendrik and William II, as well as the Grand Pensionary Jacob Cats, whose seventeen-year-old daughter had married the forty-four-year-old Musch just a few days after Cats's appointment. Many believed that it was not a coincidence that Musch died, possibly by his own hand, only five weeks after the death of his lofty patron William II. The weakness of the Republic's national institutions is borne out by the fact that Musch was left for years to indulge in such corrupt practices.

The Generality bodies were especially powerful in the so-called Generality Lands: States Flanders (now Zeeuws-Vlaanderen), States Brabant (now North-Brabant), and States Limburg (now part of the present-day province of Limburg). These lands on the outskirts of the Republic were also the most marginal from a political point of view. The part of Brabant that fell to the Republic when 's-Hertogenbosch was captured in 1629 regularly petitioned – unsuccessfully – to be admitted as the eighth province to the States General. Holland in particular protested vehemently against the addition of another voice to the choir of the anti-Holland coalition. Moreover, the House of Orange had a great deal of influence in Brabant, and it also seemed better not to strengthen its position. Ultimately, all of the provinces benefited from having a military buffer zone in the South to cushion the blows of Spanish and later French aggression. 'The Hague' could do what it liked in the Generality Lands, whereas in the 'sovereign' provinces of the North it could barely gain a foothold.

The Generality was thus forced to concentrate on foreign policy and defence and to deal with their financial ramifications, but this was no easy matter in a republic whose provinces were so often at odds. In Groningen, the provincial States were plagued by differences of opinion between the regents of the city of Groningen and the landed gentry of the Ommelands. In the States of Overijssel, voting procedures were disputed throughout the seventeenth century, causing almost every decision to be challenged. In Holland, the cities' conflicting economic interests regularly prevented action from being taken on important issues. The provincial delegates to the States General had only limited power. Whenever discussions took an unexpected turn, they were forced to return to their respective provinces to consult with their 'constituencies'. To alleviate this problem, committeeism became rife in The Hague during the rule of the stadholder Frederik Hendrik. As soon as an issue threatened to become complicated, it was referred to a committee, and if none existed, one was established for that very purpose. Committee work meant that compromises could be reached behind closed doors, which gave the prince and a select group of confidants the opportunity to dominate decision-making in The Hague.

It often seemed as though the stadholder was the only one who could cope with the complications of the Republic's political system. In the face of all dissension, he alone represented unity, appearing to be the only one willing to place the interest of the Generality above the special interests of the cities and the provinces. This is only part of the picture, however, because the stadholdership was also prone to particularism. Under Habsburg rule the stadholder had been a mere deputy, holding the reins of government in the sovereign's place, which is, after all, the literal meaning of 'stadholder'. William of Orange had been acting in this capacity on behalf of Philip II, king of Spain but also sovereign ruler of Holland, Zeeland and Utrecht. It was the stadholder's duty, for example, to appoint the cities' magistrates. In 1581, at the time of the Revolt, when Philip II was repudiated as sovereign, the stadholderate should in fact have been abolished, since from a constitutional viewpoint it no longer had grounds for existence. Instead, the stadholder's position was reinforced.

From the very beginning William of Orange had been one of the most prominent opponents of Habsburg rule in Brussels. He had emerged as a political leader whose charisma had helped the rebels through the most difficult years of the Revolt. He had also invested a great deal of his personal fortune in the struggle against Spain, and the States of Holland had rallied round him, renewing his commission as stadholder in 1581. In 1584, when the initial confusion surrounding the unexpected death of William of Orange had subsided, his son Maurits was appointed stadholder in Holland and Zeeland, but in Utrecht the States first appointed, in 1584, the field marshal Joost de Soete, lord of Villers, and in the following year Adolf van Meurs, count of Nieuwenaar, who already held the office of stadholder in Gelderland and Overijssel. Friesland and the Groningen Ommelands immediately appointed Willem Lodewijk, count of Nassau-Dillenburg and the son of the eldest brother of William of Orange, which made him Maurits's first cousin. Willem

Figure 20   Allegory of the inauguration of Ernst Casimir of Nassau (1573–1642) as stadholder of Friesland in 1620. In the seventeenth century, Friesland had its own stadholder, who came from the House of Nassau-Dietz. Ernst Casimir's father was a younger brother of William of Orange, which made him a first cousin of both Maurits and Frederik Hendrik (Printroom, Rijksmuseum fm 1423 b).

Lodewijk was subsequently recognised as stadholder by the county of Drenthe in 1593 and by the city of Groningen in 1595.

From this time on, the three northern provinces almost always chose their stadholders from the House of Nassau-Dietz, basing their right to do so on the fact that the stadholderate was a provincial and not a national institution. The ultimate failure of the rebellious provinces to find a foreign ruler willing to assume the position of sovereign prompted the provincial States to take the task upon themselves. This made the stadholders formally subordinate to the various States assemblies, though oddly enough, the stadholders continued to appoint, on behalf of the provincial States, the selfsame magistrates to whom they themselves were then answerable, since by virtue of their office the magistrates were also delegates to the provincial States assembly. Indeed, the entanglement of power was so murky and mystifying that even contemporaries asked themselves who was actually in charge. The situation became even more obscure in 1674, when the provinces of Gelderland, Overijssel and Utrecht, which had been temporarily suspended as members of the Union, were readmitted only after accepting new *Regeringsreglementen*, regulations giving the stadholders far-reaching political powers. The shaky constitutional position of the stadholderate did not automatically invest the Oranges with a greater share of authority. They had other advantages, however, not least the prestige and reputation of the House of Orange. Indeed, the glorious role they had played in the early history of the Republic was celebrated throughout the seventeenth century. In 1660, for example, when Amalia of Solms – the widow of Frederik Hendrik – visited Amsterdam, a procession of sixteen floats paraded past her, seven of which portrayed the United Provinces and seven others the princes of Nassau and Orange. A print made of the procession bore the following inscription next to the image of William I:

> This is he whom madman's bullet causes us to mourn
> He who dies for freedom's sake in death will be reborn.[11]

Their princely status, even though it derived from the insignificant principality of Orange – a tiny but sovereign state in France – lent the family prestige in the Republic and abroad. In 1637 their status rose a notch when the French court declared that Frederik Hendrik would henceforth be addressed as 'Son Altesse', His Highness, an improvement on his former title of 'Eminence'. The Oranges did everything possible to boost their standing. In Maurits's day, their household had included some 100 servants and courtiers, but under Frederik Hendrik their number swelled to 250. These grander living arrangements had been made possible by the settlement of William of Orange's estate, finally completed around 1610, and the death in 1618 of his eldest son, Philip William, who had been detained in Brussels for decades as a hostage of Spain. Thus Maurits finally gained possession of the principality of Orange, which yielded a substantial annual income. After his death in 1625, the estate devolved upon his half-brother Frederik Hendrik.

Perhaps just as important as this greater financial leeway was the example set by Frederik V, the Elector Palatine, and his wife Elizabeth Stuart, the only daughter of the English king James I, who arrived at The Hague in the spring of 1621. Frederik and Elizabeth had married in 1613 and subsequently established a splendid court at Heidelberg. In 1619, Frederik was chosen king by the Protestants of Bohemia, where he ruled

---

[11] Peter te Boekhorst, Peter Burke and Willem Frijhoff (eds), *Cultuur en maatschappij in Nederland 1500–1850. Een historisch-antropologisch perspectief* (Heerlen: Boom/Open universiteit, 1992), p. 50.

for only one winter before being driven out of Prague by the triumphant armies of the Catholic Habsburgs. Having thus acquired the epithet of Winter King, Frederik arrived in Arnhem with a retinue of 200 on 8 April 1621. From Arnhem the couple travelled to Rotterdam and on to The Hague, where they set up a court that rivalled their host's in magnificence. Although their example was wasted on Maurits, it made a deep impression on Frederik Hendrik, who in his younger years had spent eighteen months in Paris and thus had first-hand experience of a truly regal household.

Frederik Hendrik lost no time in launching an ambitious programme of building, which led to improvements on the Old Court (Oude Hof) at Noordeinde and the stadholder's quarters, conveniently located in the Binnenhof, next to the assembly rooms and offices of both the province of Holland and the Generality. New construction was also undertaken on a large scale, giving rise to the palaces of Honselaarsdijk (near Naaldwijk), Ter Nieuburg (near Rijswijk), and the Huis ten Bosch (just outside The Hague), now the residence of the Dutch royal family. Frederik Hendrik and his wife, Amalia of Solms, who had been a lady-in-waiting at the court of the Winter King, emerged as patrons of the arts. Among the most important products of their patronage were the paintings commissioned to decorate the Orange Hall (Oranjezaal) of the Huis ten Bosch – the summer residence under construction when the stadholder died – with portrayals of the life and deeds of Frederik Hendrik. The Oranges could not of course compete with the large royal families of Europe, even though they liked to think of themselves as their equals. In fact they were more on a par with the medium-sized princely families of Germany from whose ranks they were descended. However, their position as informal heads of state of the Dutch Republic – a position not always understood elsewhere – made the Oranges attractive partners for princely houses seeking to forge strategic alliances. Thus in 1641, when England was on the brink of civil war, Charles I was prepared to marry his eldest daughter, Mary, who was only nine years old at the time, to the eldest son of Frederik Hendrik, the fourteen-year-old William II. In 1677 their son William III married – also for political reasons – his first cousin Mary Stuart. The female descendants of the House of Orange had to be satisfied with less distinguished partners, however. Frederik Hendrik's eldest daughter Louise Henriette married the Elector of Brandenburg, and her sister Albertine Agnes became the wife of the Frisian stadholder Willem Frederik.

Their prestige enabled the Orange stadholders to exercise considerable authority. In addition, their status as nobles allowed them to influence the political institutions of the Republic through official channels. As

Figure 21   Frederik Hendrik takes the oath in the States of Holland in September 1625. This act emphasised that the stadholder was a servant of of provincial States, even though the reverse sometimes seemed to be true (Atlas van Stolk 1933:1).

members of Holland's *ridderschap*, they had access to assemblies of the States of Holland and also functioned as president of the Court of Holland, another relic from the period before the Revolt. In Zeeland, one of them was designated as the First Noble and bore the titles 'marquis of Veere' and 'lord of Vlissingen'. Nevertheless, the Oranges were not sovereign rulers in the Republic – far from it. Their position was described succinctly in 1638 by François van Aerssen, a confidant of the stadholder, for the benefit of the French ambassador:

The Prince of Orange is in a position different from the King [of France], who has only to express his wishes. Here he [the prince] needs money to put his ideas into effect, and this goes slowly; it can be obtained only from the provinces, which are tired and most of them exhausted, by a persuasive demonstration of some major advantage ... In the midst of such a diversity of interests and opinions, His Highness [the prince] must come to a decision and then, gradually clearing the way, bring matters to where they should be. This cannot be done without much controversy and loss of time.[12]

If this did not suffice, the stadholder had other means at his disposal. Not long after his appointment as stadholder of Holland and Zeeland, Maurits became captain-general (supreme commander of the army)

---

[12] Herbert H. Rowen, *The Princes of Orange: The Stadholders in the Dutch Republic* (Cambridge: Cambridge University Press, 1988), p. 67.

and shortly thereafter admiral-general (supreme commander of the navy). Frederik Hendrik first made his name as a general and only afterwards as a politician. William II's desire to follow in the footsteps of Frederik Hendrik led him to attempt a military occupation of Amsterdam. William III became captain-general in 1672 and assumed the stadholder-ship of Holland and Zeeland only a few months later. The role of the Oranges cannot be understood without taking into account their military duties, for it was precisely in the military sphere that the Republic's problems of coordination were most acute. As military leaders the Orange stadholders succeeded beyond all expectation, proving them-selves – with the exception of William II, who died young and did not have the opportunity to show his mettle – to be military strategists of considerable stature. The great importance of their role as military leaders was reflected by the places assigned to the mourners in Frederik Hendrik's funeral procession, in which the military officers preceded the politicians. It was inevitable, however, that their military role would have political repercussions, for the army was dominated by extensive networks of patronage. Numerous noble and middle-class families gave their loyalty to the Orange cause in exchange for commissions as officers in the army of the States General, an armed force that interfered directly in politics when the need arose. In 1618, Maurits used this army to reshuffle the local councils in cities where the Remonstrants had gained control. William II used the army in 1650 in an attempt to force a decision in his conflict with the regents of Holland. And, in 1672, William III found that the office of stadholder practically fell into his lap when the country was thrown into a military crisis.

It can hardly be a coincidence that two out of three violent confronta-tions ended in the death of the Advocate of Holland (later called the Grand Pensionary), the Oranges' great adversary. The position of the Grand Pensionary was every bit as ambiguous as that of the stadholder. As adviser to the States of Holland, he drew up their proposals and formulated the conclusions of their deliberations. He also acted as adviser to Holland's *ridderschap*, who took precedence over the cities in debates. But even though he was only a public servant – whose term of office was theoretically limited to five years – the office of Grand Pensionary grew into one of the most powerful in the land. As a member of and spokesman for Holland's delegation to the States General, he was ideally positioned to put his stamp on national policy. He corresponded privately – indeed, more or less in secret – with the Republic's foreign envoys, which made him better informed than anyone about the state of the nation. He thus acted informally as prime minister and foreign secretary combined, this being especially important at times when the Oranges were either unwilling

(Maurits in the first decade of the seventeenth century) or unable (William III during the years of his minority) to become involved in national politics. During the first decades of the Republic, when Maurits was concerned mainly with military strategy, Oldenbarnevelt grew into a prominent political figure, a role assumed by Johan de Witt in the third quarter of the seventeenth century.

De Witt was the descendant of a regent family; his father served as town councillor and burgomaster of the city of Dordrecht. De Witt's appointment as Grand Pensionary was due not only to his exceptional qualities but also to the hand of fate. In 1652 the Grand Pensionary Adriaen Pauw fell ill during his term of office. At the time, De Witt was pensionary of Dordrecht, which as the oldest city in Holland was called upon to supply a temporary replacement for Pauw. They sent De Witt, who received his official appointment the following year. De Witt was unable to wield power in the same way as the stadholders: he could not afford to build palaces, for example, nor were his ancestors so illustrious that he radiated a natural authority. De Witt's source of authority was necessarily based on networks and grounded in stability. The cornerstone of his power base was the province of Holland, where he needed to be sure of the continuing support of the nobility and the city of Dordrecht. Dordrecht, as the oldest city in Holland, was the first to speak (after the nobility) in the States assemblies. Amsterdam's vote was also of great importance.

On 16 February 1655, De Witt married Wendela Bicker, thus entering the upper echelons of Amsterdam society. The fact that no less a person than Joost van den Vondel, the semi-official town poet of Amsterdam, wrote a love poem on the occasion of their marriage underscores the public nature of these matrimonial bonds. In other cities De Witt cultivated friendly relations with burgomasters and pensionaries by means of very extensive correspondence, in which he passed on interesting information and never failed to give the impression that he valued the opinion of his correspondents. Similarly, De Witt made certain he had allies in the other provinces whom he could trust to keep him informed of the prevailing political currents and to defend his policies. Important informants during his early years as Grand Pensionary included Justus de Huybert and Adriaan Veth in Zeeland, the Overijssel nobleman Arend Jurien van Haersolte and the Nijmegen secretary Johan Singendonck. At the same time, De Witt made sure that the other provinces at least got the impression that they were not just dancing to Holland's piping. In 1656, when the conflict between Sweden and Denmark began to assume alarming proportions, it was mainly Holland's trading interests that were threatened, and it was also the Hollanders who bore the cost of fitting out a naval expedition. Nevertheless, De Witt regularly consulted the other provinces. He spent weeks, for example, as a member of the committee sent to mollify Zeeland, which thought that greater efforts should be made to protect its threatened colonies in the Americas.

Both the stadholder and the Grand Pensionary attempted, each in his own way, to keep dissension within reasonable bounds. Since there was no clear legal basis for a display of power on either side, their arsenals were limited to polite persuasion and concrete threats. The situation remained precarious, not unlike trying to maintain one's footing in a storm-tossed ship on the open sea. It was a wonder, in fact, that their attempts to steady the ship succeeded as often as they did. Authority in the Republic was not only fragmented but often hotly contested. This resulted in compromises which in turn led to another round of conflicts. At the top, however, there was no room for compromise. After the Twelve Years' Truce, either the stadholder or the Grand Pensionary was at the helm. It was no longer possible for them to steer the ship of state together.

12   A dissonant chorus

On New Year's Day 1610 a delegation representing Alkmaar's civic militias arrived in The Hague to lodge a complaint with the States of Holland about the behaviour of their town councillors. The day before, the civic militia had seized control of Alkmaar, with militiamen occupying the town hall, the gates and the walls of the city. Their reign, which was to last for nearly eight weeks, was the provisional outcome of a conflict that had started two years earlier. Like so many cities in the Republic at that time, Alkmaar was torn by religious strife. In the Reformed congregation in Alkmaar, the rigidly orthodox clergyman Cornelis Hillenius confronted the very free-thinking Adolfus Venator. Venator was the favourite of the congregation, but Hillenius had the support of the majority in the town council, which after the election of 1608 had dismissed the entire magistrates court – something that, at least in the opinion of the dissatisfied militiamen, 'had not occurred in living memory'[1] – and replaced them with adherents of the orthodox movement. The following year saw the implementation of even more extreme measures. During the election of magistrates in December 1609, the stadholder – at the insistence of Hillenius, but in violation of the local ordinance – appointed six men who had only recently acquired citizenship in Alkmaar. The new appointments resulted in some fathers and sons serving at the same time, which was also in breach of the ordinance. The orthodox group triumphed and jeered at their latitudinarian neighbours, who were chased out of the church by children who pelted them with snowballs and stones.

On 30 December the militiamen, who were overwhelmingly latitudinarian, took action to reverse this state of affairs. They demanded that their officers submit on their behalf a petition protesting the illegal appointments. The burgomasters refused to consider the petition, however, and even labelled it a 'villainous pasquil', a low-down lampoon. This enraged the militiamen, who set out at once to occupy strategic points in the city.

---

[1] P. Knevel, 'Onrust onder de schutters: de politieke invloed van de Hollandse schutterijen in de eerste helft van de zeventiende eeuw', *Holland* 20 (1988), p. 167.

They further resolved to send a delegation to The Hague, where they could count on the support of the pensionary. However, the followers of Hillenius, who had also sent a delegation, pointed out the danger of the precedent set by such a coup. The States of Holland immediately sent a commission to Alkmaar to reconcile the parties. At the end of February, by which time it had become apparent that reconciliation was impossible, the States commissioners expelled the entire orthodox group from the town council. On 4 March the newly appointed council decided to reimburse the militiamen for the expenses incurred during the riots and to fine those who had refused to do service in the same period.

Such fierce confrontations were certainly no exception in these years. In Utrecht, too, the militiamen staged a coup in January 1610, demanding that in future the town council be elected annually by the burghers, as had been customary before 1528. During the years of the Revolt it had been the leaders of the civic militias, the burgher-captains, who had assumed a leading role. Now, in 1610, the town councillors resigned immediately, declaring their disinclination to hold office against the wishes of the people. Like the disturbance in Alkmaar, the revolt in Utrecht was inspired only in part by religion. In Utrecht the rebels even formed a huge alliance of orthodox Calvinists and Catholics who for various reasons had grievances against the latitudinarian town council. Some of these grievances were economic in nature, as evidenced by their list of demands: 'that the well-being of the aforementioned commendable city of Utrecht and the prosperity of its good citizens shall be the highest law and privilege'.[2] This was immediately followed by the demand that within six months an end be put to all 'urban industries' in the countryside, which Utrecht's tradesmen and artisans saw as a threat to their livelihood. The States General attempted to mediate in the dispute, but it was not until Frederik Hendrik appeared before the town gates on 31 March with forty companies of soldiers that the rebellious militiamen surrendered. On 5 December they tried again to seize power but were quickly subdued.

Not only had the Republic been born of conflict, but in the period preceding the Revolt the Northern Netherlands had been torn by civil war and strife, fighting simultaneously against the Habsburgs and in defence of their own local and regional independence. The Revolt gave rise to a form of government that gave a wide berth to those local and regional wishes, but this had not caused domestic differences to disappear. On the contrary, throughout the seventeenth century the provinces, cities and villages were regularly at loggerheads. The nature of these clashes and the

---

[2] D. A. Felix, *Het oproer te Utrecht in 1610* (Utrecht: Oosthoek, 1919), p. ix.

attempts to resolve them reveal a great deal about the character of seventeenth-century Dutch society.

Conflicts such as those in Alkmaar and Utrecht were able to get out of hand because internal differences had caused a temporary weakening of authority. The regents were then confronted with an opposition that drew strength from a variety of sources, starting with the institutions common to civic life itself – such as civic militias, guilds and the guilds' colleges of representatives (*gemeensliedencolleges*) – which provided a means of channelling dissatisfaction. The Alkmaar militiamen, for example, were easily mobilised, since they kept the night watch and were therefore always ready for action. In their *doelen* the militiamen also had an assembly hall at their disposal. The fact that they were armed also lent weight to the seriousness of their demands. Some cities had municipal bodies designed to facilitate citizen participation. When these were lacking, as in Utrecht in 1610, the people tended to rally round old traditions in an effort to demonstrate that they had once had a right to a voice in the government and that restoring that right was a matter of some urgency. In other cases the regents were reminded that, since their authority derived from the fact that they represented the citizenry, they were obliged to listen to what those citizens had to say.

In making themselves heard, the burghers used the power of the written word. No revolt was complete without a pamphlet in which grievances were set forth and justified. Such pamphlets – varying from short explanations to extremely detailed and well-documented treatises – could be purchased for a couple of stuivers. In Alkmaar the disturbances were defended in writing by the town council's *Corte ende Waerachtige Verantwoordinghe* (Short and Truthful Account) of the measures taken in the spring against the Reverend Hillenius. Those who found all 144 pages hard going could read a greatly abridged version that appeared a short while later, titled *De Secte der Hillisten tegen de Magistraat van Alckmaar* (The Sect of the Hillists against the Magistracy of Alkmaar). It was a song consisting of ten couplets, sung to the tune of 'Ick ben een arm Pellegrim' (I'm a poor pilgrim). Such pamphlets were published by booksellers acting as publishers, of which each city had a few and some cities a great many. In Deventer, six booksellers were active between 1626 and 1650, in Gouda seven, in Middelburg nineteen and in Leeuwarden seventeen: an average of one for every 1,500 inhabitants. In Leiden, a university town, the proportion was twice and in Amsterdam three times as high. The percentage of people who could read and write was very high in the Dutch Republic. In Amsterdam in 1700, three-quarters of the men and half of the women who had their marriage banns published were able to sign the document themselves: an extremely high percentage compared with other countries. The high rate of literacy was largely due to widespread urbanisation as well as to the edifying presence of the Protestant Church, which insisted that sermons be delivered and the Bible read in the vernacular. Since the Republic scored high in both urbanisation and Protestantisation, it is hardly surprising that the ability to read and write was nowhere more prevalent than in the Northern Netherlands. Booksellers were thus supplied with a faithful clientele, and it was for this literate public that they published their pamphlets. Such broadsides often addressed the man in the street by placing him in a recognisable situation. One very popular form was the 'Schuitpraatje' (Barge Talk), in which a sailor, a farmer and a burgher, travelling together in a passenger barge, discussed a timely issue. Editions of a thousand or more were no exception.

The demands formulated in these pamphlets found their way into official petitions requesting that measures be taken to redress a certain wrong or grievance. Petitioning was a very common and generally accepted form of communication between the authorities and the people under their jurisdiction. Petitions were submitted by individuals as well as societies, but the authorities naturally gave special attention to those supported by a group of people, whether a neighbourhood, a guild or a company of militiamen. Such petitions were generally drawn up by a legal expert who was able to word them properly, and were then signed by the members of the organisation in question. Much local legislation came about in this way. When the authorities endorsed the terms of the petition – which often happened after extensive talks between the burgomasters and the signatories – the proposals outlined in the petition were adopted in a resolution formally passed by the town council. Guilds and civic militias, who were familiar with this practice, anticipated it by wording their proposals in such a way as to facilitate immediate implementation.

Though petitions sometimes succeeded because their proposals were reasonable, they often met with approval because the authorities were too weak to reject them. In the seventeenth century, local governments were dependent for their protection on a small number of municipal soldiers, but more particularly on the militiamen. When the civic militias turned against the authorities – as happened in the above-mentioned revolts in Alkmaar and Utrecht, as well as in Amsterdam's Undertakers' Riot of 1696 (see pp. 153–5) – it was very difficult to ignore their requests. Those opposing the authorities could also take advantage of the discord present in most municipal governments. Indeed, the Alkmaar militiamen succeeded in getting their way because the States of Holland were so divided that they could not act against what most regents undoubtedly saw as the undesirable interference of the citizenry in matters that concerned only the

Figure 22   Print of the 'Manly Militia of Amsterdam', produced after the Undertakers' Riot in Amsterdam in 1696. The city had a commemorative medal struck (depicted at the bottom), which was presented to the militiamen as a token of gratitude for their efforts in quelling the riot. The militiamen's cooperation was not a foregone conclusion in this case, for at first they had supported the rioters. The lack of a professional police force sometimes made it difficult to enforce authority in the cities of the Dutch Republic (Amsterdam Municipal Archives d 24220).

authorities. During the Twelve Years' Truce, such dissension was wide-spread and deep-rooted. The elites were torn by religious strife and incompatible political views. The Truce temporarily eased the pressure exerted by the war against Spain, which meant that latent differences of opinion about power relations within the government, as well as the question of whether (and under what conditions) the temporary truce should be transformed into a permanent peace, were able to take root and proliferate. Such dissension led in Holland, for instance, to an alternative assembly, beginning in July 1617, at which the eight Arminian cities met to prepare their position in the States assembly. From early 1618 they even submitted collective proposals for discussion.

In 1618, Maurits's forced replacement of local government officials before normal election time brought about some semblance of unity, but it took only a few years for old differences to raise their ugly heads. The peace talks with Spain, which took place from 1629 to 1646, led to a series of clashes between the provinces and also between the cities of Holland. The States of Zeeland continued to make demands – regarding such issues as religious tolerance and the colonies in America – which were considered unrealistic elsewhere. Discord between the cities of Holland, however, prevented them from presenting a unified front. Two groups of cities were ranged against each other: the peace faction, consisting of Amsterdam, Rotterdam and Dordrecht, supported by Alkmaar and Delft; and those advocating a continuation of the war, with Leiden and Haarlem at the forefront, followed by Gouda, Den Briel and Gorcum. The other cities either vacillated between the two or took up a middle position. The divergent standpoints were often based on fundamental differences. Cities judged the results of the peace negotiations primarily from the vantage point of local interests. Leiden and Haarlem, for instance, were afraid that a peace treaty would open up the Republic's borders to the textile products of their competitors in the Southern Netherlands. By contrast, Amsterdam, Rotterdam and Dordrecht hoped that their trading interests would profit from the cessation of hostilities. Such differences of opinion were not confined to international relations; on the contrary, they exerted an equally great influence on regional politics.

The large-scale creation of polders in the first half of the seventeenth century had rearranged the entire economic landscape of West-Friesland and the North Quarter of Holland. Most of the cities in this region were greatly dependent on trade with the surrounding countryside, which was a source of both commodities and customers. Where farmers went to market was therefore a question of vital importance to a city's economy. The answer was largely determined by the waterways, the course of which was drastically altered by empoldering. This led to continual skirmishes, which at times brought the area to the brink of civil war. One hotbed of hostility was the area between Hoorn and Alkmaar, where there had been violent disagreement during the second decade of the seventeenth century about the hydraulic consequences of creating the Beemster polder, which would impair Hoorn's connection with Amsterdam. The halfway solutions promised by the contractors were never implemented. Their laxness was applauded by Alkmaar, whose hinterland had been greatly extended to the detriment of Hoorn. In 1625 the empoldering of the Heerhugowaard again threatened to put Hoorn at a disadvantage. Alkmaar set to work with great enthusiasm, and Hoorn could not even lodge a complaint at The Hague because the States of Holland were in recess. The arbitration commission sent to Alkmaar achieved nothing, and Hoorn's town council subsequently resolved to take more drastic action, in preparation for which it supplied four companies of militiamen with gunpowder and bullets. Feverish diplomatic negotiations at The Hague ended with a temporary ruling in Alkmaar's favour: land reclamation was allowed to continue, pending the States' decision. Not surprisingly, Hoorn found this unacceptable. On Thursday, 4 September the militiamen were mobilised, and at dusk they set off towards Alkmaar, together with a troop of diggers, to destroy the excavations. Their advance did not go unnoticed, and the villagers made their opinion clearly known, jeering at the Hoorn militiamen, 'You brutes, so you don't dare to come by day?'[3] The damage done to the excavations made it impossible to complete the project before winter.

In 1634 Hoorn, acting on its own initiative, announced its plan to build a lock in the Beemster ring canal near Avenhorn, a facility that had been thought necessary for years. Alkmaar, opposing the project, mobilised the support of the town councillors of Edam and Purmerend, who were afraid that fishing vessels would prefer the route via Hoorn. The village authorities in the area also rallied round Alkmaar. Hoorn, unperturbed, began construction of the lock. By the summer the dispute had escalated to the extent that Hoorn felt compelled to have the building works guarded by municipal soldiers armed with muskets. Only when it became clear that the opponents of the project were determined to stand their ground did Hoorn agree to call a halt to the project. On 15 July the town council decided to sell the bricks that had been bought to build the lock.

The Hoorn town council was not the only government body that was prepared to settle domestic conflicts with violence. Maurits's *coup d'état* had created a precedent, and in 1650 the stadholder's court seized upon this very example to justify its secret plan to take control of the city of Amsterdam. The underlying cause was the reduction in the number of troops after the Peace of Münster. Amsterdam thought that troop reductions were not proceeding fast enough, whereas the young William II saw them as sapping the strength of the army and, by extension, his authority. On 4 June the States of Holland took it upon itself to disband some of the troops on its payroll. Immediately after passing this resolution the States recessed for Whitsuntide, but William – with the Frisian stadholder Willem Frederik and the Council of State in tow – managed the next morning to persuade the States General to send a delegation to tour the cities of Holland, which was the customary way of bringing recalcitrant cities into line.

---

[3] Diederik Aten, *'Als het gewelt comt ...': politiek en economie in Holland benoorden het IJ 1500–1800* (Hilversum: Verloren, 1995), p. 100.

Only a handful of the prince's confidants, including Willem Frederik, were privy to his plan to bring Amsterdam to its knees, by force if need be. The attack was to take place on Saturday, 30 July. The night before, troops had been brought in the greatest secrecy via the Veluwe in the direction of Abcoude, where they were to begin their march on Amsterdam. Having lost their way in the fog in the vicinity of Hilversum, they were passed by a horseman carrying the post from Hamburg to Amsterdam. Since even the commander had not been apprised of the purpose of the mission, the messenger was allowed to pass unhindered. Upon his arrival in Amsterdam, he immediately told everyone what he had seen. Having been warned, the burgomasters gave the orders to close the city gates. Meanwhile, in The Hague, William II had six of his most prominent opponents in the States of Holland arrested and taken to Loevestein Castle. Willem Frederik, who was directing the manoeuvres outside Amsterdam, soon saw that their surprise attack had failed. He could do nothing but have the letter with their demands, which he had planned to hand over triumphantly at the town hall, sent by messenger to the burgomasters. The situation rankled, and both parties were inclined to compromise, but the attempted coup had inflicted deep wounds. When William II died in November of that same year, a note was found in an Amsterdam collection bag with the words 'no better news has reached my ears in eighty years'.[4]

The events of 1650 completely changed the relationship between Holland and the stadholder. William II's arrest of his opponents and his march on Amsterdam had heightened the tension between the city's regents and his court. The stadholder had shown that he was prepared to trample the constitution underfoot, mainly in order to increase his power. His death several months later offered a completely unexpected opportunity to discuss fundamental issues surrounding the role and desirability of the stadholderate within the Republic, a subject that had scarcely been broached before this time. Moreover, in the first half of the seventeenth century there were few who felt the need to provide formal justification for the opportunistic, improvised structure which the Dutch government in fact was. At Leiden University, a tempered monarchy was held up to the students as the best form of government by professors who conveniently ignored the reality of the situation in the Netherlands.

Although the discussion flared up immediately in 1650, the Act of Exclusion passed in 1654 added fuel to the fire. Upon the disclosure of this secret appendix to the Treaty of Westminster, which excluded the

---

[4] Luuc Kooijmans, *Liefde in opdracht: Het hofleven van Willem Frederik van Nassau* (Amsterdam, Bert Bakker, 2000), p. 157.

Oranges from the stadholdership in Holland, the States of Holland felt obliged to justify its action, both to the other provinces and to the general public. This was done by means of De Witt's *Deductie, ofte declaratie van de Staten van Hollandt ende West-Vrieslandt: behelsende een waerachtich ende grondich bericht van de fondamenten der regieringe vande vrye Vereenichde Nederlanden* (Deduction, or declaration, of the States of Holland and West-Friesland containing a true and thorough account of the foundations of the government of the free, united Netherlands), which was officially sanctioned on 25 July 1654 in the States assembly. The States of Holland put forth two lines of reasoning. In the first place, it stated at great length that the Republic was a league of sovereign provinces and that Holland was therefore perfectly free to make agreements with third parties regarding the stadholdership, which was after all a provincial office. Secondly, more fundamental questions were posed about the role of the Oranges in the government of the Republic. Was it fitting for a republic to make certain crucial offices hereditary instead of simply appointing the best candidate? Everyone knew 'that all the republics in the whole world, without exception, which ever lapsed into such ... habits, yea, even most of those which only entrusted the power of its armed forces to one person ... have thereby been subjugated and reduced to a monarchical state'.[5] To drive home his point, De Witt gently reminded his readers of William II's attack on Amsterdam.

The republicanism of De Witt and the States of Holland revolved entirely around the sovereignty of the States assemblies. Others, unimpeded by the limits of official responsibility, went much further. The most interesting republican theorists were the De la Court brothers, second-generation immigrants from the Southern Netherlands and successful textile manufacturers in Leiden. After the death in 1660 of Johan de la Court – seen by some historians as the more subtle and innovative of the two – Pieter published, later in the decade, various works which contained a number of radical elaborations on the republican idea. Pieter de la Court drew the most extreme conclusions from the particularistic principles laid down in the Union of Utrecht – the protection of local and regional privileges – and from the notion that Holland was a republic unto itself. He wanted to limit Holland's military dependence on the other provinces by erecting a line of defence from the Zuider Zee to the River Lek, as a result of which only Holland, Zeeland and the western part of the province of Utrecht would be enclosed. The other provinces would

---

[5] *Deductie, ofte declaratie van de Staten van Hollandt ende West-Vrieslandt: behelsende een waerachtich ende grondich bericht van de fondamenten der regieringe vande vrye Vereenichde Nederlanden*, etc. (The Hague, 1654) (Knuttel 7547), p. 48.

have to fend for themselves. De la Court had no use for the stadholderate, which he denounced as a corruption of the republican idea and a threat to freedom. That freedom, he thought, was best served by the governors of the cities, who were Holland's strength, provided they were held accountable to the citizenry. In a discourse based largely on the work of Machiavelli, De la Court argued that an armed citizenry constituted the best defence, both against dangers from without – since they fought on their own turf to defend their own property – and against corruption from within.

Both De Witt's *Deductie* and the work of De la Court unleashed a storm of protest, yet the Orange camp could offer only a relatively weak defence against this very principled line of reasoning. Nowhere did the Orangists claim that the monarchical form of government was preferable; on the contrary, they repeatedly stressed that sovereignty resided in the provincial States and possibly the Generality. At most they suggested that the stadholderate constituted part of that sovereignty, alongside other institutions. The Oranges' claims were founded not so much on principle as on pragmatism and the lessons of history. The Republic could not exist without an 'eminent head' who took charge of its institutions, especially the army. The truth of this claim, in the Orangists' view, had been shown by historical example and confirmed by events since the outbreak of the Revolt. The leadership of William of Orange, as well as the military successes of Maurits and Frederik Hendrik, were abundant proof of this. Indeed, the Republic was greatly indebted to the House of Orange-Nassau. For all these reasons, they argued, the young William III ought to have the same dignities conferred on him – either now or when he came of age – which his father, grandfather and great-grandfather had so gloriously held.

These controversies, though they prompted much reflection and produced a host of cogent arguments – of which there was never a shortage in these years – were no less the subject of a very real political struggle. As early as the summer of 1652, when war broke out with England, the citizens of Kampen and Zwolle (through the offices of their *gezworen gemeenten*) strongly suggested that the help of the prince of Orange be enlisted. At the time he was only one year old, and any tasks assigned to him would have had to be carried out by the Frisian stadholder Willem Frederik. The following year, militiamen in Zwolle paraded around with orange ribbons on their muskets, knowing that the city governors would approve of this gesture. Things became more complicated when the discussion surrounding the role of the Oranges became entangled with a political question in Overijssel, where the provincial States were hopelessly divided over the appointment of a new bailiff in Twente. Kampen and Zwolle, backed by the nobles of Salland and Vollenhove, supported one candidate, Deventer and Twente the other. Tension mounted so much that Deventer and Twente began to hold their own States assembly in Deventer. The plot thickened when the other group, who of course considered themselves the true States assembly, appointed Willem Frederik as deputy stadholder in the hope that he would bring Deventer to its knees. By this time the situation had become so volatile that the States General had begun to discuss the possibility of all-out civil war in Overijssel. Fortunately it never came to that: in 1657 the opposing parties, at Holland's insistence, finally arrived at a compromise.

Around 1660 other provinces made substantial concessions to the Orange cause. Friesland and Groningen, for example, had decided to appoint William III as captain-general of their province and Zeeland had also held out the prospect of appointing him stadholder as soon as he reached the age of eighteen. The States of Utrecht were under great pressure to make a similar gesture, and the regents of the city, fearing a revolt, requested help from the States of Holland. Holland was more than willing to send troops to assist its 'especially good friends, neighbours and allies'.[6] Amsterdam assured the Utrechters that it was keeping another 360 men at the ready, just in case.

A decade later, in 1672, this number of troops was no longer enough to save the province of Utrecht. On 18 June, Utrecht fell to the French without offering any appreciable resistance. In Holland and Zeeland, which were not yet in French hands, the invasion led to scenes of tumult in and around the town halls. On 15 June the States of Holland had decided to enter into negotiations with both France and England. Here and there riots had already broken out. In Leiden, Monnickendam and Rotterdam civic militiamen had seized the keys to the city gates. In various cities in Zeeland the regents, anticipating trouble, entered into deliberations with the citizenry. In Middelburg, for instance, representatives of the citizens' electoral college, the clergy, the merchants and the guilds were invited to a meeting to exchange ideas with the town councillors about the negotiations with France. In Goes and Vlissingen similar gatherings took place. On 9 July, Zeeland appointed William III stadholder; Holland had already taken this step five days earlier.

The regents' sudden interest in public opinion had obviously been prompted by their fears that an opposing party of burghers, in conjunction with the stadholder's court, could make life very difficult for them. On 7 July in Middelburg the citizenry, very much aware of this, had submitted

[6] Tino Perlot, *De Staten van Utrecht en Willem III. De houding van de Staten van Utrecht tegenover Willem III tijdens het eerste stadhouderloze tijdperk (1650–1672)* (Utrecht: Vakgroep Geschiedenis der Universiteit Utrecht, 2000), p. 46.

the first in a long series of petitions placing various demands on the public authorities. Soon consultation alone was no longer considered sufficient. The guilds of Middelburg assembled on 2 August and demanded the resignation of seven regents, and the States of Zeeland did not dare to object. In Zierikzee the civic militias forced the town council to step down at the beginning of November, and eight new members were appointed. In Vlissingen a movement supported by guild brothers and sailors also resulted in the replacement of a number of town councillors, while in Veere the citizenry demanded the filling of three vacancies in the town council. In Goes the regents and the burghers were finally reconciled in January 1673, a gesture that cost a number of town councillors their seats.

The events of 1672, which led to even more turmoil in Holland than in Zeeland, go a long way towards clarifying the power relations in the Republic. The small size of the cities and the lack of a system of repression meant that the regents were subject to pressure from both within (the burghers) and without (the stadholder's court). To safeguard their interests, the regents were forced into an alliance with one of the two parties, generally preferring the citizenry. By consulting the citizens in the cities which had institutions for this purpose – such as the *gezworen gemeenten* in the cities of Overijssel – or else by lending a willing ear to the petitions of guild brothers, fellow neighbours or militiamen, the regents attempted to underline the legitimacy and representativeness of their authority. That the burgher opposition continued to demand more consultation suggests that they thought the regents should be taking more interest in their ideas. In particular, the nepotism in regents' circles, which became more and more widespread in the course of the seventeenth century, could not help but give burghers the impression that the regents were primarily promoting their own interests. In certain circumstances, however, the regents were forced to align themselves with the stadholder's court. In the landward provinces this was the only way to counterbalance Holland's supremacy. In Holland itself, alliances with the Oranges were forged in times of crisis, as in 1672, or when there was discord among the cities, as in 1650 and 1618. At such times the Orange party could usually profit by cultivating supporters in the town councils, where regents with Orangist sympathies were willing – either for ideological reasons or because of internal conflicts in the municipal government, often arising from the bestowing of offices – to side with the stadholder and his court.

In 1672 a combination of military crisis and civil revolt caused a potentially formidable degree of power to be thrown into William III's lap. In Gelderland, Overijssel and Utrecht he was able to consolidate that potential with the help of the *Regeringsreglementen* introduced there after the departure of the French. These regulations gave the stadholder wide-ranging powers to appoint government officials. Whether they liked it or not, the regent families in these provinces were dependent on the benevolence of the Orange court. In Holland, William attempted, with the help of confidential advisers in the various town councils, to achieve the same thing informally – a strategy that was most successful in places where the regents could not agree among themselves. However, his attempts to rule without the approval of Amsterdam, where the republican faction had been back in power since 1677, foundered in the long run, and in 1684 the stadholder decided that in future he would do best to attune his policies to the wishes of that powerful city.

Perhaps in doing so he was adhering to the spirit rather than the letter of the Union of Utrecht, which had attempted as early as 1579 to reconcile the discrepancy between the ambition of the cities and provinces to govern themselves and their need to cooperate to preserve their local freedoms, since everyone agreed that those freedoms were at the very heart of the Republic's identity. Any clashes that occurred were nearly always the result of disputes over the ramifications of this basic principle, not the principle itself. There was no real way to ease the friction between local independence and national cooperation, and therefore both parties continued to drag themselves from one compromise to the next. That it was possible, time and again, to arrive at such compromises was due to the shifting but ever present balance of power. Holland, of course, was the most important province, but the other six combined were able to hold their own against Holland in the States General. Within the province of Holland the shifting coalitions between cities prevented Amsterdam, for example, from lording it over the rest. In the end, it was always easier, in the Republic, to prevent things from happening than to make them happen. That the cities and provinces nevertheless continued to toe the line was due to the ready availability of money – the best lubricant for a political machine – and especially to the sobering effect that waging war always exerts on the decision-making process. When that pressure was lacking, as during the Twelve Years' Truce and after 1650, compromise suddenly proved to be much more difficult.

Part IV

An urban society

13   Religious pluralism

When he was a student, Aernt van Buchell disliked Protestants, though perhaps that was only to be expected from the son of a canon of the Utrecht chapter of St Pieter. After all, Aernt could reasonably hope that his family connections – his wealthy uncle, Hubert van Buchell, was also a canon – would ensure him a bright future in the church. It is hardly surprising, therefore, that when William of Orange was shot in 1584, Aernt – who heard the news while studying in Douai – wrote in his diary that the prince had 'died the death that he deserved'.[1] Shortly afterwards he wrote about the religious situation in his country: 'In confusion they run in so many different directions that truth can hardly be distinguished from falsehood, nor Christ from the devil, and nothing in the world is certain.'[2] Clearly, he blamed the Protestants for this state of affairs.

Van Buchell was not the only one who was worried about the spiritual health of the Low Countries. There was in fact every reason for concern, certainly in Utrecht, which had traditionally been an ecclesiastical centre whose bishop held sway over the numerous clerical exemptions and possessions – which embodied the economic power the church wielded in both city and province – and over the many church buildings, which were a solid expression of the spiritual authority of the church. The bishop, moreover, was invested with political authority and was therefore also the worldly ruler of the province of Utrecht. Although this political function had been surrendered to Emperor Charles V in 1528, the church had nevertheless remained a powerful institution in Utrecht. This made it an obvious target of opposition: the burghers, in particular, seriously objected to the constitutional change brought about by Charles in 1528 when he barred the guilds from politics. The guilds' loss of power gave rise to political objections which, in Utrecht, were to become increasingly enmeshed in religious conflicts.

---

[1] Judith Pollmann, *Religious Choice in the Dutch Republic: The Reformation of Arnoldus Buchelius (1565–1641)* (Manchester: Manchester University Press, 1999), p. 50.
[2] Ibid., p. 52.

The Reformation had got off to a slow start in Utrecht, where there were few adherents to Luther's ideas among the clergy. The church in Utrecht was not very zealous in its persecution of 'heretics', and perhaps this moderate attitude explains why in 1566 – when the Iconoclastic Fury was at its height – there was not a great deal of Protestant preaching outside the city gates, as there was in other cities. Indeed, by February 1567, when Spanish troops were billeted in Utrecht, it seemed as though Spain's authority had been completely restored. As in many places, though, it was the misbehaviour of the Spanish troops that spurred the people to action. In November 1576 the States of Utrecht decided to join the side of the Revolt in the hope of regaining their old rights, privileges and freedoms. Only after this transition did the first signs of organised Calvinism appear in Utrecht. In 1578, Werner Helmichius – a native of Utrecht who had studied in Geneva, the cradle of Calvinism – was called to the pulpit as the first Protestant minister in Utrecht.

In Utrecht's Church of St Jacob a local reformation had been taking place at more or less the same time. The priest Hubert Duifhuis had been moving slowly but surely towards reform, and had adapted his masses accordingly. In June 1578 Duifhuis broke with the Catholic Church once and for all; by the autumn a new liturgy was ready and Duifhuis began calling his church a Reformed church. This sequence of events was not unusual, for a great many of his colleagues had set similar developments in motion. Duifhuis enjoyed the support of the majority of the local elite, who were charmed by the relatively open nature of his congregation, where no church discipline was enforced and participation in the Lord's Supper was open to all who felt they had a clear conscience. In Helmichius's Calvinist church, which was much stricter, Duifhuis and his flock were condemned as a disorderly bunch who violated Calvin's precepts. Helmichius could speak from a position of authority, of course, as the first minister to be officially inducted into a Utrecht parish. Thus Utrecht started out with not one but two Reformed churches.

Duifhuis was certainly not the only priest to defect from the Catholic to the Protestant camp. In the 1590s, Aernt van Buchell did the same. Things had not been going well for him since the completion of his studies. His career prospects were less promising than expected, and when he finally succeeded in finding a position as secretary to the noble-man Walraven van Brederode, a man of no small consequence, the post appeared not to suit him at all. Unlucky in love, Van Buchell also felt lost in the tumultuous religious climate of the day. He probably distanced himself from the Catholic Church before joining another religious community. Sinking into a deep crisis of faith, he even attempted suicide. Not long afterwards, however, he met his future wife, Claesje van Voorst, and they were married on 8 May 1593 in the Geertekerk. Van Buchell's wife came from a distinguished family and was so well-to-do that Van Buchell could afford to devote much of his time to the historical research of which he was so fond. It was Van Buchell's wife who introduced him to Duifhuis's Jacobskerk.

Duifhuis died in 1581, but his work went on. His church was still supported by the majority of the elite, who had meanwhile become Protestant. In Utrecht the elite included the landed aristocracy, most of whom had a house in town, as well as the traditional town-dwelling elite consisting of regent families, rentiers and government officials. They viewed the Jacobskerk as a church whose ecumenical attitude was perfectly suited to bridging the religious differences in the city, and hoped that one day it would become a place of worship for all Utrechters. In their eyes, the membership of their church ought to coincide with the entire body of citizens. By contrast, the local Calvinists, led by Helmichius, were mostly tradesmen and artisans – traditionally the political opponents of the elite. They had vivid memories of the times when their guilds had held sway in the city. Many immigrants also felt drawn to Calvinism, whose adherents viewed themselves as the rightful heirs to Calvin and considered orthodoxy and order essential to the church. The community, in their eyes, was primarily the religious community. Though the Calvinists also thought that their ranks should ideally include all Utrechters, they were not prepared to make any concessions to this end. Unwilling to relax their standards and make their church more accessible to a broader public, they were forced to accept that the religious community and the civic community were not necessarily one and the same.

For approximately thirty years, the chasm between the libertines (as those attending the Jacobskerk were called) and the Calvinists – a split which was, on the face of it, a religious rift, though one with unmistakable social and political overtones – was the cause of much of Utrecht's political and religious turmoil. At first William of Orange tried to establish a political balance between the parties, but after his death in 1584, Utrecht again found itself in both the religious and military front lines, which reinforced the influence of the strongly anti-Spanish Calvinists. Moreover, the Utrecht civic militias were overwhelmingly Calvinist. Their cause was strengthened by the new stadholder, Adolf van Meurs, count of Nieuwenaar, who promptly appointed a distinctly Calvinist town council, which included four officers of the civic militia. In 1586 the arrival of the earl of Leicester – a staunch supporter of the Calvinists – as governor-general of the United Provinces put the libertines in an even tighter spot. A process was now set in motion which Duifhuis had foreseen as the ultimate goal of the Calvinists, namely a complete reformation of the entire community according to their lights. His Jacobskerk was closed and Catholics were harassed: the first step was to make Catholics ineligible for poor relief. In Utrecht the worst fears of Holland's regents were confirmed: the establishment of a central authority, in the person of Leicester, cooperating with the middle classes to put the local elites under ideological and political restraint.

In 1588, however, the departure and subsequent death of Leicester was followed by an about-face. The authorities – not wishing to see a recurrence of the previous situation, in which two so-called Reformed churches competed for supremacy – tried to change the Calvinists' attitude so that the followers of Duifhuis could also feel at home in their midst. All the clergymen were either dismissed or left voluntarily for callings elsewhere. Their successors were told by the authorities that admission to the Lord's Supper would have to be less restrictive than currently prescribed by the Reformed Church. The result was that many Utrecht Calvinists started to attend church in IJsselstein. The authorities then suggested various compromises, but it was not until 1605 that a solution was found which was acceptable to all parties.

In all of these developments, Aernt van Buchell, who had meanwhile started calling himself Arnoldus Buchelius, had been forced to take a stand. He had first joined the ranks of the libertines, as had many of his peers. Unlike some of his fellow townsmen, however, he did not oppose the shift towards orthodoxy. Since his crisis of faith, Buchelius placed the greatest value on order and abhorred religious discord. Finding the doctrinal vagueness of the libertines less and less appealing, he finally chose Calvinism. In his writings, he was very critical of the libertines, whom he later equated with atheists. But even though he came across in writing as an insufferable Calvinist and did his best as a member of the church council to promote the orthodox cause, at the same time he kept up warm and friendly relations with Catholics and Remonstrants. He supported his fellow scholar Caspar Barlaeus, a well-known Remonstrant, through thick and thin in the years when Barlaeus could not get work because of his religious beliefs. Buchelius's sister had remained Catholic, but that in no way hindered their family life. For years he also kept up a very friendly correspondence with Johannes de Wit, a Catholic who died in Rome in 1622. The famous Utrecht painter Abraham Bloemaert was a good friend of Buchelius, in spite of the fact that Bloemaert was a Catholic and much of his work had a distinctly Catholic character. Bloemaert exported a lot of work to the Catholic city of 's-Hertogenbosch – before 1629, at least, when the Spanish were driven out and its Catholic governors were replaced by Protestants. He had both Catholic and Reformed pupils in his studio, and his circle of family and friends also included a number of faiths. Although Bloemaert's wife was Catholic, her brother was a member of the town council and therefore must have been at least outwardly Reformed. Clearly, despite their marked differences, Utrecht's various religions had learned to coexist.

This outcome had not been obvious from the start. The Reformed had emerged in the early stages of the Revolt as a very militant minority, and the resistance they had faced was formidable. The Catholic authorities stopped at nothing in their attempts to eradicate Reformed ideas in the Netherlands. Thousands of people were condemned for their heretical views, and hundreds had been executed since 1521, when holding divergent religious beliefs became a crime punishable by death. In 1569, Friesland made church attendance on Sunday compulsory, 'to combat false teachings and heresies'.[3] In Groningen, monthly confession was still obligatory in 1588, and anyone who neglected to attend mass risked incurring a huge fine. In this way the Catholic Church attempted to preserve itself with the help of the secular authorities, and the political authorities in turn shored up their power with the help of the divine word. Nevertheless, many people joined so-called heretical movements, which existed in all shapes and sizes, though it was the Mennonites who boasted the largest following and, until the beginning of the Revolt, dominated the otherwise extremely varied Protestant landscape. The Mennonites did even more to contribute to this variety through numerous internal disputes, which resulted in various splinter groups. By the time the Iconoclastic Fury broke out in 1566, the Mennonites had in fact been seriously weakened by the discord within their own ranks.

During the tumultuous years of the Revolt, the Calvinists profited from both their tightly knit organisation and the support of the Revolt's leaders. Their own militant attitude also stood them in good stead. In 1577 Haarlem had joined the rebels on condition that public practice of the Catholic faith be allowed to continue. At the first political changeover, many vacancies in the hitherto Catholic town council were filled by the Reformed, even though at the time they represented only a small minority in the city. The Reformed were given their own place of worship – the Bakenesserkerk – and nothing was done to hinder their building up a church organisation of their own. Despite such tolerance, on 20 May 1578, the feast of Corpus Christi, soldiers ran amok around the Great or St Bavo's Church during the celebration of mass, even though the

---

[3] W. Bergsma, *Tussen Gideonsbende en publieke kerk: een studie over het gereformeerd protestantisme in Friesland, 1580–1650* (Leeuwarden/Hilversum: Verloren, 1999), p. 153.

procession usually held on that day had been cancelled. Around midday, armed soldiers forced their way into the church. In the ensuing scuffle, a number of people were wounded and one priest was stabbed to death. The perpetrators were condemned, but the church remained closed and the Catholics had to make do with several monastery and convent churches. In September there was a renewed attack on St Bavo's, but the authorities did not intervene. The guilds were ordered to remove their decorations from the church and to dismantle the guild altars. In 1580 there were still seventy-four priests active in the city, and the Protestant riots continued. It was also in this year that the States of Utrecht passed a resolution banning celebration of the mass, and in March 1581 the States of Holland followed suit. In 1581 the city of Haarlem discontinued its policy of religious coexistence; henceforth only the Reformed faith was allowed to be practised in public. The willingness of the authorities to support the cause of the Reformed Church was of decisive importance in this conflict.

Nonetheless, the Reformed had their own problems. While Catholics and Lutherans ruled a number of countries, the Calvinists did not really hold sway anywhere but Geneva. Their church organisation – built 'from the ground up', with the local community as the core – meant that while the Calvinist Church was cut out for the kind of guerrilla warfare required during the great religious conflicts of the second half of the sixteenth century, it was much less suited to the formation of a national church. The precise doctrine of the Reformed Church was disputed, and there were no church institutions with sufficient authority to make unequivocal and generally accepted pronouncements. The disputes between the Arminians and the Gomarists during the Revolt were the last (and most violent) eruption of a whole series of conflicts over Reformed dogma. Moreover, the Reformed Church did not have enough qualified people to disseminate its teachings. Until Leiden University was founded in 1575, there was no place in the Low Countries which provided theological training to Protestant ministers. Even long after the university's founding, people with a very tenuous grasp of doctrine were still preaching in the countryside. One such person was Albert Jansz – active successively in Ooltgensplaat, Ouderkerk, Leerdam and, from 1595, in Tuyll – who was found to be extremely ignorant in the teachings of the church, 'even regarding points which school children are expected to know'.[4]

Perhaps the greatest handicap was that while the political authorities endorsed the Reformed Church, they did not in fact give it their full

---

[4] A. Th. van Deursen, *Bavianen en slijkgeuzen. Kerk en kerkvolk ten tijde van Maurits en Oldenbarnevelt* (Assen: Van Gorcum, 1974), p. 9.

Figure 23   The Synod of Dordrecht (1618–19) settled the disputes that divided the Dutch Reformed Church by expelling the Arminians, who subsequently formed their own church, the Remonstrant Brotherhood. The Synod of Dordrecht, the last national church assembly to take place during the period of the Republic, was also attended by observers from the Calvinist churches of other countries. The various depictions made of this synod testify to its importance (Atlas van Stolk 1365).

support. On the one hand, they saw the 'true faith' as an important means of strengthening the Revolt and viewed Catholics as potential traitors and therefore a threat to national security. They also thought, as did the authorities everywhere in Europe, that political authority should be sustained by religious authority. On the other hand, they did not want Reformed preachers telling them what to do. In Friesland the secular authorities were closely involved in the appointment of ministers. The church council was allowed to submit a list of candidates, who were approved or rejected by the magistrates. The congregation then made its choice from the list of approved candidates. In the cities of Friesland, the municipal authorities had the last word in the allocation of church funds. In Holland, clergymen were paid from a provincial fund, established in Delft in 1578, which was administered by the States of Holland. A preacher who criticised the regents' policies consciously ran the risk of offending his employer.

Again, the Union of Utrecht managed with astonishing precision to effect what was in fact a compromise. Article 13 stated that the provinces 'shall establish such general or special regulations in this matter as they shall find good and most fitting for the repose and welfare of the provinces, cities, and individual Members thereof, and the preservation of the property and rights of each individual, whether churchman or layman, and no other Province shall be permitted to interfere or make difficulties'.[5] The article went on to say, however, that 'each person shall remain free in his religion and that no one shall be investigated or persecuted because of his religion'.[6] In other words, the political authorities in each province should regulate church organisation, taking into consideration public order and well-being without sacrificing freedom of religious thought.

Thus there arose the concept, unique in all of Europe, of the Reformed Church as the 'public church', a model introduced – with small modifications – in all seven provinces and the Generality Lands. Under this regime people were free to believe what they liked, but only the Reformed were allowed to express their beliefs openly through public worship. Indeed, all available church buildings in the Republic were put at their disposal. The other faiths were not allowed to congregate according to the letter of the law, and if they did, they risked punishment in the form of a fine, confiscation of property, imprisonment or banishment.

The Reformed Church itself viewed this situation with ambivalence. On the one hand, it required the secular authorities – in their role as 'Christian authorities' – to support the cause of the 'true Reformed faith', since the Reformed viewed the Dutch Republic as a chosen nation, a second Israel. On the other hand, it cost the Reformed Church a great deal of effort to shed its traditional image as the church of the resistance movement. In conflicts between the moderates and the strictly orthodox within the Reformed Church itself, it was the orthodox who always gained the upper hand. This emerged from the disputes taking place during the Twelve Years' Truce, and it became apparent again in the mid-seventeenth century, when another rift occurred in the Reformed Church between the orthodox and libertine streams. At that time, too, it

---

[5] Herbert H. Rowen (ed.), *The Low Countries in Early Modern Times* (London: Macmillan, 1972), p. 73.
[6] Ibid., p. 73–4.

was the theology professors who set the ball rolling. In 1634, Gisbertus
Voetius, a preacher at Utrecht, was appointed to the recently founded
Illustrious School in that city, which acquired university status two years
later. His opposite number, Johannes Cocceius, was appointed professor
of theology at Leiden University in 1650, after having taught at Franeker
University in Friesland. The two men disagreed about the observance of
the sabbath as stipulated in the Fourth Commandment. What was actually in dispute, however, was not just keeping the Lord's Day but living a
more (or less) godly life in general. Voetius was the centre of the pietistic
movement in the church which advocated a Further Reformation. This
movement, which had a large following in Utrecht, sought to combine
inner awareness and strict discipline to lift religious practice on to a higher
plane. The followers of Cocceius were moderate in the demands they
made on the faithful and strove to make the church more accessible.
Cocceius enjoyed strong support from the regents, whereas Voetius
seems to have been popular with the average churchgoer.

The high moral standards and exemplary conduct in daily life required
by the orthodox made it impossible for the Reformed Church to grow into a
true church of the people, with whose precepts most Dutchmen could
agree. The size of the congregation reflected this exclusivity. In 1587 less
than 10 per cent of the population were confirmed members of the
Reformed Church. In the following thirty years the Reformed managed
to gain some ground, but considering that the Republic had meanwhile
become an independent state and the Reformed Church its official religion,
the growth in church membership was actually very small indeed. In 1620
in Enkhuizen, a city known for being particularly orthodox, approximately
3,000 people were members of the Reformed congregation out of a total
population of 20,000. If we include all the families of confirmed members,
nearly one-third of Enkhuizen's population belonged to the public church.
In Haarlem, perhaps 20 per cent of the inhabitants were members of the
Reformed Church in 1620, and in the city of Utrecht 10–15 per cent.

These figures do not, however, paint a complete picture of the
Reformed following. The other churches were equally small, and in
many places the various denominations together accounted for less than
50 per cent of the population. In Haarlem, 20 per cent were Reformed,
14 per cent Mennonite, 12 per cent Catholic, 1 per cent Lutheran and 1 per
cent Walloon Reformed. This is not to say, however, that the other 52 per
cent were unbelievers. Reformed services were attended by a sizeable
group of listeners, or 'followers of the Reformed religion', people who
wanted to hear the sermon but had not been confirmed, and so were neither
admitted to the Lord's Supper nor subjected to church discipline. The
exact size of this informal following is not known, but we can be fairly

certain that not all of the non-confessionalised slipped in through the Reformed Church's back door, but instead became members, or at least followers, of other denominations. This emerges, first of all, from the fact that all denominations managed to increase their membership in the course of the seventeenth century, apparently by tapping the reservoir of the 'wavering faithful'. We also know that the majority of people who actually joined a church were women. Of the 708 members of the Reformed Church in Sneek in 1629, no fewer than 450 were women, and this state of affairs had prevailed for fifty years, for in 1586 the Sneek congregation had included, in addition to eighty-six married couples and twenty-five men, fifteen married women, thirty-three widows and eighteen unmarried women. The presence of married women is especially noteworthy, because a married woman was legally subject to her husband's authority. A woman's independent membership of the Reformed Church meant that her spiritual life was no longer subject to that authority. Even so, the fact that the Amsterdam burgomaster Hooft was not a member, but his wife was, was not so unusual, as these statistics make clear. Nor should we be surprised to learn that, during the Twelve Years' Truce, just under half of Delft's town councillors were members of the Reformed Church. Many men never joined a church at all.

In the course of the seventeenth century, the following of the Reformed Church certainly grew, though the ratio of confirmed members to informal followers is not known. By 1707 the Reformed Church had plainly won the day, at least in Haarlem, where its following constituted 60 per cent of the population, although the Catholics had also experienced impressive growth, their percentage having doubled since 1620, which meant they now comprised one-quarter of the population. By contrast, the Protestant dissenters – Mennonites and Lutherans, for example – had been marginalised. The growth of the most important churches in Haarlem reflected the process of confessionalisation taking place in the seventeenth century in the whole of the Dutch Republic: religious communities strengthened their grip on the faithful, and it became increasingly difficult to remain unaffiliated. These developments were influenced in large measure by the pressure exerted by the authorities. In such cities as Utrecht, Zwolle, Deventer, Zutphen, Arnhem and Nijmegen, candidates for citizenship were required to produce 'adequate certification or proof of his or her birth, conduct and religion' before being granted the rights of citizenship.[7] In Zwolle, a resolution was passed in 1646 which explicitly stated that only those who 'profess the Reformed

---

[7] Resolution passed by the Utrecht town council on 12 June 1655, Het Utrechts Archief, Stadsarchief (City Archives) II, 121, vol. XXV.

faith' could become citizens.[8] All of the above-mentioned cities excluded Catholics from citizenship. This had far-reaching consequences, for only citizens could become members of a guild and set up as independent tradesmen or craftsmen. It often happened, therefore, that people admitted to having been born Catholic but maintained that they had since had a change of heart. In 1643, Herman Berents had acquired citizenship in Deventer after making such a declaration and had subsequently opened a smithy. Three years later, however, he was suspected of being a 'papist' anyway, and was promptly stripped of his citizenship, asked to close his business, and told to leave the city by Easter.[9] The local church councils insisted upon such measures, but the fact that they could be put into practice was mainly due to the presence in these cities of burgher representation, or – in the case of Utrecht – of vivid memories of such representation. In all the cities mentioned above, the citizenry, and indirectly the guilds, had access to political power via the *gezworen gemeente* or similar bodies (see pp. 169–70). Decisions to exclude Catholics from citizenship were always taken at the suggestion of these representative bodies. In Holland, where the regents – who in fact represented the local trading elites – held sway, such proposals had no chance of being passed.

The policy of the local authorities, though not the only factor, could thus exert an important influence on the confessional balance. The distribution of the various denominations was far from uniform. In the three northern provinces, the two eastern provinces and Zeeland, the Reformed Church prevailed. By the second half of the seventeenth century, 80–90 per cent of the population was Reformed. The South, on the other hand, was overwhelmingly Catholic. By the time States Brabant and Limburg were conquered by the armies of Frederik Hendrik, more than half a century of Counter-Reformation had left its indelible mark. Although the States General made serious attempts to get the Reformed faith to take root in these so-called Generality Lands, the church could never fully free itself from the stigma of an imported religion. Religious pluriformity, therefore, could only be taken for granted in Holland and more particularly in the cities of Holland. There were certainly Catholics elsewhere as well, but it is noteworthy that they often lived in enclaves, mostly in the regions that did not become part of the Republic until quite late, and in any case bordered on Catholic areas in Germany and the Spanish Netherlands. Here there was intense traffic to the places of pilgrimage just over the border, outside the reach of the Dutch authorities

---

[8] Zwolle Municipal Archives, AAZ 01, vol. XXI, 14 December 1646 (fol. 376).
[9] Deventer Municipal Archives, Rep. I, 4, book 14, 9 February 1646.

but within reach of the faithful. In the course of the seventeenth century, such places as Handel and Kevelaer in Upper Gelderland, where miraculous events were said to have taken place, drew huge numbers of Dutch Catholics in search of relief for both body and soul. In the Republic itself the authorities attempted to discourage pilgrimages by destroying the holy places. In 1580 the Chapel of Our Lady in Renkum in Gelderland was destroyed, the following year a chapel in Eijkenduinen near The Hague suffered the same fate, and in 1590 it was the turn of the Heilige Stede of Hasselt in Overijssel. Pilgrimages to the other side of the border could not be stopped, though the pilgrims were prevented from forming processions until they were on foreign soil. In the heart of the Republic processions had to be held indoors. A public demonstration of adherence to the old faith would have been seen by the authorities as a provocation. What they were prepared to tolerate depended very much on local conditions as well as on the personal opinions of those entrusted with enforcing the law, because gatherings of a religious nature were formally forbidden for all denominations except the Reformed. Departures from this rule were tolerated at the discretion of the authorities. In Holland toleration went very far indeed, as evidenced by the proliferation of Catholic parishes in Gouda.

The Gouda magistracy, like that of Haarlem, had at first striven for a religious freedom that would force Calvinists and Catholics into peaceful coexistence. Headstrong Calvinists had thwarted this project in both cities, and the Catholic Church had gone underground in the 1570s. In 1594 the Gouda authorities reiterated the essential passage from the Union of Utrecht, which stipulated that 'no one shall be investigated or persecuted because of his religion', but the States of Holland demanded compliance with anti-Catholic regulations.[10] Consequently, Catholic spiritual care had all but disappeared by 1600, and there was no change in this until Petrus Purmerent was sent to Gouda in 1615 by Rovenius, the vicar apostolic, to rebuild the church. Since the mass had been forbidden in 1573, much missionary zeal had been aimed at Holland, where the church organisation had to be established all over again. In the absence of the usual hierarchy, the head of the church in the Netherlands was therefore not a bishop but a vicar apostolic, or bishop *in partibus infidelium*, in the land of the infidels. The first vicar apostolic, appointed in 1592, was the charismatic Sasbout Vosmeer, a man who identified with the missionary Boniface. His successor, Philippus Rovenius, looked to Willibrord, the first bishop of Utrecht, as his role model.

---

[10] Rowen, *The Low Countries*, pp. 73–4.

This shift in role models reflected the growing confidence of the Catholic hierarchy, which was due in part to the unflagging zeal of people such as Petrus Purmerent, who upon his arrival in Gouda had to rebuild the entire church and its organisation from the ground up. During the Reformation the Catholics in the Dutch Republic had been forced to give up their places of worship. In Gouda, for example, the magnificent Sint Jan (Church of St John) had been given over to Reformed services. During the first fifteen years of his priesthood, Purmerent had to celebrate mass in an ordinary house, which was in fact not far from the Sint Jan. These gatherings were regularly disrupted by the sheriff. In 1630, Purmerent bought another property, on the River Gouwe, and two houses at the rear of this property. Two years later two more houses were acquired in the same block, thus creating an enclosed and fairly sizeable Catholic complex in which a church was built that same year. In the 1680s, when new acquisitions increased the size of the property even more, a substantial addition was made to the church.

Considering Holland's status as a mission, the local Catholic organisations were not called parishes but rather 'stations'. Purmerent directed the station of St John the Baptist. In 1634 his assistant Willem de Swaen founded a second station in Gouda, with neither Purmerent's approval nor Rome's permission. De Swaen, however, was not only a native of Gouda but also wealthy, and in the semi-clandestine circumstances of the Catholic Church, no one could stop him. The same period saw the establishment in Gouda of both a Jesuit and a Franciscan station, which meant that in 1650 Catholics in Gouda had four different places of worship. Moreover, inventories show that these churches were lavishly endowed with silver and decorated with paintings, sometimes by prominent artists. The famous Gouda painter Wouter Crabeth, grandson of the renowned designer of many of the stained-glass windows in the Sint Jan, produced various pieces which were commissioned by Petrus Purmerent, including a work in which Purmerent himself is portrayed as Bernard of Clairvaux, the French theologian and reformer who converted William of Aquitaine. In this painting, the theme of missionary work among the unbelievers is obvious, but just as striking is the fact that a number of women are depicted behind the figure of Purmerent-cum-Bernard. These were almost certainly *klopjes*: lay sisters who, instead of marrying, dedicated their lives to the church. At the end of the seventeenth century, there were at least 5,000 *klopjes* in the Republic. Sometimes they boarded with other members of the congregation, sometimes they lived together in groups. Haarlem had a famous community of *klopjes* who lived near the Bakenesserkerk; in Gouda there were quite a few living in the Hofje van Buytenwech. These lay sisters often came from well-to-do families and made significant financial contributions to the church. They looked after the priests' households and assisted them in church work. *Klopjes* were not nuns, but they wore a kind of habit that distinguished them from ordinary churchgoers.

The *klopjes* fulfilled an important function, because the rapid growth of the Catholic Church meant that it did not have the personnel necessary to carry out its work. In 1612 there were reported to be only around 500 Catholics in Gouda. By 1622, several years after the arrival of Purmerent, their numbers had increased to between 3,000 and 4,000, and by 1656 to 6,000, which meant that more than one-third of Gouda's population was Catholic. Their number reflected the impressive success of the *Missio Hollandica*. For decades Catholicism had been nearly absent from Gouda, many Catholics having been subsumed by the large group of 'undecideds'. The great majority of people who attended church in 1656 at one of the four stations were either new converts or people who had been without a church for years. Few of them were people who had clung to the Catholic Church during the Revolt. Like the Reformed Church, which in only a few decades had worked itself up from a small minority to a religious community with a broad base, the Catholic Church had succeeded in mobilising a new and sizeable following. The methods it had used to achieve this closely resembled those of the Reformed Church. Both churches strongly urged active participation in religious life, demanding of their members virtuousness and deep commitment, preferably by means of daily contemplation. A strong emphasis was placed on the role of the family and the daily reading of holy scripture. Reading and singing were an important part of religious practice for Reformed and Catholics alike. Among the Reformed, the Voetians and their Further Reformation strove for a confessional spirituality which strongly resembled a similar movement within the Catholic Church, where it was fuelled by the regular clergy and the monastic orders. Even though the Calvinists and Catholics fought each other tooth and nail, they both tackled confessionalisation in their respective churches in nearly the same way.

The success of the *Missio Hollandica* was all the more remarkable because it met with considerable opposition. From around 1600 the Catholics in Gouda had an agreement with the authorities, who promised to turn a blind eye to Catholic gatherings in return for 400 guilders a year. In 1621 the amount was raised to 600 guilders, though the sheriff frequently carried out raids anyway. This ambiguous attitude on the part of the authorities was underlined the following year, when all Catholic priests were required to present themselves at the town hall as a result of the ban on the activities of Jesuits and foreign priests. Obviously their presence was fully known and in fact tolerated. In 1623 there was a raid on the housing complex where Petrus Purmerent lived and celebrated mass. The search, which lasted three hours, yielded liturgical vestments and an altar. Upon payment of a steep fine, Purmerent was allowed to collect his things and take them home. Sometimes the Catholics offered resistance, an example being the raid carried out on the feast of the Assumption of the Virgin (15 August), when the sheriff 'was stopped by force in the square in front of the church'.[11] On other occasions, however, Catholics interrupted by the authorities in the middle of mass had to find their way home as best they could, via the many hidden exits which clandestine churches and their adjoining houses always had for this purpose.

In the second half of the seventeenth century the agreements between the Catholic stations and the authorities were formalised with increasing frequency. In exchange for an annual 'contribution', usually several hundred guilders, the authorities would look the other way, at least most of the time, since payment of this so-called recognition money did not provide any guarantees. Around 1700 the de facto recognition of Catholicism came another step closer. Worsening economic conditions and the greater demand for poor relief led more and more local governments to shift the burden of rising costs on to the religious community. In Friesland this happened around 1670, in which year the Mennonite congregations in Harlingen and Sneek set up a system of poor relief intended solely for members of their congregation. In 1685 the Leeuwarden authorities tried, initially without success, to force the Catholic community to do the same. Threats were of no use in this case, since a technically non-existent fellowship could not be compelled to do anything. In 1686, however, the Catholic poor were quite simply excluded from public charity and shortly thereafter a system of Catholic poor relief appears to have been set up. From 1698 the Catholics in Rotterdam no longer received alms from the Reformed deacons. Charitable funds for Catholics were established in Haarlem in 1715 and in Leiden in 1737. To give these funds sufficient financial leverage, they were permitted to accept bequests and to hold and administer property. This semi-official status was admittedly a roundabout route, but it did make the Catholic Church a little less illegal.

The Catholic Church was far and away the thorniest problem for the authorities, because it was the traditional bugbear of Reformed preachers and church councils. In the Netherlands, the Reformed Church had acquired its place of prominence by setting itself up as the foremost rival to the Catholic Church. Its relationship to other Protestant

---

[11] Xander van Eck, *Kunst twist en devotie: Goudse Katholieke schuilkerken 1572–1795* (Delft: Eburon, 1994), p. 126.

denominations was therefore less charged. Its attitude to the Walloon Church was the most straightforward, for the Dutch Reformed Church considered it a sister organisation – Reformed but French-speaking. Relations with the Lutherans and the Remonstrant Brotherhood were cool, but not hostile. The Mennonites – who were to be found throughout the Republic, in some places even in great numbers – had emerged in the sixteenth century as a radical denomination, but by the seventeenth century this radicalism was much less in evidence. Socially, a Mennonite remained the odd man out, because he was not allowed to bear arms. By contrast, Calvinist preachers had much more difficulty with radical splinter groups such as the Socinians – a movement that had come to the Republic from Poland – who took the Bible literally and therefore denied both the Trinity and the divinity of Christ. There were also individual preachers who proclaimed their own variations of Christianity or even their own version of Calvinism. One such person was David Guilbertus, active from 1639 among the Reformed in Rotterdam, who would 'bind himself to no order other than that which could be proved to accord with God's word'.[12] Before this time, Guilbertus had been involved in a religious dispute in Amsterdam, and the church council there was happy to be rid of him. The Rotterdam church council was just as unsuccessful in silencing him. Thus the position of the Reformed Church was also threatened from within, and not only in the large cities. In Friesland the public church harboured confessors, allies, assenters, libertines, moderates, politicos – there was no end to the nonconformist tags.

The relationship of the Reformed Church to the Jewish community was a different story altogether. Because Jews were not part of Christendom, discrimination against them was considered the most natural thing in the world. In Spain and Portugal, the Jews were systematically persecuted until they converted to Christianity. This strategy was successful inasmuch as countless Jews in these countries (Sephardim) had become completely cut off from Jewish religious traditions. Persecution also induced many Jewish merchants to flee, however, and a number of cities in Holland were extremely eager to provide refuge. At first this posed no problem to religious policy. In 1598 the Amsterdam burgomasters were almost inclined to let Jews acquire citizenship, 'trusting that they were Christians'.[13] The competition between the cities put

---

[12] Jori Zijlmans, *Vriendenkringen in de zeventiende eeuw. Verenigingsvormen van het informele culturele leven te Rotterdam* (The Hague: Sdu Uitgevers, 1999), p. 74.

[13] R. G. Fuks-Mansfeld, *De Sefardim te Amsterdam: aspecten van een joodse minderheid in een Hollandse stad*, Hollandse Studiën, vol. XXIII (Hilversum: Verloren, 1989), p. 39.

Jewish refugees in a strong position to demand favourable settlement terms. In 1604 the Alkmaar authorities offered a group of Jews complete religious freedom, the opportunity to purchase exemption from civic militia duty and the same tax liability as the other inhabitants of Alkmaar. That same year the Rotterdam authorities also made an attractive offer to Jews who wanted to settle in their city. The following year Haarlem was prepared to admit a group of Jews from Amsterdam and their relatives from Portugal, Turkey and Italy. In 1610 the Rotterdammers again decided that they would extend 'certain privileges and freedoms to merchants from the Portuguese nation, for the promotion of traffic and trade',[14] inviting them to come and live in their city. For the Jewish immigrants, too, commercial considerations weighed heavily, so it is hardly surprising that most of them chose to settle in Amsterdam.

Amsterdam also offered favourable conditions to Jewish immigrants. Although the town council could not grant them formal religious freedom, it nearly always overlooked this technicality and allowed them to practise their faith undisturbed. Jews were not required to wear outward signs of identification, such as special clothing or badges, since the Union of Utrecht permitted freedom of thought. Of great importance was the fact that in 1632 the city of Amsterdam began to allow those who openly professed the Jewish faith to acquire citizenship – subject to certain conditions, that is, because Jewish citizens were expressly forbidden to practise the guild trades, being expected to confine themselves to wholesale trade. Another restriction was that Jews could not pass their citizenship on to their children, as ordinary citizens could. Nonetheless, Jewish inhabitants of Amsterdam could enhance their social standing considerably by acquiring citizenship.

It was very telling, however, that the Jews' certificates of citizenship were drawn up in both Dutch and Portuguese. The Sephardim built up their own world in Amsterdam, with their own place of worship and their own social institutions, the foundations of which were laid in 1602 with the arrival of the first rabbi, followed in 1608 by the second. At that time the services were still held in private homes, but by 1612 the building of a synagogue had progressed to the extent that the authorities were forced to respond to complaints from the Reformed church council. Construction was halted, but when the title to the property passed into the hands of Nicolaes van Campen, a member of the town council, who subsequently rented the building to the Jewish community, the authorities considered this sufficient reason to take no further action. In 1649 a second

[14] Ibid., p. 48.

Figure 24   The Portuguese synagogue in Amsterdam, depicted on the occasion of its consecration on Friday, 2 August 1675, which marked the beginning of eight days of festivities. The attendance of almost all of Amsterdam's town councillors and other local notables was ample proof of the acceptance of the Jewish community (Romeyn de Hooghe; Printroom, Rijksmuseum fm 2574 a).

Portuguese synagogue was completed, and in 1660 and 1671 synagogues were built for the Polish and German Jewish communities. In 1614 a Jewish cemetery was established just outside the city walls in Ouderkerk – before then Jews had been buried in a cemetery 40 kilometres from Amsterdam. The Jews also offered charity to their own poor, and therefore had a system of relief similar to that found in the Christian community. Portuguese Jews lived their lives largely within this network of institutions. Because they also *chose* to live close together – the Amsterdam authorities did not force them to live in a ghetto – their group culture was highly developed.

Since the Amsterdam town council took little notice of complaints lodged by the Reformed church council – in 1619, 1620, 1623 and 1639, for example – about overtly public displays of Jewish community life, the Jewish community in Amsterdam was able to grow into one of the most important in Europe. In the mid-sixteenth century, the number of Jews in the Dutch Republic had been negligible, but by 1615 there were 164 Sephardic families living in Amsterdam, numbering altogether some 550 persons. By 1640 they had roughly doubled in number, and by 1700 the Sephardic community numbered 3,000. By this time Jews from Central and Eastern Europe (Ashkenazim) had become just as numerous. In contrast to the wealthy Portuguese Jews, the Ashkenazim were often poor peddlers or beggars.

Official recognition of the Jewish community was not long in coming, but it was understood that it was socially acceptable to associate only with the wealthy Sephardim. In 1642, Frederik Hendrik – accompanied by his son William and the English queen, Henrietta Maria – paid a visit to the Amsterdam synagogue. The queen's visit was probably not a coincidence, for by this stage in the English Civil War the royal family was badly in need of money. For William III, too, this was undoubtedly a reason to seek contact with the Jewish community. In 1690 he visited the Portuguese synagogue during an official visit to Amsterdam, staying on this occasion in the house of Mozes Curiel. The stadholder–king had every reason to show his gratitude, for his crossing to England in 1688 had been financed in large part by Francisco Lopes Suasso, a prominent member of the Portuguese Jewish community.

The success stories of many of these Jewish immigrants contributed to the Republic's reputation as a tolerant society. Those living in the seventeenth century would be surprised at such a characterisation, and not only because Jews were far less welcome outside Amsterdam. There was in fact no legal basis in the Republic for a policy of religious tolerance. Nearly everywhere, people who were not Reformed were actively hindered in the practice of their religious rites. In many places they were thwarted in society in general. There was almost no one who defended tolerance as a matter of principle. Both monarchical and civic-republican notions of government presupposed a society in which the civil and religious communities largely overlapped. Elsewhere in Europe, therefore, the authorities were striving to restore the unity that had been destroyed by the Reformation and seeking to bring about a territorial division of the various religious communities. This did not happen in the Dutch Republic. Inasmuch as tolerant practices existed, however, they were the result of pragmatic considerations. Tolerance had little chance of prevailing in regions with a low degree of urbanisation, in areas where the cities experienced little growth, and in cities where representatives of the citizenry directly influenced the authorities. As a result, nearly the whole of the insular and largely rural province of Drenthe was Reformed. However, where cities dominated the social landscape and immigration caused those cities to experience strong growth, and where, moreover, the milieu of wholesale trade held sway – all of which was true of Holland – there was more likely to be a climate of tolerance, even though it could never be taken for granted, even in Holland.

In the cities in the western Netherlands a situation developed in which the civil and religious communities no longer coincided. This had various consequences: in the first place, the secular authorities were forced to find a solution to the administrative implications of this division between church and state. The church had traditionally played an important role as a bureaucratic institution: the entire civil administration, for example, was dependent on the church. Moreover, marriages were solemnised by the church, and the legal status conferred by marriage was of immense importance for such matters as the transfer of property, the settling of estates, legal liability and so on. Until the Reformation, social policies had been financed and administered largely by religious bodies. These duties devolved upon the public church almost as a matter of course, but the problem was that not everyone belonged to that church. This problem was not solved by any principle, but again, by pragmatism, which meant that the solution varied from place to place. The deacons of the Reformed Church, responsible for the distribution of poor relief, undertook in some cities to provide alms for all poor people, regardless of their religious beliefs. This worked well in Dordrecht, but elsewhere poor relief was handled very differently. In Delft, for instance, at the beginning of the seventeenth century poor relief came to be a cooperative venture: alms were distributed jointly by the deacons, who took responsibility for the Reformed poor, and the city, who provided for those of other faiths. Marriages in the whole of the Republic were solemnised in similar fashion: the ministers of the Reformed Church could perform marriage ceremonies, but people who did not wish to be married by them could go to the town hall for a civil ceremony in the presence of the magistrates. Thus there arose an ill-defined but nonetheless fundamental division between church and state.

This division also had an ideological dimension. As a counterbalance to ecclesiastical discord, the civic authorities promoted a religiously neutral civic ideology dependent on a past that need not offend anyone. In the Amsterdam Town Hall, which was built on Dam Square in the 1650s, the entire decorative programme was based on classical antiquity – safe ground as far as the churches were concerned. The town council of Haarlem consciously promoted a cult surrounding the capture of Damiate in Egypt, an event from the time of the crusades in which Haarlemmers had played a major role by sailing through a chain blocking the entrance to the harbour. In the first half of the seventeenth century, the Haarlem civic authorities commissioned various paintings and tapestries portraying this story. Whenever Haarlem presented a stained-glass window to a friendly city, it never failed to include a reference to Damiate. Each year on 1 January, the children of Haarlem marched in the New Year's parade carrying home-made replicas of Damiate ships. By underscoring their local history, the civic authorities were confirming the autonomy of the civic community, a community which could accommodate various groups of people, thanks to their social institutions. The churches were somehow incorporated in that structure, which enhanced their reputation as an indispensable part of the civic community but at the same time reduced their status to that of private-interest groups, whose desires had necessarily to be weighed against those of a host of other parties.

14 A new approach to science and philosophy

Anthonie van Leeuwenhoek was fascinated by the invisible. With his microscopes he examined plants, offal and the remains of meals picked from his teeth. The Grand Pensionary Anthonie Heinsius, an old friend from Delft, once received a letter from Leeuwenhoek containing a detailed description of the life that had sprung up between his toes during a two-week period in which he never changed his stockings. Leeuwenhoek also examined his own excrement and semen, and was one of the first to describe the development of spermatozoa – 'little animals', as he called them – and to analyse their role in reproduction. Leeuwenhoek, the first man in history to see bacteria, had gained access to the invisible world through his superior microscopes.

Enlargement was a speciality of the Dutch. In September 1608 the Middelburg spectacle-maker Hans Lipperhey gave a demonstration to Stadholder Maurits of 'a certain instrument for seeing far', for which he had applied for a patent.[1] At the same time, Jacob Metius in Alkmaar invented the same instrument independently. The very next spring, telescopes were being sold in Italy, and the astronomer Galileo Galilei built from the Dutch example a telescope of his own, with which he studied the surface of the moon and discovered that it was full of mountains and craters. Using an improved telescope, the famous Dutch scientist Christiaan Huygens discovered in 1655 that Saturn had a satellite – later named Titan – and ascertained a year later that Saturn was surrounded by rings.

Some ten years after the appearance of the first binoculars, the first compound microscope – which combined a concave and a convex lens – was made in Middelburg by a father and son, Johan and Zacharias Jansen. Later in the century, the better microscopes were equipped with only one tiny convex lens. Such lenses were blown into the correct form and then ground and polished. Though seemingly primitive, these lenses enabled

---

[1] Klaas van Berkel, Albert van Helden and Lodewijk Palm (eds.), *A History of Science in the Netherlands: Survey, Themes and Reference* (Leiden: Brill, 1999), p. 28.

Leeuwenhoek, who built hundreds of microscopes, to obtain astonishing results. His lenses normally offered magnification of 170 times, and the best of his surviving microscopes achieved a magnification of up to 266 times. Just what sparked Leeuwenhoek's scientific curiosity is still a mystery. The son of a basket-maker, he did not seem destined for a career in science, having neither a university education nor much knowledge of Latin or other foreign languages. The following words, written in 1673, show that despite his remarkable achievements, this self-taught man was not unaware of his own shortcomings:[2]

I have several times been pressed by various gentlemen to put on paper what I have seen through my recently invented microscopes. I have constantly declined to do so, first because I have no style or pen to express my thoughts properly, secondly because I have not been brought up in languages or art, but in trade, and thirdly because I do not feel inclined to stand blame or refutation from others.

Leeuwenhoek was a draper by trade, but later in life he derived most of his income from various civic offices he held in his native Delft. Many of his official duties were probably carried out by others, however, in exchange for a share of the proceeds. This left him more time for his hobby, which quickly earned him a great reputation. In the 1670s he was inundated with questions from fellow researchers, especially those active in London, and in 1680 he was even made a Fellow of the Royal Society, an honour of which he was extremely proud. It is owing to Leeuwenhoek's correspondence with the Royal Society that the results of his research became known, since he published very little. The public eventually became acquainted with his research by reading the editions of his letters.

Like other Dutch natural scientists, such as Jan Swammerdam and Frederik Ruysch, Leeuwenhoek was a master in the art of laying bare the normally invisible world of insects, spermatozoa and lymph vessels. All of these men allowed interested parties to examine the results of their work. The collections of Swammerdam and Ruysch in Amsterdam were veritable tourist attractions, and Leeuwenhoek complained that if he were to admit everyone who showed up at his door he would never have time for research. Despite these complaints, however, he was flattered by the interest taken in his work, the purpose of which, in his eyes, was not merely scientific advancement. For all three of these men, science was also a means of achieving social recognition. Indeed, Ruysch and Leeuwenhoek were very secretive about their methods, in an attempt to

---

[2] Klaas van Berkel, 'Intellectuals against Leeuwenhoek. Controversies about the Methods and Style of a Self-Taught Scientist', in L. C. Palm and H. A. M. Snelders (eds.), *Antoni van Leeuwenhoek 1632–1723: Studies on the Life and Work of the Delft Scientist Commemorating the 350th Anniversary of his Birthday* (Amsterdam: Rodopi, 1982), p. 188.

preserve their exclusivity. Ruysch, moreover, tried for years to sell his anatomical collection to a foreign prince, finally succeeding in 1717, when the Russian court bought his whole collection for the vast sum of 30,000 guilders. Tsar Peter the Great had already become acquainted with Ruysch and his collection while staying in the Republic in 1697, at which time he had also paid a visit to Leeuwenhoek.

Though lacking a university education, Leeuwenhoek had received formal training in at least one field, having qualified in 1669 as a surveyor. This required a knowledge of mathematics, a fact which is not insignificant, since at this time it was mathematics that underpinned scientific progress in all fields. In the Republic, the foundation of mathematical instruction was laid by Simon Stevin. Stevin, who grew up in Flanders and Brabant, came from the world of commerce. His background meant that his particular brand of mathematics leaned heavily towards practical application. After settling in the Republic – he was active from 1581 in Leiden and The Hague – he wrote a number of books for a wide-ranging readership: his book on the decimal system, for example, was dedicated to 'Astronomers, Surveyors, Tapestry-measurers, Wine-gaugers, Measurers of bodies in general, Mint masters, and all Merchants'.[3] Stevin wrote on principle in Dutch, which in his opinion was worthy of being the official language of all scientific discourse. Perhaps it had also been the language barrier – at the universities the official language was Latin – that initially discouraged Leiden (the oldest university in Holland) from including mathematics in its curriculum. The first lecturer in mathematics, Rudolf Snellius, was appointed in 1579 at the insistence of the students. Of perhaps even greater importance than mathematical instruction at university level was the para-academic training offered at Leiden for engineers. This training programme, designed by Stevin and launched in 1600, was aimed especially at educating military specialists – designers and builders of fortifications, for example, as well as artillerists – though carpenters and masons also attended the classes. Among those lecturing at this institute were father and son Van Schooten. Frans van Schooten Jr owed his reputation mainly to his synthesis and systematisation of the work of others. He had also taught mathematics to both Johan de Witt – whose treatise on annuities, published during his term as Grand Pensionary, had a strong mathematical bias – and Christiaan Huygens, whose knowledge of mathematics enabled him to invent, among other things, the pendulum clock. Van Schooten was an important sounding board for the French mathematician René Descartes and even translated the latter's *Géométrie* into Latin. It was this

[3] Van Berkel et al., *A History of Science*, p. 19.

translation, and especially the expanded edition that Van Schooten published a year before Descartes's death, which was generally cited in scholarly debate, for Latin was then the official language of scholarship, much as English is today.

René Descartes, who lived and worked in the Dutch Republic from 1629 to 1649, was the first to provide a framework for systematising the new scientific insights fermenting everywhere in Europe at this time. Traditional scientific views harked back to Aristotle, who attributed inherent qualities and a purpose to all things. A stone, for example, falls downward because it is returning to its natural place. Such reasoning had been criticised with increasing frequency, but until Descartes there was no serious alternative to the Aristotelian view. Descartes now put forward the theory that all material was composed of small particles which behaved according to the laws of mechanics and could therefore be described in mathematical terms. Descartes had hit upon this idea as a result of conversations and correspondence with Isaac Beeckman, whom he had met in 1618 in Breda. Beeckman had studied mathematics under Snellius in Leiden and, after a spell as a candle-maker, had become a schoolmaster in Utrecht, Rotterdam and finally Dordrecht. Beeckman himself left only his unpublished notes. Though he had been on the right track, he lacked the mathematical knowledge necessary to develop his theories fully.

In the systematised mould into which Descartes poured it, the mechanistic world view revolutionised scientific thought, not only in the Republic but all over Europe. In time it became clear that Descartes's theory also had shortcomings, the most important of which was that it was based on deduction rather than empirical observation. His best-known proposition, 'Cogito, ergo sum' (I think, therefore I am), actually proves nothing in itself. The mathematical model he employed was also difficult to reconcile with such phenomena as atoms and the vacuum. Admittedly, Descartes had attempted by means of essays on optics, geometry and meteorology to collect evidence for his propositions, but they appeared not to have a firm foundation, as Huygens demonstrated, for example, with respect to the Cartesian laws of impact. Such criticism eventually undermined Descartes's authority but left intact the fundamental principle of his work – namely that natural phenomena are subject to laws that can be expressed in terms of mathematical formulae – which laid the foundation of modern science.

Although it is difficult to ascertain the origins of ideas like Descartes's, it is not difficult to identify circumstances in the Republic that were conducive to the development and dissemination of new scientific insights. As mentioned earlier, the high degree of urbanisation in the

Republic made Dutch society a literate one, and this certainly provided fertile ground in which to cultivate new scientific ideas. Even people lacking a university education, such as Leeuwenhoek, could make important contributions. The interest in natural phenomena was given a strong impetus by the hitherto unknown objects and exotic flora and fauna flowing into the Netherlands at this time, thanks in large part to the Dutch East India Company (VOC). Collectors and scholars asked VOC employees to gather specimens for their collections. Amsterdam and Leiden boasted dozens of cabinets of *curiosa*, in which objects made by artisans were displayed side by side with *naturalia*. Delft, the home of Leeuwenhoek, also had several such collections. These cabinets were the museums of the seventeenth century, prime places of interest to foreign princes and scholars visiting the Republic, though ordinary Dutchmen also showed considerable interest. The visitors' book of Petrus Paludanus, whose cabinet in Enkhuizen was listed in all the guidebooks, contains no fewer than 1,900 names. The Amsterdam damask merchant Levinus Vincent, who owned another huge collection, received around 250 visitors annually.

The high degree of literacy and the great interest shown in all manner of natural and historical phenomena led to a huge increase in the demand for books and prints. Publishers and booksellers witnessed a spectacular increase in business in the seventeenth century. In 1600, there were around sixty-eight printers and publishers active in twenty cities in the Republic. By 1650, thirty-four cities had at least one printer or publisher, and 247 businesses – three-quarters of them in Holland – were competing for customers. Amsterdam, which in 1650 had ninety-one printers and publishers, had become the most important centre of publishing in Europe. More than 100,000 titles, many of which were destined for export, were published in the Republic in the seventeenth century. Dutch publishers in Holland supplied English Bibles to the British, Hebrew and Yiddish texts to the Jews in Poland, and yet other reading material to the Catholics in Germany. Though their orientation was clearly very cosmopolitan, Dutch publishers were not always fastidious about what they put into print. Publishers in Amsterdam unhesitatingly produced pirated editions of French books, alongside such highly original and influential works as the *Nouvelles de la République des Lettres*, a periodical edited by the French philosopher Pierre Bayle which appeared from 1684 in Amsterdam. Moreover, it was the Amsterdam publisher Elzevier who was responsible for putting the works of Descartes within reach of an international public.

The book trade also profited from relatively great freedom, though by no means did the authorities in the Republic allow everything to appear in print. In the years leading up to the Twelve Years' Truce, for example, it was forbidden to publish anything that might prejudice the interests of the Republic in the peace negotiations. In January 1621 the States General banned books considered unacceptable 'in both ecclesiastical and political affairs'.[4] In 1624 it was forbidden to publish anonymously, and in 1651 both the States of Holland and the States General issued general rules for weeding out undesirable reading matter. Later in the century these rules were followed by bans on specific titles, nearly all of which had to do with politics or religion. The implementation of such prohibition orders was often erratic, however. Descartes's *Discours de la méthode*, for instance, was published anonymously in Leiden in 1637. Jealousy between the cities in the sphere of cultural achievements greatly benefited the freedom of the press. Many civic authorities simply refused to exercise censorship, Amsterdam being in the vanguard in this respect. It is indeed telling that Jan Rieuwertsz, the publisher of Spinoza and a number of other writers whose works had been banned, was also the city's official printer. To be sure, Rieuwertsz regularly resorted to subterfuge, such as printing the name of a foreign city as the place of publication or even producing completely fictitious title pages, such as those used for the edition of Spinoza's *Tractatus theologico-politicus*, but it could hardly escape notice that his shop in Amsterdam served as a meeting place for free-thinkers.

These free-thinkers and scholars were often immigrants or the children of immigrants. Stevin was a native of the Southern Netherlands, Descartes and Pierre Bayle had made their way to the Republic from France, and Spinoza's father had come from Portugal. In the sixteenth century, intellectuals – among them Erasmus – had left the Northern Netherlands and moved to the South, but in the seventeenth century the direction of migration was reversed. Sometimes their stay in the Republic was temporary – the English philosopher John Locke, who lived in Holland from 1683 to 1689, is a case in point – but Descartes was one of those who adopted the Republic as their new home. The presence of great numbers of immigrants with a wide variety of cultural backgrounds made the Republic – especially Amsterdam – a cosmopolitan melting pot where the discussion and publication of new ideas gave rise to an exceptionally dynamic cultural climate.

[4] S. Groenveld, 'Mecca of Authors? States Assemblies and Censorship in the Seventeenth-Century Dutch Republic', in A. C. Duke and C. A. Tamse (eds.), *Too Mighty to be Free. Censorship and the Press in Britain and the Netherlands* (Zutphen: De Walburg Pers, 1987), vol. IX, p. 70.

Institutionally, this international orientation was boosted by the Republic's expanding scientific infrastructure. In 1600 there were only two universities: Leiden, established in 1575 and Franeker in Friesland, founded in 1585. By 1650, however, every province had at least one institution of higher education – either an Illustrious School (a civic institution which offered no doctoral degrees) or a fully fledged university. Although the number of institutions offering undergraduate education had grown from two to thirteen, they were not all of equally high quality. The universities at Leiden and Utrecht, both of which attracted large numbers of foreign students, were the undisputed frontrunners, whereas Harderwijk had become known for the ease with which one could earn a degree.

There was considerable demand in the Republic for knowledge of an intellectual or academic nature, and in the course of the seventeenth century, academic training became something of a requirement for many professions. Among the town councillors of Leiden, only one in seven had a university degree in the first half of the century, whereas in the last quarter of the century two-thirds of them were university graduates. A similar increase was seen among the town councillors in Zwolle, a city which had no university of its own. In other professions it was not so much an academic degree as expertise in some subject that was required. For artillerists, surveyors and the navigators of ocean-going vessels – to name but a few of the professionals in great demand in the seventeenth-century Dutch Republic – elementary and even advanced knowledge of mathematics was a must. Intellectual debates, certainly those in which mathematics played an important role, attracted the interest of a large and knowledgeable public. And the lack of a long academic tradition – and therefore of vested interests – meant that debate could take place with unusual candour.

These conditions undoubtedly influenced the radical philosophers active at this time in the Republic, the best known being of course Descartes and Spinoza. From the very beginning, the polemic prompted by Descartes's ideas was much more than a scientific dispute. In 1641, Gisbertus Voetius – Reformed minister, professor of theology and rector of Utrecht University – bitterly attacked his colleague Henricus Regius, professor of medicine at the same institution, for discussing Descartes's ideas in his lectures. According to Voetius, the doubt underpinning Descartes's philosophical system inevitably led to the denial of the authority of the Bible. Thus Utrecht University, the first in the world where Descartes's theories were discussed, also became, on 17 March 1642, the first where they were officially banned. The ensuing controversy led to a battle fought on numerous fronts – not just in the fields of science and philosophy, but spilling over into political and theological discourse – and when Descartes entered the fray, he did not always show himself to best advantage. He accused Voetius of being a slanderer and a threat to public order. If he expected the Utrecht town council, which was given a copy of Descartes's rebuttal, to take measures against Voetius, he was sorely disappointed. After all, Voetius was at the time the leading Reformed theologian in the Republic. Having fought a losing battle, a disappointed Descartes finally left the Republic in 1649.

Although Descartes's disappointment was due mainly to the official opposition he had encountered, he had in fact failed to appreciate the tolerance with which his ideas were received by the universities, for despite official censure, the Cartesians managed to gain a foothold nearly everywhere. Even Utrecht University appointed professors who were known to be adherents of Descartes. To stabilise the situation, however, it was important for the Cartesians to come to a compromise with the theologians and, astonishingly enough, they managed to do so. Descartes himself had always emphasised that his ideas were compatible with church doctrine. Christopher Wittichius, a professor at Leiden, argued that the Bible focused mainly on the conditions for salvation. His colleague Abraham Heidanus, a Reformed theologian whose orthodoxy was never in doubt, went so far as to maintain that a refusal to recognise the division between philosophy and theology was a typically Catholic trait. This uneasy truce between the philosophers and the theologians was blown wide open by the radical ideas of Spinoza.

Baruch de Spinoza was a contemporary of Leeuwenhoek; both were born in 1632. His father, Michael d'Epinosa, was an Amsterdam merchant of Portuguese Jewish descent and active in the Jewish community of Beth Jacob. Baruch, or Bento as he was normally called, was educated at synagogue schools but left school early to help his father in his business. Over the years the family experienced a number of setbacks. Bento's mother died in November 1638, and his father, left with five young children, remarried two and a half years later. During the First Anglo-Dutch War his firm suffered heavy losses when its cargoes were repeatedly confiscated by the English. Spinoza's stepmother died in October 1653, followed by his father five months later, leaving Bento completely on his own at the age of twenty-one. The business he had inherited was deeply in debt, and the family's contributions to the Jewish community dropped sharply in the following months. The young Bento did not confine himself to business, however. It is likely that he attended some kind of evening classes, where he presumably vented a number of dissenting views. Though his exact words are not known, this assumption is borne out by the fierce condemnation voiced by the *parnassim*, the governing board of Beth Jacob, which on 27 July 1656 pronounced judgement on the 'evil opinions and acts of Baruch de Spinoza': '[H]aving failed to make him mend his wicked ways, and, on the contrary, daily receiving more and more serious information about the abominable heresies which he practised and taught and about his monstrous deeds',[5] the board decided to banish him from the community. Banishment was not unusual in itself, but the fierceness with which this particular sentence was pronounced was remarkable, as was the fact that it was never repealed. The mention of his 'heresies' suggests that Spinoza had meanwhile begun to devote a lot of time and effort to his new calling: philosophy. Although the source of his philosophical training is unknown, his intellectual development clearly proceeded with lightning speed. In the years following his banishment from the Jewish community, he became closely associated with the Latin school run by another radical thinker, Franciscus van den Enden, who was eventually convicted of conspiracy against Louis XIV, sentenced to death and subsequently hanged in the Bastille. Van den Enden had come from the Southern Netherlands and had briefly been a Jesuit, but in Amsterdam he grew into a radical utopian. Van den Enden exerted a great influence on the young Spinoza, though there were a number of other radicals in Amsterdam with whom Spinoza also remained in contact until he moved in 1661 to Rijnsburg, near Leiden. Rijnsburg, the headquarters of the Rijnsburg Collegiants, was another breeding ground for dissidents. The Collegiants, who formed a radical-democratic movement within the Reformed Church, championed toleration. Spinoza boarded with a Collegiant and earned some money by grinding and polishing optical lenses: 'the Jew of Voorburg [where Spinoza had meanwhile settled] finishes his little lenses by means of the instrument and this renders them very excellent',[6] wrote Christiaan Huygens in 1667. Spinoza also received financial assistance from friends and admirers in Amsterdam, which enabled him to work on his remarkable philosophical oeuvre.

Spinoza's philosophy has two distinguishing features, the first being its systematic nature: instead of the random ideas put forward by his predecessors and contemporaries, Spinoza developed a comprehensive philosophy. Only Descartes had been equally ambitious. The second distinguishing feature, which derived from the first, was the ability of his philosophy to connect fresh scientific insights with ethical issues. Spinoza's work has a reputation for being inaccessible, owing to its high level of abstraction and thoroughgoing logic. Even so, the systematic nature of his work makes it relatively easy to outline its basic principles. It may come as a surprise to learn that a philosopher who is reputed to be

---

[5] Steven Nadler, *Spinoza: A Life* (Cambridge: Cambridge University Press, 1999), p. 120.
[6] Ibid., p. 183.

the founder of modern atheism chose God as his starting point and based his entire philosophy on the qualities he attributes to God. Spinoza's God is infinite and all-embracing, from which it follows that nothing can exist apart from this all-embracing God. Thus God is all things, and all things derive from God, God being tantamount to Nature. Indeed, Spinoza used these two concepts, God and Nature, synonymously. God (or Nature) is not only infinite and all-embracing, He is also perfect. From this perfection it follows that nothing is accidental: everything is preordained and happens according to set rules that can be equated with natural laws. From this it follows that God cannot – and indeed would have no reason to – intervene in human affairs. Thus there is no God who passes judgement on human behaviour, punishing or rewarding accordingly. Judgement, after all, would only be appropriate in the case of behaviour resulting from an individual's free choice, but the very existence of such 'freedom' would gainsay divine providence and predetermination, implying that God is imperfect and that alongside Him there is another substance or reality which makes 'free' human behaviour possible. This, in Spinoza's philosophy, is a priori impossible.

In Spinoza's work these basic assumptions have important moral, religious and political implications. Because everything is preordained, there is no 'good' or 'evil' in the usual sense. Moral behaviour presupposes a choice, which Spinoza denies humankind. However, he does acknowledge that humankind has an imperfect understanding of its own situation, and this is the source of human emotions. People must act in their own self-interest, but a correct understanding of this concept would make them realise that it is in everyone's interest to live in harmony with one another. It is a lack of understanding, and the emotions thereby aroused, which precludes this harmony. Moreover, the churches, with their mistaken ideas about God and human destiny, only aggravate the situation, evidence of this being – as Spinoza noted on various occasions – the disputes that occurred during the Twelve Years' Truce. To curb human emotions, therefore, the state must make laws, which Spinoza prefers to call rules, to distinguish them from the immutable natural laws. These rules must protect people's natural rights, giving them every opportunity to gain a correct understanding of their destiny and the self-interests deriving from it. Where natural rights have been preserved, freedom can be said to exist.

Spinoza's political notions were controversial enough, though they did conform to some extent to the ideas of other radical republicans, such as the De la Court brothers, who enjoyed the patronage of the Grand Pensionary Johan de Witt. Spinoza, too, hoped for his protection, but De Witt refused to receive him because of his questionable religious ideas.

Although Spinoza was always writing about God, his notion of God was far removed from that of the Christian religions. Spinoza's attitude towards organised religion reveals that he considered it a threat to human salvation. The churches countered by doing everything they could to prevent the dissemination of his ideas – and did so with some measure of success. After the appearance of one short early work, Spinoza published only one more book during his lifetime: the *Tractatus Theologico-Politicus*. In 1671, when Spinoza heard that kindred spirits in Amsterdam were preparing a Dutch edition of his *Tractatus*, he begged them to abandon the project. Such caution did not, however, stop the religious authorities from voicing bitter criticism of the Latin edition, which had been published anonymously in 1670. At the instigation of the Reformed church council, the Leiden town council passed a resolution as early as May 1670, ordering a search for the book to be carried out in all local bookshops. In June 1670 the Amsterdam churches denounced the *Tractatus* as 'blasphemous and dangerous',[7] and in July churches in The Hague followed suit. In the summer of 1671 further dissemination of the book was forbidden, first in the city of Utrecht and then in the entire province. In June 1675 Spinoza's work was condemned by the church council in The Hague, where he had meanwhile gone to live. Despite these attempts to suppress his ideas, his friends in Amsterdam undertook to publish his work immediately upon his death in The Hague on 21 February 1677. The very next day all his manuscripts were removed from his room for safekeeping and shipped in a portable writing bureau to Amsterdam, where Jan Rieuwertsz prepared the *Opera Posthuma* for simultaneous publication in Latin and Dutch. The immediate impact made by these publications is apparent from the great number of contemporary reactions.

Descartes and Spinoza were two of the most important philosophers of the seventeenth century. Stevin, Huygens and Leeuwenhoek were among the century's chief innovators in the natural sciences. All of these men were active in the Republic. Spinoza, Huygens and Leeuwenhoek were born there, Stevin and Descartes came as immigrants. Descartes left the Republic after twenty years, and Huygens spent part of his adult life in Paris. In the seventeenth century, science was, as it is now, an international undertaking. No country could claim to have invented the new science and world view that developed in the seventeenth century and is known as the Scientific Revolution. It cannot be denied, however, that the Republic played a pioneering role in these developments. This was not due to the inherent superiority of Dutch scholarship: on the contrary,

---

[7] Ibid., p. 296.

one might say, since before 1600 hardly any scientific research was being carried out in the Northern Netherlands. Instead, it was precisely the lack of entrenched scientific and philosophical beliefs, combined with the expansion of the academic infrastructure, the flourishing book trade, the high degree of literacy and the widespread urbanisation in the Republic – with its cosmopolitan culture marked by a healthy rivalry among the cities – which offered ample opportunity for scientific innovation. That not one of the five scientists mentioned above was connected with a university suggests that in this period non-academic factors played an important role in the development of new ideas. The Republic's large economic and cultural hinterland enabled these new ideas to spread rapidly: Germany, the Scandinavian countries and the Baltic were supplied not only with French wines and Oriental spices but also with the latest scientific and philosophical insights. France, too, was very receptive to Spinoza's ideas in the last decades of the seventeenth century, by which time the conditions in the Republic itself were becoming less favourable – the economy was stagnating, the universities were being forced to make cutbacks, and the stream of immigration was drying up – so that the cosmopolitan Republic inevitably deteriorated into a provincial backwater.

15   The Dutch school of painting

In the latter part of the eighteenth century, the renowned English painter Sir Joshua Reynolds travelled through the Low Countries. In his journal, which was published in 1781, Reynolds naturally described the paintings he had seen along the way. For example: 'Cattle and a shepherd, by Albert Cuyp, the best I ever saw of him; the figure is likewise better than usual [Cuyp was known mainly for his landscapes]; but the employment which he has given the shepherd in his solitude is not very poetical: it must, however, be allowed to be truth and nature; he is catching fleas or something worse.'[1] And he described a work by Metsu thus: 'A woman reading a letter; the milk-woman who brought it is in the meantime drawing a curtain, a little on one side, in order to see the picture under it, which appears to be a sea-view.' Reynolds himself was well aware that his descriptions did not do justice to the undeniable qualities of these seventeenth-century masters. He noted, almost apologetically, that in order to appreciate the works fully, one had to see them first-hand. His descriptions also strike a chord of puzzlement, for what on earth had inspired Metsu to depict such a scene? In the case of the Cuyp there are even overtones of disapproval: catching fleas was surely not a suitable subject for a true work of art.

Reynold's opinion was no doubt a candid one, but his view of Dutch art was far from original. As early as 1538, a treatise on art had been published whose authorship was attributed to no less a luminary than Michelangelo. Comparing the descriptive qualities of Netherlandish art – having in mind mainly the art of Flanders and Brabant – with the narrative style of Italian art, Michelangelo maintained that the Netherlanders were unsurpassed in the depiction of reality. Their subjects – figures, landscapes, cityscapes, still lifes, church interiors – were rendered with such precision that the painted image was indistinguishable from the real

---

[1] Svetlana Alpers, *The Art of Describing: Dutch Art in the Seventeenth Century* (Harmondsworth: Penguin Books, 1989), p. xvii.

Figure 25   Gabriel Metsu, *Woman Reading a Letter*, *c*. 1662–5 (National Gallery
of Ireland, Dublin).

thing. In his view, however, Northern painting had no feeling for harmony or proportion, and lacked the lofty ideas that a work of art was
supposed to express. Italian art, which could indeed boast all these
characteristics, was therefore superior to Dutch art.

Such notions were common, and were even voiced in Holland itself
during the Golden Age. The collection of paintings started by Frederik
Hendrik had no room for flea-catching shepherds or letter-reading dam-
sels. The stadholder wanted art that articulated grand ideas and was
executed in the classicist style fashionable at the other courts of Europe.
Many commissions were therefore granted to Utrecht painters, who had
been strongly influenced by the Italian master Caravaggio, especially
since many had themselves spent a number of years working in Italy.
Similarly, in the mid-seventeenth century, when it came time to decorate
Amsterdam's new Town Hall, the burgomasters did not want 'typical
Dutch art' to adorn their monument to civic pride. The enormous canvases commissioned to decorate the walls and mantelpieces of the Town

Hall displayed episodes from tales of classical antiquity. Obviously these were not the paintings that interested Reynolds in the eighteenth century. He was interested in art of the kind Michelangelo had already acknowledged (and condemned), but which had since grown into what was perhaps the most immediately recognisable aspect of Dutch culture: works of art depicting everyday life and the Dutch landscape in an unadorned, realistic way – much like today's photographs.

In the sixteenth century there were scant signs that the Northern Netherlands would one day produce an important school of painting. Great art had traditionally come from the Southern Netherlands: from Bruges and Ghent as early as the fourteenth century and from Antwerp in the sixteenth century. These were the cities where such prominent artists as Jan van Eyck, Hugo van der Goes, Hans Memling and Rogier van der Weyden lived and worked. An artist with any ambition settled in one of these places. To be sure, the North had Jan van Scorel in Utrecht and Maerten van Heemskerck in Haarlem – both artists of international stature – but their reputations were not to be compared with those of the above-mentioned Flemish artists. A unique set of circumstances changed this state of affairs drastically in the decades around 1600.

In those days, too, art was a luxury product. Paintings had traditionally been produced to adorn public buildings or the homes of the wealthy. The most important patron of the arts was the church, though many works of art were commissioned by private individuals who subsequently presented them to the church. Such art naturally depicted religious subjects inspired by the Bible or the lives of the saints. When the work of art in question was intended as a donation, the donor saw to it that his likeness was incorporated in the composition. In Flanders, important studios had a stock of panels with biblical representations suitable for use as the central panel of a triptych, and a generous donor would order two side panels bearing his and his wife's portraits.

People who could afford to donate works of art to the church were usually inclined to buy art for their own enjoyment as well. Such art lovers were often either members of the nobility or wealthy burghers aspiring to an aristocratic lifestyle. They were enthusiastic adherents of the 'higher' artistic ideals Michelangelo had expounded: compositions based on classical precepts, representing lofty subjects. The paintings they bought thus belonged for the most part to the type known as history painting: representations of subjects from classical antiquity, literature or the Bible. In their view, art was not only a source of enjoyment but also a means of displaying their cultural attainments and impeccable taste. Their acquisitions were mostly commissioned works, though they sometimes purchased paintings from an artist's ready-made stock. Artists whose work was much

in demand resorted more and more to repeating successful subjects, applying the details with the help of cartoons: drawings made as designs to be
used over and over again – a procedure that greatly increased productivity.
Van Scorel's studio, for example, repeated the subject of 'Madonna and
Child' a great many times, presumably because it was very popular. These
paintings were not exact copies, because the Madonna was placed in a
different setting each time. Instead, Van Scorel and his assistants cleverly
combined both standard and unique elements to produce art at competitive prices. Whole generations of artists after Van Scorel continued to
benefit from similar cost-cutting techniques.

The Dutch Revolt seriously disrupted the art market in the Southern
provinces. Political and religious turmoil – not to mention open hostilities –
caused a sharp drop in the demand for art. When the cities of Flanders and
Brabant, which were bulwarks of Protestantism, fell to the Spanish, those
who refused to convert to Catholicism fled, and many artists ended up in
the Northern Netherlands. Artists specialising in landscape and still-life
painting settled in the most important cities, such as Middelburg, Utrecht,
Haarlem and Amsterdam. These cities, which lacked artistic traditions of
their own, provided fertile ground for experimentation and innovation.
Haarlem, for example, was introduced to the most recent 'inventions' of
Mannerism by the engraver Dirck Volkertsz Coornhert and his German
pupil Hendrick Goltzius, as well as by the painters Bartolomeus Spranger
and Karel van Mander. Van Mander, who had moved to Haarlem from
Flanders, gave new impetus to the artistic life of Haarlem by collaborating
with Cornelis Corneliszoon and Hendrik Goltzius in an informal 'academy',
which probably consisted in gatherings at which they drew together and
Van Mander shared his experiences in Italy and his ideas on painting with
his young friends. His famous *Schilderboeck* (Book of Painters and
Painting), published in 1604, tells the story of Northern Netherlandish
painting up to the end of the sixteenth century.

One huge problem confronting Northern Netherlandish art at the dawn
of the Golden Age was the fact that the traditional patrons – the church and
the nobility – had largely disappeared. Many nobles had emigrated in the
opposite direction, from North to South, and the Catholic churches had
been turned over to the Reformed, who were strongly opposed to images
and idols in the house of God. Artists were thus forced to find or create
other markets, and were fortunate in finding ample opportunity to do so.
The cities in the province of Holland were mushrooming, and it was
proving much easier to sell paintings to town-dwellers than to country
folk. Broad segments of society, profiting from the economic boom, suddenly had enough money to buy luxury products. To corner their share of
this growing market, however, artists had to change course completely.

The average town-dweller now had money to spare but was still far from wealthy; for such people traditional, large-scale history paintings were out of the question. Thus artists not only had to produce more affordable paintings but also had to cater for the different tastes of their new clients. While it was difficult to persuade them to buy depictions of lofty subjects, there did appear to be a great demand for scenes from everyday life – kitchen interiors, a lady playing a spinet, a quiet street, or even a brothel, for paintings were also allowed to be racy at times.

To exploit these new markets, painters had to change their production methods. Efficiency, which had already been a significant factor in the competitive markets of Flanders and Brabant in the fifteenth and sixteenth centuries, was now of overriding importance. Just how important is typified by a wager allegedly laid in the mid-seventeenth century by the landscape painters François Knibbergen and Jan van Goyen and the marine painter Jan Porcellis, each of whom boasted that he could produce the best painting in only one day. The best-known works of the minor master Knibbergen of The Hague and of the considerably more famous Van Goyen of Leiden display sketchily rendered landscapes executed in a very subdued palette. It is not difficult to imagine that such canvases could be produced in a relatively short time. Because the price of a picture was largely determined by the amount of work put into it, a painting produced so rapidly could not cost more than a few guilders. Such inexpensive works brought art within the reach of even a simple artisan.

Efficiency was realised in a variety of ways. Formats often remained small and the manner of painting sketchy, because a wealth of detail simply cost too much time. Painters did not wait for commissions, but went ahead and made paintings for customers to choose from. Successful depictions were unashamedly copied, or reworked with small modifications. Around 1670 Jacob van Ruisdael painted a view of Haarlem depicting, in the foreground, the bleaching fields for which the city was famous, with the profile of the city on the horizon, dominated by the imposing Church of St Bavo, and above the whole the typical cloudy sky of Holland. The work proved to be popular and Ruisdael painted so many variations of it that it eventually acquired its own name: a 'Haarlempje'. Popular painters set up studios and enlisted the help of assistants, many of them pupils or former pupils, in an attempt to keep up with demand. Rembrandt, for example, had just such a 'painting factory' in St Anthonies Breestraat (now Jodenbreestraat) in Amsterdam. His 'workers' paid for the privilege of studying with him, and so the great master, who was a shrewd businessman, profited doubly from their presence. His pupils and assistants included such talents as Ferdinand Bol, Carel

Fabritius, Govert Flinck and Nicolaes Maes, all of whom were to become famous in their own right.

The most important step to cutting production costs was rigorous specialisation. Sometimes artists went so far as to call in the help of fellow painters to apply certain elements, such as figures or animals, which they felt could be done better – and more quickly – by someone else. More commonly, however, they avoided such situations altogether by specialising in one type of painting. Jan van Goyen, for example, made only landscapes in quite a small format, executed with rapid brushstrokes in predominantly yellow and brown hues. Pieter Saenredam concentrated exclusively on the rendering of precisely measured church interiors and exteriors. Willem van de Velde the Elder made extremely accurate depictions of sea battles observed at first hand. Mostly drawn with pen on white canvas, these drawings are so painterly in appearance that they are referred to as 'pen paintings'. Frans Hals confined himself to portraiture, Simon de Vlieger to seascapes, Frans van Mieris to so-called 'merry companies', or interiors with a few figures, often engaged in some activity, such as making music. Hendrik Averkamp – who was a special case because he was a deaf-mute and, moreover, one of the few successful painters who lived and worked outside Holland – devoted himself completely to winter scenes.

These changes in the market pushed the more distinguished history paintings to the sidelines. This was due in part to the format in which many history painters worked, producing paintings so large that few people had drawing rooms that could accommodate them. Changing tastes also contributed to the drop in the demand for history paintings. As mentioned above, the burghers of Holland had a greater affinity for depictions with which they could easily identify – recognisable scenes from everyday life – such as civic militiamen keeping the night watch, kitchen maids at work, Twelfth Night festivities, an interior with a view to adjoining rooms, merry companies making music, and such winter diversions as skating and sledging. These were the typical subjects of what is called genre painting. Much of it, though deceptively realistic, in fact contains both hidden and overt allusions to a subtext. An example of such symbolism is Gabriel Metsu's letter-reading woman, who caught the attention of Joshua Reynolds. The maidservant, who fills the right-hand side of the painting, holds up a curtain, revealing a painting of a storm-tossed ship at sea. The full meaning of this painting-within-a-painting becomes apparent when we realise that this canvas has a pendant in which a man sits writing a letter. The stormy sea clearly refers to the woman's state of mind as revealed by her maid. Other elements in the painting allude to the same theme. The little dog, for example, symbolises loyalty.

A less innocent reference is the slipper, which almost certainly refers to female sexuality, a subject on which seventeenth-century artists were decidedly unsubtle. A simple depiction of reality was obviously not enough, however. Like today's viewers of television soaps, the seventeenth-century Dutch demanded a near-perfect reflection of reality, distorted just enough to make it more exciting than their own humdrum existence.

It would be wrong, however, to think that genre paintings completely dominated the Dutch art market. History paintings did in fact continue to be held in high regard. Rembrandt's success demonstrates that history painters could also find work in seventeenth-century Holland. Painstaking and time-consuming research carried out in Amsterdam probate inventories – notarial acts listing every item in a person's estate – has shown that the art hanging in seventeenth-century households was not confined to 'typically Dutch' works. Genre paintings accounted for less than 10 per cent of all the art mentioned, the same percentage as still lifes. Portraits, landscapes and even history paintings occurred much more frequently. Small landscape paintings in particular were extremely popular, accounting for nearly one-third of the paintings listed in these inventories. Many Amsterdammers also had biblical or mythological scenes and, in a few cases, depictions of events from recent history. That genre paintings nonetheless attracted so much attention is mainly due to their originality. In other countries, scenes from everyday life were rarely the subject of paintings.

In addition to landscapes, another type of painting that became very popular from around 1660 was the townscape. Since the fifteenth century, cities had been figuring – often recognisably so – in Netherlandish paintings, such as those of the Van Eyck brothers, where they are clearly in evidence behind Madonnas and in the background of other biblical scenes. In the first half of the seventeenth century, Pieter Saenredam painted several church exteriors, including St Mary's in Utrecht, in their urban settings. While staying for several weeks in 's-Hertogenbosch in the summer of 1632, he also made a number of stunning drawings of the city in profile, a tradition developed earlier by map-makers and book illustrators. The second half of the seventeenth century saw the development – particularly in Delft, Haarlem and Amsterdam – of a new type of painting which featured a specific location in a city. Pieter de Hooch in Delft specialised in small-scale, intimate 'through-views', often featuring a view to a street through a house or courtyard. Gerrit Berckheyde in Haarlem and Jan van der Heyden (also known as the inventor of the fire pump) in Amsterdam painted well-known sites in their respective cities: such as the Grote Markt and St Bavo's in Haarlem, and the new Town Hall on Dam Square and the

Westerkerk in Amsterdam. Such works proved to be in great demand, and Berkheyde, Van der Heyden and various other masters were only too willing to supply them, often by repeating the same subjects over and over again with only minor changes in the composition.

Dutch painters thus catered for the wide-ranging tastes of the art-buying public, and did so with great success. Foreigners were amazed not only at the great numbers of paintings in Dutch houses but also at the wide diffusion of art: even ordinary people owned one or two paintings. Their random impressions are corroborated by other data, such as the number of artists active in the Republic. In 1650, for example, there were probably between 650 and 750 artists living and working in the Republic, or 1.5–2 artists per 1,000 inhabitants. In Delft, with its population of 24,000, there were thirty painters registered with the Guild of St Luke in 1650. That this was an impressive number is borne out by the fact that the painters' guild of Seville – a city four times the size of Delft and unquestionably Spain's most important artistic centre – had fewer than thirty members in 1599. The Dutch painters, moreover, were extremely productive. Though precise figures are lacking, it is estimated that at least 5 million paintings were produced in the Dutch Republic in the seventeenth century. Most of these paintings have been lost, but a great many of them were undoubtedly of little artistic merit. The ones we admire in museums today represent only the tip of the iceberg.

The names of many of these painters no longer mean anything to us. Who has ever heard of the Delft history painter Willem Verschoor, who enrolled in the local Guild of St Luke on 6 January 1653? Or of his fellow painters Hans Jordaens and Abram van Beijeren – specialising respectively in landscapes and still lifes – who joined the same guild four years later? Even Leonard Bramer, a Delft artist who was well known in those days, is now known only to a handful of connoisseurs. In the seventeenth century, however, all these artists lived by the brush and provided their customers with a wide range of products to choose from. Even so, the art on sale in any given city was usually limited to the work of local guild members. At least two-thirds of all the art recorded in Delft households had been made by Delft artists. In Haarlem, where the preference for local masters was even more pronounced, more than three-quarters of the paintings had been produced in the city itself.

This preference for local painters did not arise spontaneously. Like the manufacture of many products, the production of paintings was also organised in guilds. In the sixteenth century, painters often belonged to a more general guild incorporating all manner of professions. In Utrecht, for example, the painters belonged to the saddler's guild, whose members also included book illuminators, wood-carvers, moquette workers and, from 1540, even clog-makers. Haarlem was the only city which had a separate painters' guild before the Revolt. This guild was called the Guild of St Luke, after the patron saint of painters, and could even pride itself on having a small piece of the saint's bones in its possession. In 1579, almost immediately after Amsterdam joined the side of the Revolt, a painters' guild was established during a general reorganisation of the guilds. Middelburg saw the establishment of a painters' guild in 1585, as did Gouda and Rotterdam in 1609 and Utrecht and Delft in 1611. In 1631 a painters' guild was founded in Alkmaar. Leiden followed suit much later, in 1648, and Hoorn later still, in 1651.

The Guilds of St Luke arranged apprenticeships for young painters and protected the market by ensuring a monopoly of art production in their respective cities. At the same time they acted as the official channel through which customers could lodge complaints. Painters' guilds sprang up in the larger cities, where there were enough artists to make a separate guild worthwhile. The painters of the Dutch Golden Age did not conform to the image – later propagated by the Romantic movement – of the artist as an inspired genius. On the contrary, many of these painters were simply artisans who produced and sold a product to make a living. The price of that product was largely determined by the materials used (canvas, pigments, brushes) and by the time needed to complete the painting. Only an established artist with a good reputation could ask for more money than other painters.

Most of the larger cities could boast a number of well-known painters, often belonging to a group specialised in a certain type of painting. In Haarlem, for example, there was an important circle of painters which included Esaias van de Velde, Salomon van Ruysdael and later his nephew Jacob van Ruisdael, who specialised in Dutch landscapes, as well as Claes Berchem, who excelled at Italianate landscapes. In Utrecht it was the history painters who set the tone, with the Catholic painter Abraham Bloemaert dominating the city's artistic circles in the early seventeenth century. He passed the torch to Hendrick ter Brugghen and Gerard van Honthorst, who had been strongly influenced by the Italian painter Caravaggio. In Middelburg there was a short-lived blossoming of the flower still life, with Ambrosius Bosschaert and Balthasar van der Ast as its most important exponents, while in Delft there emerged around the middle of the century a recognisable school of architectural painters who specialised in interiors of both public buildings and private houses. This school included Gerrit Houckgeest, Hendrick van Vliet, Emanuel de Witte, Pieter de Hooch, and in a certain sense also Johannes Vermeer. The Leiden *fijnschilders* ('fine painters'), especially Gerrit Dou and Frans van Mieris, gained international fame with their meticulously executed scenes of domestic life. Only Amsterdam was large enough to accommodate various schools of painting alongside one another. In addition to harbouring a recognisable group of history painters, to which Rembrandt and his teacher Pieter Lastman belonged, Amsterdam was a centre of marine and landscape painting. The rise of these local schools of painting was probably stimulated by the activities of the recently founded painters' guilds. The guilds protected the market, giving local masters the edge on competitors and at the same time providing a framework for training and cultivating young talent.

The local schools of painting were so successful that their products were sought, both at home and abroad, by collectors willing to pay very high prices. This gave rise to a paradoxical situation: the typical Dutch genre painting had originally been intended for the lower end of the art market, for the less cultured customers who were frightened off by references to classical mythology and had no affinity with Mediterranean landscapes. Specialisation, however, had enabled some genre painters to hone their skills to such an extent that ordinary customers could no longer afford their highly polished work. Such painters as Dou and Van Mieris, whose subjects were often simple and unpretentious, were nonetheless so highly esteemed for their fine workmanship that they could ask 1,000 guilders or more for a painting. Another example of a genre painter who became extremely skilled and polished was Johannes Vermeer.

Nowadays Vermeer is counted among the great masters of the seventeenth-century school of Dutch painting. Such recognition was not forthcoming in his lifetime, though he was not entirely unknown either. In 1669 the Hague patrician Pieter Teding van Berkhout wrote in his diary that on 14 May he had visited 'an excellent painter by the name of Vermeer',[2] who had shown him several of his works. Five weeks later Teding van Berkhout visited this 'celebrated painter'[3] again. All the same, a detailed description of the city of Delft published in 1667 mentioned Vermeer only in passing. In 1696, however, when twenty-one of his canvases were sold at auction, it was reiterated that they were 'vigorously and glowingly painted'.[4] Even allowing for the customary exaggeration of advertising, one must admit that those words describe Vermeer's qualities nicely. Even so, in the seventeenth century he was definitely not the prominent Dutchman he is today.

Vermeer's comparative obscurity perhaps explains why we know so little about him. We do have a reasonably good knowledge of his small oeuvre, however, which probably contained no more than thirty works.

[2] Montias, *Vermeer en zijn milieu* (Baarn: de Prom, 1993), p. 377.
[3] Ibid., p. 377.   [4] Albert Blankert, *Vermeer of Delft* (Oxford: Phaidon, 1978), p. 154.

This astonishingly small number leads one to ask how on earth Vermeer could have supported himself and his family. Little is known of his life, though we do know that he was born in 1632 in Delft, where he was baptised on 31 October in the New Church. His father, Reynier Jansz Vermeer, kept an inn called 'De Vliegende Vos' (The Flying Fox). His family had moved North from Flanders at the end of the sixteenth century. Before he started calling himself Vermeer, he was called Vos, or De Vos, and it is reasonable to assume a connection with the name of his inn. On 13 October 1631, exactly one year before the birth of Johannes, Reynier Vos became a member of the Delft Guild of St Luke, not as a painter but as a 'master art dealer'. His guild membership put him in a position to sell works of art at his inn, not an unusual practice in those days.

Vermeer must therefore have come into contact early on with art and artists, though it is not known from whom he received his training. One reason to assume that he was trained in Utrecht rather than Delft is the prominence of a Utrecht painting, made by Dirck van Baburen, in two of Vermeer's own works. This painting by Van Baburen, *The Procuress*, was owned by Vermeer's mother-in-law, and could well have been what inspired Vermeer to paint a canvas of a similar subject – a brothel scene – early in his career. Like two early history paintings, it is not yet a 'typical' Vermeer. Besides the presence of a painting by a Utrecht master in Vermeer's household, a Utrecht apprenticeship is also supported by the fact that he married, at the unusually early age of twenty-one, a girl connected with the circle of Utrecht painters. This woman, Catharina Bolnes, was related through her mother to Abraham Bloemaert, who is known to have had a great many pupils. While it is possible that Vermeer was one of them and met his wife in this way, this is mere conjecture.

What we do know is that Catharina Bolnes's mother objected at first to the marriage, though she did not forbid it outright. One reason for her lack of enthusiasm might have been the social differences between bride and groom. Vermeer did not come from the back streets of Delft by any means, yet his father's occupation put him in the social class of small tradesman. By contrast, Vermeer's mother-in-law, Maria Thins, was well-to-do. Her father owned a brickworks and they were part of the upper crust of Gouda, where their forefathers had been members of the town council until the Revolt. There was another obstacle to the marriage: Johannes Vermeer and Catharina Bolnes belonged to different churches. Vermeer was Reformed, as emerges from his baptism in the New Church in Delft, but his wife came from a family that had remained Catholic after the Revolt. It is likely that Vermeer converted to Catholicism. Vermeer's mother-in-law was to play an important role in his life. Vermeer and Catharina moved in with her mother soon after their marriage, and it was her fortune that released Vermeer from the worry of selling his paintings and enabled him to devote himself entirely to his art. At the end of his life, when he and his family were short of money, Vermeer received several commissions from Catholic circles which had no doubt been secured by his mother-in-law.

Vermeer's choice of subject matter was certainly not unique. He worked in the tradition of the 'conversation piece': a picture showing several figures discussing a subject which may or may not be apparent from the depiction. When the subject is clear, it is nearly always love, or simply sex. Some of these scenes contain only one figure, and the conversation takes place by letter. At other times such depictions include an observer, such as the maidservant in Metsu's painting who has just delivered a letter and alludes to its contents by revealing the picture of the stormy sea. Vermeer in fact made a similar painting – *The Love Letter* – though he usually preferred not to make such overt allusions. In an early painting of a woman reading a letter by a window, he painted over the Cupid he had initially depicted on the back wall. It is only through an x-ray that we know of the one-time presence of this Cupid, whom Vermeer presumably considered, on reflection, to be an overly blatant reference to the contents of the letter.

Another important influence on Vermeer must have been the architectural paintings made by his fellow painters in Delft. In the same years that Vermeer set himself up as an independent master – he enrolled in the local Guild of St Luke on 29 December 1653 – Delft was witnessing the development of a new school of architectural painting, whose practitioners produced not only townscapes but also depictions of geometrically accurate interiors. Even if we do not know exactly how Vermeer worked, everything points to the probability that a great deal of preparation went into composing his paintings. That he might have used a camera obscura to project the scenes set up in his studio is indicated by the fact that he rendered certain highlights – clearly visible, for example, in *The Milkmaid* – with thick daubs of paint. The comparatively primitive lenses common in the seventeenth century yielded similar visual effects. However, the presence of a tiny hole at precisely the vanishing point in a number of his paintings suggests another working method. A nail fixed at that spot could have held a chalked string which was pulled across the prepared canvas, then lifted up and released, causing chalk to spatter in a straight line on the canvas. This method could have been used to construct a scene in proper perspective.

All of this indicates that Vermeer was interested in the visual effect produced by his work more than anything else, especially since his work seldom seems to bear a message to the viewer. Attempts to read meanings into Vermeer's paintings nearly always prove futile. His work consists

Figure 26   Johannes Vermeer, *Woman in Blue Reading a Letter*, c. 1660–5
(Rijksmuseum, Amsterdam).

mainly of carefully composed scenes of everyday life. Most of his works
depict interiors: the corner of a room, for example, with light falling into
the picture from the upper left. Usually only one figure is visible, portrayed three-quarter length and engaged in an activity in which movement has been suspended for an instant. The viewer is invited, as it were,
to participate in this quiet moment. The hushed atmosphere is created

largely by the uniformity of the light bathing the scene, leaving the viewer in a state of uncertainty as to the exact season or time of day, all of which contributes to the sense of timelessness.

The small size of Vermeer's oeuvre and the painstaking execution of his paintings clearly suggests that he spent a great deal of time on each canvas. His work must therefore have been relatively expensive. Monsieur de Monconys, a French tourist who visited Delft in the summer of 1663, recorded in his diary that he had seen – at the home of a baker, no less – a painting by the renowned 'Peintre Vermer' which had cost all of 600 guilders, 'even though it contained only one figure'.[5] De Monconys thought it a scandalous sum for such a simple depiction. In fact, Vermeer's paintings did not fetch such high prices later on. At the 1696 auction of an entire collection – at which no fewer than twenty-one Vermeers were sold, including several which are now the most famous – the most expensive was the *View of Delft*, which fetched 200 guilders. The *Milkmaid* was sold for 175 guilders, and a third canvas for 155 guilders, but the rest went for less than 100 guilders. The fact that so many of his works were in one collection – the sale probably contained more than half of all the paintings ever completed by Vermeer – suggests that they were inaccessible to the public, which may have put something of a damper on the impact he made. Vermeer was largely dependent on a single buyer, the brewer and rentier Pieter Claesz van Ruijven, and it was his collection that was auctioned off in 1696. A few Vermeers found homes outside Delft: 'a young lady playing the clavichord', for example, was to be found in Antwerp in the collection of the banker Diego Duarte. Duarte maintained close contacts with the elite of The Hague, especially Constantijn Huygens the Younger. Another native of The Hague, the sculptor Jean Larson, owned a '*tronie* [a study of a head] by Vermeer'. Part of Vermeer's oeuvre remained unsold, however, as evidenced by the inventory drawn up after his death, which listed at least four paintings presumed to be by his hand. When the artist died in December 1675 at the age of forty-three, he left his widow in such straits that in September 1676 the Delft magistrates finally intervened to straighten out the finances of the Vermeer family, appointing a curator of Vermeer's estate and of Catharina Bolnes's assets. That curator was none other than Anthonie van Leeuwenhoek, the famous inventor of the microscope (see pp. 222–3.).

After his death, Vermeer sank into oblivion and remained there for more than a century and a half, until he was discovered by the French art critic Théophile Thoré, who in 1866 wrote in the *Gazette des Beaux-Arts*: 'By all means let us include Van der Meer [Vermeer] in the *pleiade* of

---

[5] Ibid, p. 147.

"minor" Dutch masters, namely as their equal. Like them, he is original in character and what he made is perfect.' In the following years Thoré emerged as an ardent advocate of Dutch painting and an indefatigable champion of Vermeer. He was also the first to compile an overview of the master's works. Thoré's defence of naturalism caught on, and eventually Vermeer was held in such high esteem that the French Impressionists took him as their example. Suddenly a collection of Dutch masters was no longer complete without at least one Vermeer. Museums that had none made every effort to acquire one, so it is hardly surprising that when various unknown works of the young Vermeer appeared on the market in the 1930s they found eager buyers. After the Second World War, however, it was discovered that these unknown Vermeers had been painted by the master forger Han van Meegeren, who thereby took revenge on the connoisseurs who had failed to appreciate his own work.

Vermeer is now assured of a permanent place in the pantheon of great Dutch painters. An exhibition of his work held in The Hague in 1995–6 attracted nearly half a million visitors. For the artist himself, fame came 300 years too late. At the end of his life, he was broken in spirit and unable to earn a living. According to his widow, he had taken his problems so much to heart that he had 'fallen into a frenzy' and within a day, or a day and a half, 'he had gone from being healthy to being dead'.[6]

Vermeer's financial problems were due to more than just his inability to find sufficient clients or to the death of his patron Van Ruijven. In a petition submitted to the High Court in 1676, his widow stated that 'during the long and ruinous war with France' her husband had been 'unable to sell any of his art'.[7] Not only had the sale of Vermeer's own work come to a standstill, but the demand for art had dried up to such an extent that dealing in the work of other artists, which had always been his sideline, was no longer profitable either. In the end he was forced to sell canvases for a fraction of their original price in order to support his wife and their eleven children.

The problems of the Vermeer family reflected the problems of the art market in general. In Utrecht, which had been occupied by the French for a year and a half, the art market collapsed completely and its school of painting never recovered from the blow. Elsewhere, too, it became increasingly difficult for painters to find work. Their customers, who until this time had always been willing to support the latest developments in painting, began to turn their backs on contemporary work. In 1650,

---

[6] Montias, *Vermeer and his Milieu: A Web of Social History* (Princeton: Princeton University Press, 1989), p. 212.
[7] Ibid.

living masters were responsible for half of all the paintings in private collections in Amsterdam, but by the end of the century their share had dropped to one-sixth. Art buyers showed such a strong preference for works of the 'classical' Dutch school, of which there were so many in circulation, that the demand for art could easily be supplied by the second-hand market. Everywhere we see, especially after 1672, a dramatic decrease in membership of the painters' guilds. One or two artists managed to rise above this sad state of affairs. The Rotterdam artist Adriaen van der Werff built up a great reputation with his classicist works. He became extremely wealthy from his art, which, though it resembled the work of the 'fine painters' in style, expressly broke with the Dutch tradition in subject matter. The rise of Dutch classicism in the last years of the seventeenth century therefore marked the end of the characteristic look and enormous productivity of the Dutch school of painting of the Golden Age.

16   The urban landscape

In 1625 a volume of poetry by Constantijn Huygens was published in Dutch, Latin, French and Italian. Huygens – the future secretary to Frederik Hendrik but at this time still learning the finer points of statesmanship while carrying out various diplomatic missions – was a man of many talents. A poet and politician, he was also the stadholder's most valued adviser on artistic matters and a sounding board for the most prominent architects of his day. Huygens's book contained a series of poems extolling the virtues of the towns and villages of Holland. In these verses, full of erudite allusions to antiquity and finely crafted turns of phrase, Huygens sang the praises of what he apparently viewed as an important part of Dutch society: the city. He was, of course, most impressed by Amsterdam, which he presented, like the other cities, personified as a woman. Inevitably, the strangers visiting her were astonished at what they saw:

> How come thee, O golden fen, to be by heaven blessed?
> All water and all street art thou, storehouse of East and West ...[1]

Huygens praises Haarlem for its artistic life, Hoorn for its fishermen and cheese, and Leiden for withstanding the Spanish siege and for its Reformed university. Clearly, he was deeply impressed by the cities of Holland, expressing both admiration of their achievements and recognition of their diverse characters.

What was true of Holland was also true to some extent of the country as a whole. Its urban character, already noticeable in 1600, became even more marked in the course of the seventeenth century. The Republic was a nation of towns and townspeople, though just what constituted a town or city was a matter of some dispute. Sloten, in Friesland, had been enfranchised since the early fifteenth century and was therefore formally a city, even though its population of 448 (in 1689) made it more the size of a village. The Hague, by contrast, had some 20,000 inhabitants (in 1665),

[1] Constantijn Huygens, *Stede-Stemmen en Dorpen*, edited by C. W. de Kruyter (Zutphen: Thieme, 1981), p. 40.

but because it was not invested with municipal rights it was scornfully referred to as the largest village in Holland. In 1600 approximately one-fourth of the population of the Republic lived in towns of 10,000 people or more. By 1670 this percentage had increased to one-third, or even one-half, if we include small cities like Sloten. Such high percentages of town-dwellers were unheard-of in the rest of Europe. In most countries the urban population was less – often far less – than 15 per cent. The only region that approached the Republic in this respect was the Southern Netherlands, where in 1700 nearly one-fourth of the people were living in cities. The Low Countries were by far the most urbanised region of Europe, followed at some distance by northern Italy.

There was another remarkable thing about the Republic's special brand of urbanisation: instead of being concentrated in one or two metropolises, the urban population was spread over a large number of towns. Naturally there was a world of difference between Sloten, with its 448 inhabitants, and Amsterdam, with more than 200,000. Between these two extremes, however, there were a great number of medium-sized towns. Around 1700 the Republic had twenty-one cities with at least 10,000 inhabitants, whereas England, which was nearly three times as populous, had only eleven. London, with more than half a million inhabitants, was more than twenty times the size of Bristol, then the second-largest city in England. In comparison, Leiden, the second-largest city in the Republic, was only three times smaller than Amsterdam, and in 1700 the Republic had seven cities, in addition to Amsterdam, which were just as large or larger than Bristol.

The cities of the Dutch Republic – all of which had been founded well before 1600 – began to grow rapidly during the seventeenth century. The most spectacular growth was seen in the west of the country, particularly in Holland. The Republic's 'two-speed' economy emerges most clearly from population trends in the urban areas. Between 1560 and 1670 the number of inhabitants of the voting cities – the cities represented in the provincial States assemblies – showed no growth whatsoever in Overijssel and Gelderland; indeed, the only apparent changes marked a drop in population. Utrecht, on the other hand, showed growth of 16 per cent in the same period, and the city of Groningen grew by 25 per cent. The difference in growth rates between these two provinces and the three western provinces was, however, enormous. Between 1560 and 1670 the eleven cities of Friesland grew by no less than 64 per cent, those of Zeeland by 129 per cent, and the cities of Holland – far and away the frontrunner – by more than 250 per cent. The result was that by 1670 more than two-thirds of all the city-dwellers in the Republic were living in Holland, as contrasted with one-half a century before.

The rapid growth in population did not coincide with the beginning of the Revolt. On the contrary, during the Revolt many cities experienced a sharp drop in population. In 1590 Maastricht, 's-Hertogenbosch, Nijmegen, Zutphen, Zwolle, Deventer and Kampen had 25 to 40 per cent fewer inhabitants than in 1550. In 1570 the cities in the provinces of Holland, Utrecht and Groningen had approximately the same number of inhabitants as twenty years earlier. This trend was reversed in the 1580s. The population of Haarlem, which in 1577 was around 18,000, increased to approximately 30,000 by 1600. In Dordrecht, too, the years between 1585 and 1609 saw strong population growth. Leiden, which had 12,000 inhabitants in 1581, had grown by 1622 into a city of nearly 45,000, an increase of 375 per cent. Amsterdam, which had sided with the Spanish king until 1578 and had therefore remained isolated, had scarcely more inhabitants in 1585 than in 1550, but in the twenty-five years after 1585 its population doubled. During the last two decades of the sixteenth century and the first two decades of the seventeenth, urban populations experienced spectacular growth, owing almost entirely to the large numbers of immigrants streaming into the young Republic. Some cities even managed to achieve sustained growth when the influx of immigrants slackened. Elsewhere we see a levelling off of the growth curve starting in the 1630s. Growth did not come to a complete standstill – this did not happen until around 1670 – but spectacular increases in population were seen in only a couple of places, namely Amsterdam and Rotterdam, both of which doubled in population after 1620.

Although there was no longer a meteoric rise in population after 1630, urbanisation in the west of the Republic was given a whole new dimension by the construction in 1631 of a *trekvaart* – a canal intended for passenger barges (*trekschuiten*) – between Amsterdam and Haarlem. This waterway was built for the purpose of providing regular passenger services, the punctuality of which could be guaranteed because the system was unaffected by the elements. Instead of being propelled by wind, the barges were pulled by horses, hence the need for tow-paths along their entire route. Moreover, even winter frost could not disrupt the timetable: when the canals froze, the same scheduled services were provided by sledges instead of barges.

The passenger barge caught on. In 1636 the States of Holland granted permission to Leiden and Delft to construct a canal connecting the two cities, a route to which The Hague was connected in 1638. Meanwhile a canal had been dug between Amsterdam and Weesp, and in 1640 between Amsterdam and Naarden. Barge canals were constructed in the northern provinces as well. By the mid-seventeenth century fifteen cities had invested 1.5 million guilders in 243 kilometres of canals, though an overall network had not yet materialised. In 1647, when investment in these waterways temporarily slackened, there were four separate networks: a

Figure 27 The network of *trekvaarten*, or canals specially built for passenger barges, in 1665 (taken from Jan de Vries, *Barges and Capitalism*, Utrecht, 1981).

route between Maassluis and Leiden, with a branch to The Hague; a canal running from Vreeswijk via Utrecht and Amsterdam to Haarlem; a route in the north from Workum via Leeuwarden to Dokkum and an alternative route from Harlingen to Dokkum; finally, in the province of Groningen, the city of Groningen was connected to Delfzijl and Winschoten. In the years between 1656 and 1665 these separate routes were finally incorporated into two large systems, one in the Holland–Utrecht area and one in the Friesland–Groningen area. In 1665 the two networks together totalled 658 kilometres and connected thirty cities, and were themselves connected by regular services to various harbours in Friesland. Every evening, for example, one could take a night barge from Amsterdam or Enkhuizen to Harlingen, Workum, Staveren or Lemmer, and find a connection in any of these cities to the northern canal system.

The passenger barge was slow – approximately seven kilometres per hour – but the barges were a wonder of comfort and punctuality. A bell was rung to announce their departure, and foreigners noted with amazement that there was no waiting for latecomers. When a barge was full – they could generally hold about twenty people – an extra one was pressed into service. Passengers leaving from Rotterdam could get a barge every hour, starting at 5 a.m., which would take them to Delft in 1 hour 45 minutes, where there was a barge nine times a day to Leiden, a journey of three hours. From Leiden there were nine barges a day to Haarlem, three times a day to Utrecht, and a special night barge leaving at 8 p.m. which arrived at 6 a.m. in Amsterdam.

Passenger barges mainly served the urban areas. In the North, where the cities were few and far between, the barges also stopped at villages. In the rural areas of Holland, however, villagers regularly used the market ferry, which allowed them to take cattle and produce to market. In the Holland–Utrecht network, more than 90 per cent of all travellers used the passenger barge to journey from one city to another, and it was these cities, of course, which took the initiative to raise the necessary capital and dig the canals. That burghers encouraged town councils to invest in this form of transport is evidenced by a petition submitted in 1640 to the Leiden authorities by a group of fifty prominent merchants, who urged the construction of a connection with the existing canal between Haarlem and Amsterdam in the hope that the reduction in travelling time would make Leiden more attractive to traders. The capital was raised by means of a bond issue. The city governors often succeeded in interesting social institutions – which they themselves conveniently controlled – in this form of investment. Socially speaking, the extraordinary thing about the passenger barge was that it grew into an efficient system of transport without any appreciable coordination from above. Awareness of the advantages of economic integration, as well as fear of missing the boat, as it were, were usually enough to move local governors to grant substantial sums of money to such projects. Even after the canals had been built, town councils remained closely involved in their operation by appointing commissioners, at least one of whom was required to be present at each scheduled departure. The network of cities thus created – in fact a foreshadowing of the Randstad, the present-day agglomeration of cities in the west of the Netherlands – was in fact maintained by the voluntary participation of all the cities involved.

Naturally the feasibility of the *trekvaart* system was greatly enhanced by the topographical suitability of the coastal provinces to this form of transport. The passenger barge was viable because of the flatness of the land and the presence of water. Indeed, to the south of Rotterdam there was even such an abundance of water that one could dispense with the digging of canals altogether. Elsewhere large-scale investment in the system was forthcoming only because of the sharply rising demand for transport, a demand that probably came least from the upper crust of society. Regents had either their own means of transport or the municipal yacht at their disposal. It seems, however, that all other social classes used the passenger barge: merchants maintaining business contacts, government officials travelling to The Hague, ordinary people looking for work elsewhere or simply going to the annual fair. Such fairs invariably meant peak season for the passenger barges.

In the inland provinces one had to make do with the stage-coach, which was two to three times as expensive and scarcely any faster than the passenger barge. Moreover, the schedule was much more difficult to maintain, since the weather largely determined the quality of the roads, which were generally no more than sandy tracks or muddy lanes. It was, however, not only natural conditions but also insufficient demand that hindered the development of a better system of transport in these inland provinces, which lacked the necessary combination of numerous urban centres and strong population growth.

The passenger barge was just one way in which the cities in the west of the country displayed their supremacy over the rural districts, a supremacy that was in itself nothing new. As early as 1531, the States of Holland had, at the insistence of the cities, passed an ordinance curbing the development of rural industry. The economic superiority of the cities had made rural industry largely dependent on urban markets. Important drainage schemes – such as those carried out in Holland's North Quarter – had been financed mainly by merchants from the cities, especially Amsterdam, who had mansions built and splendid gardens laid out, not only in the new polders but also in the dunes of Kennemerland, for example, and more to the south, along the River Vliet outside Leiden and Delft, and especially along the River Vecht between Utrecht and Amsterdam. In the early seventeenth century, however, the colonisation of the countryside entered a new phase when large numbers of city-dwellers began to buy manors, doubling their share of the country estates in the Rijnland district of Holland between 1585 and 1620.

What happened around Maarssen, to the west of Utrecht, is typical of these developments. In 1641 this domain came into the possession of Johan Huydecoper, whose son Johan we met in a previous chapter (see p. 128). In 1629 Huydecoper senior had become a member of the Amsterdam town council and in the years 1638–42 had built a monumental canal-side house on the Singel, designed by the prominent architect Philips Vingboons. Huydecoper was extremely interested in architecture: his children had drawing lessons from Vingboons, and he himself made architectural sketches on any paper he could find, including old letters. In Maarssen he owned the mansion Goudestein, directly on the River Vecht, but also made the rest of his grounds available for the building of country villas, of which no fewer than fourteen were built within twenty years. Some of the property was sold on the express condition that the new owner build a villa on it. The former farmstead of Endelhoef was even sold together with the design of the house to be built on the site and a penalty clause if the building did not go ahead as planned. Thus Maarssen developed in a short time into an exclusive residential area, where wealthy Amsterdammers could relax and escape from the unbearable stench of the canals in summer.

In 1637 Vingboons had designed Elsenburch, situated in Maarssen beside Huydecoper's mansion Goudestein. He also designed another mansion in Maarssen called Gansenhoef, and further up the River Vecht one called Vegtvliet. For Reinier Pauw, another prominent Amsterdam regent, he designed the country estate of Westwijck in the Purmer polder, and for the merchant Frederick Alewijn a house in the Beemster polder, though Alewijn's house was eventually built from the design of another architect. It was in the city itself, though, that Vingboons found his most important clients. For an architect, Amsterdam in the first half of the seventeenth century was a veritable paradise. Clients presented themselves by the dozens, each and every one jockeying for position in the extremely dynamic social life of the city. Money, it seemed, played no role whatsoever. There was plenty of building land available, thanks to the large extension approved almost immediately after the signing of the Twelve Years' Truce. Thirty years earlier, after Amsterdam joined the side of the Revolt in 1578, the city had been enlarged substantially for the first time in a century, partly to absorb the growth that had taken place before 1560 and partly for military and strategic reasons: the harbour and the 'Lastage' – the industrial areas to the east of the city – were extremely vulnerable and needed urgently to be brought within the city walls. In the 1580s a relatively small strip of land had been added around the rest of the city, but this was not enough to accommodate the population explosion. From 1609, therefore, work was begun on much more ambitious plans to enlarge the city. The realisation of this extension to the west of the city would put the city walls approximately twice as far from Dam Square and double the surface area of the city. The plan, as it was finally carried out, sought to accommodate two social milieux in more or less separate environments. A new neighbourhood – which later became known as the Jordaan – was planned for the area just inside the new wall, where the layout of the streets followed the existing allotment of the pastures now brought inside the city walls. Ditches were vaulted over or changed into canals. Along those canals, lots suitable for tradesmen and artisans were created. The connecting streets and alleys were intended for the working classes. The plans also included the construction – just outside the old city walls, and therefore close to the Stock Exchange and the Town Hall – of three parallel canals, called the Herengracht, the Prinsengracht and the Keizersgracht (the Gentlemen's, Princes' and Emperors' canals). Industry was forbidden in this area and wide lots were laid out for the benefit of the well-to-do, many of whom bought two or three adjacent lots and had wide-fronted mansions built. This was the neighbourhood where Vingboons's clients settled down. In the 1660s another extension completed the ring on the south and east sides of the city, again creating a large number of building lots. In contrast to the extension of 1610, this one was never fully developed, because the expected growth in population failed to occur. These two enlargements gave Amsterdam its characteristic shape which is still visible today.

Other cities were extended as well. Between 1591 and 1606, Rotterdam was enlarged in two directions, primarily to increase the capacity of the harbour but also to provide more housing. Leiden underwent extensions in 1611 and again in 1644 and 1658. Haarlem was extended in the 1670s. One very important argument in favour of these three extensions was the need for more housing for the well-to-do, and, as in Amsterdam, the plans expressly provided for the building of stately canals to provide the proper setting for their prestigious mansions. In Utrecht, too, this was the most important consideration when drawing up the plans for a city extension in the 1660s. Utrecht's extension was designed by Hendrick Moreelse, burgomaster of the city and son of the famous portrait painter Paulus Moreelse. In Moreelse's view, an extension of the city was urgently needed 'to attract a greater influx of people, primarily by opening up suitable, pleasant and wonderful opportunities for powerful and rich people, for the purpose of reviving and relieving our increasingly declining tradesmen and artisans, increasing consumption, and consequently improving all public and private incomes'.[2] Moreelse thus described in a nutshell the chain reaction he expected from attracting the well-to-do to the city. The money they spent and invested would breathe new life into Utrecht's declining middle classes and boost both private and public expenditure, leading to greater prosperity for all.

Moreelse's plans were as ambitious as his theories were extravagant. A vast quarter was to be built, chiefly to the west of the city, with lots twice the size of those along Amsterdam's principal canals. A draft shows palatial houses with extremely large gardens. The whole plan – designed in accordance with the latest fashion, following a strict geometric pattern –

---

[2] Ed Taverne, *In 't land van belofte: in de nieue stadt; Ideaal en werkelijkheid van de stadsuitleg in de Republiek 1580–1680* (Maarssen: Gary Schwartz, 1978), p. 252.

exuded an air of quiet beauty. For Moreelse's colleagues, however, it was simply too ambitious. The city's economic decline – which was Moreelse's strongest argument for the necessity of adopting his plan – was the very thing that prevented the city governors from risking their limited financial resources. The town council dithered endlessly; the French occupation of 1672 and its aftermath eventually caused the plan to be shelved. Only at the beginning of the nineteenth century was it accidentally discovered by the ambitious burgomaster Van Asch van Wyck, who not only wrote a short biography of Moreelse but also presented his own town-planning scheme and hailed it as the direct descendant of Moreelse's plan.

The city extensions – and, it should be borne in mind, even more building within the existing city walls – created a huge demand for private housing as well as for a number of new public buildings. Someone who was especially successful in this market was the Haarlem-born architect Pieter Post. Post began his career as a draughtsman in the employ of another Haarlem artist and architect, Jacob van Campen. Van Campen, who had been strongly influenced by classical traditions, guided Huygens in his study of Vitruvius, the influential architect-theorist of ancient Rome. Huygens eventually designed his own house in The Hague, based on the principles of classicism. These consisted mainly of regularity, harmonious proportions, taut lines and antique elements, such as pilasters and tympana. A classicist building was immediately recognisable by these details, as well as by its symmetry. In the house built after Van Campen's design next to the Binnenhof for Johan Maurits of Nassau-Siegen – now known as the Mauritshuis, the home of the Royal Cabinet of Paintings – these principles were consistently applied. This architectural style, interestingly enough, caught on among aristocrats and regents alike. The former had a traditional bond with classical antiquity, while the latter saw it as an important source of inspiration for their republican ideas.

Pieter Post profited from this interest in classicism. After the itinerant Maurits – who had remained something of a soldier his whole life long, even after the difficult years of the Revolt – Frederik Hendrik was determined to raise the status of the Oranges until it was on a par with that of the Republic itself. To bring this about, he not only sought for his children marriage partners from the most prominent courts, but also threw himself into a building programme designed to provide visual proof that the Oranges were the equals of foreign princes. In 1645 Post officially became 'His Highness's architect', though he had actually filled this role since 1640. Post was put in charge of the renovations carried out on the stadholder's quarters at the Binnenhof in The Hague, the renovation of

Noordeinde Palace (now the queen's working quarters), the extension of Honselaarsdijk Palace (which has disappeared) and the building of a new summer house for Amalia of Solms, the wife of the stadholder. This last building, the Huis ten Bosch (now the queen's residence), was originally planned as a modest country house, but gradually became larger and more ambitious in scope.

Though Post retained his position as court architect after 1650, there was no longer any question of large-scale building during the stadholder-less era. However, the States of Holland and other government bodies more than made up for this shortage of princely commissions. The large number of commissions Post received from civic authorities included a new weigh-house in Gouda; a weigh-house, a butter hall and a gatehouse in Leiden; a town gate (the Wittevrouwenpoort) in Utrecht; a church (the Oostkerk) in Middelburg; and finally his most eye-catching creation, the town hall in Maastricht. Everywhere in the Republic, town halls were being built or renovated.[3] Between 1590 and 1621, new town halls were built in Franeker (1591–4), Leiden (1592), Dokkum (1608), Bolsward (1613–17) and Delft (1618) and existing town halls were renovated in Leiden (1604), Bergen-op-Zoom (1611) and Hattem (1619). Later on the authorities also decided to build new town halls in Lochem (1634–40), Amsterdam (begun in 1648), Maastricht (1659–64) and Enkhuizen (1686–88), while thorough renovations were carried out in Haarlem (1633), Deventer (1662 and 1692–4), 's-Hertogenbosch (1670), Gouda (1675) and again Leiden (1660).

The commission in Maastricht proved to be complicated, owing to the difficulties presented by the location and the complex political situation. The square where the building was to be erected was very irregular in shape and therefore unsuited to the strictly regular forms of classicism. Post's clever solution to this problem entailed demolishing various buildings and planting trees on two sides of the square to produce the illusion of a perfect square, and on this seeming square he built his creation.

The Maastricht town hall consists of a square block, all four sides of which measure 100 feet. The façades are divided by means of pilasters into nine sections, or bays. The cellar and the ground floor housed the least glamorous facilities, such as storage rooms, prison cells, the civic carpenter's yard and the civic militia's guardrooms. The first floor, reached via a double staircase at the front, is completely symmetrical in design. Naturally this was one of the precepts of the classicist architectural style, but in this case there was another important reason to divide

---

[3] This overview concerns only the so-called voting cities. I am indebted to Koen Ottenheym for supplying me with this information.

the building in this way. Since the thirteenth century Maastricht had been ruled jointly by Liège and Brabant. When Maastricht was conquered by Frederik Hendrik in 1632, Brabant's rights were transferred to the States General. Under this form of dual government, Maastricht's governing bodies were composed of representatives of both Liège and Brabant, each with their own staircase and, in the colleges of justice, their own court-rooms. The magistrates and town councillors, however, held a general assembly. Post grouped the rooms around a monumental central hall crowned by a dome reaching up to the roof.

Although Post was successful as a designer of public buildings, he was not awarded the most prestigious commission of all – the new Amsterdam Town Hall. Various payments made to him show that he was very much involved in the planning stage, though no independent designs of his are known. The most important candidates for the commission were the ubiquitous Philips Vingboons, even though his experience did not extend beyond private houses, and the equally ubiquitous Jacob van Campen. It was Van Campen who finally received the commission – at a very late stage. The Amsterdam regents had been seriously considering plans for a new town hall since 1639. The existing town hall was much too small, and the incorporation of neighbouring houses had created a labyrinth of corridors and stairwells. The building's state of disrepair and the danger of collapse had already led to the decision to build a new town hall when the old one, as fate would have it, was destroyed by fire in early July 1652.

By then, however, the building of the new Town Hall was well under way. In May 1643 a start had been made by demolishing the houses around Dam Square to make room for it. On 20 January 1648, ten days before the signing of the Peace of Münster, the first pile was driven into the ground, even though a design had yet to be approved. A total of 13,659 trunks of Scandinavian conifers, each some 12 metres long, were driven by hand into the marshy ground at an average rate of sixty per day, until a solid sand flat was reached on which the entire building could stand. Six months later the decision was made to rotate the design ninety degrees and to expand its area considerably. It was probably at this time that Van Campen produced his definitive design.

It was taken for granted that Van Campen's design would meet the classicist requirements of regularity, harmonious proportions and antique elements. The antique elements were ably represented by pila-sters of the Composite and the Corinthian Order, as well as by the tympana on both front and back. The harmonious proportions were to be in keeping with the natural proportions of the human body and the cosmos. The front and back were therefore subdivided into units of 40, 60, 80, 60 and 40 feet, and these proportions were carried through to all

Figure 28   The Amsterdam Town Hall in Dam Square was officially opened on 29 July 1655, even though after twelve years of construction it was not yet finished. The Town Hall, the largest public building project undertaken in the Republic in the seventeenth century, served to illustrate - both inside and out - the ambitions of the Amsterdam civic authorities (Amsterdam Municipal Archives d 6258).

the subdivisions. The Amsterdam Town Hall was built in mirror-image over the longitudinal axis, by means of two inner courtyards, which provided the building with natural light. The ingenious part of Van Campen's design was that he not only succeeded in providing a place for all civic functions – from the prison and the court of justice to the treasury, and from the Exchange Bank to the headquarters of the civic militia – but managed to do it in such a way that the power relations were adequately expressed by their location. To this end Van Campen patterned his building after the model of the ancient forum.

It was therefore no coincidence that the very centre of the building was given over to an enormous hall, called from the very beginning the Citizens' Hall (Burgerzaal). The floor of this hall consisted of a mosaic depicting the terrestrial hemispheres – with Amsterdam prominently displayed in the northern hemisphere – and the northern celestial hemisphere. The richly carved decorations also gave expression to the cosmic meaning of the Town Hall. The building was a statement of power – in stone. Joost van den Vondel, the most famous Dutch poet of his day, did not mince his words in the poem the town council commissioned him to write for the official opening on 29 July 1655 (long before the building was actually completed):

> The Seven Peoples,[4] who from one German tribe do stem,
> Confess that God and Amsterdam have granted them
> Salvation, falling like the morning dew and blessing.[5]

In 1,378 rich lines of verse Vondel portrayed the Town Hall as a *Gesamtkunstwerk*, which in all manner of ways expressed the reality and the ambitions, the past and the present, the economy, the politics and the arts of Amsterdam. Huygens summarised it succinctly in a poem composed for the same occasion. Reciting it during the banquet laid on for the town councillors, he addressed the gentlemen as the 'founders of the eighth wonder of the world'.[6] Such praise from the lips of the courtier Huygens must have been music to the ears of Amsterdam's regents.

---

[4] The Seven Peoples personify the seven provinces.
[5] Saskia Albrecht et al., *Vondels' Inwydinge van 't Stadthuis t' Amsterdam* (Muiderberg: Coutinho, 1982), p. 187, lines 1371–3.
[6] Ibid., p. 28.

17 The end of the Golden Age

Some time between 1672 and 1715 the Golden Age came to an end. It is impossible to give a precise date, but in the winter of 1715, when the Union treasury had to be closed because there was no money left to pay the interest on government bonds, insiders saw the writing on the wall. The state bankruptcy, for that is what it was, lasted nine months, after which creditors had to settle for lower interest rates on their investments. As the Dutch ambassador in London wrote in a letter dated 26 November 1715, 'The Republic is in a bad state and other countries know this all too well.'[1]

These financial troubles were no coincidence, but rather a symptom of deep-seated problems that had been brewing for decades. The growth of the cities, which had been such a dynamic factor in the rise of the Republic, had come to a standstill in the last decades of the seventeenth century. Only Amsterdam was still expanding, owing in part to its relaxation of the requirements for citizenship, such as the lowering of citizenship fees, which enabled less well-to-do burghers to acquire citizenship. Despite these efforts to boost population growth, the fourth extension to the city, carried out in the 1660s, did not become fully developed until the nineteenth century. More tellingly, large-scale public works became less and less frequent. Among the voting cities in the States of Holland, Enkhuizen was the only one to build a new town hall after 1672, the Year of Disaster.

A levelling-off of urban population growth, and in many cases even outright decline, was in turn the tangible result of underlying economic problems. In agriculture the decline had set in as early as the mid-seventeenth century. The prices of agricultural products had been dropping in all European markets since the 1650s, and because the majority of

---

[1] J. Aalbers, *De Republiek en de vrede van Europa. De buitenlandse politiek van de Republiek der Verenigde Nederlanden na de Vrede van Utrecht (1713), voornamelijk gedurende de jaren 1720–1733: achtergronden en algemene aspecten* (Groningen: Wolters Noordhoff, 1980), p. 330, n. 20.

Europeans lived in the countryside and were therefore dependent, either directly or indirectly, on incomes deriving from agriculture, a drop in the price of farm products meant a corresponding drop in purchasing power. In this shrinking market, moreover, other countries began to take steps to protect their own producers. The English Navigation Act of 1651 had marked the start of a string of protectionist measures, first in England itself and from 1664 also in France. These measures, aimed especially at the Hollanders, had adverse effects on such activities as the cloth industry in Leiden (production began to drop around 1670), shipbuilding (an English law passed in 1676 prohibited English shipowners from using any but English ships) and earthenware manufacturers (an English embargo was in effect throughout the 1670s and 1680s). Dutch pipe manufacturers and sugar refiners suffered heavy losses as a result of French regulations.

The domestic market worsened as well. Johannes Vermeer was certainly not the only painter in financial trouble: after 1672, sales of new paintings dropped dramatically everywhere in the Republic. At the same time, the heavy taxes necessary to finance the continuing war effort were pushing prices up, and the government loans contracted in support of those same wars were draining capital from the productive sector, since the government guaranteed an admittedly modest but nevertheless risk-free return on one's money. The decline was scarcely visible at first, but by the mid-eighteenth century it was evident for all to see. The English writer James Boswell, forced to study in Utrecht by a father who talked endlessly about the beauty of Dutch cities, was disillusioned when he saw the country with his own eyes. In 1764 he wrote of his disappointment to a friend in England:

Most of their principal towns are sadly decayed. Instead of finding every mortal employed, you meet with multitudes of poor creatures who are starving in idleness. Utrecht is remarkably ruined ... You see, then, that things are very different here from what most people imagine. Were Sir William Temple to revisit these Provinces, he would scarcely believe the amazing alteration which they have undergone.[2]

Because the economy had been the driving force behind advancements in many fields, the prospect of increasing hardship had a domino effect. The well-to-do suffered relatively little, however. By cutting back on their trading activities and investing all available capital in the national debt, they shielded themselves from the cold economic winds that blew across

[2] Frederick A. Pottle (ed.), *Boswell in Holland 1763–1764* (London: McGraw-Hill, 1952), p. 281.

the polders. The middle classes, though, and especially the working classes, were left out in the cold.

In 1685 the Haarlem town councillors forbade the transport of vagrants by passenger barge from Amsterdam to Haarlem, though such transport in the opposite direction was still allowed. The number of immigrants decreased noticeably: in Amsterdam, 40 per cent of those marrying in the 1640s had been foreigners. By the end of the century, this had declined to 25 per cent. In many places the institutions administering poor relief found themselves in financial straits. To ease the burden, members of the tolerated, but technically illegal churches, such as the Catholics and the Lutherans, were forced increasingly to care for their 'own' poor. Even though this inadvertently offered greater freedom to these oppressed religious communities, it did little to alleviate general social ills.

The political consequences were severe indeed. To protect Holland's trading interests – sometimes even its very existence – the Republic had been forced continually to expand its armed forces. The wars against the English had shown the necessity of an extensive programme of shipbuilding. The series of wars with France, which broke out in 1672 and ended only in 1713 with the Peace of Utrecht, placed an almost unbearable financial burden on the Republic. In this period Holland's debt doubled and that of the Union quadrupled. In 1715 more than half of the ordinary revenues of the province of Holland went directly to creditors. The closing of the Union treasury, albeit temporary, had in fact meant the end of a period in which the Republic, despite its relatively small population, had been able to maintain its status as a great power by borrowing huge sums of money. By 1715 there was no more room for manoeuvring, and the conclusion was inevitable: the country would have to maintain strict neutrality and its armed forces would no longer be able to intervene to protect vital trading interests. Dutch merchants would henceforth have to fend for themselves.

This forced withdrawal to the position of second-rate power had in turn a significant effect on employment opportunities. Until 1713 the army had been far and away the largest employer in the Republic. During the War of the Spanish Succession (1702–13), the Republic had more than 100,000 men in military service. Immediately afterwards, troop reductions cut their numbers to 40,000, and by 1725 to fewer than 30,000, 12,000 of whom were garrisoned in the 'barrier' towns in the Southern Netherlands, which served as a buffer against a possible French offensive. In the second half of the 1720s, when the number of men in the armed forces again increased to more than 50,000 – a result of the Republic's commitments to its allies – the effect on the Generality's budget was felt immediately. Amsterdam lost no time in demanding

Figure 29   Utrecht's town hall at the time of the negotiations for the Peace of Utrecht (1713), which put an end to the War of the Spanish Succession. Although the Republic had been on the winning side in the war, it lost the peace, so to speak, to the English. As a result of the war, the Dutch Republic had to bow out of its leading role on the international stage (I. Smit, 1712; Atlas van Stolk 3407).

cutbacks in the form of troop reductions. As Amsterdammers said, not without reason, 'Having no money but wanting to be rich is a bad thing.'[3]

This policy of military aloofness had grave consequences for domestic politics. During the seventeenth century it had been difficult enough to agree on a common policy and to share its cost, but now it was almost impossible. Holland was torn by internal strife. The cities that were experiencing a drop in population insisted on a redistribution of the financial burden. For years Amsterdam had blocked redistribution,

[3] J. Aalbers, 'Het machtsverval van de Republiek der Verenigde Nederlanden 1713–1741', in J. Aalbers and A. P. Van Goudoever (eds.), *Machtsverval in de internationale context* (Groningen: Wolters Noordhoff/Forsten, 1986), p. 11.

since it was still growing and therefore profiting by the existing situation. By way of revenge, the other cities obstructed the decision-making process in matters that were of particular interest to Amsterdam. Many provinces could not fulfil their obligations. In 1716 Friesland, where agriculture had been hard hit by the cattle plague, paid less than one-quarter of the amount it was expected to contribute to the Generality's coffers, and in 1717 and 1718 its contribution was only one-third of what it should have been. Between 1715 and 1725 the province of Groningen contributed absolutely nothing towards paying off the interest on the Generality's debt. In the past, Holland had always helped to solve such problems by acting as a moneylender or making up the deficit itself, but Holland, too, had exhausted its resources. The province did what it could, including taking such initiatives as issuing so-called lottery loans, whereby a normal interest-earning bond doubled as a lottery ticket. This, of course, was not a sound method of financing a government. The other provinces, which had always viewed the national debt as Holland's affair, were even less inclined than before to lend their support. 'It's a republic of persuasion',[4] sighed Amsterdam's representatives in 1731, when the umpteenth attempt at financial reform had failed. That pronouncement would have been just as applicable to the seventeenth-century Republic, although then particularism had been tempered by the need to negotiate, a situation brought about by the succession of wars. After 1713, the determination to pursue a policy of neutrality had done away with that need, which meant that decisions could be put off for ever, while public and private interest groups in the cities and provinces lobbied to undermine the opposition. 'We're in favour of fair words, except when our own interests are at stake',[5] said the same Amsterdammers, thus offering an apt description of the political disintegration of the country.

Of course the Republic did not go completely to ruin. In the second half of the eighteenth century there was even a slight economic recovery, though everyone understood that a new era had dawned. Particularly in the 1780s, during the Patriot revolution, there was a constant call for reform, motivated by the Republic's loss of prosperity and standing in the world. In 1785 the Patriots of Holland published a programme that promised to make the Republic 'happy from within and formidable from without'.[6] Nothing came of it, however. The pressure of the French occupation, which began in the winter of 1794–5, followed by renewed negotiations that dragged on for years, led to a coup on 21–22

---

[4] Aalbers, *De Republiek en de vrede van Europa*, p. 117.   [5] Ibid.
[6] 'Ontwerp, om de Republiek door eene heilzaame vereeniging der belangen van regent en burger van binnen en van buiten gedugt te maaken' (Leiden: Herdingh, 1785).

January 1798. As a result, the structure of the federal state was replaced by a centralised government in The Hague, while the provinces lost all of their former autonomy. Provincial and civic bodies were degraded to the status of executive agencies, serving only to implement the guidelines issued by the national government.

On that fateful night in January, events conspired to put a definite end to a historic experiment, an end that had been in the offing since 1715. Slowly but surely, the late-medieval and early-modern European societies had been changing in character under the influence of two great processes: the breakthrough of capitalism and the formation of the modern state. Although the market had previously played a role in economic life, that role had been limited. Trade was small-scale and overwhelmingly regional. International, let alone intercontinental, trade was the exception. For manufacturers, the low level of commercialisation was scant inducement to innovation and efficiency. Trade focused on the cities, and the low level of urbanisation was thereby indicative of the market's limited influence on the economy.

The increasing importance of trade in Europe between 1500 and 1800 is evidenced by the corresponding increase in the degree of urbanisation, which roughly doubled in this period. This development, however, did not take place everywhere with the same intensity or speed. In 1500, Italy and the Low Countries had been the undisputed frontrunners, with an urban growth rate of two to four times the European average. The Italian cities did not keep up this pace, but in the Republic the degree of urbanisation doubled again between 1500 and 1650. The prominent role played by the cities of the Italian peninsula and the Low Countries is also apparent from their commercial leadership. In the fourteenth and fifteenth centuries, Venice had been the largest European centre of international trade, owing mainly to the fact that Asian spices routinely made their way to Europe via the Middle East. Venice, once the western outpost of the Byzantine Empire, was ideally placed to receive these goods, which were subsequently shipped – at first over the Alps and later via the Straits of Gibraltar – to the rest of Europe. In the sixteenth century, however, the economic heart of Europe began to shift from the Mediterranean region to the Atlantic seaboard and the North Sea, owing in part to the Portuguese discovery of an alternative route to the Indies. This new route, around the southern tip of Africa, allowed the Portuguese to bypass the Mediterranean. Only a small part of the spices they imported could be sold in Portugal itself, however, and Portugal was off the beaten path when it came to the important markets in continental Europe. Since the Portuguese could hardly sell their spices in Italy, they sought an alternative, finding it in the Southern Netherlands. In 1501 the

Portuguese spice entrepôt was established at Antwerp, making Antwerp the successor – or at least a rival – to Venice. In the seventeenth century, Antwerp was succeeded by Amsterdam as the centre of world trade. The rise of these cities transformed the economic life of Europe's hinterlands, the commercialisation of which in turn stimulated the further development of international trade. This meant that Europe now had two regions where commercialisation was well advanced and commercial capitalism firmly entrenched. These two regions were connected by a belt of cities stretching all the way from Italy to the Low Countries. Europe's urban backbone was formed not only by a number of larger cities situated along the Rhine and in southern Germany – such as Cologne, Frankfurt and Augsburg – but also by Basel and Zürich in Switzerland, which, though actually quite small, exerted a great influence on the surrounding rural areas.

Remarkably enough, the process of state formation in Europe displayed a pattern of geographical symmetry. In the belt of cities, the modern state gained a foothold only late or not at all. In the late Middle Ages, principalities began to strengthen their authority by extending the powers of central government. Under the feudal system, central authority had been continually weakened by splitting up territories in order to give feudal estates to nobles in return for military services. Public expenditure had been financed by the return on crown property. Starting in the fifteenth century, princes tried to levy taxes more systematically and to exert more control on lawmaking and the administration of justice. In the sixteenth century this process was speeded up by the military revolution, which required a standing army of well-drilled troops. After the Reformation, governments also began to concern themselves with the opinions of their subjects. This interaction was especially successful in the more agrarian parts of Europe, in the British Isles, France, Spain, Prussia and Russia, not to mention the Scandinavian countries, where monarchical absolutism reached its apex in the seventeenth century. The urban areas largely remained free from this centralisation and bureaucratisation of the state machinery. Neither the Italian nor the German territories were united until the second half of the nineteenth century, and the Swiss state is remarkably unintegrated even today. The resistance to the growing power of the state derived directly from the economic structure of these regions. The cities were collection points for capital flows, and this capital was easily siphoned off for public expenditure. The inhabitants of these areas were willing to part with their money, provided they could exert some influence on how it was spent. Attempts to pressure them or to take their money by force were thwarted by the extreme mobility of capital, as the Habsburgs found out in 1585 when they conquered

Antwerp. Trading contacts were not easy to control politically. Thus the centres of commerce coupled small-scale politics and decentralisation with an extensive network of trading contacts. By contrast, the territorial states were large, with governments that were more centralised and at the same time economies that were more introverted.

Contemporaries realised all too well that the various regions that formed Europe's urban backbone had something in common. Amsterdam began to compare itself to Venice even before it succeeded in outstripping Antwerp. In 1544, Cornelis Anthonisz made an aerial perspective of Amsterdam, the idea for which had been taken from a Venetian example of 1500. In 1609 the regulations of the Amsterdam Exchange Bank were shamelessly copied from those of the Banco della Piassa di Rialto, which had been founded in Venice in 1587. Writers who concerned themselves with the governmental institutions of the Dutch Republic saw in Venice an example which the Republic would do well to follow. One such writer was Pieter de la Court, who made a careful study of the history and constitution of Venice, from which he gleaned various ideas which he then submitted in the form of recommendations to the regents of Holland. One particularly praiseworthy characteristic of the Republic of Venice, in his opinion, was the way it prevented its rulers from forming cliques. Venice was not De la Court's only source of inspiration, however. In 1671, when he wished to demonstrate that all of Holland's larger cities – 'no less than any other republic consisting of one city'[7] – could be defended against attacks by foreign powers, he took as his examples the Imperial Cities of Germany (such as Hamburg, Bremen, Cologne, Frankfurt, Strasbourg, Ulm and Nuremberg), the Swiss 'republics and cities' (namely Basel, Schaffhausen, Zürich, Lucerne, Berne and Fribourg) and the Italian city of Lucca.

The Swiss looked in turn upon the Dutch Republic as an example to be followed. They adopted Holland's social innovations, such as its houses of correction, and also took inspiration, as did many countries, from the military reforms introduced by Prince Maurits of Nassau. Moreover, they modelled their political reforms on the Dutch system of establishing institutions to deal with the inevitable problems of coordination arising in an internally divided republic. A treatise from the 1630s, for example, recommended the establishment of a Council of State (*Stand-Rath*) in the Swiss confederation, 'based on the manner and form of the Council of State of the gentlemen in the States General, who reside at The Hague in

---

[7] (Pieter de la Court), *Aanwysing der heilsame politike gronden en maximen van de Republike van Holland en West-Vriesland* (Leiden/Rotterdam: Hakkens, 1671), p. 351.

Figure 30 Details of engravings of Venice (above) and Amsterdam (below). Interestingly enough, the depiction of Venice was made in 1614 in Amsterdam by Willem Jansz Blaeu, while the depiction of Amsterdam was made around 1620 in Venice by Giovanni Femini and Giorgio Salmisio, apparently as a pendant to Blaeu's depiction. The similarities in composition are striking. Amsterdam saw itself as the direct descendant of Venice, but other cities in the Dutch Republic also considered Venice an example well worth following (Royal Dutch Maritime Museum, Amsterdam).

Holland, and have until now ruled so happily and with such great success, despite their humble beginnings'.[8]

In the seventeenth century Venice, itself a long-standing model of an exemplary city-state, began to follow Amsterdam's example. Venetian prints depicting the city took their inspiration – to the extent of including numerous topographically incorrect details – from similar prints of Amsterdam. In Holland these perspectives of Venice were made as pendants to similar perspectives of Amsterdam.

Within Europe's belt of cities, however, the Dutch Republic was not simply a state cast in the Venetian mould. The Dutch Republic differed essentially in size and complexity. Though in the early fifteenth century Venice had conquered a sizeable territory (the Terra Ferma), it remained in essence a city-state. The Dutch Republic, by contrast, was never a city-state in the proper sense. In the province of Holland alone, eighteen cities, both large and small, had to manage to work together somehow; on a larger scale, the seven provinces had to cooperate in the same way. As has repeatedly emerged from the preceding pages, this was no easy task. Even so, for much of the seventeenth century the cities and provinces succeeded in welding the Republic not just into a workable whole but into a power of the first order. It is indeed amazing that such a young and relatively small state could play a leading role on the international stage for nearly a century, growing, in the words of Sir William Temple, into 'the envy of some, the fear of others, and the wonder of all their neighbours'.[9] The previous pages have shown that the Republic achieved this not in spite of, but rather because of, the loosely woven fabric of its state structure, which formed the ideal backdrop for the development of trade, which in turn provided the money needed to achieve dominance in international relations. For nearly a century the Republic thus succeeded in being both a major player in the economic sphere – as Venice and Antwerp had previously been – and a formidable military opponent to countries eager to encroach on its territory and economic interests. Seen from this perspective, the state bankruptcy of 1715 did indeed mark the end of an era. The Republic could no longer withstand attempts to harm its vital interests. In the end, its weakened state led to the loss of political independence in the French era at the beginning of the nineteenth century. The country regained its freedom, but only under a completely different form of government, one in which the cities were largely subordinate to

---

[8] Frieder Walter, *Niederländische Einflüsse auf das eidgenössische Staatsdenken im späten 16. und frühen 17. Jahrhundert* (Zürich: Rohr, 1979), p. 62.

[9] Sir William Temple, *Observations upon the United Provinces of the Netherlands*, edited by Sir George Clark (Oxford: Clarendon Press, 1972), p. 1.

provincial and national authority. Clearly, the Netherlands was no longer the country it had been during the Golden Age.

The history of the Dutch Republic can also be viewed from another angle. The greatness of the Republic rested on the unique ability of the Dutch to exploit the advantanges of both smallness at home and expansiveness abroad. The transparency of urban society was conducive to trust, and it was this trust that prompted people to enter into joint business ventures. Moreover, it was their faith in local and provincial government that enabled those governments to borrow money at extremely low rates of interest. Such trust was not to be taken for granted in the seventeenth century; indeed, many countries at this time were experiencing violent and repeated clashes between the populace and the authorities. The small scale of the Republic made it easier to find a modus vivendi, but smallness proved to be a disadvantage when the state was confronted with powerful opponents boasting more sizeable populations and greater financial resources. In the arms race of early-modern times, this was a potentially fatal shortcoming. The Republic managed to overcome this drawback through the voluntary cooperation of local and provincial communities. Despite its republican diversity, it somehow managed to achieve the unity necessary for an effective foreign policy, which was essential to protect its worldwide economic interests. The Republic had a powerful trading network out of all proportion to its small size, and a proportionately greater effort was therefore required of its small population to maintain it. By 1715, however, the burden had become too great. For more than a century, that curious blend of unity and discord, urban and rural, large and small, cosmopolitan and provincial which constituted the Dutch Republic had worked to remarkable effect. Although the Golden Age had come to an end, it left the Dutch with a valuable legacy. At the beginning of the nineteenth century, the Netherlands still had the highest per capita income in Europe and possibly the entire world, and until well into the twentieth century it remained a world power, a position from which the Dutch profited greatly. Dutch culture became known throughout the world, and its enduring fame is due in large measure to the lasting achievements of a single century – the Golden Age of the Dutch Republic.

Further reading

So much has been written on the Dutch Golden Age that there is no point in attempting to list all the relevant literature. Anyone intending to read widely and exhaustively would be better served by the bibliographies found in specialised works. I have concentrated here on mentioning recently published works that may help those wishing to delve more deeply into the subject. The literature appearing between 1945 and around 1980 is discussed in the two articles that Guido de Bruin contributed to W. W. Mijnhardt (ed.), *Kantelend geschiedbeeld. Nederlandse historiografie sinds 1945* (Utrecht, 1983). Recently published literature is discussed, usually around a year after its appearance, in the *Bijdragen en Mededelingen betreffende de Geschiedenis der Nederlanden*. It is useful to know that many monographs written in Dutch also contain English summaries.

Footnotes have been used in this book only to reference quotations. Otherwise I have listed the sources (and recommendations for further reading) by chapter. To avoid unnecessary searching, titles that occur in more than one chapter are mentioned in full in each chapter; shortened titles are used only upon subsequent mention within a given chapter. These sources sometimes include references to museums and websites that are worth a visit. The website www.historischhuis.nl contains, under the heading 'nieuwe geschiedenis', a great deal of information on the history of the Republic and the relevant museums, archives and so on.

INTRODUCTION: THE ENIGMA OF THE REPUBLIC

Of course this is not the first book to be written on the seventeenth-century Dutch Republic, and after reading this book the reader may profitably turn to others which contain more detailed information or information of a different kind. Such worthy predecessors as Robert Fruin, *De drie tijdvakken der Nederlandsche Geschiedenis* (1865, reprinted in his *Verspreide Geschriften*, The Hague, 1900–5), P. L. Muller, *Onze Gouden Eeuw: de Republiek der Vereenigde Nederlanden in haar bloeitijd* (Leiden, 1908), Johan Huizinga, *Dutch Civilisation in the Seventeenth Century* (London, 1968, originally published in Dutch in 1941) and Pieter Geyl, *The Netherlands in the Seventeenth Century*, 2 vols. (London, 1961) (first published in English in 1936 as *The Netherlands Divided*) are especially interesting for those wishing to know how earlier generations viewed the Republic. The most detailed book on the subject is Jonathan I. Israel, *The Dutch Republic: Its Rise, Greatness, and Fall 1477–1806* (Oxford, 1995), which contains more than a thousand pages, most of which treat the Golden Age. It deals with the economy, social structure, the religious situation, etc., and is especially valuable for its chronological ordering of events. Much of the information it contains cannot be found elsewhere. The fifteen-volume *Algemene Geschiedenis der Nederlanden* (Bussum, 1980) was edited by D. P. Blok et al. Numerous experts worked on this project. Volumes V–IX treat a variety of aspects of the seventeenth century, volume V being of particular importance.

Several books view the Republic from a certain angle, but do it in such a comprehensive way that they actually illuminate the whole of society. This is true of Willem Frijhoff and Marijke Spies, *1650: Hard–Won Unity* (Assen: Van Gorcum and Basingstoke: Palgrave, 2004), which treats both high and low culture from the vantage point of the mid-seventeenth century, and of A. Th. van Deursen, *Plain Lives in a Golden Age: Popular Culture, Religion and Society in Seventeenth-Century Holland* (Cambridge, 1991), which views society from its lower rungs. Van Deursen confines his story to Holland and stops at mid-century because he was mainly interested in how ordinary folk experienced the Revolt. The recent work of J. L. Price, *Dutch Society 1588–1713* (Harlow, 2000), concentrates especially on the social aspects of the Republic. The essays in Karel Davids and Jan Lucassen (eds.), *A Miracle Mirrored: The Dutch Republic in European Perspective* (Cambridge, 1995), view the peculiarities of the Republic compared with the situation in other European countries. The same holds true for the history of ideas in Jonathan I. Israel, *Radical Enlightenment: Philiosophy and the Making of Modernity 1650–1750* (Oxford, 2001), a great deal of which is devoted to the Dutch debates, which it places in an international context. Perhaps the most original approach is that of Willem Frijhoff, *Wegen van Evert Willemsz. Een Hollands weeskind op zoek naar zichzelf, 1607–1647* (Nijmegen, 1995), which familiarises the reader with the Republic through the fate of one individual who was anything but ordinary.

1   A TURBULENT BEGINNING

The story of the Netherlands in the fifteenth and the first half of the sixteenth centuries is generally described as one of growing unity under Burgundian and later Habsburg rule. An excellent survey of these developments is to be found in W. Blockmans and W. Prevenier, *The Promised Lands. The Low Countries under Burgundian Rule, 1369–1530* (Philadelphia, 1999). Also to be recommended is James D. Tracy, *Holland under Habsburg Rule 1506–1566: The Formation of a Body Politic* (Berkeley, Calif., 1990).

If, however, one surveys the situation from the viewpoint of areas that long remained outside the Burgundian–Habsburg sphere, a completely different picture emerges. In writing this book I have made use of various provincial histories, namely: J. J. Kalma et al. (eds.), *Geschiedenis van Friesland* (Drachten, 1968); J. Frieswijk et al. (eds.) *Fryslân, staat en macht 1450–1650* (Hilversum, 1999); W. J. Formsma et al. (eds.), *Historie van Groningen Stad en Land* (Groningen, 1981); P. J. Meij et al. (eds.), *Geschiedenis van Gelderland 1492–1795* (Zutphen, 1975); B. H. Slicher van Bath et al. (eds.), *Geschiedenis van Overijssel* (Deventer, 1970); C. Dekker et al. (eds.), *Geschiedenis van de provincie Utrecht*, vol. I (Utrecht, 1997). Interesting details can also be found in J. E. A. L. Struick, *Gelre en*

Habsburg 1492–1528 (Arnhem, 1960); C. A. van Kalveen, *Het bestuur van bisschop en Staten in het Nedersticht, Oversticht en Drenthe, 1483–1520* (Utrecht, 1974); and R. Reitsma, *Centrifugal and Centripetal Forces in the Early Dutch Republic. The States of Overyssel 1566–1600* (Amsterdam, 1982).

There is an abundance of literature about the Dutch Revolt. The best modern survey is offered by Geoffrey Parker, *The Dutch Revolt* (Harmondsworth, 1977). A number of specific aspects, including the Spanish mutinies and the international dimension of the Revolt, are treated in an earlier book by the same author: *The Army of Flanders and the Spanish Road, 1567–1659. The Logistics of Spanish Victory and Defeat in the Low Countries* (Cambridge, 1972). Important insights are developed in the work by J. J. Woltjer, several of whose essays have been brought together in *Tussen vrijheidsstrijd en burgeroorlog: over de Nederlandse Opstand 1555–1580* (Amsterdam, 1994). The terrible reality of the Revolt as it influenced the Hollanders' daily lives is described by Henk van Nierop, *Het verraad van het Noorderkwartier: oorlog, terreur en recht in de Nederlandse Opstand* (Amsterdam, 1999). The telling text of the Union of Utrecht, as well as an explanation of its genesis and application, are to be found in S. Groenveld and H. L. Ph. Leeuwenberg (eds.), *De Unie van Utrecht: wording en werking van een verbondsacte*, Geschiedenis in veelvoud, vol. VI (The Hague, 1979); an English translation of the text is included in Herbert H. Rowen (ed.), *The Low Countries in Early Modern Times* (New York, 1972). The website http://dutchrevolt.leidenuniv.nl provides a summary, sources from the period itself (including the entire text of the Union of Utrecht), illustrations and links to other interesting websites.

2   AN INDEPENDENT STATE (1609–1650)

An overview of the situation in 1609 is included in the contributions of S. Groenveld, H. L. Ph. Leeuwenberg, N. Mout and W. M. Zappey to the third part of *De kogel door de kerk? De Opstand in de Nederlanden 1559–1609* (Zutphen, 1983). The information on Deventer and Twente was taken from Paul Holthuis, *Frontierstad bij het scheiden van de markt. Deventer militair, demografisch, economisch 1578–1648* (Houten, 1993) and Cor Trompetter, *Agriculture, Proto-Industry and Mennonite Entrepreneurship. A History of the Textile Industries in Twente, 1600–1815* (Amsterdam, 1997). The entire period is described in chapters 17–22 and 25 of Jonathan I. Israel, *The Dutch Republic: Its Rise, Greatness, and Fall 1477–1806* (Oxford, 1995), though in fact one would do better to consult an earlier book by the same author: *The Dutch Republic and the Hispanic World 1606–1661* (Oxford, 1982).

The central figures in the drama of the years of the Twelve Years' Truce have all been given excellent biographies, though of very different kinds. J. den Tex, *Oldenbarnevelt* (Haarlem, 1960–72) – five volumes, three containing text and two with appendixes – is a monumental and very detailed work; the abridged English edition (Cambridge, 1973) contains two volumes. A. Th. van Deursen, *Maurits van Nassau. De winnaar die faalde* (Amsterdam, 2000) is concise and aims rather at painting an overall picture. Both authors, while showing understanding for their protagonists' opponents, are mainly concerned with comprehending the reasons for their protagonists' actions. Van Deursen sheds light on the religious angle in his classic *Bavianen en slijkgeuzen. Kerk en kerkvolk ten tijde van Maurits en Oldenbarnevelt* (Assen, 1974).

The period of Frederik Hendrik has not attracted so much attention, but a somewhat baroque biography was written about this 'conqueror of cities' by J. J. Poelhekke, *Frederik Hendrik. Prins van Oranje* (Zutphen, 1978). The Peace of Münster was commemorated not so very long ago with exhibitions and conferences. The most comprehensive publication was the three-volume catalogue, edited by Klaus Bussmann and Heinz Schilling, published in conjunction with the exhibition in Münster itself: *1648: Krieg und Frieden in Europa* (n.p., 1998). In the Netherlands there appeared, among other publications, Jacques Dane (ed.), *1648, Vrede van Munster: feit en verbeelding* (Zwolle, n.d.) and a special issue of the periodical *De Zeventiende Eeuw: 1648. De Vrede van Munster. Handelingen van het herdenkingscongres te Nijmegen en Kleef, 28–30 augustus 1996* (Hilversum, 1997), which deals with numerous aspects of the treaty, as well as society at that time. The attack on Amsterdam is treated in chapter 5 of Luuc Kooijmans, *Liefde in opdracht. Het hofleven van Willem Frederik van Nassau* (Amsterdam, 2000) and in S. Groenveld, *De prins voor Amsterdam. Reacties uit pamfletten op de aanslag van 1650* (Bussum, 1967).

The department of history at the Rijksmuseum has various objects from this period of Dutch history on display, including Oldenbarnevelt's famous cane. The rich collection of the Amsterdam Historical Museum elucidates the seventeenth century from the local perspective. Depictions of seventeenth-century history have been made accessible on the internet by the Atlas van Stolk in Rotterdam: the collection is to be found at www.atlasvanstolk.nl. Some of these engravings have appeared in print, together with pieces from the collections of the Rijksprentenkabinet (Printroom of the Rijksmuseum) and the Museum Simon van Gijn in Dordrecht, in J. F. Heijbroek (ed.), *Geschiedenis in beeld* (Zwolle, 2000).

3   A WORLD POWER (1650–1713)

For an overview of the events, see once again Jonathan I. Israel, *The Dutch Republic: Its Rise, Greatness, and Fall 1477–1806* (Oxford, 1995). Chapters 29–32 discuss the period 1650–1702. Those in search of even greater detail will be grateful for the nearly 900 pages of Herbert H. Rowen, *John de Witt, Grand Pensionary of Holland, 1625–1672* (Princeton, N. J., 1978), which gives a detailed treatment of the foreign policy pursued in the years 1650–72. There is an abridged version of this book: *John de Witt: Statesman of the 'True Freedom'* (Cambridge, 1983), which focuses, more so than the unabridged version, on the personality of the Grand Pensionary. The conflicts with England are elucidated in J. R. Jones, *The Anglo-Dutch Wars of the Seventeenth Century* (London, 1996), but equally worthwhile is a somewhat older work by Charles Wilson, *Profit and Power: A Study of England and the Dutch Wars* (London, 1957). The Republic's position between the powers and the development of its diplomatic apparatus is treated by J. Heringa, *De eer en hoogheid van de staat* (Groningen, 1961).

No monumental work has been devoted to the last quarter of the seventeenth century, but recent biographies by Wout Troost, *Stadhouder-koning Willem III: een politieke biografie* (Hilversum, 2001) and Tony Claydon, *William III* (London,

2002) attempt to fill this gap. Political developments are also outlined in M. A. M. Franken, *Coenraad van Beuningen's politieke en diplomatieke aktiviteiten in de jaren 1667–1684* (Groningen, 1966). Relations between Amsterdam and the stadholder's court, also discussed in Franken, are pursued in Petra Dreiskämper, *Aan de vooravond van de overtocht naar Engeland. Een onderzoek naar de verhouding tussen Willem III en Amsterdam in de Staten van Holland, 1685–1688*, Utrechtse Historische Cahiers, vol. XVII/4 (Utrecht, 1996). There is an excellent discussion of the Glorious Revolution, also from the Dutch perspective, in Jonathan I. Israel (ed.), *The Anglo-Dutch Moment: Essays on the Glorious Revolution and its World Impact* (Cambridge, 1991). The prelude to the wars with France is examined by Paul Sonnino, *Louis XIV and the Origins of the Dutch War* (Cambridge, 1988); see also C. J. Eckberg, *The Failure of Louis XIV's Dutch War* (Chapel Hill, N. C., 1979). The end of the first war with France is examined from various angles in J. A. H. Bots (ed.), *The Peace of Nijmegen, 1676–1679* (Amsterdam, 1980). Heinz Duchhardt (ed.), *Der Friede von Rijswijk 1697* (Mainz, 1998) discusses a subsequent stage in the conflict.

Domestic imbroglios during the Year of Disaster are the subject of D. J. Roorda, *Partij en factie. De oproeren van 1672 in de steden van Holland en Zeeland, een krachtmeting tussen partijen en facties* (Groningen, 1961), summarised in 'Party and Faction', *Acta Historiae Neerlandicae* 2 (1967) pp. 188–221. A number of other studies by the same author which treat this period have been compiled in S. Groenveld et al. (ed.), *Rond Prins en Patriciaat. Verspreide opstellen van D. J. Roorda* (Weesp, 1984), but the most help is actually his popularised overview, *Het Rampjaar 1672* (Bussum, 1971). The situation in the occupied provinces is grippingly described in J. den Tex, *Onder vreemde heren. De Republiek der Verenigde Nederlanden 1672–1674* (Zutphen, 1982).

4   THE ARMED FORCES

A general survey of the subject of this chapter was published recently: Jaap R. Bruijn and Cees B. Wels (eds.), *Met man en macht. De militaire geschiedenis van Nederland 1550–2000* (n.p., 2003); see especially the chapters by Kees Schulten, Adri P. van Vliet, Olaf van Nimwegen and Ronald Prud'homme van Reine. The history of the army is, however, treated much less adequately than that of the navy. Of the older works on the seventeenth-century Dutch navy, see especially J. E. Elias, *Schetsen uit de geschiedenis van ons zeewezen*, 6 vols. (The Hague, 1916–30), and *De vlootbouw in Nederland 1596–1655* (Amsterdam, 1933) by the same author. The most complete treatment, however, is also a source of exceptional insights: Jaap R. Bruijn, *The Dutch Navy of the Seventeenth and Eighteenth Centuries* (Columbia, N. Y., 1993), which contains an ample bibliography. The first phase of the organisation of the Admiralties is described in Marjolein 't Hart, *The Making of a Bourgeois State. War, Politics and Finance during the Dutch Revolt* (Manchester, 1993). Michiel de Ruyter's career is recounted in Ronald Prud'homme van Reine, *Rechterhand van Nederland. Biografie van Michiel Adriaenszoon de Ruyter* (Amsterdam, 1996).

There is no comparable overview of the development of the army at the time of the Republic, although Olaf van Nimwegen is planning to write such a book.

A detailed picture of the state of the army at the beginning of the seventeenth century is given in J. W. Wijn, *Het krijgswezen in den tijd van Prins Maurits* (Utrecht, 1934), which is still a standard reference work on the subject. In addition, one should become acquainted with Michiel de Jong, '*Staet van oorlog': wapenbedrijf en militaire hervorming in de Republiek der Verenigde Nederlanden (1585–1621)* (Hilversum, 2004), and with Olaf van Nimwegen, 'Het Staatse leger en de militaire revolutie van de vroegmoderne tijd', *Bijdragen en mededelingen betreffende de geschiedenis der Nederlanden* 118 (2003), pp. 494–518. Wijn also described the army at the beginning of the following century in *Het Staatsche leger*, vol. VIII: *Het tijdperk van de Spaanse Successieoorlog 1702–1715* (3 vols., The Hague, 1956–64), the last volume in a series of very poorly organised books by F. J. G. ten Raa and F. de Bas. Regarding the international background, Frank Tallett, *War and Society in Early Modern Europe, 1495–1715* (London, 1992), is a useful handbook. As regards the building of fortifications, see Charles van den Heuvel, *Papiere bolwercken. De introductie van de Italiaanse stede- en vestingbouw in de Nederlanden (1540–1609) en het gebruik van tekeningen* (Alphen a/d Rijn, 1991), as well as Frans Westra, *Nederlandse ingenieurs en de fortificatiewerken in het eerste tijdperk van de Tachtigjarige Oorlog, 1573–1604* (Alphen a/d Rijn, 1992). Additional information is to be found in H. L. Zwitzer, '*De militie van den staat'. Het leger van de Republiek der Verenigde Nederlanden* (Amsterdam, 1991), in M. van der Hoeven (ed.), *Exercise of Arms. Warfare in the Netherlands, 1568–1648* (Leiden, 1997) and in Jan A. F. de Jongste and Augustus J. Veenedaal Jr (eds.), *Anthonie Heinsius and the Dutch Republic 1688–1720. Politics, War, and Finance* (The Hague, 2002).

The siege of 's-Hertogenbosch is described in *Het beleg van 's-Hertogenbosch in 1629. Tentoonstelling ter gelegenheid van de 350-jarige herdenking van de belegering en inname van 's-Hertogenbosch* (Den Bosch, 1979). The eye-witness report of one of the besieged is printed in *Negen schoten met grof canon. Bossche oorlogsdagboeken 1629, 1794, 1944*, compiled and with an introduction by Coen Free (Den Bosch, 1993). The building of the fortifications at Deventer has been investigated by Paul Holthuis, *Frontierstad bij het scheiden van de markt. Deventer militair, demografisch, economisch 1578–1648* (Houten, 1993). Finally, it is possible to experience a seventeenth-century battle by reading the eye-witness account of Antonis Duyck, *De slag bij Nieuwpoort: Journaal van de tocht naar Vlaanderen in 1600*, retold by Vibeke Roeper and published by Wilfried Uitterhoeve (Nijmegen, 2000). Realia from Dutch military history are preserved and exhibited in the Army Museum in Delft. In Noord-Groningen the defence works of Fort Bourtange have been reconstructed and are open to the public. To learn about naval history, visit the martime museums in Rotterdam and Amsterdam.

5 FINANCIAL MIGHT

A fair amount of research has been done in recent years on the public finances of the Republic. The basic reference work is Marjolein 't Hart, *The Making of a Bourgeois State: War, Politics and Finance during the Dutch Revolt* (Manchester, 1993). Although the book confines itself to the first half of the seventeenth century, both the information and the way in which it is analysed have had a great impact on the whole debate. The same author has edited a survey on the subject, together with Joost Jonker and Jan Luiten van Zanden: *A Financial History of the Netherlands* (Cambridge, 1997), to which 't Hart contributed an essay on public finances in the seventeenth century. An overview with a slightly different slant is to be found in chapter 4 of Jan de Vries and Ad van der Woude, *The First Modern Economy: Success, Failure, and Perseverance of the Dutch Economy, 1500–1815* (Cambridge, 1997). The latest insights have been aired in W. Fritschy, 'A "financial revolution" reconsidered: public finance in Holland during the Dutch Revolt, 1568–1648', *Economic History Review* 46 (2003), pp. 57–89. The sixteenth-century changes in Holland in the area of public finance are described in James D. Tracy, *A Financial Revolution in the Habsburg Netherlands: Renten and Renteniers in the County of Holland, 1515–1565* (Berkeley, Calif., 1985).

An important contribution on the development of the quota system was written by H. L. Zwitser, 'Het quotenstelsel onder de Republiek der Verenigde Nederlanden, alsmede enkele beschouwingen over de Generale Petitie, de Staat van Oorlog en de Repartitie', which first appeared in 1982 and was later included in '*De militie van den Staat*' (Amsterdam, 1991). Local finances are treated in P. Nagtegaal, 'Stadsfinanciën en lokale economie: invloed van de conjunctuur op de Leidse stadsfinanciën, 1620–1720', *Economisch-en Sociaal-Historisch Jaarboek* 52 (1989), pp. 96–147. The information on Deventer was taken from Paul Holthuis, *Frontierstad bij het scheiden van de markt. Deventer militair, demografisch, economisch 1578–1648* (Houten, 1993). The comparison between prices in Kampen and Alkmaar is to be found in J. L. van Zanden, 'Kosten van levensonderhoud en loonvorming in Holland en Oost-Nederland 1600–1850: de voorbeelden van Kampen en Alkmaar', *Tijdschrift voor sociale geschiedenis* 11 (1985), pp. 309–23. The role of Francisco Lopes Suasso is discussed in Daniël Swetschinski and Loeki Schönduve, *De familie Lopes Suasso, financiers van Willem III* (Zwolle/Amsterdam, 1988), and that of the Doubleth family in Marjolein 't Hart, 'Staatsfinanciën als familiezaak tijdens de Republiek: de ontvangers-generaal Doubleth', in J. Th. de Smidt et al. (eds.), *Fiscaliteit in Nederland: 50 jaar Belastingmuseum 'Prof. Dr. Van der Poel'* (Zutphen/Deventer, 1987), pp. 57–66, a book containing a number of other contributions germane to this subject. The Tax and Customs Museum in Rotterdam has a website – www.le.ac.uk/hi/bon/ESFDB/dir.html – giving access to a database of information about the public finances in a large number of European countries in early-modern times. Another address – www.inghist.nl/Onderzoek/Projecten/GewestelijkeFinancien – gives access to information on provincial finances at the time of the Republic.

6   A MARKET ECONOMY

Two fascinating books have been published in English on tulips and the speculation in tulip bulbs: Anna Pavord, *The Tulip* (London, 1999) and Mike Dash, *Tulipomania. The Story of the World's Most Coveted Flower and the Extraordinary Passions It Aroused* (London, 1999). For the broader cultural context, see also Simon Schama, *The Embarrassment of Riches. An Interpretation of Dutch Culture in the Golden Age* (London, 1987).

For several years now the standard reference work on the economic history of the Republic has been Jan de Vries and Ad van der Woude, *The First Modern*

Economy: Success, Failure, and Perseverance of the Dutch Economy, 1500–1815 (Cambridge, 1997), a detailed, in-depth analysis based on the proposition that the Republic had a modern economy even before the Industrial Revolution. Important introductory essays, treating the various sectors and aspects, are to be found in Karel Davids and Leo Noordegraaf (eds.), *The Dutch Economy in the Golden Age: Nine Essays* (Amsterdam, 1994), which also appeared as vol. IV in the series *Economic and Social History in the Netherlands*. In 1976, H. P. H. Jansen gave an important lecture on Holland's 'great leap forward': 'Holland's Advance', *Acta Historiae Neerlandicae* 10 (1978), pp. 1–19. A stimulating sequel to his suggestions is to be found in J. L. van Zanden, *The Rise and Decline of Holland's Economy: Merchant Capitalism and the Labour Market* (Manchester, 1993), chapter 2. Quantitative estimates of the development of Holland's economy were presented by J. L. van Zanden in 'De economie van Holland in de periode 1650–1850: groei of achteruitgang? Een overzicht van bronnen, problemen en resultaten', *Bijdragen en mededelingen betreffende de geschiedenis der Nederlanden* 102 (1987), pp. 562–609, and 'Economic Growth in the Golden Age. The Development of the Economy of Holland, 1500–1650', in Davids and Noordegraaf, *Dutch Economy*, pp. 5–26.

Developments in the rural areas are discussed in detail in various regional studies carried out by the so-called Wageningen School, namely B. H. Slicher van Bath, *Een samenleving onder spanning: geschiedenis van het platteland in Overijssel* (Assen, 1957; reprinted Utrecht, 1977); A. M. van der Woude, *Het Noorderkwartier: een regionaal-historisch onderzoek in de demografische en economische geschiedenis van westelijk Nederland van de late middeleeuwen tot het begin van de negentiende eeuw*, AAG-Bijdragen, vol. XVI (Wageningen, 1972; reprinted Utrecht, 1983); J. A. Faber, *Drie eeuwen Friesland: economische en sociale ontwikkelingen van 1500 tot 1800*, AAG-Bijdragen, vol. XVII (Wageningen, 1972; also published Leeuwarden, 1973); H. K. Roessingh, *Inlandse tabak: expansie en contractie van een handelsgewas in de 17e en 18e eeuw*, AAG-Bijdragen vol. XX (Wageningen, 1976); J. Bieleman, *Boeren op het Drentse zand: een nieuwe visie op de 'oude' landbouw*, AAG-Bijdragen, vol. XXIX (Wageningen, 1987). A synthesis of the agricultural–historical aspects of this research is to be found in J. Bieleman, *Geschiedenis van de landbouw in Nederland 1500–1950* (Amsterdam/Meppel, 1992). A later publication is the excellent work by P. Priester, *Geschiedenis van de Zeeuwse landbouw circa 1600–1910*, AAG-Bijdragen, vol. XXXVII (Wageningen, 1998). Also of great value in studying this period is Jan de Vries, *The Dutch Rural Economy in the Golden Age, 1500–1700* (New Haven, Conn. 1974), in which the differences between the western and eastern Netherlands is strongly emphasised. J. Bieleman put these differences into perspective in his essay 'Dutch Agriculture in the Golden Age, 1570–1660', in Davids and Noordegraaf, *Dutch Economy*, pp. 159–83. On peat excavation in the North, see M. A. W. Gerding, *Vier eeuwen turfwinning. De veenderijen in Groningen, Friesland, Drenthe en Overijssel tussen 1550 en 1950*, AAG-Bijdragen, vol. XXXV (Wageningen, 1995). See also Richard W. Unger, 'Energy Sources for the Dutch Golden Age: Peat, Wind, and Coal', *Research in Economic History* 9 (1984), pp. 221–53.

No similar studies have been done on the history of Dutch industry, which is the least well studied of the three economic sectors. Most accounts confine themselves to one branch of industry, such as Richard Unger, *A History of Dutch Brewing 900–1900: Economy, Technology and the State* (Leiden, 2001), often in a single city, such as Arjan Poelwijk, *'In dienste vant suyckerbacken'. De Amsterdamse suikernijverheid en haar ondernemers, 1580–1630* (Hilversum, 2003). The information on the tobacco industry comes from the previously mentioned work by Roessingh, *Inlandse tabak.* The efforts made by local governments to promote 'their' economy are illuminated from various angles in the essays in Clé Lesger and Leo Noordegraaf (eds.), *Ondernemers en bestuurders. Economie en politiek in de Noordelijke Nederlanden in de late Middeleeuwen en vroegmoderne tijd* (Amsterdam, 1999). The information on Deventer was taken from Paul Holthuis, *Frontierstad bij het scheiden van de markt. Deventer militair, demografisch, economisch 1578–1648* (Houten, 1993).

On the Amsterdam guilds, see Piet Lourens and Jan Lucassen, 'Ambachtsgilden binnen een handelskapitalistische stad: aanzetten voor een analyse van Amsterdam rond 1700', *NEHA-Jaarboek voor economische, bedrijfs- en techniekgeschiedenis* 61 (1998), pp. 121–62. I. H. van Eeghen, *De gilden: theorie en praktijk* (Bussum, 1974) also contains information on the Amsterdam guilds. The situation in the clothing sector is discussed by Bibi Panhuysen, *Maatwerk: Kleermakers, naaisters, oudkleerkopers en de gilden (1500–1800)* (Amsterdam, 1999). The information on the art market was taken from John Michael Montias, 'Art Dealers in the Seventeenth-Century Netherlands', *Simiolus* 18 (1988), pp. 244–56. See also, by the same author, *Artists and Artisans in Delft: A Socio-Economic Study of the Seventeenth Century* (Princeton, N. J., 1982), a book which, despite its off-putting title, paints a fascinating picture of a group of artisans, some of whom (Johannes Vermeer!) eventually became world-famous; see also chapter 15 of the present publication. The reasoning that guilds were good for the development of painting is elucidated in Maarten Prak, 'Guilds and the Development of the Art Market during the Dutch Golden Age', *Simiolus* 30 (2003), pp. 236–51. The requirements for guild membership are discussed in Piet Lourens and Jan Lucassen, '"Zunftlandschaften" in den Niederlanden und im benachbarten Deutschland', in Wilfried Reininghaus (ed.), *Zunftlandschaften in Deutschland und den Niederlanden im Vergleich* (Münster, 2000), pp. 11–43.

Numerous studies have been published on the development of trade. The grain trade in the early period is the subject of M. van Tielhof, *The 'Mother of all Trades': The Baltic Grain Trade in Amsterdam from the Late 16th to the Early 18th Century* (Leiden, 2002). There is also a great deal about trade in De Vries and Van der Woude, *The First Modern Economy.* Moreover, Jonathan I. Israel, *Dutch Primacy in World Trade 1585–1740* (Oxford, 1989) is devoted completely to this sector. His propositon that Holland's dominance was due mainly to the introduction of the rich trades to Amsterdam by the Antwerp merchants who settled there has been commented on by J. L. van Zanden and L. Noordegraaf in *Bijdragen en Mededelingen betreffende de Geschiedenis der Nederlanden* 106 (1991), pp. 451–79, which also includes Israel's reply. A recent publication is David Ormrod, *The Rise of Commercial Empires. England and the Netherlands in the Age of Mercantilism, 1650–1770* (Cambridge, 2003). Three recent monographs on trade around 1600 also deal with the crucial transfer of Antwerp's wealth to the North: Victor Enthoven, *Zeeland en de opkomst van de Republiek. Handel en strijd in de Scheldedelta c. 1550–1620* (Leiden, 1996); Oscar Gelderblom, *Zuid-Nederlandse kooplieden en de opkomst van de Amsterdamse stapelmarkt (1578–1630)* (Hilversum, 2000) and Oscar Gelderblom, 'From Antwerp to Amsterdam: The Contribution of Merchants from the Southern Netherlands to the Commercial Expansion of Amsterdam (*c.* 1540–1609)', *Review* 26 (2003), pp. 247–82; Clé Lesger, *Handel in Amsterdam ten tijde van de Opstand. Kooplieden, commerciële expansie en verandering in de ruimtelijke economie van de Nederlanden ca. 1550–ca. 1630* (Hilversum, 2001). See also the list of sources for chapters 7 and 8 below.

A classic description of trends in population growth in the Republic is to be found in A. M. van der Woude, 'Demografische ontwikkeling van de Noordelijke Nederlanden 1500–1800', in D. P. Blok et al. (eds.), *Algemene geschiedenis der Nederlanden*, vol. V (Bussum, 1980), pp. 102–68. That information is supplemented by data from Ronald Rommes, 'Pest in perspectief. Aspecten van een gevreesde ziekte in de vroegmoderne tijd', *Tijdschrift voor sociale geschiedenis* 16 (1990), pp. 244–66, and *Oost, west, Utrecht best? Driehonderd jaar migratie en migranten in de stad Utrecht (begin 16e-begin 19e eeuw)* (Amsterdam, 1998) by the same author. Leo Noordegraaf and Gerrit Valk, *De gave Gods. De pest in Holland vanaf de late middeleeuwen* (Bergen, 1988) is a survey of the plague years.

The expansion of the Republic's economy took place against the background of general economic expansion in the whole of Europe, which has often been called the 'rise of capitalism', but nowadays is frequently treated from the perspective of economic growth. Both points of view are discussed in Maarten Prak (ed.), *Early Modern Capitalism. Economic and Social Change in Europe, 1400–1800* (London, 2001) and in S. R. Epstein, *Freedom and Growth. The Rise of States and Markets in Europe, 1300–1750* (London, 2000). The best overview of the European economy in this period is still Jan de Vries, *The Economy of Europe in an Age of Crisis, 1600–1750* (Cambridge, 1976). To get a visual picture of the various aspects of economic life it is worth paying a visit to the Netherlands Open Air Museum in Arnhem, the Zuiderzee Museum in Enkhuizen, and the Maritime Museums in Amsterdam and Rotterdam. At 'Zaansche Schans' one can still get an idea of what the largest industrial area in the seventeenth-century Netherlands looked like by viewing various mills and other buildings from that period. The website www.geheugenvannederland.nl contains information on the trade with Russia and the Baltic.

7 A WORLDWIDE TRADING NETWORK

C. R. Boxer, *The Dutch Seaborne Empire 1600–1800* (London, 1965) is a classic, but so much has since been published on the subject that it would be better to start with a more recent work. The story of Dutch colonial expansion is clearly told in Jur van Goor, *De Nederlandse koloniën. Geschiedenis van de Nederlandse expansie 1600–1975* (The Hague, 1997). A good introduction to trade with the West is Henk den Heijer, *De geschiedenis van de WIC* (Zutphen, 1994); on trade with the East one should read Femme Gaastra, *The Dutch East India Company. Expansion and Decline* (Zutphen, 2003). The reader should not be put off by the dry titles of these books; they were written by top experts in the field and are not only extremely informative but also richly illustrated. Both concentrate on the seventeenth century. The relations between colonial vicissitudes and the development of the Dutch economy is clearly discussed in J. L. van Zanden, *The Rise and Decline of Holland's Economy: Merchant Capitalism and the Labour Market* (Manchester, 1993), chapters 4 and 5, as well as in Jan de Vries and Ad van der Woude, *The First Modern Economy: Success, Failure, and Perseverance of the Dutch Economy, 1500–1815* (Cambridge, 1997), chapters 9 and 10.

The life of Reverend Bogardus is told in Willem Frijhoff, *Wegen van Evert Willemsz. Een Hollands weeskind op zoek naar zichzelf, 1607–1647* (Nijmegen, 1995), and an account of New Netherland is to be found in Jaap Jacobs, *New Netherland: A Dutch Colony in Seventeenth-Century America* (Leiden, 2005). The slave trade based on the coast of West Africa is concisely described in P. C. Emmer, *De Nederlandse slavenhandel 1500–1850* (Amsterdam, 2000). The standard reference work on the subject is J. M. Postma, *The Dutch in the Atlantic Slave Trade 1600–1815* (Cambridge, 1990). See also Johannes Postma and Victor Enthoven (eds.), *Riches from Atlantic Commerce: Dutch Transatlantic Trade and Shipping, 1585–1817* (Leiden, 2003). Cornelis Ch. Goslinga, *The Dutch in the Caribbean and on the Wild Coast, 1580–1680* (Gainesville, Fla., 1971), and its sequel, *The Dutch in the Caribbean and in the Guianas, 1680–1791* (Assen/Dover, 1985), are the reference works on the Dutch settlement in the Antilles and in what would later be called Surinam. The most recent monograph on the Republic's short-lived Brazilian colonies is still C. R. Boxer, *The Dutch in Brazil 1624–1654* (Oxford, 1957), although Goslinga also treated this subject. The cultural digestion of the New World is discussed in Benjamin Schmidt, *Innocence Abroad: The Dutch Imagination and the New World, 1570–1670* (Cambridge, 2001).

The East Indies, always a favourite subject among historians, have been written about extensively. In addition to the above-mentioned books by Van Goor and Gaastra, I have relied mainly on J. L. Blussé van Oud-Alblas, *Strange Company. Chinese Settlers, Mestizo Women and the Dutch in VOC Batavia* (Dordrecht, 1986); Roelof van Gelder, *Het Oost-Indisch avontuur. Duitsers in dienst van de VOC* (Nijmegen, 1997); G. J. Knaap, *Kruidnagelen en christenen. De Verenigde Oost-Indische Compagnie en de bevolking van Ambon 1656–1696* (Dordrecht, 1987); Johan Talens, *Een feodale samenleving in koloniaal vaarwater. Staatsvorming, koloniale expansie en economische onderontwikkeling in Banten, West-Java (1600–1750)* (Hilversum, 1999). The VOC's provisioning post at the Cape of Good Hope has been examined in minute detail by Ad Biewenga, *De Kaap de Goede Hoop. Een Nederlandse vestigingskolonie, 1680–1730* (Amsterdam, 1999). The intimate workings of colonial society are revealed in Leonard Blussé, *Bitter Bonds: A Colonial Divorce Drama of the Seventeenth Century* (Princeton, N. J., 2002) and in the previously mentioned book by Frijhoff. Both stories tell a tale of personal tragedy.

A very different story is told about the European trading settlements of the Dutch in Jan Willem Veluwenkamp, *Archangel. Nederlandse ondernemers in Rusland 1550–1785* (Amsterdam, 2000); Erik Wijnroks, *Handel tussen Rusland en de Nederlanden, 1560–1640. Een netwerkanalyse van de Antwerpse en Amsterdamse kooplieden op Rusland* (Hilversum, 2003); and Marie-Christine Engels, *Merchants, Interlopers, Seamen and Corsairs. The 'Flemish' Community in Livorno and Genoa (1615–1635)* (Hilversum, 1997). A survey of these European settlements is to be found in J. W. Veluwenkamp, 'Merchant Colonies in the

Dutch Trade System (1550–1750)', in C. A. Davids, W. Fritschy and L. A. van der Valk (eds.), *Kapitaal, ondernemerschap en beleid. Studies over economie en politiek in Nederland, Europa en Azië van 1500 tot heden* (Amsterdam, 1996), pp. 141–64. The Tropical Museum in Amsterdam contains a great deal of information on colonial history. In Lelystad and Amsterdam (Netherlands Maritime Museum) one may see life-size replicas of East Indiamen; the *Batavia* in Lelystad was built after a seventeenth-century example. The internet is a good source of information on the Dutch East India Company (VOC): begin your search at http://voc-kenniscentrum.nl and enter the world of New Netherland via www.geheugenvannederland.nl.

8 RICHES

The story of Elias and Louis Trip was taken from P. W. Klein, *De Trippen in de 17e eeuw. Een studie over het ondernemersgedrag op de Hollandse stapelmarkt* (Assen, 1965). Additional information, including a lot about the Trippenhuis (now the home of the Royal Dutch Academy of Sciences), is to be found in R. Meischke and H. E. Reeser (eds.), *Het Trippenhuis te Amsterdam* (Amsterdam, 1983). The Dutch arms trade is illuminated from many angles in Jan Piet Puype and Marco van der Hoeven (eds.), *Het arsenaal van de wereld. De Nederlandse wapenhandel in de Gouden Eeuw* (Amsterdam, 1993) and in Michiel de Jong, '*Staet van oorlog': wapenbedrijf en militaire hervorming in de Republiek der Verenigde Nederlanden (1585–1621)* (Hilversum, 2004). Far too little has been written about merchants as a social group, but this situation is slowly being remedied, even though the literature published thus far mainly dwells on their entrepreneurial role: C. Lesger and L. Noordegraaf (eds.), *Entrepreneurs and Entrepreneurship in Early Modern Times. Merchants and Industrialists within the Orbit of the Dutch Staple Market*, Hollandse Historische Reeks, vol. XXIV (The Hague, 1995); as well as the books by Gelderblom, Veluwenkamp, Wijnroks and Engels mentioned in the sources for chapter 7. Access to somewhat older literature is facilitated by P. W. Klein and J. W. Veluwenkamp, 'The Role of the Entrepreneur in the Economic Expansion of the Dutch Republic', in Karel Davids and Leo Noordegraaf (eds.), *The Dutch Economy in the Golden Age: Nine Essays* (Amsterdam, 1993), pp. 27–53.

For information concerning wealth and incomes it is best to start with Lee Soltow and Jan Luiten van Zanden, *Income and Wealth Inequality in the Netherlands, 16th–20th Century* (Amsterdam, 1998). Another source of my data is J. A. Faber, 'De Noordelijke Nederlanden van 1480–1780: structuren in beweging', in D. P. Blok et al. (eds.), *Algemene geschiedenis der Nederlanden*, vol. V (Bussum, 1980), pp. 196–250; P. W. Klein, 'De heffing van de 100e en 200e penning van het vermogen te Gouda, 1599–1722', *Economisch-Historisch Jaarboek* 31 (1965–6), pp. 41–62.

A good source of information on the regents is J. L. Price, *Holland and the Dutch Republic in the Seventeenth Century: The Politics of Particularism* (Oxford, 1994), chapter 3. Otherwise one must rely on local studies. An older source that is well worth consulting is Johan E. Elias, *Geschiedenis van het Amsterdamsche Regentenpatriciaat* (The Hague, 1923), based on the information published by the same author in *De vroedschap van Amsterdam*, 2 vols. (Haarlem, 1903–5), which in turn serves as the source for Peter Burke, *Venice and Amsterdam: A Study of Seventeenth-Century Elites* (Cambridge, 1994), a comparison of the elites in those two trading centres. A short but interesting book on seventeenth-century regents is Dirk Jaap Noordam, *Geringde buffels en heren van stand. Het patriciaat van Leiden, 1574–1700* (Hilversum, 1994). The Zwolle information was taken from J. C. Streng, '*Stemme in staat': de bestuurlijke elite in de stadsrepubliek Zwolle 1579–1795* (Hilversum, 1997). The social isolation of the patriciate has been written about by H. van Dijk and D. J. Roorda in their article 'Social Mobility under the Regents of the Republic', *Acta Historiae Neerlandicae* 9 (1976), pp. 76–102. They further developed their Zierikzee data in *Het patriciaat van Zierikzee tijdens de Republiek* (n.p., n.d.). The most important exception to this pattern of local studies is C. Schmidt, *Om de eer van de familie: het geslacht Teding van Berkhout; een sociologische benadering* (Amsterdam, 1986), an intelligently written book. Personal relationships in this milieu are treated in the equally fascinating book by Luuc Kooijmans, *Vriendschap en de kunst van het overleven in de zeventiende en achttiende eeuw* (Amsterdam, 1997).

The treatment of the 'middling sort' relies heavily on G. Groenhuis, *De predikanten: de sociale positie van de gereformeerde predikanten in de Republiek der Verenigde Nederlanden voor ± 1700* (Groningen, 1977) and on Willem Frijhoff, 'Non satis dignitatis . . . : over de maatschappelijke status van geneeskundigen tijdens de Republiek', *Tijdschrift voor Geschiedenis* 96 (1983), pp. 379–406.

H. F. K. van Nierop, *The Nobility of Holland: from Knights to Regents* (Cambridge, 1993), the best book about the aristocracy in the Republic, unfortunately stops at mid-century. This also holds true for Sherin Marshall, *The Dutch Gentry 1500–1650: Family, Faith and Fortune* (New York, 1987), which deals with the Utrecht nobility. Frisian nobles are given quite extensive treatment in J. A. Faber, *Drie eeuwen Friesland: economische en sociale ontwikkelingen* (Leeuwarden, 1973; also published as AAG-Bijdragen, vol. XVII (Wageningen, 1972)); the landed gentry of the Veluwe region are described in S. W. Verstegen, *Gegoede ingezetenen: jonkers en geërfden op de Veluwe 1650–1830* (Zutphen, 1990), the Groningen gentry in H. Feenstra, *Adel in de Ommelanden; Hoofdelingen, Jonkers en Eigenerfders van de late middeleeuwen tot de negentiende eeuw* (Groningen, 1988). The information on the Isendoorn à Blois family was taken from D. J. G. Buurman (eds.), *De Cannenburch en zijn bewoners* (Zutphen, 1990). The peat excavation undertaken by the Ewsums is described in M. A. W. Gerding, *Vier eeuwen turfwinning: de verveningen in Groningen, Friesland, Drenthe en Overijssel tussen 1550 en 1950*, AAG-Bijdragen, vol. XXXV (Wageningen, 1995). The possession of manorial domains by the Leiden regents is discussed in L. van Poelgeest and D. H. H. van Heest, 'Leidenaars en hun heerlijke titels', *Leids Jaarboekje* 75 (1983), pp. 119–38. The story about Adriaan van Bredehoff was taken from L. Kooijmans, *Onder regenten: de elite in een Hollandse stad; Hoorn 1700–1780* (n.p., 1985).

For an impression of the lifestyle of the well-to-do, pay a visit to the Museum Willet-Holthuysen in Amsterdam, which is housed in a canal-side house that once belonged to a merchant's family. Quite a few aristocratic country estates, including Canneburch Castle, in the possession of the Isendoorn à Blois family for centuries, are open to the public, though they seldom display purely seventeenth-century furnishings.

9   TOIL AND TROUBLE

This chapter discusses social relations in the Republic, which have been the subject of many monographs. Portraits of such 'types' as sailors, soldiers, women and the poor are to be found in H. M. Beliën, A. Th. van Deursen and G. J. van Setten (eds.), *Gestalten van de Gouden Eeuw: een Hollands groepsportret* (Amsterdam, 1995). The story of the life of Hermanus Verbeeck, *Memoriaal ofte mijn levensraijsinghe*, has been edited by Jeroen Blaak (Hilversum, 1999). See also Jeroen Blaak, 'Worstelen om te overleven: de zorg om het bestaan in het Memoriaal van Hermanus Verbeeck (1621–1681)', *Holland* 31 (1999), pp. 1–18. The lives of Dutch artisans in general are described in Rudolf Dekker, 'Handwerkslieden en arbeiders in Holland van de zestiende eeuw tot de achttiende eeuw: identiteit, cultuur en protest', in Peter te Boekhorst, Peter Burke and Willem Frijhoff (eds.), *Cultuur en maatschappij in Nederland 1500–1850: Een historisch-antropologisch perspectief* (Heerlen, 1992), pp. 109–47. The data on the apportionment of wealth in Gouda were taken from P. W. Klein, 'De heffing van de 100e en 200e penning van het vermogen te Gouda, 1599–1722', *Economisch-Historisch Jaarboek* 31 (1965–6), pp. 41–62.

The social funds of the Amsterdam guilds are surveyed in Sandra Bos, *'Uyt liefde tot malcander': Onderlinge hulp binnen de Noord-Nederlandse gilden in internationaal perspectief (1570–1820)* (Amsterdam, 1998). The situation in the Amsterdam orphanages is described in detail and analysed in Anne E. McCants, *Civic Charity in a Golden Age: Orphan Care in Early Modern Amsterdam* (Urbana, Ill., 1997). There are numerous descriptions of particular orphanages. A study summarising such information is S. Groenveld, J. J. H. H. Dekker and Th. R. M. Willemse (eds.), *Wezen en boefjes: zes eeuwen zorg in wees- en kinderhuizen* (Hilversum, 1997), which contains a detailed section written by Groenveld on the era of the Republic (pp. 45–251).

The fate of Hendrikje Slackebaarts and her relatives is recorded in Hilde van Wijngaarden, *Zorg voor de kost: armenzorg, arbeid en onderlinge hulp in Zwolle, 1650–1700* (Amsterdam, 2000). The standard of living of labourers in Holland is discussed in Leo Noordegraaf, *Hollands welvaren? Levensstandaard in Holland 1450–1650* (Bergen, 1985) and in chapter 12 of Jan de Vries and Ad van der Woude, *The First Modern Economy: Success, Failure, and Perseverance of the Dutch Economy, 1500–1815* (Cambridge, 1997). Comparisons with other countries are made in Leo Noordegraaf and Jan Luiten van Zanden, 'Early Modern Economic Growth and the Standard of Living: Did Labour Benefit from Holland's Golden Age?', in Karel Davids and Jan Lucassen (eds.), *A Miracle Mirrored: The Dutch Republic in European Perspective* (Cambridge, 1995), pp. 410–37.

The workings of the labour market are explained in Jan Lucassen, 'Labour and Early Modern Economic Development', in Davids and Lucassen, *A Miracle Mirrored*, pp. 367–409, and chapter 12 of De Vries and Van der Woude, *First Modern Economy*. The data on the size of certain branches of industry were taken from Femme S. Gaastra, *The Dutch East India Company. Expansion and Decline*

(Zutphen, 2003); Piet Lourens and Jan Lucassen, 'Ambachtsgilden binnen een handelskapitalistische stad: aanzetten voor een analyse von Amsterdam rond 1700', *NEHA-Jaarboek voor economische, bedrijfs- en techniekgeschiedenis* 61 (1998), pp. 121–62.; John Michael Montias, *Artists and Artisans in Delft: A Socio-Economic Study of the Seventeenth Century* (Princeton, N. J., 1982); N. W. Posthumus, *De geschiedenis van de Leidsche lakenindustrie*, 3 vols. (The Hague 1908–39). Much information on one very important group, namely those involved in seafaring, is to be found in Piet Boon, *Bouwers van de zee: zeevarenden van het Westfriese platteland, c. 1680–1720*, Hollandse Historische Reeks, vol. XXVI (The Hague, 1996); P. C. van Royen, *Zeevarenden op de koopvaardijvloot omstreeks 1700*, Hollandse Historische Reeks, vol. VIII (Amsterdam/ The Hague, 1987); Adri P. van Vliet, 'Zeevarenden op de vissersvloot, 1580–1650', *Tijdschrift voor sociale geschiedenis* 22 (1996), pp. 241–59.
    Those wishing to know more about immigration can best start with Jan Lucassen and Rinus Penninx, *Newcomers. Immigrants and their Descendants in the Netherlands 1550–1995* (Amsterdam, 1999). A work concentrating more on the seventeenth century is Jan Lucassen, 'The Netherlands, the Dutch, and Long-Distance Migration in the Late Sixteenth to Early Nineteenth Centuries', in Nicholas Canny (ed.), *Europeans on the Move: Studies on European Migration 1500–1800* (Oxford, 1994), pp. 153–91. Another interesting source of information on this subject is Ad Knotter and Jan Luiten van Zanden, 'Immigratie en arbeidsmarkt in Amsterdam in de 17e eeuw', *Tijdschrift voor sociale geschiedenis* 13 (1987), pp. 403–31, which was reprinted (in an English translation) in J. L. van Zanden, *The Rise and Decline of Holland's Economy: Merchant Capitalism and the Labour Market* (Manchester, 1993); Lotte van de Pol, 'The Lure of the Big City: Female Migration to Amsterdam', in Els Kloek, Nicole Teeuwen and Marijke Huisman (eds.), *Women of the Golden Age. An International Debate on Women in Seventeenth-Century Holland, England and Italy* (Hilversum, 1994), pp. 73–82; Solvi Sogner, 'Young in Europe around 1700: Norwegian Sailors and Servant-Girls Seeking Employment in Amsterdam', in *Mesurer et comprendre: mélanges offerts à Jacques Dupâquier* (Paris, 1991), pp. 515–32; Cor Trompetter, 'De migratie van Twente naar Amsterdam in de zeventiende en achttiende eeuw. Ontwikkelingen en lokale verschillen', *Tijdschrift voor sociale geschiedenis* 21 (1995), pp. 145–65. For other cities refer to Leo Lucassen and Boudien de Vries, 'Leiden als middelpunt van een Westeuropees textiel-migratiesysteem, 1586–1650', *Tijdschrift voor sociale geschiedenis* 22 (1996), pp. 138–67; Ronald Rommes, *Oost, west, Utrecht best? Driehonderd jaar migratie en migranten in de stad Utrecht (begin 16e–begin 19e eeuw)* (Amsterdam, 1998).
    The story of Joost Arienszoon of Delft and his family was taken from Ingrid van der Vlis, *Leven in armoede. Delftse bedeelden in de zeventiende eeuw* (Amsterdam, 2001). For this section I also relied upon A. Th. van Deursen, *Een dorp in de polder: Graft in de zeventiende eeuw* (Amsterdam, 1994); H. Gras, *Op de grens van het bestaan: armen en armenzorg in Drenthe 1700–1800* (Zuidwolde, 1989); Maarten Prak, 'Een verbazende menigte armen. Zorg en samenleving', in Aart Vos et al. (eds.), *'s-Hertogenbosch: de geschiedenis van een Brabantse stad 1629–1990* (Zwolle/ 's-Hertogenbosch, n.d.), pp. 79–93; Joke Spaans, *Armenzorg in Friesland 1500–1800: publieke zorg en particuliere liefdadigheid in zes Friese steden:*

Leeuwarden, Bolsward, Franeker, Sneek, Dokkum en Harlingen (Hilversum/ Leeuwarden, 1997); C. W. van Voorst van Beest, *De katholieke armenzorg te Rotterdam in de 17e en 18e eeuw* (The Hague, 1955). See also Maarten Prak, 'Armenzorg 1500–1800', in Jacques van Gerwen and Marco H. D. van Leeuwen (eds.), *Studies over zekerheidsarrangementen. Risico's, risicobestrijding en verzekeringen in Nederland vanaf de Middeleeuwen* (Amsterdam/The Hague, 1998), pp. 49–90.

The history of the workhouse is told from an international perspective in Pieter Spierenburg, *The Prison Experience: Disciplinary Institutions and their Inmates in Early Modern Europe* (New Brunswick, 1991); regarding the Zwolle workhouse, see Hilde van Wijngaarden, 'Het Zwolse werkhuis: liefdadige instelling of zakelijke onderneming?', in C. Lesger and L. Noordegraaf (eds.), *Ondernemers en bestuur. Economie en politiek in de Noordelijke Nederlanden in de late middeleeuwen en vroegmoderne tijd* (Amsterdam, 1999), pp. 603–20. A vivid picture of life on the edge of society is painted in Lotte van de Pol, *Het Amsterdams hoerdom. Prostitutie in de zeventiende en achttiende eeuw* (Amsterdam, 1996).

For an impression of life on the lower rungs of society's ladder, pay a visit to the Zuiderzee Museum in Enkhuizen and the Netherlands Open Air Museum in Arnhem, both of which have some older pieces on display amidst mostly nineteenth-century objects.

10 COMMUNITY

Joris Craffurd's eye-witness account of the Undertakers' Riot is to be found in *Oproeren in Holland gezien door tijdgenoten: ooggetuigeverslagen van oproeren in de provincie Holland ten tijde van de Republiek (1690–1750)*, published by Rudolf Dekker (Assen, 1979). For a sociological and anthropological analysis of the events, see Maarten Prak, 'Velerlei soort van volk – sociale verhoudingen in Amsterdam in de zeventiende eeuw' and Lotte C. van de Pol, 'Hoeveel soorten volk?', both in *Jaarboek Amstelodamum* 91 (1999), pp. 29–54 and 55–61.

Holland's civic militias are discussed in detail in Paul Knevel, *Burgers in het geweer. De schutterijen in Holland, 1550–1700*, Hollandse Studiën, vol. XXXII (Hilversum, 1994). A beautifully illustrated and highly informative volume is the exemplary Haarlem exhibition catalogue by M. Carasso-Kok and J. Levy-Van Halm (eds.), *Schutters in Holland. Kracht en zenuwen van de stad* (Zwolle/ Haarlem, 1988). The periodical *Tijdschrift voor sociale geschiedenis* 26 (1997) contains four articles on civic militias which also present their counterparts in other countries. The *Night Watch* as a militia piece is analysed in E. Haverkamp-Begemann, *Rembrandt: The Nightwatch* (Princeton, N. J., 1982).

Amsterdam citizenship rights are analysed in Maarten Prak, 'Cittadini, abitanti e forestieri. Una classificazione della popolazione di Amsterdam nella prima età moderna', *Quaderni storici* 30 (1995), pp. 331–57. See also Gabrielle Dorren, 'De eerzamen. Zeventiende-eeuws burgerschap in Haarlem', in Remieg Aerts and Henk te Velde (eds.), *De stijl van de burger. Over Nederlandse burgerlijke cultuur vanaf de middeleeuwen* (Kampen, 1998), pp. 60–79; Ronald Rommes, *Oost, west, Utrecht best? Driehonderd jaar migratie en migranten in de stad Utrecht (begin 16e- begin 19e eeuw)* (Amsterdam, 1998), chapter 2; J. A. Schimmel, *Burgerrecht te*

Nijmegen 1592–1810, geschiedenis van de verlening en burgerlijst (Tilburg, 1966); J. C. Streng, *'Stemme in staat': de bestuurlijke elite in de stadsrepubliek Zwolle 1579–1795* (Hilversum, 1997). The problem of citizenship and religion in the eastern Netherlands is discussed in Maarten Prak, 'The Politics of Intolerance: Citizenship and Religion in the Dutch Republic (17th–18th C.)', in Ronnie Po-chia Hsia and Henk van Nierop (eds.), *Calvinism and Religious Toleration in the Dutch Golden Age* (Cambridge, 2002), pp. 159–75.

A systematic overview of the number of guilds per city around the years 1400, 1560 and 1670 is to be found in Piet Lourens and Jan Lucassen, 'De oprichting en ontwikkeling van ambachtsgilden in Nederland (13de–19de eeuw)', in Catharina Lis and Hugo Soly (eds.), *Werelden van verschil: ambachtsgilden in de Lage Landen* (Brussels, 1997), pp. 43–77. The guilds of one city in particular are described in the well-illustrated book by Koen Goudriaan et al., *De Gilden in Gouda* (Gouda/Zwolle, 1996). The Dordrecht guild graves are discussed in Eric Palmen, 'De gilden en hun sociale betekenis', in Willem Frijhoff, Hubert Nusteling and Marijke Spies (eds.), *Geschiedenis van Dordrecht van 1572 tot 1813* (Hilversum, 1998), pp. 221–33; the graves of the Utrecht guilds are treated in Maarten Prak, 'Politik, Kultur und politische Kultur: die Zünfte in den Nördlichen Niederlanden', in Wilfried Reininghaus (ed.), *Zunftlandschaften in Deutschland und in den Niederlanden im Vergleich* (Münster, 2000), pp. 71–83. The documents of the Haarlem Guild of St Luke are published in *De archiefbescheiden van het St. Lukasgilde te Haarlem*, 2 vols. published by Hessel Miedema (Alphen a/d Rijn, 1980). Several other items of information in this section are based on archival research carried out for a survey of the guilds which I intend to publish together with Piet Lourens and Jan Lucassen. See also the list of sources for chapter 9.

The neighbourhoods have only recently been discovered as interesting subject matter, but a book which appeared before the subject was fashionable is Ton Kappelhof, *Armenzorg in Den Bosch: de Negen Blokken 1350–1810* (Utrecht, 1983). A good introduction to the subject is Herman Roodenburg, 'Naar een etnografie van de vroegmoderne stad: De "gebuyrten" in Leiden en Den Haag', in Peter te Boekhorst, Peter Burke and Willem Frijhoff (eds.), *Cultuur en maatschappij in Nederland 1500–1850. Een historisch-antropologisch perspectief* (Heerlen, 1992), pp. 219–43. The situation in Haarlem is described in a short book by Gabrielle Dorren: *Het soet vergaren: Haarlems buurtleven in de zeventiende eeuw* (Haarlem, 1998). See also her *Eenheid en verscheidenheid: de burgers van Haarlem in de Gouden Eeuw* (Amsterdam 2001). The Snippevlucht neighbourhood in Utrecht is treated in a fine article by Llewllyn Bogaers, 'Geleund over de onderdeur: doorkijkjes in het Utrechtse buurtleven van de vroege Middeleeuwen tot in de zeventiende eeuw', *Bijdragen en mededelingen betreffende de Geschiedenis der Nederlanden* 112 (1997), pp. 336–63.

One can meet the burghers of Graft in A. Th. van Deursen, *Een dorp boven de polder: Graft in de zeventiende eeuw* (Amsterdam, 1994), chapter 12. Guilds in rural areas are discussed in F. D. Zeiler, '"Men segt, dat hier so een gilde is . . .": semi- en buitenstedelike gilden in Noordwest-Overijssel in de zeventiende en achttiende eeuw', *NEHA-Jaarboek voor economische, bedrijfs- en techniekgeschiedenis* 57 (1994), pp. 91–106. The rules and regulations of the village militias in Brabant are discussed in detail in E. Van Autenboer, *De kaarten van de schuttersgilden van het Hertogdom Brabant (1300–1800)*, 2 vols. (Tilburg, 1994). A well-documented local example is to be found in Max Farjon, *Het gilde St.-Jan Baptista en Leenderstrijp: 350 jaar historie en gebruiken* (Leenderstrijp, 1995). The mark communities are discussed in Jan Luiten van Zanden, 'The Paradox of the Marks: The Exploitation of Commons in the Eastern Netherlands, 1250–1850', *Agricultural History Review* 47 (1999), pp. 125–44.

The Republic as a corporate society is treated in Streng, '*Stemme in staat*'; Willem Frijhoff and Marijke Spies, *1650: Hard–Won Unity* (Assen: Van Gorcum and Basingstoke: Palgrave, 2004), chapter 3; Maarten Prak, *Republikeinse veelheid, democratische enkelvoud: sociale verandering in het Revolutietijdvak: 's-Hertogenbosch 1770–1820* (Nijmegen, 1999); Goffe Jensma, 'Het theater "Leeuwarden"', in René Kunst et al. (eds.), *Leeuwarden 750–2000: hoofdstad van Friesland* (Franeker, 1999). In the civic militia gallery of the Amsterdam Historical Museum one comes face to face with that corporate society. The museum, moreover, is housed in what was once the Civic Orphanage, itself one of those corporate structures. The museum's website also provides information on these subjects: www.ahm.nl.

11 THE AUTHORITIES

The career of Coenraad van Beuningen is recounted in C. W. Roldanus, *Coenraad van Beuningen: staatsman en libertijn* (The Hague, 1931). See also M. A. M. Franken, *Coenraad van Beuningen's politieke en diplomatieke aktiviteiten in de jaren 1667–1684* (Groningen, 1966). Other regent-diplomats are encountered in J. Heringa, *De eer en hoogheid van de staat* (Groningen, 1961). An exhaustive overview is to be found in O. Schutte, *Repertorium der Nederlandse vertegenwoordigers residerende in het buitenland 1584–1810* (The Hague, 1976).

The national institutions of the Republic are described in two older works: Robert Fruin, *Geschiedenis der Staatsinstellingen in Nederland tot den val der Republiek*, published by H. T. Colenbrander, with an introduction by I. Schöffer (originally 1901; The Hague, 1980) and S. J. Fockema Andreae, *De Nederlandse staat onder de Republiek* (Amsterdam, 1961). Modern treatments of this subject to be recommended include A. Th. van Deursen, 'Staatsinstellingen in de Noordelijke Nederlanden 1579–1780', in D. P. Blok et al. (eds.), *Algemene Geschiedenis der Nederlanden*, vol. V (Bussum, 1980), pp. 350–87, and Guido de Bruin, *Geheimhouding en verraad: de geheimhouding van staatszaken ten tijde van de Republiek (1600–1750)* (The Hague, 1991), chapter 8. The text of the Union of Utrecht is to be found in S. Groenveld and H. L. Ph. Leeuwenberg (eds.), *De Unie van Utrecht: wording en werking van een verbond en een verbondsacte*, Geschiedenis in veelvoud, vol. VI (The Hague, 1979) and in an English translation in Herbert H. Rowen (ed.), *The Low Countries in Early Modern Times* (New York, 1972).

The municipal government and Zwolle's 'town-hall traditions' are the subject of J. C. Streng, '*Stemme in staat': de bestuurlijke elite in de stadsrepubliek Zwolle, 1579–1795* (Hilversum, 1997). On the 'Holland model' we still have the superbly readable pioneering work by Johan E. Elias, *Geschiedenis van het Amsterdamsche Regentenpatriciaat* (The Hague, 1923) and the concise work of Dirk-Jaap Noordam, *Geringde buffels en heren van stand: het patriciaat van Leiden, 1574–1700* (Hilversum, 1994). The situation in Leeuwarden is described in

Hotso Spanninga, 'Om de vrije magistraatsbestelling. Machtsverhoudingen en politiek in Leeuwarden', in René Kunst et al. (eds.), *Leeuwarden 750–2000: hoofdstad van Friesland* (Franeker, 1999). Peter Schotel, 'Strijd om de macht', in Willem Frijhoff, Hubert Nusteling and Marijke Spies (eds.), *Geschiedenis van Dordrecht van 1572 tot 1813* (Hilversum, 1998) and Jozef Hoekx, Beatrix Jacobs and Bert Looper, 'De "Stadstaat": politiek, bestuur en rechtspraak', in Aart Vos et al. (eds.), *'s-Hertogenbosch: de geschiedenis van een Brabantse stad 1629–1990* (Zwolle/'s-Hertogenbosch, n.d.) treat both the seventeenth and eighteenth centuries. Other town histories mentioned in the sources for chapter 16 contain shorter sections on governance and politics.

A very readable book on the Hague bureaucracy was published a few years ago: Paul Knevel, *Het Haagse bureau: zeventiende-eeuwse ambtenaren tussen staatsbelang en eigenbelang* (Amsterdam, 2001). The relationship between the Hague and the Generality Lands, especially States Brabant, is treated in M. P. Christ, *De Brabantsche Saecke: het vergeefse streven naar een gewestelijke status voor Staats-Brabant, 1585–1675* (Tilburg, 1984) and A. C. M. Kappelhof, *De belastingheffing in de Meierij van Den Bosch gedurende de Generaliteitsperiode, 1648–1730* (Tilburg, 1986).

The first two stadholders of the seventeenth century have been the subject of modern biographies: A. Th. van Deursen, *Maurits van Nassau: de winnaar die faalde* (Amsterdam, 2000) and J. J. Poelhekke, *Frederik Hendrik, Prins van Oranje: een biografisch drieluik* (Zutphen, 1978). Their life and work is placed in a wider context in several fine exhibition catalogues: Kees Zandvliet (ed.), *Maurits, Prins van Oranje* (Amsterdam/Zwolle, 2000); Marika Keblusek and Jori Zijlmans (eds.), *Princely Display: The Court of Frederik Hendrik of Orange and Amalia van Solms in The Hague* (The Hague/Zwolle, 1997); Peter van der Ploeg and Carola Vermeeren (eds.), *Princely Patrons: The Collection of Frederick Henry of Orange and Amalia of Solms* (The Hague/Zwolle, 1997). Portraits of all the seventeenth-century stadholders of the House of Orange-Nassau are to be found in C. A. Tamse (ed.), *Nassau en Oranje in de Nederlandse geschiedenis* (Alphen a/d Rijn, 1970) and Herbert H. Rowen, *The Princes of Orange: The Stadholders in the Dutch Republic* (Cambridge 1988). The importance of the stadholder's court for the political culture of the seventeenth-century Republic is underlined by Olaf Mörke, *'Stadtholder' oder 'Staetholder'? Die Funktion des Hauses Oranien und seines Hofes in der politischen Kultur der Republik der Vereinigten Niederlande im 17. Jahrhundert*, Niederlande-Studien vol. XI (Münster, 1997). A modern biography of William III has also appeared: Wout Troost, *Stadhouder-koning Willem III: een politieke biografie* (Hilversum, 2001). A probing picture of life at court in Leeuwarden and The Hague is given in Luuc Kooijmans, *Liefde in opdracht: het hofleven van Willem Frederik van Nassau* (Amsterdam, 2000). The courtier is discussed in H. A. Hofman, *Constantijn Huygens (1596–1687): een christelijk-humanistisch bourgeois-gentilhomme in dienst van het Oranjehuis* (Utrecht, 1983). On Huygens, see also S. Groenveld, '"Een out ende getrouw dienaer, beyde van den staet ende welstant in t'huys van Orangen": Constantijn Huygens (1596–1687), een hoog Haags ambtenaar', *Holland* 20 (1988), pp. 3–32.

For information on the role of the Grand Pensionaries, see the detailed biographies of Oldenbarnevelt and De Witt: Jan den Tex, *Oldenbarnevelt*, 2 vols.

(Cambridge, 1973) and Herbert H. Rowen, *John de Witt, Grand Pensionary of Holland, 1625–1672* (Princeton, N.J., 1978).

The Royal Palace 'Het Loo' in Apeldoorn has been restored to its original, seventeenth-century state, as has its garden. The furnishings, however, often date from later periods. The Royal Palace on the Dam, built as the Town Hall of Amsterdam, gives an overwhelming, if atypical, picture of the power of local governments. It is generally open to the public in the afternoon.

12   A DISSONANT CHORUS

The story of the disturbances caused in Alkmaar by the civic militiamen is taken from P. Knevel, 'Onrust onder de schutters: de politieke invloed van de Hollandse schutterijen in de eerste helft van de zeventiende eeuw', *Holland* 20 (1988), pp. 158–74. On the Utrecht conflict, see D. A. Felix, *Het oproer te Utrecht in 1610* (Utrecht, 1919) and Benjamin J. Kaplan, *Calvinists and Libertines: Confession and Community in Utrecht, 1578–1620* (Oxford, 1995), chapter 6.

Rebelliousness in Holland is treated in Rudolf Dekker, *Holland in beroering: oproeren in de 17de en 18de eeuw* (Baarn, 1982). More rebellious militiamen are to be found in chapter 10 of Paul Knevel, *Burgers in het geweer: de schutterijen in Holland, 1550–1700*, Hollandse Studiën, vol. XXXII (Hilversum, 1994). D. J. Roorda, *Partij en factie: de oproeren van 1672 in de steden van Holland en Zeeland, een krachtmeting tussen partijen en facties* (Groningen, 1961), is always seen as a book about regents' politics, but it also contains a lot of interesting material on civil unrest in the Year of Disaster; see also the English summary: 'Party and faction', *Acta Historiae Neerlandicae* 2 (1967), pp. 188–221.

Regarding printed pamphlets, see especially W. P. C. Knuttel, *Catalogus van de pamflettenverzameling berustende in de Koninklijke Bibliotheek* vols. I–III (The Hague, 1889–1900). As the title reveals, this is a catalogue, not a book to be read, but perusing this list provides a very interesting picture of the lively public debate in the Republic. For a treatment of these pamphlets, see Craig E. Harline, *Pamphlets, Printing and Political Culture in the Early Dutch Republic* (Dordrecht, 1987). The practice of petitioning is a neglected facet of seventeenth-century political life, but one of the first studies of the subject is to be found in H. F. K. van Nierop, 'Popular Participation in Politics in the Dutch Republic', in Peter Blickle (ed.), *Resistance, Representation, and Community* (Oxford, 1997), pp. 272–90.

The discord between the cities is fully elucidated by Jonathan I. Israel, 'The Holland Towns and the Dutch-Spanish Conflict, 1621–1648', *Bijdragen en Mededelingen betreffende de Geschiedenis der Nederlanden* 94 (1979), pp. 41–69. This subject is treated in a general way by S. Groenveld, *Evidente factiën in den staet: sociaal-politieke verhoudingen in de 17e-eeuwse Republiek der Verenigde Nederlanden*, Zeven Provinciën Reeks, vol. I (Hilversum, 1990). See also Diederik Aten, *'Als het gewelt comt . . .': politiek en economie in Holland benoorden het IJ 1500–1800* (Hilversum, 1995). The attack on Amsterdam is described in detail in chapter 5 of Luuc Kooijmans, *Liefde in opdracht: het hofleven van Willem Frederik van Nassau* (Amsterdam, 2000). The reactions were analysed by S. Groenveld, *De prins voor Amsterdam: reacties uit pamfletten op de aanslag van 1650* (Bussum, 1967).

Since the publication of Roorda, *Partij en factie*, the idea that there was an 'Orange party' or a 'States party' has no longer been taken seriously, though there were doubtless groups that worked to further the cause of either the stadholder or republicanism. They were prompted to do so by a mixture of self-interest and ideological zeal, as may be gleaned from the general political literature on that era. A very recent example is Tino Perlot, *De Staten van Utrecht en Willem III. De houding van de Staten van Utrecht tegenover Willem III tijdens het eerste stadhouderloze tijdperk (1650–1672)*, Utrechtse Historische Cahiers, vol. XXI/4 (Utrecht, 2000). The war of words of that period has already been analysed by P. Geyl in his 'Het stadhouderschap in de partij-literatuur', originally published in 1947 but made accessible in his *Pennestrijd over staat en historie* (Groningen, 1971). A more systematic treatment of Orangist views is G. O van der Klashorst, '"Metten schijn van monarchie getempert": de verdediging van het stadhouderschap in de partijliteratuur, 1650–1686', in H. W. Blom and I. W. Wildenberg (eds.), *Pieter de la Court in zijn tijd (1618–1685): aspecten van een veelzijdig publicist* (Amsterdam/Maarssen, 1986), pp. 93–136. The republican idea is discussed in a volume still to be published: *Republiek*, edited by Martin van Gelderen and Wyger Velema. In the meantime, see Eco O. G. Haitsma Mulier, *The Myth of Venice and Dutch Republican Thought in the Seventeenth Century* (Assen, 1980) and E. O. G. Haitsma Mulier and W. R. E. Velema (eds.), *Vrijheid: een geschiedenis van de vijftiende tot de twintigste eeuw* (Amsterdam, 1999), especially the contribution of G. O. van der Klashorst, 'De "ware vrijheid", 1650–1672'. The scant attention paid to republican ideas during the first half of the seventeenth century has already been pointed out by E. H. Kossmann, 'Politieke theorie in het zeventiende-eeuwse Nederland', *Verhandelingen der Koninklijke Nederlandse Akademie van Wetenschappen, afdeling Letterkunde* 67/2 (1960), now translated in E. H. Kossmann, *Political Thought in the Dutch Republic: Three Studies* (Amsterdam, 2000).

13   RELIGIOUS PLURALISM

The section on Utrecht is based mainly on Judith Pollmann, *Religious Choice in the Dutch Republic: The Reformation of Arnoldus Buchelius (1565–1641)* (Manchester, 1999) and Benjamin J. Kaplan, *Calvinists and Libertines: Confession and Community in Utrecht, 1578–1620* (Oxford, 1995). The information on the Bloemaert family comes from the biographies by Marten Jan Bok in Marcel G. Roethlisberger, *Abraham Bloemaert and his Sons. Paintings and Prints* (Doornspijk, 1993).

Anyone wishing to know more about religion in the seventeenth-century Dutch Republic can best start with A. Th. van Deursen, *Plain Lives in a Golden Age: Popular Culture, Religion and Society in Seventeenth-Century Holland* (Cambridge, 1991), part 4, in which the positions of the Catholics, the Mennonites and, of course, the Reformed are sharply delineated. A quantitative picture is given by Hans Knippenberg, *De religieuze kaart van Nederland: omvang en geografische spreiding van de godsdienstige gezindten vanaf de Reformatie tot heden* (Assen/Maastricht, 1992), chapter 2. It is impossible here to give a complete list of the various religious streams to be found in the Republic and for the sake of brevity one is referred to the very detailed and recently compiled list of literature accompanying chapter 6 in Willem Frijhoff and Marijke Spies, *1650: Hard–Won Unity* (Assen: Van Gorcum and Basingstoke: Palgrave, 2004).

The history of the Reformation in the Northern Netherlands from the time of the Revolt is analysed in detail in a number of recent studies of a regional or local nature. Important new insights are developed in the essays by Alastair Duke, included in his *Reformation and Revolt in the Low Countries* (London, 1990). The works that treat more than just the first decades of the seventeenth century (most of them end around 1620) are, in order of publication, Joke Spaans, *Haarlem na de Reformatie: stedelijke cultuur en kerkelijk leven, 1577–1620*, Hollandse Historische Reeks, vol. XI (The Hague, 1989); P. H. A. M. Abels and A. Ph. F. Wouters, *Nieuw en ongezien: kerk en samenleving in de classis Delft en Delfland 1572–1621*, 2 vols. (Delft, 1994); the above-mentioned book by Kaplan, *Calvinists and Libertines*; Charles de Mooij, *Geloof kan bergen verzetten: Reformatie en katholieke herleving te Bergen op Zoom 1577–1795* (Hilversum, 1998); W. Bergsma, *Tussen Gideonsbende en publieke kerk: een studie over het gereformeerd protestantisme in Friesland, 1580–1650* (Leeuwarden/Hilversum, 1999); Christine Kooi, *Liberty and Religion: Church and State in Leiden's Reformation, 1572–1620* (Leiden, 2000). A. Th. van Deursen, *Bavianen en slijkgeuzen. Kerk en kerkvolk ten tijde van Maurits en Oldenbarnevelt* (Assen, 1974) is still exemplary for studies of the Reformed Church in this period, offering a probing picture of the church and its organisation in Holland. This phase ended with the synod of 1619, which is discussed in W. van 't Spijker et al., *De Synode van Dordrecht in 1618 en 1619* (Houten, 1987). A detailed description of the religious engagement of one individual in particular is given in Willem Frijhoff, *Wegen van Evert Willemsz.: een Hollands weeskind op zoek naar zichzelf, 1607–1647* (Nijmegen, 1995).

The historical literature has paid an inordinate amount of attention to the Reformed congregation, considering the relatively small percentage of the population that actually joined the Dutch Reformed Church in the seventeenth century. Most of the studies mentioned, however, also treat Catholics and Protestant dissenters to some extent. De Mooij, *Geloof kan bergen verzetten*, even gives the Catholics detailed treatment, although the standard work remains J. L. Rogier, *Geschiedenis van het katholicisme in Noord-Nederland in de 16e en 17e eeuw*, 3 vols. (Amsterdam, 1947). J. A. de Kok, *Nederland op de breuklijn Rome-Reformatie: numerieke aspecten van Protestantisering en Katholieke Herleving in de Noordelijke Nederlanden 1580–1880* (Assen, 1964) has also attempted to give some idea of the size of the Catholic community, though doubt has been cast on his figures by A. M. van der Woude, J. A. Faber and H. K. Roessingh in 'Numerieke aspecten van de protestantisering in Noord-Nederland tussen 1656 en 1726', *A. A. G. Bijdragen*, vol. XIII (Wageningen, 1965), pp. 149–80. Important recent publications treating the religious practices of Catholics in the Republic include Xander van Eck, *Kunst, twist en devotie: Goudse katholieke schuilkerken 1572–1795* (Delft, 1994); Marc Wingens, *Over de grens: de bedevaart van katholieke Nederlanders in de zeventiende en achttiende eeuw* (Nijmegen, 1994); F. J. M. Hoppenbrouwers, *Oefening in volmaaktheid: de zeventiende-eeuwse rooms-katholieke spiritualiteit in de Republiek* (The Hague, 1996); Marit Monteiro, *Geestelijke maagden: leven tussen klooster en wereld in Noord-Nederland gedurende de zeventiende eeuw* (Hilversum, 1996). I also made use of several as yet unpublished articles by Christine Kooi, who is writing a book about the Catholics in Holland in the seventeenth century. See her 'Katholieken en tolerantie in de Gouden Eeuw', *Tijdschrift voor Nederlandse Kerkgeschiedenis* 2 (1999), pp. 112–17. The story of the Jewish population of the Netherlands in the seventeenth century takes place largely in Amsterdam. Three important works have recently been published on Amsterdam's Portuguese Jews: R. G. Fuks-Mansfeld, *De Sefardim te Amsterdam: aspecten van een joodse minderheid in een Hollandse stad*, Hollandse Studiën, vol. XXIII (Hilversum, 1989); Miriam Bodian, *Hebrews of the Portuguese Nation: Conversos and Community in Early Modern Amsterdam* (Bloomington, 1997); and Daniel M. Swetschinski, *Reluctant Cosmopolitans: The Portuguese Jews of Seventeenth-Century Amsterdam* (London, 2000). A general survey is to be found in the contributions by J. I. Israel and Y. Kaplan to J. C. H. Blom, R. G. Fuks-Mansfeld and I. Schöffer (eds.), *Geschiedenis van de Joden in Nederland* (Amsterdam, 1995). Another very worthwhile publication is J. I. Israel's *European Jewry in the Age of Mercantilism, 1550–1750* (London, 1998), owing to the wealth of information about the Republic and the European background.

Many of the works mentioned thus far also broach the subject of the relations between the churches. This particular problem is treated in S. Groenveld, *Huisgenoten des geloofs: was de samenleving in de Republiek der Verenigde Nederlanden verzuild?*, Zeven Provinciën Reeks, vol. XI (Hilversum, 1995) and the seminal article by Olaf Mörke, '"Konfessionalisierung" als politisch-soziales Prinzip? Das Verhältnis von Religion und Staatsbildung in der Republik der Vereinigten Niederlande im 16. und 17. Jahrhundert', *Tijdschrift voor sociale geschiedenis* 16 (1990), pp. 31–60. The relations between church and state are discussed in various essays by Heinz Schilling, compiled and translated in two volumes: *Civic Calvinism in Northwestern Germany and The Netherlands, Sixteenth to Nineteenth Centuries* (Kirksville, Mo., 1991) and *Religion, Political Culture and the Emergence of Early Modern Society: Essays in German and Dutch History* (Leiden, 1992). See also Andrew Pettegree, 'The Politics of Toleration in the Free Netherlands, 1572–1620', in Ole Peter Grell and Bob Scribner (eds.), *Tolerance and Intolerance in the European Reformation* (Cambridge, 1996), pp. 182–98 and Ronnie Po-chia Hsia and Henk van Nierop (eds.), *Calvinism and Religious Toleration in the Dutch Golden Age* (Cambridge, 2002). Simon Schama, in his controversial book *The Embarrassment of Riches: An Interpretation of Dutch Culture in the Golden Age* (London/New York, 1987), argues that, although religion had a strong impact on people's everyday lives and world view, their religious ideas were mixed with all kinds of pre- and non-Christian notions and rituals. This is also borne out in Gerard Rooijakkers, *Rituele repertoires. Volkscultuur in oostelijk Noord-Brabant 1559–1853* (Nijmegen, 1994).

Many church buildings still bear silent witness to religious life in the seventeenth century. The Museum Catherijneconvent in Utrecht is devoted completely to this subject. Also highly recommended is a visit to the Museum Amstelkring in Amsterdam, which is housed in a seventeenth-century clandestine church – a unique experience. The Jewish Historical Museum, likewise in Amsterdam, paints a lively picture of the history of the Jewish community. One can take a virtual tour of this museum through www.jhm.nl.

14 A NEW APPROACH TO SCIENCE AND PHILOSOPHY

Anthonie van Leeuwenhoek's biography was last written by A. Schierbeek, *Measuring the Invisible World: The Life and Works of Antoni van Leeuwenhoek* (London/New York, 1959). For more recent insights, see L. C. Palm and H. A. M. Snelders (eds.), *Antoni van Leeuwenhoek 1632–1723: Studies on the Life and Work of the Delft Scientist Commemorating the 350th Anniversary of his Birthday* (Amsterdam, 1982) and Edward G. Ruestow, *The Microscope in the Dutch Republic. The Shaping of Discovery* (Cambridge, 1996). Leeuwenhoek's fellow naturalist Frederik Ruysch is the subject of a biography by Luuc Kooijmans *De doodskunstenaar: De anatomische lessen van Frederik Ruysch* (Amsterdam, 2004). The general outlines of Dutch science in the seventeenth century are sharply drawn by Klaas van Berkel in chapters 1 and 2 of Klaas van Berkel, Albert van Helden and Lodewijk Palm (eds.), *A History of Science in the Netherlands: Survey, Themes and Reference* (Leiden, 1999). For the general context of the Scientific Revolution it is best to start with John Henry, *The Scientific Revolution and the Origins of Modern Science* (Basingstoke, 2002).

The information on social backgrounds was taken mainly from Paul Hoftijzer, 'Metropolis of Print: The Amsterdam Book Trade in the Seventeenth Century', and Karel Davids, 'Amsterdam as a Centre of Learning in the Dutch Golden Age, c. 1580–1700', both in Patrick O'Brien, Derek Keene, Marjolein 't Hart and Herman Van der Wee (eds.), *Urban Achievement in Early Modern Europe. Golden Ages in Antwerp, Amsterdam and London* (Cambridge, 2001), pp. 249–263 and 305–325, respectively. On censorship, see Ingrid Weekhout, *Boekencensuur in de Noordelijke Nederlanden: de vrijheid van drukpers in de zeventiende eeuw* (The Hague, 1998), and S. Groenveld, 'Mecca of Authors? States Assemblies and Censorship in the Seventeenth-Century Dutch Republic', in A. C. Duke and C. A. Tamse (eds.), *Too Mighty to be Free. Censorship and the Press in Britain and the Netherlands*, vol. IX (Zutphen 1987), pp. 63–86. This last article also contains an interesting table illustrating the size of the book business. University life is analysed in W. Th. M. Frijhoff, *La société néerlandaise et ses gradués, 1575–1814* (Amsterdam, 1981). The standard reference work on cabinets of *curiosa* is Ellinoor Bergvelt and Renée Kistemaker (eds.), *De wereld binnen handbereik. Nederlandse kunst- en rariteitenverzamelingen, 1585–1735* (Zwolle, 1992).

The best introduction to the philosophical debates in the seventeenth-century Republic is Wiep van Bunge, *From Stevin to Spinoza. An Essay on Philosophy in the Seventeenth-Century Dutch Republic*, Brill's Studies in Intellectual History, vol. CIII (Leiden, 2001). A wealth of information on the radicals and Spinoza in particular is offered by Jonathan Israel's monumental monograph, *Radical Enlightenment. Philosophy and the Making of Modernity 1650–1750* (Oxford, 2001). The few known facts about Spinoza's life have been assembled by Steven Nadler in *Spinoza. A Life* (Cambridge, 1999). An entire academic industry has sprung up around this philosopher: a good beginning is Roger Scruton, *Spinoza* (Oxford, 1986). Those interested in delving more deeply into his writings are advised to consult Richard Mason, *The God of Spinoza. A Philosophical Study* (Cambridge, 1997). Modern English editions are available of all Spinoza's works. The most recent is Baruch Spinoza, *The Complete Works*, edited and with an introduction by Michael L. Morgan, trans. Samuel Shirley (Indianapolis, Ind., 2002). However, many Spinoza scholars consider a superior edition to be *The Collected Works of Spinoza*, vol. I (the only volume published so far), ed. Edwin Curley (Princeton, N. J., 1985). Both editions contain, among other writings, the *Korte Verhandeling (Short Treatise)*, an excellent introduction to Spinoza's ideas and style, and the *Ethics*, the most highly developed version of his philosophy.

15   THE DUTCH SCHOOL OF PAINTING

The best way to become acquainted with the art of the Dutch Golden Age is to visit a suitable museum. The Rijksmuseum in Amsterdam and the Mauritshuis in The Hague have superb collections, as do provincial museums such as the Frans Halsmuseum in Haarlem and the Dordrechts Museum. Many museums outside the Netherlands also have important collections of Dutch paintings. In Great Britain, the most notable collections of Netherlandish art are to be found in London (the National Gallery, the Dulwich Picture Gallery, the Wallace Collection, the Victoria and Albert Museum and Kenwood House, Iveagh Bequest), Oxford (the Ashmolean Museum), Cambridge (the Fitzwilliam Musuem), Edinburgh (the National Gallery of Scotland), Manchester (the City Art Gallery) and Birmingham (the Barber Institute of Fine Arts). The most important collections of Dutch art in the United States are to be found in the Metropolitan Museum of Art (New York), the Museum of Fine Arts in Boston, the National Gallery of Art in Washington, D.C., the Art Institute of Chicago, the Cleveland Museum of Art, the Detroit Institute of Arts and, on the west coast, the J. Paul Getty Museum, the Los Angeles County Museum of Art and the Norton Simon Museum in Pasadena.

Those wishing to read more about Dutch art of the seventeenth century will not be disappointed, for no aspect of the Golden Age has been so well illuminated as its painting. Various books offer introductions or overviews, the best being Bob Haak, *The Golden Age: Dutch Painters of the 17th Century* (London, 1984) and Seymour Slive, *Dutch Painting 1600–1800* (New Haven, Conn., 1985). The latter is organised by genre and devotes much attention to the 'big three' – Hals, Rembrandt, and to a lesser extent Vermeer – keeping largely within the bounds of the Netherlandish canon. Haak's book treats the schools of painting of the various cities, which makes it more wide-ranging in scope. Both are exceptionally informative in their own way. Every year the art-historical periodicals *Oud-Holland* and *Simiolus* (the latter published in English) publish a number of interesting and well-illustrated articles on seventeenth-century Dutch art.

The innovations in fifteenth-century Flemish art are discussed in Jean C. Wilson, *Painting in Bruges at the Close of the Middle Ages: Studies in Society and Visual Culture* (University Park, Pa., 1998). The sixteenth-century art of the Northern Netherlands was the subject of a large exhibition held in the Rijksmuseum, *Kunst voor de Beeldenstorm*, the catalogue of which (Amsterdam, 1986) provides a good introduction. Jan van Scorel's Madonnas are discussed in Molly Faries and Liesbeth Helmus, *De madonna's van Jan van Scorel 1495–1562: Serieproduktie van een geliefd motief* (Utrecht, 2000). The transition to the Golden

Age was treated in another large exhibition held in the Rijksmuseum, *Dawn of the Golden Age: Northern Netherlandish Art, 1580–1620*, with accompanying catalogue (Amsterdam, 1993).

Biographies, often accompanied by a *catalogue raisonné*, have been written about numerous artists of the Golden Age. The 'big three' have been written about by Bob Haak, *Rembrandt: His Life, his Work, his Time* (New York, 1969); Gary Schwartz, *Rembrandt: His Life, his Paintings* (New York, 1985); S. Slive et al., *Frans Hals* (exhibition catalogue Washington/Haarlem/London 1989–90); Albert Blankert, John Michael Montias and Gilles Aillaud, *Vermeer* (Amsterdam, 1992); John Michael Montias, *Vermeer and his Milieu: A Web of Social History* (Princeton, N. J., 1989). The last two books supplied the information for the section on Vermeer in this chapter. See also Ivan Gaskell (ed.), *Vermeer Studies* (Washington, 1998); Walter Liedtke, *A View of Delft: Vermeer and his Contemporaries* (Zwolle, 2000) and Wayne E. Franits (ed.), *The Cambridge Companion to Vermeer* (Cambridge, 2001). The career of a more average artist is described in Gary Schwartz and Marten Jan Bok, *Pieter Saenredam: The Painter and his Time* (The Hague, 1990).

The local schools of painting are discussed in the previously cited overview by Haak. Recommended reading from more recent literature includes Peter Hecht, *De Hollandse fijnschilders: Van Gerard Dou tot Adriaen van der Werff* (exhibition catalogue Amsterdam, 1989), which treats mainly the Leiden School, and Joaneath A. Spicer and Lynn Federle Orr (eds.), *Masters of Light: Dutch Painters in Utrecht during the Golden Age* (exhibition catalogue San Francisco/Baltimore/London, 1997–8). The cityscape is discussed in Richard J. Wattenmaker et al., *Opkomst en bloei van het Noordnederlandse stadsgezicht in de 17de eeuw / The Dutch Cityscape in the 17th Century and its Sources* (exhibition catalogue Amsterdam/Toronto, 1997) and Leonore Stapel, *Perspectieven van de stad: Over bronnen, populariteit en functie van het zeventiende-eeuwse stadsgezicht* (Hilversum, 2000). The so-called Haarlem Academy is discussed at length in Pieter J. J. van Thiel, *Cornelis Cornelisz van Haarlem* (Doornspijk, 1999), pp. 59–65.

In recent decades the discussion of seventeenth-century Dutch art has concentrated on two aspects: the influence exerted by the economy on the kind of paintings produced is treated by John Michael Montias in his book *Artists and Artisans in Delft: A Socio-Economic Study of the Seventeenth Century* (Princeton, N. J., 1982), as well as in numerous articles, of which one deserves special mention: 'Cost and Value in Seventeenth-Century Dutch Art', *Art History* 10 (1987), pp. 455–66. Among those following in Montias's footsteps are David Freedberg and Jan de Vries (eds.), *Art in History, History in Art: Studies in Seventeenth-Century Dutch Culture* (Santa Monica, Calif., 1991); Michael North, *Art and Commerce in the Dutch Golden Age* (New Haven, Conn./London 1997) and Marten Jan Bok, 'Vraag en aanbod op de Nederlandse kunstmarkt, 1580–1700' (dissertation, Utrecht University 1994). The importance of the guilds is discussed in Maarten Prak, 'Guilds and the development of the art market during the Dutch Golden Age', *Simiolus* 30 (2003), pp. 236–51.

Eddy de Jongh first questioned the realism that many connoisseurs consider typical of the Dutch school of painting in *Zinne- en minnebeelden in de schilderkunst van de zeventiende eeuw* (Amsterdam, 1967) and in numerous later publications, several of which are included in *Questions of Meaning: Theme and Motif in Dutch Seventeenth-Century Painting* (Leiden, 1999). De Jongh's views have in turn become a subject of discussion. A frontal attack was undertaken by Svetlana Alpers, *The Art of Describing: Dutch Art in the Seventeenth Century* (Chicago, 1983), though her ideas, too, are hotly disputed. The discussion, which is still raging, is concisely summarised in Wayne Franits (ed.), *Looking at Seventeenth-Century Dutch Art: Realism Reconsidered* (Cambridge, 1997). Above all, however, one should take the title of Franits's book to heart and see the paintings with one's own eyes. Many illustrations with explanations are to be found on the websites of the large museums, such as www.centraalmuseum.nl (Utrecht), www.mauritshuis.nl (The Hague) and www.rijksmuseum.nl (Amsterdam).

16 THE URBAN LANDSCAPE

Patterns of urbanisation are discussed in Jan de Vries, *European Urbanization 1500–1800* (London, 1984). See also Henk Schmal, 'Patterns of Urbanization and De-urbanization in the Netherlands between 1650 and 1850', in Herman Van der Wee (ed.), *The Rise and Decline of Urban Industries in Italy and the Low Countries* (Louvain, 1988), pp. 287–306. An overview of numbers of inhabitants per city is to be found in Piet Lourens and Jan Lucassen, *Inwoneraantallen van Nederlandse steden ca. 1300–1800* (Amsterdam, 1997). The fascinating story of the passenger barge is told in Jan de Vries, *Barges and Capitalism: Passenger Transportation in the Dutch Economy (1632–1839)* (Utrecht, 1981).

Urban development in the Netherlands in the seventeenth century was systematically discussed for the first time in G. L. Burke, *The Making of Dutch Towns: A Study in Urban Development from the 10th to the 17th Centuries* (London, 1956). The best modern study is Ed Taverne, *In 't land van belofte: in de nieue stadt; Ideaal en werkelijkheid van de stadsuitleg in de Republiek 1580–1680* (Maarssen, 1978). See also Ed Taverne and Irmin Visser (eds.), *Stedebouw: De geschiedenis van de stad in de Nederlanden van 1500 tot heden* (Nijmegen, 1993). On the Amsterdam extensions, see B. Bakker, 'De stadsuitleg van 1610 en het ideaal van de "volcomen stadt": Meesterplan of mythe?', *Jaarboek Amstelodamum* 87 (1995), pp. 71–96, and J. E. Abrahamse and H. Battjes, 'De optimale stad: Grondgebruik, structuur en stedenbouwkundige theorie in de 17de-eeuwse stadsuitbreidingen van Amsterdam', *Jaarboek Amstelodamum* 92 (2000), pp. 95–108.

The layout and development of the cities is also treated in various city histories which have been appearing in recent years with increasing frequency: (in order of publication) W. Th. M. Frijhoff et al. (eds.), *Geschiedenis van Zutphen* (Zutphen, 1989); G. F. van der Ree-Scholtens et al. (eds.), *Deugd boven geweld: Een geschiedenis van Haarlem, 1245–1995* (Hilversum, 1995); A. Vos et al. (eds.), *'s-Hertogenbosch: De geschiedenis van een Brabantse stad, 1629–1990* ('s-Hertogenbosch, n.d.); Willem Frijhoff, Hubert Nusteling and Marijke Spies (eds.), *Geschiedenis van Dordrecht van 1572 tot 1813* (Hilversum, 1998); Arie van der Schoor, *Stad in aanwas: Geschiedenis van Rotterdam tot 1813* (Zwolle, n.d.); René Kunst et al. (eds.), *Leeuwarden 750–2000: Hoofdstad van Friesland* (Franeker, 1999); A. Pietersma et al. (eds.), *'Een paradijs vol weelde': Geschiedenis van de stad Utrecht* (Utrecht, 2000); S. Groenveld (ed.), *Leiden: de geschiedenis van een Hollandse stad,* vol. II: *1574–1795* (Leiden, 2003); Willem Frijhoff and Maarten Prak (eds.), *Geschiedenis van Amsterdam,* vol. 2.I: *Centrum van de wereld, 1578–1650* and vol. 2.II: *Zelfbewuste stadstaat, 1650–1813* (Amsterdam, 2004–5). All of these books are published in large format and richly illustrated. The relations between the various cities are discussed in C. M. Lesger, *Hoorn als stedelijk knooppunt. Stedensystemen tijdens de late middeleeuwen en vroegmoderne tijd,* Hollandse Studiën, vol. XXVI (Hilversum, 1990).

The best treatment of the architecture of Dutch classicism is to be found in several monographs on individual architects: Jacobine Huisken, Koen Ottenheym and Gary Schwartz (eds.), *Jacob van Campen: Het klassieke ideaal in de Gouden Eeuw* (Amsterdam, 1995); J. J. Terwen and K. A. Ottenheym, *Pieter Post (1608–1669), architect* (Zutphen, 1993); Koen Ottenheym, *Philips Vingboons (1607–1678), architect* (Zutphen, 1989). Regarding the cities as patrons of the arts, see also Koen Ottenheym, 'Tot roem en sieraad van de stad. Hollandse stedelijke en regionale overheden als opdrachtgevers van architectuur in de zeventiende eeuw', in Harald Hendrix and Jeroen Stumpel (eds.), *Kunstenaars en opdrachtgevers* (Amsterdam, 1996), pp. 119–40.

A great deal has been written about the construction of the Amsterdam Town Hall. Much is contained in the above-mentioned books about Van Campen, Post and Vingboons. In addition to the standard reference work by Katherine Fremantle, *The Baroque Town Hall of Amsterdam* (Utrecht, 1959), there are a number of more recent publications, including Pieter Vlaardingerbroek, 'Het stadhuis van Amsterdam: Bouw, verbouw en restauratie' (dissertation, Utrecht University 2004); Sjoerd Faber, Jacobine Huisken and Friso Lammertse, *Van Heeren die hunn' stoel en kussen niet beschaemen: Het stadsbestuur van Amsterdam in de 17e en 18e eeuw* (Amsterdam, 1987), which describes the use to which the various rooms were put; Saskia Albrecht et al., *Vondels' Inwydinge van 't Stadthuis t' Amsterdam* (Muiderberg, 1982), which contains not only Vondel's eulogy but also a detailed analysis of it; Eymert-Jan Goossens, *Treasure Wrought by Chisel and Brush: The Town Hall of Amsterdam in the Golden Age* (Amsterdam/Zwolle, 1996), an accessible introduction to both exterior and interior of this magnificent building. The best approach, of course, is a visit to the building itself, which is now the Royal Palace (Paleis). Regarding town halls in other cities, see C. Boschma-Aarnoudse, *'Een huijs om te vergaderen ende tgerecht te houden': Renaissance-raadhuizen boven het IJ* (Zutphen, 1992). The Amsterdam Historical Museum has a good website with much illustrative material: www.ahm.nl.

17   THE END OF THE GOLDEN AGE

The economic decline of the Republic is described in Jan de Vries and Ad van der Woude, *The First Modern Economy: Success, Failure, and Perseverance of the Dutch Economy, 1500–1815* (Cambridge, 1997). The problems of poor relief emerge in Joke Spaans, *Armenzorg in Friesland 1500–1800: Publieke zorg en particuliere liefdadigheid in zes Friese steden: Leeuwarden, Bolsward, Franeker, Sneek, Dokkum en Harlingen* (Hilversum/Leeuwarden, 1997) and C. W. van Voorst van Beest, *De katholieke armenzorg te Rotterdam in de 17e en 18e eeuw* (The Hague, 1955). The collapse of the art market is elucidated in J. Michael Montias, 'Cost and Value in

Seventeenth-Century Dutch art', *Art History* 10 (1987), pp. 455–66 and Marten Jan Bok, *Vraag en aanbod op de Nederlandse kunstmarkt, 1580–1700* (Utrecht, 1994).

The disintegration of the political system is described most grippingly in J. Aalbers, *De Republiek en de vrede van Europa. De buitenlandse politiek van de Republiek der Verenigde Nederlanden na de Vrede van Utrecht (1713), voornamelijk gedurende de jaren 1720–1733: achtergronden en algemene aspecten* (Groningen, 1980), summarised in J. Aalbers, 'Holland's Financial Problems (1713–1733) and the Wars against Louis XIV', in A. C. Duke and C. A. Tamse (eds.), *Britain and the Netherlands*, vol. VI: *War and Society* (The Hague, 1977), pp. 79–93. By the same author, see also 'Het machtsverval van de Republiek der Verenigde Nederlanden 1713–1741', in J. Aalbers and A. P. van Goudoever (eds.), *Machtsverval in de internationale context* (Groningen, 1986), pp. 7–36. On Holland's financial problems, see also R. Liesker, 'Tot zinkens toe bezwaard. De schuldenlast van het Zuiderkwartier van Holland 1672–1794', in S. Groenveld, M. E. H. N. Mout and I. Schöffer (eds.), *Bestuurders en geleerden* (Amsterdam, 1985), pp. 113–25.

The idea, originally developed by the Norwegian political scientist Stein Rokkan, of the league of cities is elucidated in the introductory and concluding chapters of Karel Davids and Jan Lucassen (eds.), *A Miracle Mirrored: The Dutch Republic in European Perspective* (Cambridge, 1995), though it had already been explored in some other publications: Marjolein 't Hart, *The Making of a Bourgeois State. War, Politics and Finance during the Dutch revolt* (Manchester, 1993); Maarten Prak, 'Citizen Radicalism and Democracy in the Dutch Republic. The Patriot Movement of the 1780s', *Theory and Society* 20 (1991), pp. 73–102; and Charles Tilly, *Coercion, Capital, and European States, AD 990–1990* (Oxford, 1990). Historical material on the relations between the Dutch Republic and Venice is to be found in Margriet de Roever (ed.), *Amsterdam: Venetië van het Noorden* ('s-Gravenhage/Amsterdam, 1990) and Eco O. G. Haitsma Mulier, *The Myth of Venice and Dutch Republican Thought in the Seventeenth Century* (Assen, 1980). On the relations between the Dutch Republic and Switzerland during this period, see Frieder Walter, *Niederländische Einflüsse auf das eidgenössische Staatsdenken im späten 16. und frühen 17. Jahrhundert* (Zürich, 1979).

Index

Aardenburg, 66
Act of Abjuration (1581), 21
Act of Exclusion (1654), 48, 193–4
admiralties, 81
  Amsterdam, 132
  Dokkum, 62
  Enkhuizen and Hoorn, 62
  Harlingen, 62
  Rotterdam, 62, 132
  Veere, 62
Aelianus, 73
Aerssen, Cornelis van (1545–1627), 176
Aerssen, François van (1572–1641), 182
Africa, 49, 61, 98, 109, 111–12, 115, 117, 268, 284
agriculture, 109, 280
  cattle-grazing, 92, 93
  madder production, 91
  tobacco cultivation, 93
Albany, 114
Albertine Agnes, Princess of Orange (1634–96), 181
Albrecht of Saxony (1464–1500), 11, 15
Aleppo, 98
Alewijn, Frederick (1603–65), 256
Alkmaar, 78, 87–9, 102, 106, 149, 186–7, 188, 189, 191–2, 217, 242, 280
almshouses, *see* poor relief, *under individual cities*
Alteration, the (1578), 156
Alva, duke of (1507–82), 16, 17, 18
Ambon, 118
America
  colonisation of, 112–15, 120, 191
  Native Americans, treatment of, 114–15, 116
  trade with, 93, 98, 101, 109, 115, 116, 121
Amersfoort, 20, 40, 172
ammunition, 122–3
  standardisation of, 72
Amsterdam, 14, 17, 28, 96, 97, 106, 109, 125, 126, 148, 157, 159–60, 166–7, 171, 188, 191, 218, 226, 232, 235, 252–4, 265, 271
  citizenship, 289
  civic orphanage, 138, 159
  extensions to the city, 27–8, 256–7
  guilds, 104, 137–8, 242, 282, 287
  immigration, 142–3, 155, 227
  local government, 171, 285
  militia, 153–6, 190 *see also* riots, militia
  painters, 105, 238
  political importance, 14
  poor relief, 146, 148, 216–19, 287
  population, 28, 144, 171, 252, 283
  religion, 32, 218–19, 232
  schools of art, 240
  Town Hall, 221, 235, 259, 260, 261, 293, 301
  VOC, 100
  William II's attack on (1650), 44, 192–3, 277
Anglo-Dutch Wars, 46
  The First War (1652–4), 47, 61, 63, 64, 195
  The Second War (1665–7), 49, 79, 81
  The Third War (1672–4), 79, 80, 278, 293
Anjou, duke of (1556–84), 20–1
Anthonisz, Cornelis (c. 1499–1566), 270
Antilles, 115, 284
Antwerp, 13, 19, 20, 21, 22, 28, 65, 69, 270, 272, 282
  large-scale emigration from, 109
  importance as commercial centre, 28, 95–7, 282
  painting, 236, 247
  Portuguese spice trade, 269
  Spanish Fury, 20
architecture (*see also* classicism), 124, 255–62
Arienszoon, Joost, 145, 288
Armada (1588), *see* Spanish Armada
Arminians, *see* Remonstrants

Arminius, Jacobus (1560–1609), 29–30
army, Dutch, 5, 65, 74, 82, 183, 278
    foreigners serving in, 70
    garrison system, 69, 70, 73
    payment of, 70–1, 73
    quartering and billeting of, 69
    tactics and training, 71–2
Arnhem, 12, 51, 132, 160, 161, 210
Arnhem, van, family, 132
art market, 236
    effects of economic hardship on, 237, 302
    guilds' influence on, 241
Aruba, 98
Asch van Wyck, H. M. A. J. van
    (1774–1843), 258
Asia, 28, 98, 100, 109, 117, 121, 140
asiento, 99
Ast, Balthasar van der (1593/4–1657), 242
Augsburg, 8, 269
Avenhorn, 192
Averkamp, Hendrik (1585–1634), 239
Ayscue, Sir George, 81

Baburen, Dirck van (c. 1595–1624), 244
Bahia, 98
Banda Islands, 119
Banning Cocq, Frans (1605–55), 157, 158
Banten (Bantam), 117
Barentszoon, Willem (c. 1550–97), 99
Barlaeus, Caspar (1584–1648), 204
Basel, 269, 270
Batavia, 119
Bayle, Pierre (1647–1706), 226–7
Beeckman, Isaac (1588–1637), 225
Beemster (polder), 94
Beemster (canal), 192
Bentinck, family, 132
Berchem, Claes (1620–83), 242
Berckheyde, Gerrit (1683–98), 240
Berents, Herman, 211
Beresteyn, Margaretha Duyst, 127
Berg, 13
Bergen-op-Zoom, 27, 66, 69, 170, 259
Berkhout, Jan (1510/16–87), 127
Berkhout, Pieter Janszoon (1472/6–1558),
    127
Berne, 270
Bernard of Clairvaux, 213
Beuningen, Coenraad van (1622–93),
    166–7
Bevernigh, Hieronymus van (1614–90), 157
Beverwijck (Albany), 114
Bible, see States Bible
Bicker, Andries (1586–1652), 125
Bicker, Cornelis (1592–1654), 126

Bicker, Elisabeth, 125
Bicker, Jacob (1588–1646), 125
Bicker, Jan (1591–1653), 126
Bicker, Wendela (1635–68), 184
Bie, Joris de (1587–1628), 176
Bitter, Johan (b. 1638), 120
Blaeu, Willem Jansz (1571–1638), 271
Bloemaert, Abraham (1564–1651), 204–5,
    294
Blood Council, 17
Bogardus, Everardus see Willemszoon,
    Evert
Bohemia, 180
Bol, Ferdinand (1616–80), 238
Bolnes, Catharina (c. 1631–88), 244–7
Bolsward, 259
Bommel, 12
Bommelerwaard, 12
Bonaire, 98
Boniface, 212
borders, of the Dutch Republic, 27
Boreel, Jacob, 153
Bosschaert, Ambrosius (1573–1621), 242
Boswell, James (d. 1795), 264
Bourtange, 66
Boyne, Battle of the (1690), 59
Brabant, duchy of (see also States Brabant),
    9, 10, 14, 16, 17, 211, 290
    economy, 9, 95, 134
    government, 170
    immigrants from, 109, 141
    merchants from, 28, 109
    military operations in, 27, 38, 50
    religion, 42
    society, 165
Bramer, Leonard (1596–1674), 241
Brandenburg, Elector of, 55, 181
Brazil, 61, 99, 111–12, 115
Breda, 27, 38–9, 41, 69, 76
Bredehoff, François (1648–1721), 133
Brederode, family, 133
Brederode, Walraven van (1547–1614),
    202
Brederode, Wolfert van (d. 1679), 133
Bredevoort, 28, 29
Bremen, 270
Bristol, 251
Bruges, 9, 20, 95, 236
Brugghen, Hendrick ter (1588–1629), 242
Brussels, 7
    Habsburg government, 13, 15, 23–4, 37,
        38, 176, 178
Buat, Henri (d. 1666), 50
Buchell, Aernt van (Arnoldus Buchelius)
    (1565–1641), 201, 202–3, 204

Buchell, Hubert van (d.1599), 201
Büderich, 51
budget, Dutch state, 35, 39, 55, 76, 265
burgher, 158
    representation, 169–71
Burgundy, 9, 10
Burgundy, House of, 9, 275
Byzantine Empire, 268

Cabeljauws, 12
Cadzand, 66
Calvin, John (1509–64), 29, 202, 203
Calvinism, see Reformed Church
Campen, Jacob van (1596–1657), 258, 260
Campen, Nicolaas van, 217
canals, 252–5
Cape of Good Hope, 119
capitalism, 268
Caravaggio, Michelangelo Merisi da
    (1571–1610), 235, 242
Caribbean, 61, 98, 115
Carlos II, king of Spain, 59
Catalonia, 41
Catholic Church, 205, 211, 294, 295–6
cattle, 92–3
Cats, Jacob (1577–1660), 177
Central America, 112, 115–16
Ceylon, 119
Champagne, 9
Charles I, king of England (1600–49), 46,
    47, 181
Charles II, king of England (1630–85), 49
Charles the Bold (1433–77), 10
Charles V, king of Spain, Holy Roman
    Emperor (1500–58), 15
    abdication (1555), 7–8, 16
    constitutional changes in the
        Netherlands, 13–14
    financial reforms, 19
    military reforms, 65
    ruler of Low Countries, 24, 168, 170, 201
    Peace of Augsburg (1555), 16
Chatham, 49
cheese, 94
citizenship, 105–6, 160, 210, 211, 217, 290
classicism (in art and architecture), 249,
    258–9, 301
clergymen, 130–1
Cleves, 13
    duke of, 13
Clusius, Carolus (1526–1609), 87
Cnoll, Pieter, 120
Cocceius, Johannes (1603–69), 209
Coen, Jan Pieterszoon (1587–1629), 119
Coevorden, 23, 66, 69, 92

Colchester, 106
Coligny, Louise de (1555–1620), 34
collegiants, 230
Cologne, 20, 96, 269, 270
Company of Adventurers, 49
Constantinople, 87
Coornhert, Dirck Volkertsz (1522–90), 237
Corneliszoon, Cornelis, 102, 237
Council of State, 132
Counter-Remonstrants (Gomarists), 31,
    32, 127
country houses (estates, mansions), 161,
    220, 255, 269, 286
Court, Johan de la (1622–60), 194, 231
Court, Pieter de la (1618–85), 79, 105,
    194–5, 231, 270, 294
Court van der Voort, Pieter de la
    (1664–1739), 79, 194–5
Courtrai, 145
Coymans, Aletta (1641–1725), 128
Coymans, family, 128
Crabeth, Wouter (c. 1595–1644), 213
Craffurd, Joris (d. 1733), 155
Cromwell, Oliver (1599–1658), 46–8, 64
Curaçao, 115
Curiel, Mozes (1618/9–after 1695), 219
Cuyp, Albert (1620–91), 234

Damiate, 221
Declaration of Rights, 59
Delden, 164
Delft, 14, 40, 106, 149, 191, 208, 223, 226,
    255, 259, 279, 282, 295
    admiralty, 62
    canal network, 252
    economy, 106, 140, 143
    guilds, 242
    local government, 171, 210
    neighbourhoods, 161
    Orange dynasty, 21, 175
    painters, 105, 240–1, 242, 243–4, 245–7,
        299
    poor relief, 145, 146, 220
    population, 103
    VOC, 100
Delftware, 140
Delfzijl, 253
Den Bosch ('s-Hertogenbosch), 27, 259
    Catholicism, 204
    local government, 170
    poor relief, 146
    population, 14, 252
    siege (1629), 39, 40, 67, 66–9, 71, 279
Den Briel (Brill), 17, 22, 62, 106, 130, 191
Denmark, 46, 90, 93, 184

Denmark, king of, 58, 107
Descartes, René (1596–1650), xii, 224–5, 226, 227, 228–9, 230, 232
Deshima, 119
Deventer, 23, 28–9, 69, 210, 259, 276
  booksellers, 188
  citizenship, 105–6, 160, 210
  Dutch Revolt, 23
  economy, 105–6, 280, 281, 282, 283
  fortifications, 65–6, 82, 279
  population, 252
  States of Overijssel, 196
Doesburg, 51, 66, 69
Dokkum, 62, 253, 259
Dordrecht (Dordt), 40, 62, 161, 184, 191
  economy, 101, 107–8
  De Witt family, 184, 185
  guilds, 161, 171, 290
  local government, 171
  poor relief, 220
  population, 252
  trade, 107–8
  States of Holland, 14, 19
  Synod (1618–19), xii, 35, 36–7, 45, 207
Dou, Gerrit (1613–75), 242, 243
Douai, 201
Doubleth, family, 83–4
Doubleth, Johan (1580–1650), 84
Doubleth, Philips (1566–1612), 83–4
Doubleth Jr., Philips (1590–1660), 84
Doubleth, Philips (1600–74), 84
Dover, 47, 50
Downing, Sir George (c. 1623–84), 49
Drago, Jacob Franco, 101
Drenthe, 77, 92, 92–3, 220
  poor relief, 146
  population, 103
drill, military, 71–2
Duarte, Diego, 247
Dublin, 59
Duifhuis, Hubert (1531–81), 202–3
Dunkirk, 23, 76, 81
  privateers (Spanish), 39, 63, 64
Dutch East India Company (VOC), see VOC
Dutch Revolt, 276
  Alva's attempts to suppress, 16
  iconoclasm (1566), 16, 17
  international repercussions, 40–1
  leadership, 16
  origins, 15, 17
  peace talks with Spain, 20
  quest for independence, 24
Dutch West India Company (WIC), see WIC

Duyst van Beresteyn, Margaretha (1581–1635), 127

East India Company, Dutch, see VOC
Edam, 32, 192
'Ecluse, Charles de (1526–1609), 87
Edict of Nantes, revocation of (1685), 56, 141
education
  general level of literacy, 226
  engineers' training, 224
  Illustrious Schools, 209
  universities, 224, 228, 229, 233 see also Leiden; Utrecht
  theological training, see clergymen
  mathematics, see mathematics
  of orphans, 138
Egypt, 221
Eighty Years War, see Dutch Revolt
Eindhoven, 165
Elizabeth I, queen of England (1533–1603), 22
Elizabeth Stuart, queen of Bohemia (1596–1662), 180
Emden, Jacob van, 101
Enden, Franciscus van den (1602–74), 230
England, 17, 22, 24, 57, 90, 139
  Civil War period (1642–60), 46, 64
  colonial rivalry, 116
  Dutch ally, 50
  Dutch invasion (1688), 57–8, 83
  Dutch Wars, see Anglo-Dutch Wars
  dynastic relations, see William II, William III
  earl of Leicester, 22
  economic rivalry, 105
  peace with Dutch, 48
  protectionism, see Navigation Act
  William and Mary, 49
English Civil War, see England, Civil War period
Enkhuizen, 40, 226, 259, 263
  Admiralty, 62
  economy, 107
  local government, 171
  religion, 32, 209
  VOC, 100
Enschede, 28
Episcopius, Simon (1583–1643), 37
Erasmus, 227
Ernst Casimir of Nassau (1573–1632), 179
Ewsum, Anna van, 131
Ewsum, van, family, 131
Exchange Bank, in Amsterdam, 106, 123
Eyck, Jan van (c. 1390–1441), 236, 240

Fabritius, Carel (1622–54), 238
Fagel, Caspar (1634–88), 167

Femini, Giovanni, 271
Ferdinand of Habsburg, 16
fire pump (invention of), 102, 240
First Noble (Zeeland), 172
fishing, *see* herring industry
Fivelingo, 172
Flanders (county; *see also* States Flanders),
    9, 10, 16
  blockade of, 22
  civic militias, 165
  Dutch Revolt, 8, 17
  economy, 9, 14, 16, 95, 134
  French annexations, 50
  immigrants from, 141
  painters, 234, 236–8, 298
Flinck, Govert (1615–60), 239
Flora, goddess of flowers, 88
flute (ship), 96, 101
fortifications, 279
  building of, 65–6
  Stercktenbouwinge (Stevin), 66
France, 59, 90–1
  Dutch Revolt, 17
  Dutch War (1672–8), 51, 55, 80, 278
  Huguenots, 56
  Nine Years War (1689–97), 59
  protectionism, 48
  relations with Dutch Republic, 24, 48, 59
Franeker, 106, 209, 228, 259
Frankfurt, 96, 269, 270
Frederik Hendrik, prince of Orange
    (1584–1647), 34, 39, 42, 178, 183,
    187, 292
  England, 47
  funeral, 74, 183
  Jews, 219
  military leadership, 38, 39–40, 66–7
  naval reforms, 63
  Orange dynasty, 180
  patron of the arts, 235
  political leadership, 41, 182
Frederik V, Elector Palatine (d. 1632),
    180–1
Frederik Willem, Elector of Brandenburg
    (1620–88)
Fribourg, 270
Friesland, 17, 27, 76
  Admiralty, 62
  agriculture, 11
  before Dutch Revolt, 10, 69
  canal network, 253
  Dutch Revolt, 17
  financial contributions, 77
  Generality, 176
  nobility, 11, 132

  peace with Spain, 40, 42
  population, 103
  religion, 32, 33, 205, 207, 216
  social welfare, 148, 215
  stadholder, 11, 179
  States of Friesland, 173
  taxation, 12
  towns, 250–1
  trade, 11, 108
  Year of Disaster (1672), 52
'Frisian Freedom', 11
Frijhoff, Willem, 3
Fronde, 48
Fruin, Robert (1823–99), 3
Further Reformation, 209, 214

Galilei, Galileo, 222
garrison, military, *see* army Dutch,
Geer, Johanna de (1627–91), 123
Geer, Louis de (1587–1652), 123
Geer, Maria de (1574–1609), 122
Geer, Mathias de, 123
Geertruidenberg, 23, 27, 66, 69
Gelderland (Gelre, Guelders), 33, 74, 170
  before Dutch Revolt, 11, 12, 15, 17
  constitution, 55
  Dutch Revolt, 20, 23
  duke of, 11
  economy, 93
  financial contributions, 77
  local government, 170
  military situation, 40, 73
  nobility, 131, 132, 172
  population, 103, 143, 251
  States of Gelderland, 90
Generaliteitsrekenkamer (National
    Auditing Office), 127
Generality Lands, 66, 83, 177, 211, 292
Geneva, 206
Genoa, 9, 14, 23
Germany (Holy Roman Empire), 8
  border, 107
  Dutch ally, 12
  Dutch influence in, 149, 233
  migrants from, 141
  regiments from, 70
  religion, 211, 226
  Thirty Years War (1618–48), 37, 41
  trade, 93, 97, 122
  urbanisation, 269
gezworen gemeente (sworn representatives),
    169, 197, 211
Ghent, 7, 9, 14, 16, 20, 95, 236
Gheyn, Jacob de (1565–1629), 71, 73
Glorious Revolution, 59, 278

Goes, Hugo van der (*c.* 1440–82), 196, 197, 236
Goltzius, Hendrick (1558–1616/17), 237
Gomarists, *see* Counter-Remonstrants
Gomarus, Franciscus (1563–1641), 29, 31, 32
Goor, 28, 29
Gorcum, 40, 53, 62, 191
Gouda, 40, 105, 106, 125, 137, 149, 188, 191, 212–15, 242, 259, 287
Goyen, Jan van (1596–1656), 238, 239
Graeff, Jacob van der, 52
Graeff, Pieter van der, 55
Graft, 146, 164
Grand Pensionary, 173, 183, 185, 292
Grand Privilège (1477), 10
Grave, 55, 66, 69
Great Assembly, 45
Groenlo, 27, 28, 29, 65, 69
Groningen (city), 23, 69, 92, 170
    and province, 11, 172
    canal network, 253
    Dutch Revolt, 23
    economy, 92
    population, 251–2
    social policies, 149
Groningen (province), 11, 77, 174
    Dutch Revolt, 23
    economy, 90, 93
    nobility, 11, 131, 132, 172, 177
    peace with Spain, 40, 42
    population, 103
    religion, 32, 33, 205
    stadholder, 178
Groot, Hugo de (Hugo Grotius) (1583–1645), 51
Groot, Pieter de (1615–78), 51, 52
Grotius, Hugo, 35 (*see also* Groot, Hugo de)
Guelders, *see* Gelderland
Guicciardini, Lodovico (1521–89), 175
Guilbertus, David (b. *c.* 1603), 216
guilds, 104, 160, 163, 290
    burial vaults, 161, 290
    citizenship requirement, 211, 217
    influence on local politics, 188, 201
    painters' guilds, 104, 161, 241–2, 282
    sickness benefits, 135, 137
Guinea, 106
Gustavus Adolphus, king of Sweden (1594–1632), 123
Guyana, 98, 115

Haarlem, 221, 259
    architects, 258–60
    canal network, 252–4

civic militias, 156, 158
Dutch Revolt, 19
economy, 106
expansion, 257
guilds, 104, 161, 242
Jews, 217
local history, 221
neighbourhoods, 161–2, 290
painters, 105, 236, 237–8, 240, 242
peace with Spain, 40, 191
population, 252–4
religion, 205–6, 209, 210
social policies, 149, 265
Habsburg, House of
    Dutch Revolt, 96
    dynastic lands, 168
    government in Low Countries, 13–14, 178, 269, 275
    pan-European interests, 22
Haersolte, Arend Jurien van (1621–73), 184
Hague, The (Den Haag), 41, 84, 174–5, 178, 232
    ambassadors in, 49, 75
    bureaucracy, 176, 292
    canal network, 191–2, 252
    cannon foundry, 72
    De Witt murder (1672), 53–4
    Generality, 82, 174, 177
    neighbourhoods, 161
    population, 250
    religion, 32–3, 232
    States of Holland, 174–5
Hainault, 9
Hals, Frans (1581/5–1666), 239, 298, 299
Hamburg, 96, 193, 270
Handel, 212
Hanseatic League, 14
Harlingen, 62, 215, 253
Hasselt, 212
Hattem, 259
Heemskerck, Maerten van (1498–1574), 236
Heeren XVII (Gentlemen XVII), 100
Heerhugowaard, 94, 191
Heidanus, Abraham (1597–1678), 229
Heidelberg, 180
Hellevoetsuis, 63
Helmichius, Werner (1568–1600/1), 202–3
Hendrikszoon, Jan, 68
Henri IV (of Navarre), king of France (1553–1610), 22
Henrietta Maria, queen of England, 219
herring industry, 94–5
Hertogenbosch, 's-, *see* Den Bosch
Heusden, 66

Heyden, Jan van der (1637–1712), 102, 240
Heyn, Piet (1577–1629), 39, 63, 111
Hillenius, Cornelis, 186
Hoeks and Cabeljauws, 14
Hoge Raad (Supreme Court), 30
Hogerbeets, Rombout (1561–1625), 35
Holland (*see also* States of Holland), 9, 16,
    39, 74
  agriculture, 93
  before the Revolt, 14–15
  canal network, 252, 254
  Dutch Revolt, 4, 19, 187
  economy, 77, 109–10, 134, 251
  fishing, 94–5
  Generality institutions, 198
  migration to, 109
  industry, 101–2, 255 (windmills), 102–3
  Jews, *see* Jews
  nobility, 132
  painters, 235, 239, 240
  painters' guilds, 241
  polders, 191
  population, 103, 252
  religion, 208
  social welfare, 148
  standard of living, 139
  towns, 191
  trade, 108
  urban elites, 134
Holy Roman Empire (*see also* Germany), 8
Hondschoote, 142
Honthorst, Gerard van (1590–1656), 242
Hooch, Pieter de (1629–84), 240, 242
hoofdelingen, 10–11, 131
Hooft, Cornelis Pietersz (1547–1626), 31,
    126
Hooft, Pieter Cornelisz (P. C.)
    (1581–1647), 126
Hoorn, 94, 191–2
  Admiralty, 62
  civic militia, 192–3
  economy, 107
  local government, 171
  painters' guild, 242
  peace with Spain, 40
  VOC, 100
horses, 93
Houckgeest, Gerrit (*c*.1600–61), 242
Houtman, Cornelis de (*c*.1565–99), 99
Hudson, Henry (1565–1611), 112
Huguenots, 17, 106
Huizinga, Johan (1872–1945), 1–2, 3
Hulst, 69
Hunsingo, 172
Huybert, Justus de, 184

Huydecoper van Maarsseveen, Johan
    (1625–1704), 128–9
Huydecoper, Constantia (1636–96), 128–9
Huydecoper, family, 128, 129
Huydecoper, Johan (Sr) (1599–1661), 128,
    255
Huygens the Younger, Constantijn,
    (1628–97), 247
Huygens, Christiaan (1629–95), 176, 222,
    224, 225, 230, 232
Huygens, Constantijn (1596–1687), 250,
    292

Iconoclastic Fury (1566), 202
IJssel, River, 65
IJsselstein, 13, 204
IJzendijke, 66
Illustrious Schools, *see* education
immigration, immigrants, 109, 141, 288
Imperial Cities, 168
In- en Kniphuizen, George Willem van, 131
India, 100
Indies (Dutch East), 24, 28, 42, 95–6,
    99–100, 114, 119–21, 140, 144, 284
Indonesia, 100, 120
industry, 281–2, 287
  linen-bleaching (Haarlem), 107
  pipe-making (Gouda), 107
  pottery (Delft), 140
  shipbuilding (Zaan area), 101
  sugar-refining (Amsterdam), 101, 140
  textiles (Leiden), 106, 107, 140, 141–2,
    143
  tobacco (Veluwe), 93, 101
  Amsterdam, 140
Inquisition, Spanish, 141
Ireland, 22, 59, 61
Isendoorn à Blois, family, 132, 286
Israel, Jonathan, 3
Italy, 9, 98, 217, 234, 235, 251, 268, 269,
    270

Jacoba of Bavaria, 9
Jacobskerk, 202–4
James II, king of England, 57, 59
Jansen, Johan and Zachanas, 222
Jansz, Albert, 206
Japan, 100, 119
Java, 117–19
Jews, xii, 101, 111, 115, 141, 216, 218, 296
  Ashkenazim, 219
  citizenship, 160, 217
  immigrants (cities' policies towards), 216–19
  Sephardim, 216–19
  wholesale trade, 217

Johan Maurits, count of Nassau-Siegen
    (1604–79), 72, 73, 111, 258
Johan Willem Friso, prince of Orange
    (1687–1711), 60
Johann of Nassau, 73
Jordaens, Hans (1616–80), 241
Jülich, 13, 51
Junius, Hadrianus (1511–75), 158

Kaiser, Nanning, 167
Kampen, 78, 92, 168, 195, 280
Karel of Egmond (1467–1538), 11, 12–13
Kennemerland, 255
Kensington, 60
Kevelaer, 212
klopjes (lay sisters), 213–14
Knibbergen, François (1597/8–1665?), 238
Knuyt, Johan de (1587–1654), 42
Kosovo, 87

Lampsins, brothers, 61
landscape painting, see painting
Larson, Jean, 247
Lastman, Pieter (1583–1633), 243
Leenderstrijp, 165
Leerdam, 206
Leeuwarden, 11, 148, 149, 170, 188, 215,
    291
Leeuwenhoek, Anthonie van (1632–1723),
    222, 223, 224, 226, 229, 232,
    247, 297
Leicester, Robert Dudley, earl of
    (1533–88), 22, 203–4
Leiden, 126, 174, 226, 259
    bookshops, 232
    canal network, 252
    civic militia, 157–8, 196
    cloth industry, 28
    economy, 27, 106
    elite, 125
    expansion, 27
    immigrants, 28, 141–2
    neighbourhoods, 161
    painters, 105, 242, 299
    peace with Spain, 40
    population, 27, 252
    social welfare, 215
    States of Holland, 14
    university, xii, 29, 30, 37, 66, 87, 132,
        193, 206, 224, 228
Lemmer, 253
Lerma, Don Francisco Gómez de Sandeval
    y Rojas, duke of (1554–1625), 37
Levy, Abraham, 101
Lewe van Ulrum, Abel Coenders, 131

Liège, 122
Lier, 20
Lille, 50
Lillo, 69
Limburg (duchy), 9, 27, 52, 211
Lingen, 20, 28
Lipperhey, Hans, 222
literacy, see education
loans, state, 79–80, 82, 84
Lochem, 29, 259
Locke, John, 227
Lodewijk of Nassau, see Willem Lodewijk
Loevestein Castle, 193
London, 96
    occupation by William III (1688), 58
    seat of government, 59
    size, 251
    standard of living, 139
Lopes Suasso, Francisco (1634–93), 83,
    219
Lorraine, 10
lotteries, 161, 162
Louis XI, king of France, 10
Louis XIV, king of France (1638–1715), 48,
    51, 52–3, 56, 59, 64
Louis, count of Nassau, 19
Louise Henriette, princess of Orange
    (1627–67), 181
Louise de Coligny, 34
Louvain, 133
Lowestoft, 49
Lucca, 270
Lucerne, 270
Luther, Martin (1483–1546), 15
Lutheran Church, 216
Luxemburg, 9, 16
Lyons, 107

Maarsseveen, 129, 255–6
Maassluis, 253
Maastricht, 40, 66, 69, 91,
    252, 259
Machiavelli, Niccolò (1469–1527),
    195
Madder, 91–2
Madrid, 19, 21, 37–42
Maes, Nicolaes (1634–93), 239
Mander, Karel van (1548–1606), 237
Manhattan, 113
Maranhão (Brazil), 115
Mark, 13
mark societies, 165, 291
Mars, god of war, 38
Mary of Burgundy (1457–82), 10
Mary of Hungary (1505–58), 7

Mary Henrietta Stuart, sister of Charles II, wife of William II, mother of William III (1631–60), 49, 181
Mary Stuart, daughter of the duke of York, wife of William III, queen of England (William and Mary) (1662–94), 56, 58, 181
Matanzas (Cuba), 39
mathematics (see also education), 224–8
Maurits of Nassau, prince of Orange (1567–1625), 65, 70, 71–3
countermarch, 71
coup d'état (1618), 35, 191
Johann of Nassau (military academy), 73
military commander, 23, 72, 182, 184
military reforms, 65, 70, 71–3
modernisation of weaponry, 71
and Oldenbarnevelt, 33
religion, 34
stadholder, 33, 38–9, 82, 178, 292
standardisation of artillery and ammunition, 72
Wapenhandelinge (Jacob de Gheyn), 73
Willem Lodewijk, 71
Maximilian of Habsburg, archduke of Austria (1459–1519), 10, 11
Max Havelaar (Multatuli), 121
Mazarin, Jules, cardinal (1602–61), 48
Mechelen (Malines), 18
Medemblik, 171
Meegeren, Han van, 248
meente, see burgher representation
Meerman, Johan (1624–75), 167
Meierij, the (Brabant), 27
Memling, Hans (c. 1433–94), 236
Mennonite Church, 205, 206, 209, 210, 215, 216, 294
Meppel, 92
Merchant Adventurers, 107
Metius, Jacob, 222
Metsu, Gabriël (1629–67), 234, 235, 239, 245
Meurs, Adolf van, count of Nieuwenaar (c.1545–89), 178, 203
Michelangelo (1475–1564), 234–6
Michielsdochter, Neeltge, 145
Middelburg, 96, 188, 222, 259
economy, 96, 101, 106
guilds, 242
local government, 170, 196–7
painters, 242
population, 91
social welfare, 149
Year of Disaster (1672), 196–7
VOC, 100

Mieris, Frans van (1635–81), 239, 242, 243
militias, civic, 153–4, 156–9, 164, 289
duties, 156–7
influence on local politics, 160, 186–7, 189, 196
rural, 165
supplementing regular army, 153–4, 156
Missio Hollandica, 214
modernity, 3–4, 6, 108
Moers, 28
Moluccas, 118, 301
Monconys, 291
Monnickendam, 127, 196
Montecuculi, Raymond, count (1609–80) 40
Montfoort, 172
Mookerheide, 19
Moreelse, Hendrick, 257, 258
Moreelse, Paulus (1571–1638), 257
Mossel, Jan, 161
Mouree, 111
Mud Beggars, 32
Muller, P. L., 1, 3
Münster, 43
Münster, bishop of (see also Peace of), 49, 56
Musch, Cornelis (1592/3–1650), 177
Multatuli, 121
mutinies, Spanish army, 19–20
Myle, Cornelis van der (1579–1642), 133

Naaldwijk, 181
Naarden, 18, 55, 252
Nagasaki, 119
Nagtegaals, Anna, 163
Namur, 9
Nancy, 10
Nassau, 180
Nassau-Dietz, House of, 179, 182
Navigation Act (1651), 47, 49
navy, 61, 73, 278 see also Admiralties
financing of, 61–2, 81
personnel, 63
professionalisation, 65
ships, 63, 64
tactics, 64
Nedersticht, see Utrecht
neighbourhood organisations, 161–4, 290
New Netherland Company (Nieuw Nederland Compagnie), 98
New York (city), 116
New York (state), 114
Nienoord, 131
Nieuw Nederland, 112–15
Nieuw-Amsterdam (New York City), 113, 114

Nieuwerbrug, 53
Nieuwervliet, 90
Nieuwpoort, Battle of (1600), 71, 72
Nieuwveen, 90
Nieuwwolde, 90
Nijenroode, Cornelia van (b.
    1629), 120
Nijmegen (see also Peace of Nijmegen), 13,
    35, 108
    before the Revolt, 13, 20
    citizenship, 210
    fortifications, 66, 69
    guilds, 161
    Maurits and, 35
    military situation, 51
    nobles, 172
    population, 252
nobility, 14, 131, 133, 172
Noord-Brabant, 296
Northern War, 46

Oldambt, 172
Oldenbarnevelt, 31, 32, 33–6, 76, 100, 133,
    134, 174, 184, 185, 292
Oldenzaal, 28
Ommelands, see Groningen
Ooltgensplaat, 206
Oosthuizen, 133
Orange, House of, 133, 172, 197
Orange, principality of, 180
Orangism, 195, 294
Orléans, 127
Orliens, David van, 66
orphanage (weeshuis), 138, 159
Orsoy, 51
Ouderkerk, 206
Overijssel (Overstricht), 170, 195–6, 197
    before the Revolt, 12
    during the Revolt, 17, 131
    constitution, 55
    economy, 139
    financial contributions, 77
    military situation, 65
    population, 103
    provincial government, 171
    voting procedures, 177
    Year of Disaster (1672)
Overstricht, see Overijssel

Pacification of Ghent, 20
painting, 298
    architectural, 242
    flower painting, 242
    genre painting, 239, 243
    landscape painting, 242
    (see also art market; guilds)

Paludanus, Petrus (1550–1633), 226
pamphlets, see printing and publishing
Paris, 17, 48, 50–3, 59, 139, 157,
    166, 181
Parma, Alexander Farnese, duke of
    (1545–92), 21, 22
Parma, Margaret of (1522–86), 21
passenger barges (see alsotrekvaart), 252–5
Patriots, 267
Pauw, Adriaen (1581–1653), 175, 184
Pauw, Reinier (1564–1636), 256
Pawn Banks, 106
Peace of Augsburg (1555), 16
Peace of Breda (1667), 50, 168
Peace of Münster (1648), 43, 44, 46, 64, 82,
    168, 173, 192
Peace of Nijmegen (1678), 56, 59
Peace of Utrecht (1713), 60, 266
peat, 90, 147
    excavation of, 102
    importance as fuel, 103
pensionary
    Grand Pensionary, 183, 222 see also
        De Witt; Oldenbarnevelt
    Amsterdam, 166, 175
    Dordrecht, 184
    Hoorn, 167
    Monnickendam, 127
Pernambuco, 111, 115
Perpetual Edict, 52, 53
Peter the Great, Tsar, 224
petitions, 189, 293
Philip II, king of Spain (1527–98), 7, 16, 19,
    20, 22, 24, 79
Philip of Anjou, 60
Philip the Bold (1342–1404), 9
Philip the Good (1396–1467), 10
Philip William, prince of Orange
    (1554–1618), 180
philosophy, 228–33, 297
physicians, 130
Picardt, Hendrik, 131
Picardt, Johannes (1600–70), 130
Picardy, 9
Piershil, 53
Pieterszoon, Claes, see Tulp, Nicolaes
Pijlsweert, 133
pilgrimages (Catholic), 212
Pinto, David de, 155
plague, 103–4
Poland, 46, 97, 166, 216, 226
polders, 94, 191
poor relief, see individual cities
population growth, see individual cities
Porcellis, Jan (c. 1584/7–1632), 238

Portugal
  and Brazil, 111–12
  and Indies, 268
  and Spain, 41
  trade, 98, 268
Post, Pieter (1608–69), 258–60
Pragmatic Sanction (1549), 8
Prague, 181
Prak, Johan (1868–1936), 1
Prak, Wim (b. 1908), 1
Price, J. L., 2
printing and publishing
  books, 226
  pamphlets, 188–9, 293
privateers
  Dutch, see Sea Beggars
  Dunkirk, 39
Prussia, 269
Puerto Rico, 98
Punta de Araya, 98
Purmer, 94
Purmerend, 32, 192
Purmerent, Petrus (1588–1663), 213–14, 215

Rammekens, 22
Rasphouse (Amsterdam), 149
Ravensberg, 13
receiver-general (ontvanger-generaal), 83–4
Recife, 111
Reformation, 7, 202, 213, 220, 295
Reformed (Calvinist) Church, 5, 16, 29,
  145, 186, 203, 205, 207, 208, 220, 294
regents, 127, 188, 197, 204, 285, 293
Regeringsreglement (government regulation,
  1674/5), 55, 60, 180, 197
Regius, Henricus (1598–1679), 228
Rembrandt van Rijn (1606–69), xii, 157,
  240, 243, 298, 299
  Anatomy Lesson of Doctor Tulp, The, 88
  Night Watch, The, 289
  pupils, 238–9
  workshop production, 238
Remonstrant Brotherhood, 207, 216
Remonstrants, 31, 32
Rengers, family, 131
Renkum, 212
Rennenberg, Georges de Lalaing, count of
  (c. 1540–81), 20
repartition, 83
Republicanism, 194
Reynolds, Sir Joshua (1723–92), 234, 236,
  239
Rheinberg, 28, 51
Rhenen, 172
ridderschap, see nobility

Rieuwertsz, Jan, 227, 232
Rijnsburg, 230
Rijswijk, 59
riots
  Alkmaar (1610), 186–7
  Amsterdam (1696), 153–6, 190, 289
  Utrecht (1610), 187
Roermond, 12, 40, 172
Rogman, Geertuyt (1625–51/7), 144
Rome, 73, 204, 213, 258
Rosaeus, Henricus (d. 1637), 32, 33
Rossum, Maarten van (1478–1555), 13,
  132
Rotterdam, 92, 101, 191
  Admiralty, 62, 132
  canal network, 253
  civic militia, 196
  economy, 92, 101, 107
  expansion, 257
  guilds, 242
  Jews, 217
  neighbourhoods, 161
  painters, 105, 242
  poor relief, 146
  peace with Spain, 40, 191
  population, 252
  social welfare, 215
  VOC, 100
Rouen, 96
Rovenius, Philippus (1574–1651), 212
Ruijven, Pieter Claesz van (1624–74), 247,
  248
Ruisdael, Jacob van (1628/9–82), 238, 242
Russia, 98, 125, 269
Ruysch, Frederik (1638–1731), 223, 224,
  297
Ruysdael, Salomon van (1600/3–70), 242
Ruyter, Michiel de (1607–76), 48, 49, 51,
  74
  Chatham (1667), 49
  honours, 63–4, 159
  naval career, 51, 55, 61, 81, 167
rye, 92

Saenredam, Pieter (1597–1665), 239, 240,
  299
Salland, 195
Salmisio, Giorgio, 271
Scandinavia, 90, 119, 141, 142, 166, 269
Schaffhausen, 270
Schiedam, 62
Schoonhoven, 171
Schooten, Frans van (1615–60), 224–5
Sciences, Royal Academy of, 124
Scientific Revolution, 232

Scorel, Jan van (1495–1562), 236–7, 298
Scotland, 22, 70
Sea Beggars (see also privateers), 17, 23, 63
Seville, 96
shipbuilding, see industry
Siegen, 73
silver fleet, Spanish, 111
Singendonck, Johan, 184
Sittard, 40
Slackebaarts, family, 138–9, 146, 147, 148
Slackebaarts, Hendrickje, 138–9, 143, 287
Slackebaarts, Jan, 138
Slackebaarts, Maaike, 138
Sloten, 250
Sluis, 39, 66
Smith, Adam (1723–90), 105
Sneek, 147, 210, 215
Snellius, Rudolf (1546–1613), 224, 225
Soete, Joost de (stadholder of Utrecht), 178
solliciteurs-militair, 73
Solms, Amalia of (1602–75), 180, 181, 259
South America, 95, 100, 111
Southern (Spanish) Netherlands, 236, 265
    Dutch blockade of, 37
    economic relations with, 32, 94, 191
    French claims on, 48, 50
    immigration from, 141
    merchants from, 98
    military situation, 48, 59
    urbanisation, 251
Spain (see also Philip II), 99, 202
    army mutinies, 19, 20, 23
    finance, 23
    Jews from, 216, 217–19
    king of, see Philip II
    military operations in the Low Countries, 40
    non-European empire, 100
    and Portugal, 41
    peace negotiations with, 23, 38, 41
    recognises Dutch Republic, 41
    Revolt against, 4, 18
    trade with, 100
Spanish Armada, 22
Spanish Fury, see Antwerp
Spanish Netherlands, see Southern Netherlands
Sparo, Martinus (captain), 153
spice trade, see trade
Spies, Marijke, 2
Spinola, Ambrogio (1569–1630), 23, 29, 38–9
Spinoza, Baruch (1632–77), xii, 227, 228–33, 297–8
Spranger, Bartolomeus (1546–1611), 237

St Bartholomew's Day Massacre, 17
St George d'Elmina, 98
Stad en Lande, see Groningen
stadholderate, 45, 47, 50, 62, 182, 193, 195, 197
stadholders, 178, 185, 197, 292
stadholderless eras, 259
States Bible, 37
States Brabant, 42, 52, 66, 73, 165, 177
States Flanders, 27, 37, 42, 66, 177
States-General (see also Great Assembly), 10, 23, 27, 32, 174
    foreign policy, 42
    military issues, 41, 43, 65, 82
States Limburg, see Limburg
States of Holland, 89, 172, 173, 189
    Act of Seclusion (1654), 193–4
    before the Revolt, 14–15
    foreign policies, 48
    Glorious Revolution (1688–9), 59, 278
    Grand Pensionary see pensionary
    military issues, 44
    navy, 62
    peace with Spain, 44
    and other provinces, 106, 174, 177
    public finances: contributions to national revenues, 82
        debt, 80
        taxation, 77, 80
    stadholder, 182
    voting procedures, 174
Staveren, 253
Steenbergen, 66
Steenwijk, 23, 69
Stevin, Simon (1548–1620), 66, 73, 224, 225, 227
Sticht, see Utrecht
Stralen, 12
Strasbourg, 270
Stuyvesant, Pieter (1592–1672), 116
Sumatra, 117
Supreme Court, see Hoge Raad, 30
Surinam, 99, 115, 116, 284
Swaen, Willem de (1607/8–74), 213
Swammerdam, Jan (1637–80), 223, 224
Sweden, 46, 50, 123–4, 166–7, 184
Switzerland, 70, 269, 270
Synod of Dordrecht (Dutch Reformed Church) (1618–19), 45, 295
Syria, 98

tariffs (French), 48
taxation, 75, 173
    'contributions', 80
    convooien and licenten (import and export duties), 81–2

excises, 77–8, 82
fixed quotas, 76, 280
property, 78, 82
   Hundredth Penny, 17, 78
   tax-farmers, 80
Teding van Berkhout, Adriaan
   (1571–1620), 127–8
Teding van Berkhout, family (see also
   Berkhout), 127
Teding van Berkhout, Pieter (1643–1713),
   243
Tedingsdochter, Cornelia Jan
   (1567–1633), 127
Teeng (Teding), Jan (1549–1633), 127
Temple, Sir William (1628–99), 75, 77,
   108, 147, 171, 272
Ter Apel, 1
tercios, 17, 18
Ternate, 118
Terneuzen, 66
Terra Ferma, 272
Texel, 99
Thins, Maria (c. 1593–1680), 244
Thirty Years War, 37, 41, 46
Tholen, 91, 92
Thoré, Théophile, 247
Tichelaer, Willem (c. 1642–c.1714), 53
tobacco, see agriculture and industry
Torbay, 58
town halls
   Amsterdam Town Hall, 221, 235, 259,
      260, 261, 293, 301
   construction of new town halls, 259
   renovations of town halls, 259
trade, 111, 282–3
   Americas (Dutch West India Company),
      see WIC
   Baltic, 97, 107
   colonial trade, 109, 111
   East (Dutch East India Company), see
      VOC
   grain, 90–1, 96
   Mediterranean, 98
   rich trades, 282
   salt, 95
   slave, 49, 98–9, 111–12, 115, 284
   spices, 95, 99, 117, 269
   sugar, 111
Treaties of Rijswijk (1697), 59
Treaty of Dover (1670), 50
Treaty of the Pyrenees (1659), 48
Treaty of Westminster (1654), 64, 116,
   168, 193
trekvaart (canals for passenger barges), 253
Trip, Elias (c. 1570–1636), 122, 125

Trip, Hendrick(1607–66), 118, 123, 301
Trip, Jacob (c. 1576–1661), 123
Trip, Jacob (1604–81), 123,
Trip, Louis (b.1405), 118, 123–5, 128
Trip, Pieter(1579–1655), 123
Trip, Sophia(1615–79), 128
Triple Alliance (1668), 50
Trippenhuis, the, 125
Tromp, Maarten Harpertsz (1598–1653), 63
tulips, 87, 88, 280
Tulp, Nicolaes (1593–1674), 88
Turkey, 22, 87, 217
Tuyll, 206
Twelve Years' Truce (1609–21), 24, 27, 33,
   37, 38, 66, 190, 198, 208, 210, 231, 276
Twente, 23, 27, 29, 73, 142, 165, 195–6,
   276

Uitgeest, Cornelis Corneliszoon van, 102
Ulm, 270
Union of Arras (1579), 20
Union of Utrecht (1579), 20, 29, 33, 75,
   82–3, 131, 167–8, 194, 196, 198, 208,
   217, 276, 291
Upper Gelderland, 66, 212
urbanisation, 172–3
Utrecht (city) (see also Union of Utrecht),
   90, 149, 286, 287
   citizenship, 160
   civic militia, 187, 188, 189, 203, 293
   constitution, 13, 35, 55
   defence, 55, 65
   expansion, 103, 257
   guilds, 161, 242
   immigrants, 143
   neighbourhoods, 161
   painters, 235, 242, 248
   population, 103
   public buildings, 259, 266
   religion, 201, 202, 203, 204, 205, 206,
      210, 232
   social welfare, 148
   university, 228–9
   Year of Disaster (1672), 196
Utrecht (province), 12, 40
   financial contributions, 77
   nobility, 131, 132, 172–3
Uyttenbogaert, Johannes (1557–1644),
   30–1, 32

Vaassen, 132
Valckenier, Gilles (1623–80), 124
Veere, 197
Vélazquez, Diego Rodrigues da Silva y
   (1590–1660), 39

Velde, Esaias van de (1590/1–1630), 242
Velde the Elder, Willem van de
    (c. 1611–93), 239
Veluwe, 12, 93, 131, 286
    quarter, 132
Venator, Adolfus (d. 1619), 186
Venezuela, 98
Venice, 271, 286
    centre of trade, 9
    competition with Republic, 46, 302, 303
Venlo, 13, 20, 40
Verbeeck, Hermanus (1621–81), 135–7,
    141, 287
Vermeer, Johannes (1632–75), xii, 242–8,
    264, 298
Vermeer, Reinier Jansz (c. 1591–1652), 244
Verschoor, Willem (d. 1678), 241
Veth, Adriaan, 184
Vianen, 136
Vienna, 55
Vincent, Levinus (1658–1727), 226, 280
Vingboons, Justus (1620/1–98), 118, 124,
    301
Vingboons, Philips (1607–78), 124, 255,
    256, 260, 301
Vitruvius, 258
Vlieger, Simon de (c. 1600–53), 239
Vliet, Hendrick van (1611/12–1675), 242
Vlissingen, 22, 61, 96, 106, 172, 197
VOC (Verenigde Oostindische Compagnie,
    Dutch East India Company), 28, 100,
    106, 116, 118, 125, 138, 140, 144, 284
Voet, Carel (1631–79), 128
Voetius, Gisbertus (1589–1676), 209,
    228–9
Vollenhove, 195
Vondel, Joost van den (1587–1679), 126,
    184, 262
Voorst, Claesje van, 202
Vosmeer, Sasbout (1548–1614), 212
Vredenburg Castle, 65
Vreeswijk, 252
Vries, Jan de, 2
Vrije (of Bruges), 20
Vroedschap (town council), 170

waardgelders, 33–6, 34, 35, 36
Wachtendonk, 28
Wageningen, 12, 93, 281
Walaeus, Antonius (1573–1639), 36
Wallonia, 21
Walloon Reformed Church, 209
Walraven, Lodewijk, 147
War of the Spanish Succession (1702–13),
    60

Wassenaer van Duvenvoirde, family, 133
Water Line, 52, 73
Waterloo, 46
Weesp, 252
welfare, see poor relief
Werff, Adriaen van der (1659–1722), 249
Wesel, 51
West Friesland, 171, 191, 194
West India Company, see WIC
West Indies, 42
Westerhoff, Coenraad van, 128–9
Westerkwartier, 172
Westerwolde, 172
Westphalia, 40
Weyden, Rogier van der (c. 1400–64), 236
wheat, 91
WIC (Westindische Compagnie, Dutch
    West India Company), 28, 39, 40, 49,
    98–9, 111–15, 115–16, 121, 283
Wijk bij Duurstede, 172
Wildt, Job de, 74
Willem Frederik, count of Nassau
    (1613–64), 45, 170, 181, 192–3, 195
Willem Lodewijk, count of Nassau
    (1560–1620), 71, 178
Willemstad, 66
Willemszoon, Evert (Everardus Bogardus)
    (1607–47), 111, 112–14, 115,
    121, 284
William I, prince of Orange (1533–84), 21,
    180, 203
    and Charles V, 7
    civic militia reforms, 156
    death (1584), 21
    leader of Revolt, 17, 18, 22
    personal fortune, 17
    reputation, 180
    stadholder, 178
William II, prince of Orange (1626–50), 16,
    42–4
    attack on Amsterdam (1650), 173, 183,
    192–3
    death of (1650), 193
    financial policies, 173
    and provincial sovereignty, 173–4
    stadholder, 42–4
    and Stuarts, 42
William III, prince of Orange, king of
    England (1650–1702), 51, 55,
    55–60, 79, 124, 179, 183, 195, 196,
    277, 292
    army, 55
    childhood, 47
    and France, 50
    Glorious Revolution (1688–9), 58

government regulations (1674), *see Regeringsreglement*
and Holland, 196
Jewish connection, 57, 219
and Stuarts, 56
Year of Disaster (1672), 197
William of Aquitaine, 213
Winkel, Wouter (d. 1636), 87, 88
Winschoten, 253
Wirtz, Paulus, baron Holm, 51
Wit, Johannes de, 204
With, Witte de (1599–1658), 63
Witt, Cornelis de (1623–72), 53–4
Witt, Jacob de (1589–1674), 167, 194
Witt, Johan de (1625–72), 46, 47, 48, 49–50, 52, 53–5, 64, 73–4, 173–4, 184, 185, 231, 277, 292
Witte, Emanuel de (1617–92), 242
Wittichius, Christopher (1625–87), 229
Woerden, 53, 111
wool, 93
working class, 139–40, 156
Workum, 253
Wormer, 94, 102, 146
Woude, Ad van der, 2

Year of Disaster (1672), 79, 80, 196–7, 278, 293
Ypres, 20

Zaan, 101–2, 103
Zaltbommel, 122
Zeeland, 47, 196
    agriculture, 90, 91–2
    before the Revolt, 9
    during the Revolt, 17–19, 20
    economy, 134
    financial situation, 77
    First Noble, 172
    Generality, 176
    navy, 62
    peace with Spain, 27, 42
    population, 103
    privateering, 39
    religion, 32, 33, 211
    social welfare, 148
    stadholder, 39
    towns, 172
    trade, 108
    VOC, 106–7
Zeeuws-Vlaanderen, 27, 52, 73, 90, 177
Zierikzee, 106, 126, 197
Zuid-Holland, 90
Zürich, 270, 272
Zutphen (city), 13, 18, 23, 66, 69, 210, 252
Zutphen (county), 12, 20, 27, 165, 172
Zwijndrecht, 123
Zwolle, 92, 130, 195, 210
    citizenship, 210
    elites, 228
    economy, 92
    fortifications, 66
    local government, 126, 168–70, 286, 291
    poor relief, 146, 148
    population, 252
    social welfare, 139

DATE DUE

JUN 2 2 2010